LOOKING
for ALASKA

LOOKING
for ALASKA

Peter Jenkins

St. Martin's Griffin
New York

www.stmartins.com

Book design by Michelle McMillian

Maps on xii–xiii by Paul M. Breeden

Grateful acknowledgment is given for permission granted to the author to quote from the works of Leslie Fields, Joe Runyan, and Jim Varsos.

Library of Congress Cataloging-in-Publication Data

Jenkins, Peter, 1951–
    Looking for Alaska / Peter Jenkins.—1st St. Martin's Griffin edition.
        p. cm.
    ISBN 0-312-26178-0 (hc)
    ISBN 0-312-30289-4 (pbk)
    1. Alaska—Description and travel. 2. Jenkins, Peter, 1951—Journeys—Alaska.
3. Indians of North America—Alaska—Social life and customs. 4. Alaska—Social life
and customs. 5. Alaska—History, Local. I. Title.

FP10.5.J46 2001
979.8—dc21   2002048871

First St. Martin's Griffin Edition: September 2002

10 9 8 7 6 5 4 3 2 1

To my six highly intelligent,
extremely creative,
hard-working,
beautiful, and handsome,
perfect children:
Julianne, Luke, Jed,
Rebekah, Brooke,
and Aaron

Contents

Contents

Acknowledgments

Looking for Alaska would not have been possible without the caring and assistance and friendship of the following people: my great family, Fred and Coleen Jenkins and Molly, Sarah, Derick, Colin, and Evie. Winky and Randy Rice and Alex, Jesse, and Tyler. Scott and Bonnie Jenkins and their children. Elizabeth and Abigail, my little sisters. Mom and Dad Jorgensen. Kevin and Val Karikomi and Matt, Mike, Dave, and Dan. Mike and LeAnn Turner and John, Michael, and Scott. Eric and Michele Jorgensen and Tammi, Kari, Rachael, Derick, Cheyanne, Chris, Brandon, and Brittany. Aaron and Robin Jorgensen, Gena, Julie, Jerry, Cory, Taylor, and Page. Chris Jorgensen and Anna Stowell. Archie and Janice Buttrey. And a special thanks to Rhoda Jenkins, who inspired me very early to be an adventurer.

There were many terrific people in Alaska who helped out and offered their assistance. Many of them are in the book. Those that are not I wish to thank here: Gale Vick and Richard Lowell. Mary Pignalberi. Linda Sylvester. Dawn Starke. Tina Lingren. Colonel Glenn Godfrey. Julie Guy. Linda Thompson. The following people at APRN: Dale Harrison, Ron Zastrow, Steve Franklin, Liz Fullerton, and Jessica Cochran. Cindy Matson. Ron Spatz. Scott Taylor. Lee Gorsuch. Ann Parrish. Kathy Newman. Mel Kalkowski. Terri Graham. Tom and Mary Tougas and family. Mavis Blazy and Ken Lancaster. Jim and Kathleen Barkley. Kenai Fjords Tour staff. Sharon Anderson. Lori Draper. Randy Becker. Mark and Betsy Bartholomew. Doug Lechner and Bay Vista B&B. Gail Phillips. John Torgerson. The University of Alaska, Anchorage. The University of Alaska, Fairbanks. Kodiak College. Maggie Wall. The brilliant staff at the

Acknowledgments

Alaska State Library. Mike Hyde. Gerry, Margie, and Guy Riley. Brian Porter. Lisa Murkowski. Gary Wilken. Robbie Graham. Craig Matkin. Diane Kaplan. Richard Foster. Scott Henderson. Joyce Thomas. Steve Langdon. Alan and Ginnie Austerman. Peter Ecklund. Kyle Johansen. Karen Hofstad. Stan Hooley. Jim Tilly. Jennifer Foltz. David and Elizabeth Odell. Kerry Cline. Neal and Juanita O'Shea. Macen Kinne. Genie and Joe Smith. Pat and Lorali Carter. Drew Pierce. Kris Norcoz. Arne Fugloug. Harold Kalve. Don Young. Hertz of Seward and Rosie. Dale and Carol Ann Lindsey. Dennis and Jackie Wheeler. Bob Malone. The ALPINI's. Artie at BJ's. Jim Menard. And in general, the outstanding people of Alaska, so many who were so helpful.

Speaking of Alaskans, a very special thanks to the supporters of The University of Alaska's Writer in Residence Program, of which I was a part. Thank you so much, National Bank of Alaska (now Wells Fargo), Alaska Railroad, Alaska Heritage Tours (CIRI), NorthRim Bank, and Holland America Westours. Thanks especially to Al Parish, Ed Rasmuson, Gov. Bill Sheffield, Johne Binkley, Dennis Brandon, and Mark Langland.

Thanks to my longtime great friends, Skip Yowell and Winnie Kingsberry and, of course, JanSport. And Bill and Mary Lucy Fuqua, great friends. Bill, thanks for all the doctoring and especially the friendship. And our terrific friends and neighbors, Ray and Cindy Williams. Thanks to Tammy and Tony Jamison and A.J., Sam, and Lucy, who took care of stuff while we were gone. Thanks to our great friends Tom, Belinda, and Tanner Long. Thanks to Christ Community Church, Scotty Smith, and congregation. To my friend and one of the few people who can read my handwriting, Glenda Andrews, who typed much of this book as I wrote it by hand. It has been great working together again. And to Paul and Anne Breeden. Paul has made the excellent maps in all my books since my first, published in 1979. And to Tom Smith, my mentor at National Geographic. And Harvey Arden. Thanks to Pat Golbitz, my first book editor and beloved friend who influenced me in so many ways. Thanks for inspiration and friendship to Luther and Kay Jones and family, and the Minnow Bucket Crowd.

Thanks to my excellent agents, Michael Carlisle, Whitney Lee, Byrd Leavell, Michelle Tessler, and Christy Fletcher at Carlisle and Company. And to Neal Bascomb. Special thanks to my good friend and adviser, Barbara Morgan.

I am especially pleased with my new publisher, St. Martin's Press. First, to the voice of St. Martin's, Helen Plog. In a world of sameness and the shunning of accents, Helen sets the tone for St. Martin's! I love it. Thanks to Sally Richardson for her outspoken belief in this project. And thanks to the other talented folks at St. Martin's I've had the pleasure to work with: John Sargent, John Cunningham, John Murphy, George Witte, Joe Rinaldi (Go get 'em, Joe), Alison Lazarus and her outstanding sales people, Ben Sevier, Steve Snider, Matthew Baldacci, and Matthew Shear. And especially to my talented, calm editor with the perfect personality for me, the outstanding driver Kelley Ragland. Thanks so much, Kelley. And thanks, Kent Ragland, for giving your little daughter a book you really liked, A *Walk Across America*, and suggesting that she read it.

A fond tribute to that pivotal moment, known to but a few, now immortalized as "Three moons over the Kenai."

And especially to Rita, my loving wife.

ARCTIC

Point Ho

Kotzebue

Deering

Nome

Unalakleet

YUKON

IDITAROD

Bethel

OCEAN

Barrow

BROOKS RANGE

Chandalar Lake

Wiseman
Coldfoot

CHANDALAR RIVER

ARCTIC CIRCLE

RIVER

ALASKA

Fairbanks

Healy
Cantwell

MT. McKINLEY

Tok

ALASKA RANGE

Merrill Pass

Talkeetna

GRIZZLY
FLATS

Anchorage

Prince William Sound

Soldotna
Seward

Cordova

KENAI
PENINSULA

MONTAGUE I.

HARVESTER I.

Resurrection Bay

KODIAK ISLAND

UNITED STATES

CANADA

Juneau

ADMIRALITY ISLAND

Angoon

Ketchikan

Craig

Hydaburg

PRINCE OF WALES ISLAND

ART & MAP BY Paul M. Breeden

Dream in the Daylight

Four feet of the whitest, most gorgeous snow was on the ground north of Moose Pass, Alaska. It looked so deep and so perfect it seemed as if I could jump out of a plane from five thousand feet and land in it with a poof, without a parachute. The top foot was fine powder; most of it had fallen ever so lightly from the sky last night. The sun does not light things for very long this time of year, and at this time of the afternoon the snow and the sharp-faced mountains glow a deep yellow-pink. The sky is the deepest, purest blue I have ever seen.

I spotted something far to the right in my peripheral vision. A magnificent long-legged, mature lynx was bounding through the snow. The clouds of snow that rose all around it hid whatever it was chasing. This scene was so exhilarating to me; it seemed to be happening in slow motion. The lynx was light and dark gray and surrounded by the clouds of yellow-pink-colored crystals of snow kicked up around it. I may have seen the lynx for only five seconds. It, and whatever it was chasing, took a sharp turn into the snow-coated spruce. I was the only person in Alaska who witnessed that moment of high inspiration. How many tiny pieces of wild animals' lives are we humans blessed to see?

Who will see the twin moose calves, warmed by spring's penetrating Alaskan sun, as they both try to stand for the first time on wobbly legs? They almost fall; one hits its nose on the ground and that keeps it from completely losing its balance. They attempt to take their first steps; they must be able to run soon. Only their mother and a few ravens watch.

Who will see the female mountain goat, who is having her kid on a beach right before Bear Glacier in a place safe from so many aggressive predators?

This lone female climbed down an almost vertical rock face to this beach on Resurrection Bay where a freshwater spring drains down the rock. No bear, no wolf, no wolverine, could follow. She would not look up often, but that is where the golden eagle came from, to take her kid in its talons.

Who gets to notice fifteen snow-white ptarmigan, the state bird, fly over the ivory meadow, the black marks on their tails looking like flying black triangles on a giant piece of clean white paper?

A pack of four black wolves pad down a frozen creek. They spook a couple thousand caribou, part of a herd of several hundred thousand. At first the wolves are not visible, just the caribou moving across the white-on-white-on-white tundra. The running caribou string out and move as if they were a school of fish, darting, alternating their course, and shifting so slightly, in unison. Then the black wolves appear surrounded by an eternity of white, and the reason for the caribou's movement is clear. No human stands on this massive piece of tundra but me.

There is so much life and death that plays out on the land and water of Alaska, and only a tiny bit of it is ever seen. But because of how Alaska thrilled and surprised me, I'm getting ahead of myself. Before we could come here, there was so much to do, so much to consider. But thanks to friends and family, it turned out to be no big deal getting access to the last frontier.

Two weeks after we arrived, riding down the hill in Seward, Alaska, on this borrowed mountain bike made me feel like a kid again, a feeling that is getting harder and harder to capture. I'd practically skidded around the curve by the abandoned orphanage, maybe fifty yards from the house we were renting, and was gaining speed on the straightaway of this paved road. The blue Schwinn mountain bike I rode had so many gears, if I shifted into the highest one, I could keep pedaling and still gain speed. People interested in my continued good health would accuse me of going too fast.

I hoped one of Seward's horses wasn't standing in the road around the next sharp, blind corner. The Bardarsons' horses lived on that corner, and one or two were often out of the corral, where the grass was greener. At the bottom of the hill a group of huge, black ravens often perched in a stand of dead spruce, making bizarre sounds. They sounded nothing like birds; hearing them I could understand why Natives felt ravens had powerful spirits. Later in the summer, when my son Luke used his bike to get back and forth to work, I would walk up this hill and try to mimic the ravens. They were too intelligent to respond.

It was early June, yet I had on a black fleece vest, blue cotton sweatpants, and Adidas cross trainers. On our farm in Tennessee, where we normally lived, it was hot and humid in June; wearing fleece would be impossible this time of year. As I sped down the hill, Alaskan air flavored by glaciers and the sea blew hard in my face. To be able to dress like this in the summer was a simple yet surprisingly profound pleasure, especially because the daylight stayed out to play until 2 A.M. Oh, to be away from the shriveling humidity.

Some of our friends thought we might be moving here forever, but Rita and I had made no plans to stay longer than a year or so. Rita and I and most of our children had been living in Alaska for only two weeks, and I hadn't traveled anywhere yet, except around and around this coastal town, really a village walled in by jagged mountains and otherworldly blue glaciers on three sides. The road to Seward ended in the sea; "downtown," where the city hall, library, and movie theater were, this town was not even three-quarters of a mile wide. In 1964 much of it had been destroyed by one of the ten worst earthquakes in the world in the last hundred years—three of the ten worst have occurred in Alaska.

I know people who travel across several countries on their two-week vacations, but this was not our vacation. While we were in Alaska, we had decided to settle down in Seward (pop. 2,830), about 130 miles south of Anchorage, on the Kenai Peninsula. I'd heard the name Seward—he was the man who "bought" Alaska for two cents an acre. But I'd never heard of Seward the city until my friend Ben Ellis told me about it. Ben, a former newspaperman, worked at the Sea Life Center there.

I didn't know where to begin this odyssey. I'd fought the feeling these two weeks that I was wasting priceless time. I was not burning up the roads headed for some Eskimo village, nor was I making any lists or filling up my calendar with interview dates and visits. Fortunately, I have a wife who understands that some people, including her husband and her father, a farmer, don't work like many people do.

Different seasons of the year, of life, demand different kinds of output. There is a time to sow and a time to reap. Sometimes it's more mental, sometimes it's almost purely physical. And at times your heart and spirit rule. There are similarities between writers and farmers; you prepare the ground, then plant the seed. You patiently allow Nature to do as she will. You take away the weeds, you allow the sun to shine and the rain to fall, then you harvest what is there.

Alaska seemed too big of a field to harvest. People I respected said, though, that Alaska was more like a big small town. Everyone knew everyone. That was easy for them to say.

I did not feel at home in Alaska yet. I wondered if I ever would. But on these journeys, I always feel this way at first. It's part of the pressure of adjusting to a new place. It might take me a while to feel comfortable. I learned a long time ago that it's best to allow myself to be reprogrammed to the pace of a new place. It's better to relax and respect my way into a new world than to force myself on it.

And there is always sadness about what we've left behind. If it hadn't been for our friends Nona and Rusty Jones, we would probably not have been here at all. Certainly we wouldn't have relocated as a family, and then the adjustment would have been much more wrenching for me. In my life, tiny, apparently un-related moments have had great influence. This whole trip had started with a simple introduction over lunch.

Over the last few years Rusty and Nona had become two of our closest friends. In the fall of 1994, Rusty invited me to come for lunch in Nashville to meet one of his clients. Rusty's an entertainment attorney and represents me when I do something entertaining. Lately I hadn't been doing much. I was pre-pared to accept that now that I was older, and like other adventurers, whether they be explorers or athletes or entrepreneurs, my best adventures in life were over. Leave the intense challenges for the young. But I didn't want to give them up. I like to compliment Rusty and tell him he is the lawyer with half a heart; at times he really seems to care about people. For months, he'd been telling me I needed to go somewhere, take off and explore, so that I would have something to write about. He knew how I was feeling and what I needed. Although he tried to make a joke of it, he knew my situation wasn't funny.

The client Rusty wanted me to meet was an Alaskan folksinger, songwriter, and true eccentric named Hobo Jim. Hobo's given name is Jim Varsos. He's ac-tually not eccentric, just ferociously himself. He has carved out his own kind of life; he's the kind of guy who has never worked in a cubicle. In the seventies he hitchhiked to Alaska with two women from Texas. They landed in Homer. Rusty had been itching to introduce us to each other. He was fond of saying that Hobo was his favorite anarchist. And, based on some comments I've made about politicians and the government, Rusty seemed to think that Hobo and I might share some views. Hobo is no anarchist; it's just that Rusty's a liberal democrat.

After lunch Hobo invited me to come visit him and his family in Alaska. I decided to take him up on his offer; about six months before I was supposed to leave, Rusty's wife, Nona, stepped in. The Joneses' youngest daughter, Grayson, had become our youngest daughter's good friend; they were both seven and *loved* the Spice Girls. Usually I did all I could to avoid hearing their music. One day, however, Rusty and I took them to a Spice Girls concert. While we were at the concert, Nona and Rita were going to see *There's Something About Mary*. (They thought it was a chick flick. Whoops.)

Nona is the kind of woman who makes things happen. She's from Memphis and she could probably run a small country. She is *not* your image of a shy and subtle southern girl. Rita fits that description more, except she's from southern Michigan. When the movie grossed them out, they went for coffee. When we all met back at the Joneses', Rita and Nona were ready for something.

"You guys, sit down," Nona commanded us, as only Nona can do.

Nona is forceful but only when she thinks there is something good for you involved. You can't help but love her because you know she loves you, even if she's a bit dominating. I am used to Nona's type of personality; my father was just like her. My dad expressed his opinion about *everything* we did—everything that he knew about, anyway. Somehow he seemed to know much more about what we did than we thought he did, almost as if he had done the same things when he was young. I used to think he wanted all of his children to do just what he said, but I learned that he expected us to respect his opinion and then make up our own minds.

When we came in from the concert, Rusty went to make us each a mint julep, but decided to wait when he discerned Nona and Rita's seriousness. Rusty surely knew something was up. Being an attorney, he is used to being thrown any kind of pitch, so he smiled comfortably as if nothing were out of the ordinary. Maybe he was still thinking about Posh Spice.

"Honey," Rita said sweetly, "Nona and I have been talking and she has something important to say for me."

My brain dashed around in search of places of difficulty in our relationship, but before I could find any, Nona took over.

"You're going to Alaska, going there to work on your next book. Well, why not take the family with you? Rita wants to move up there with you, no matter how long you plan to stay. You can take Julianne, she can go to school up there somewhere, and the older kids can come up in the summers. What do you think?"

Rusty looked as if he'd swallowed a law book. Rita watched my face and smiled one of her "this is going to happen" smiles. I felt sick just attempting to work through the logistics, and aggravated with Nona for putting me on the spot.

"That would be nice," I said, and I was only sort of lying.

It would be nice, but finding a place for all of us to stay and then moving at least the three of us up there would be difficult. Finding places to rent in the summer is hard to do. It would have to be big enough for all the kids to visit, and Alaskans as a rule don't have large homes—too much to heat for too long. Plus, every Alaskan told me that when you live in Alaska, suddenly friends and family remember you and miss you and can't wait to see you—that is, as long as you're willing to be their personal tour guide. Then there was the thought of bringing our other five children, ages fourteen, sixteen, eighteen, twenty, and twenty-three, up for the summers. Quite a frisky bunch they are. My mind raced—finding jobs for the older ones, paying for all of it, the travel, the expenses. But what Nona and Rita were suggesting did sound wonderful, and suddenly I knew that sharing Alaska was the right thing to do. Could we pull it off? Did the kids even want to?

The logistics made my brain want to burn some wires and short-circuit. It wasn't just getting them to Alaska; it was the wanting everyone to be happy and fulfilled by it. And of course there was the major challenge of truly discovering Alaska. In twisting my arm, Nona said that our children could be a big part of our Alaskan experience, that their enthusiasm would be a bonus for me. We talked with our children, and to our surprise they all wanted to experience Alaska too. They were willing to make the sacrifice of us being away from home for the time we would be together in the last frontier. Alaska was so enormous, so distinct; it had such an unusual presence. I hadn't been this overwhelmed since I began my walk across America as a twenty-two-year-old. Could I possibly handle the plate I had set for myself and now serve it up successfully to our whole family?

Rita, Julianne, Luke, Jed, Aaron and I arrived in Anchorage on the plane with one duffel bag each in late May. Rebekah and Brooke would be here soon. The duffels were huge black things with wheels on one end, made by JanSport

Somewhere along the road to Anchorage from Seward. PHOTO BY PETER JENKINS

of ballistics cloth. Each one holds over ten thousand cubic inches and weighs six pounds eight ounces empty. As big as they are, they didn't hold chairs, sofas, beds, a TV, the kitchen sink. We did bring six sleeping bags. Rita brought her set of linen napkins. She'd set those napkins up on top of a cardboard box, covered with some lovely tablecloth she had found buried at a garage sale with a vase filled with Alaskan wildflowers if she had to. She has a way of making things beautiful. That spirit of hers has even softened me.

Rita did pack a Krup's coffeemaker, which she wrapped in mismatched sheets. One essential piece of our life we made sure followed us to Alaska was our monthly delivery of coffee. Starbucks sends two pounds of coffee beans every month to our farm, usually French roast. Rita had it forwarded to Seward. There is no door-to-door mail delivery in Seward; everyone picks mail up at the post office. Our address was P.O. Box 761, zip 99664. I never thought I would have a zip code that began with a nine, much less a double nine. Where I was born, it begins with zero; where I have been living since the early eighties, it begins with three.

The street where we lived in Seward went another hundred yards or so and intersected with Seward's main street, which was the one and only road out of town. Go left to Anchorage and the rest of North America; go right about a mile to downtown Seward and the ocean.

I rode my bike on a path that paralleled the road. After two weeks I could fly down it. These horses seemed to know not to come toward the main road. Somebody's horses had been running around on Seward's airport runway, where they had to compete for grazing with the moose that lived off in the willows by the runway.

Being surrounded as we are here by the wilderness, endless mountains, water, and glaciers, with only one road out, Seward has little crime, even though most of the worst criminals in Alaska live here. On the other side of Resurrection Bay by Fourth of July Creek and Spring Creek is Alaska's maximum-security prison. It sits alone crammed a long way down a closed mountain valley.

Seward's only recent bank robbery took place in the seventies. To rob a bank in Seward, where the road dead-ends into the ocean and goes for sixty miles north with no outlet, is not going to get you listed in the who's who of successful bank robbers. A bank robber trying to escape would not park a getaway car and attempt to climb over the mountains and glaciers that hem us in. These glaciers have carved out the bit of flat land that Seward perches on by the sea; these inspired sculptors have carved much of Alaska and are still grinding away. Sometimes the glaciers look silver, sometimes ice blue; sometimes they are immaculate, covered with snow. They keep us in on the east and the west and stretch for miles and miles to the north. There are only narrow passageways out of town, some blasted by man and others created by the glaciers' flow.

The ocean waters of Resurrection Bay, which flow in from the Gulf of Alaska, block us, except of course for boats. The waters bring to within view of town pods of orcas, several salmon runs a year, sea otters floating on their backs. Even a humpback can sometimes be seen breaching a mile or more offshore.

The mountains, sharp as a scalpel, that rise on all sides make us feel secure some days, trapped on others, and when the sun, clouds, and glacial mists cooperate, extremely inspired. Sometimes the mountain walls can be seen so clearly that their grandeur can almost knock you over. When people from Outside, which is what Alaskans call the rest of the United States, hear that Mount Alice, directly to our east, is just 5,265 feet in elevation, they act disappointed. People are looking for big numbers, but numbers can be deceiving. The mountains all around us rise up from sea level. The mountains I've walked over in Colorado start at eight or nine thousand feet, and the grandest rise to something over thirteen thousand. Here what are called hanging glaciers are sus-

8

A bull orca surfaces near us in Resurrection Bay, Seward. PHOTO BY PETER JENKINS

pended in among the surrounding peaks; they were like blue mirages floating inside openings in the clouds. There just is no easy way out of Seward, and there had been no easy way to get out of my stagnation, a feeling I'd felt for a few years, until coming here.

Seward is one of those rare communities where you can turn your kids loose and let them roam around town. People don't have to worry about not being able to find husbands or wives. Turn them loose. Even if a husband is prone to hang around at bars or other places he shouldn't—which I am not—he can be found quickly. There are only so many bars and only so many streets. Many people think that Alaska would be a great place to disappear to or hide out, but that's not true in Seward.

I rode Joe's bike across the main street, which is called either the Seward Highway or Third Avenue depending on where you are, and headed toward the city docks. I have always loved hanging around boat docks. By Icicle Seafoods, a cannery, there's a railroad car or two set up with shops in them. One corner is the bike shop, where fourteen-year-old Joe Tougas got his really advanced new mountain bike, the yellow and black one, which is why I was riding his old one. Redheaded, shorthaired Joe is a hard worker, and he pays for his bikes with his own money. He even put studded tires on his new one for winter. I watched the way the teenagers rode their mountain bikes, down the stairs and up the stairs. They would ride up a couple stairs slowly, almost coming to a stop, fighting for balance. I tried to do what they did.

The guy who runs the bike shop and his family spend the summer here and drive to Mexico in their camper and live there after tourist season. I was always seeing him in the bay in his kayak or riding fast around town on one of his bikes.

I pedaled over to Captain Jack's. Captain Jack is Jack Scoby. Several years ago, he and his wife, Sheila, and some other pioneering Sewardites started taking visitors on their boat into the bay to see the orcas and humpbacks and Steller's sea lions and bald eagles and Dall porpoise and peregrine falcons and mind-blowing glaciers. They then sold out to Kenai Fjord Tours, who continued their tradition and added more boats to their fleet. At Captain Jack's, they process the fresh salmon and halibut tourists catch each day on the local charter boats. Our sons Luke and Aaron would have summer jobs there cutting up and vacuum-packing the fish, then shipping it FedEx frozen back to the fisherman's home. If you caught an eighty-pound halibut and six silvers, you could send sixty to seventy pounds of fresh fish back home.

Part of the reason I was not jumping face first into Alaska was that I wanted to make sure the family was settled in. Our other son, Jed, sixteen, would work at the local Helly Hansen store. They sold the kind of high-quality wet-weather gear favored by commercial fishermen and outdoor gear that was quickly being discovered by adventurers and outdoorsy people.

It was about four o'clock and getting crowded on the docks, since many charter-fishing boats come in around this time. They say that late in the afternoon in summer you can climb to the top of Mount Marathon, one of the thousands of mountains around Seward, and see the whole fishing fleet heading home, making white wakes in the turquoise-blue-green ocean.

I took off again, past Miller's Daughter, where we went for homemade bread and soup. I loved being able to eat hot soup in the summer. I rode through a parking lot and around the corner to two old school buses that were sort of pushed together. Inside the small one was Red. He sold the best hamburgers and fries in town. He'd set up a soda machine outside and kept a few picnic tables for his customers. Everyone said that Seward in the summer and Seward in the winter were two different cities; we would find out, they'd tell us, and watch for our reaction. I had none. I had no idea what an Alaskan winter was like, and I wasn't quite ready to learn yet. I was still getting my feet wet.

Leaving Red's gravel parking lot was a man in a motorized wheelchair. He pulled out onto our main street and headed down the road, out of town, at about five miles an hour. He didn't drive in the main car lane but just to the side. I was headed to our little bitty movie theater to see which kids we could take to the movie, which we would do once a week all summer, but I turned around and pulled alongside the man in the wheelchair. When he saw me, he pulled farther over so I wouldn't be nailed by some of the traffic. He said he was headed to Eagle, a grocery store on the edge of town just before the huge metal coffee cup called Espresso Simpatico. A guy named Darien sold Americanos and lattes and all kinds of other fancy coffee there.

I must have registered surprise on my windburned face because he said, "That's no big deal. I've taken this wheelchair all the way to the Pit Bar." The Pit Bar stays open until 5 A.M. and opens again a few hours later. It's a few miles out the road.

I told him to have a nice ride, he wished me the same. I rode past Terry's Tire and Lube, a gas station right out of the fifties, where Terry and his wife repair tires and change oil. Before Terry's on the left was National Bank of Alaska. It had small plots of ground by the side road entrance where people tend little gardens. After we'd been to the bank once, Cheryl, at the far right window, knew our names. She lived about halfway up our hill in an apartment complex. We'd run into Cheryl all over the place, as you do everyone you love, hate, or are indifferent about in a small place like Seward.

I try not to hate anyone, but there is an occasional person in life that you just don't want to see, and that is what's bad about Seward's post office. I pedaled there before checking into the movie playing at the Liberty Theater. Everyone in Seward has to go to the post office every day to get mail. Eventually you notice who gets their mail at what time of day, and if you want to see a friend or meet someone or avoid someone else, you know when to go. If you hate people in general, you could go to the post office at 3 A.M. If you had a big package, they'd put a key in your box that fit a larger box and keep your big package there. If you love most people and have time to spare, you could hold the front door for people and strike up conversations. Just as long as you didn't get in the way of the people who hold their eyes straight ahead and are in a hurry to get back to work. Though there aren't many of these types in Seward.

I often volunteered to stand in line at the post office to buy some stamps for the family just to check out the platinum blond window clerk. One day I had mailed a package and noticed she wore yellow contacts that made her eyes look like snake eyes. A few days later she wore red ones that made her eyes look like the devil, someone you wouldn't expect to see working at the post office. The next week she wore purple ones because they matched her sweater, or black ones because she'd ridden her Harley to work and they matched her leathers. I told her I liked the statement she was making; she said thanks, that at least half the people didn't look her in the eye.

A few blocks over and down, getting closer all the time to Resurrection Bay, was Liberty Theater. I rode up and stopped. I stared through the glare on the glass at the movie posters. This week *The Mummy* was playing, and coming soon was *A Simple Plan*. The Liberty is almost exactly like the first movie theater I ever went to, back in Connecticut in the early sixties. I remembered having my father drop me off a few blocks away on my first date so that Kathy Flanigan wouldn't see me getting out of our old car. We always seemed to have cars that were ten years older than everyone else's. It took me at least half the movie to put my arm around the back of her chair. My knee touched hers, I forget if it was accidental, what a surprising thrill. I don't remember what was playing—it didn't matter.

I do remember another night in that theater in Connecticut, a night my life was altered, seriously and profoundly. It was a couple years before I put my arm around Kathy. A few hours in the dark being consumed by what was happening on-screen had actually influenced this moment on this borrowed blue bike in Seward, Alaska. The movie I saw that evening, over thirty-five years ago, would crawl deep into my subconscious to the place where my dreams were born, where my fears originated. The movie was *Lawrence of Arabia*. I saw it when I was eleven or twelve.

The opening scene from *Lawrence of Arabia* has haunted me on and off all these years. It gripped me like a prophecy that would someday come true. I had this feeling, even then as a sixth-grader, that sometime much later in life I would die, like Lawrence, on a narrow country street surrounded by green fields and contented, quiet people.

Why would that scene, a scene about an adventurer's death, haunt a sixth-grader? I'd not known anyone who'd died, I'd never feared for my life. I loved life. In the opening of this movie, which won seven Academy Awards, T. E. Lawrence is done with the desert and done with Arabia, where he had led a rebellion, and he heads out for a ride on a powerful motorcycle away from his cuddly, tree-shaded, petite cottage in the English countryside. The walls of his cottage must have become so confining. He fuels up his Brough motorcycle, wipes up some spilled drops, and takes off, shifting rapidly, gaining speed. His goggles keep the bugs out of his eyes. The road is not smooth; he bounces with the thrill of the ride, he feels it. He is going too fast but he must go faster. After all he's done in Arabia, to feel anything takes more and more. T. E. Lawrence needs to be thrilled again, even if it's just for the few minutes of the ride. He needs to risk something. Some unsuspecting bicyclists, meandering in the countryside, are in his lane; he is going far too fast, he's on the edge of being out of control. Still, there is life in his eyes, concentration. Then he begins to skid, then he slides off the road, then he is dead.

I got a Mustang GT right before I turned forty. Every time I'd get to going outrageously fast in it out on some country road near our farm that used to be only wide enough for a wagon, this scene from the movie would come up in my mind. When I got my hand stuck between two logs, attached to a logging chain, attached to my Ford 5000 gas tractor, and was trapped there for three hours, I thought of this scene. I did not really think I would die but wondered if I would lose my right hand if no one found me until nighttime. Finally, my neighbors Cindy and Ray Williams heard my screams, and Ray released me. That hand still goes numb. Whenever I pull out onto the main road near the end of our gravel driveway and about get smashed by a concrete truck because I am preoccupied with something stupid or silly, I think of this scene.

I'm not sure why it has been so hard for me to leave home for the last several years. The kind of writing I do, if I don't leave home, I don't have anything to write about. Part of it may be that I've always yearned for a home and never really found one until I moved to this farm. Growing up, we lived in a federal housing project. Now I know every square foot of these 150 acres of farm; it is my island, our peace. I know where the coyotes crawl under the fence to get to the back hayfield, where recently one tried and failed to haul the leg bone of one of my neighbor's dead cows underneath it. I know where the flock of wild turkeys scratches in the leaves of the forest around the straight red oaks looking for acorns and bugs. I have seen where springs bubble out of the ground in April after heavy rains. For the last three years a great horned owl has nested, first in a half-dead oak a hundred yards from our front porch and then in an oak thirty feet from the back door. Last spring one of the baby owls blew out of the nest into the yard; somehow it flew back. I've seen the spot where red-tailed hawks have killed cottontail rabbits. I know each cow and who her father was.

When I take walks to the larger half of the farm, back to the woods, I always look toward Kedron Road and see the dream home that my ex-wife, Barbara, and I built, just a few hundred yards from where I live now. Barbara owns it now and rents it out to strangers. She lives up the road about thirty-five miles with our three children. We restored a 1901 farmhouse, added on an oak timber-frame structure, put in a hot tub, and thought it would be perfect. I found a great deal on walnut lumber at the sawmill in Culleoka, when no one wanted walnut. I had gorgeous tongue-and-groove flooring made, cheap, at some guy's shop behind his house in Lewisburg. Part of that dream, the part with our children, has been put back together, albeit imperfectly. The other part, about Barbara and me, is focused on our children and it works well because we love them so much.

The home Rita and I live in now is just up the hill. A ranch house that used to be owned by Jess and Mary Lou Morton, we've added on to it. It is painted gray, but the paint is constantly peeling. Paint just does not seem to stick to it. Jess told me he always had the same problem.

Red and gray foxes come out at night; we sometimes see them in the fields when we're coming home after dark. The coyotes often howl on the ridge behind us; five of them can sound like twenty, although, who knows, maybe there *are* twenty of them up there. As I listen to them, I wonder, do they howl to celebrate life or are they crying? I wish they would let me join them. Instead, I go to church to get my release. At the farm, for the first time in my life I can understand how someone could sit on a front porch in a rocking chair, just sit. I used to criticize people for that.

As much as I love that piece of land and my family, lately though, I'd become too sedate, too Buddha-like, too contented. Until now.

I rode over to Second Avenue and coasted down the hill toward the sea. I turned left, onto the bike path. When I got to the city's skateboarding ramps, I went up and over one and glided back along Resurrection Bay. A couple local teens looked at me like "You're too old to be doing that!" A gull glided to my right, hovering to see if two Steller's sea lions would leave any scraps.

I got back to Phoenix Road and turned right. It was a hard, uphill pedal; I refused to get off and walk, even though I felt like it, even in the lowest gear. Two black ravens sat in the top of a swaying spruce and made odd clucking sounds. I thought again about how we would not be here in Alaska if it hadn't been for true friends. But here we were.

I was riding past the orphanage, almost home, when I remembered a quote from T. E. Lawrence's book *Seven Pillars of Wisdom*. It rushed to me now: *All men dream: but not equally. Those who dream by night in the dusty recesses of their minds wake up in the day to find it was vanity: but the dreamers of the day are dangerous men, for they may act their dreams with open eyes, to make it possible. This I did.*

So far in life I'd dreamed and made my dreams live in the light. Each one brought to life far surpassed the dream. Right this minute a dream was coming to life, being lit by the almost constant daylight of an Alaskan summer.

When I got home, Rita wanted me to plant some flowers she'd bought over in Soldotna, shopping with our friend Linda. So I did.

2

Ted

A man I met named Ted Spraker probably sees about as much as any human can because of what he does for a living. What a life Ted has. When I was between nine and eighteen, I dreamed about being like him. You could say he is a type of referee in one of the wildest places in the world. Ted spends much of his time saving wild animals from themselves and each other, saving wild animals from humans, saving humans from wild animals. The most horrifying and, fortunately, rare part of his job is investigating the death of a human by the claws or teeth of an animal.

Ted Spraker has lived in Alaska since July 1973. As an Alaska Fish and Game area wildlife biologist he gets just as many calls for help at the office as he does at home. Doesn't matter what's going on at home—the phone rings, he must stop what he's doing and take action. Ted must be prepared for everything a wild animal can do to people, their property, or themselves.

People call him needing help with two moose in a backyard pool, suicidal squirrels chewing through wires charged with electricity, brown bears killing chickens, bats flying too close to the TV screen, and wolves on the porch. They dial his number because of a quill-slinging porcupine or a bald eagle that's got a fishing lure in its foot. They call because a wolverine tore up a shed, a caribou calf is lost or orphaned, or a coyote killed Julie's cat. They call when a human has been killed by one of the wild animals on the Kenai Peninsula.

Ted earned his B.S. in wildlife management and his M.S. in range management from the University of Wyoming. He's half dusty-dry westerner from Wyoming and half Cajun from near Houma, Louisiana. He's got some of Clint

Eastwood's strong, quiet side, some of Jack Nicholson's playful irony, and the nonjudgmental portion of your best friend's personality wrapped up in his own unique self.

Ted says there have been no calls recently about field mice attacks, but then the winters have been mild lately, which leads to less drinking. Like so many who work unpredictable high-excitement/high-boredom jobs, Ted seems unexcitable. Similar to detectives and SWAT team members, the job with Fish and Game can be mundane almost to the point of comatose. But then some bear or wolf, wolverine or moose, does something upsetting to the public; perhaps it even kills something or someone. When a human is killed, there is the potential for the highest, most terrible drama. In the spring of 1998, Ted got one of those dreadful calls. A forty-year-old man working on a seismic crew was mauled by a brown bear and lost his life near Soldotna. Nothing can prepare Ted, and the rest of Alaska Fish and Game, for some of the scenarios they encounter.

Sometimes the calls to Fish and Game are framed in the hardwood of sheer terror. One damp, foggy night a longtime Alaska resident called. She seemed close to losing control. It was during the short dark time of an Alaskan summer night, at 2:57 A.M. Ted remembers some late-late-night calls and even what time some of them woke him. He can still see the numbers that tell the time glowing obnoxiously large and red on his alarm clock that night.

The first sound he heard on the phone, drowning out the caller, was a chilling roaring that could only be a brown bear. His first thought, based on the intensity and volume of the roaring, was that a bear had either gotten in the house and the callers were being attacked, or that someone was calling on a cell phone while their dome tent was being invaded.

The woman's voice was so charged, so altered by terror, that though Ted knew her, he did not recognize her at first, not until she said her name. She and her husband were friends of his; in fact, they'd had a problem with a sow and her two cubs a few days before. These brown bears had come to their yard and destroyed their chicken house and most of their chickens. They came back a couple days later to see what else they could eat and tear up. Ted and his associates had set three supposedly close-to-indestructible culvert traps in their yard.

It was difficult carrying on a conversation because, although the woman was inside her well-built and well-insulated home, the roaring of the mother bear outside was so loud. Every few minutes Ted heard what sounded loud enough to be the bear tearing down their house. Actually, it sounded more like the bear was tearing apart their car, because it was the sound of metal being destroyed.

Turned out both cubs had gotten trapped, and the sow was literally trying to rip apart the metal traps, rolling them over, smashing them with her paws, biting—whatever she could, all the while filling up the woods and this home with her desperate roaring and sounds of destruction. While telling me this story, Ted repeated a few times that he could not believe the mother bear's sounds were that loud inside the house. The sow did turn over one trap, somehow tore open the door, and released one of her cubs. They were gone before Ted got there. Ted and his associates retrieved the one cub still in a trap and moved it far away.

"I would not want to imagine what would happen if I got between that mother bear and her cubs. Just call the funeral director, and he better be expert at restoring the head area because that's what they go for first," Ted told me.

One night, at 12:32 A.M., in the fall, the caller was a new Alaskan, the real tenderfoot type, just moved up from Massachusetts. He was trying the wilderness thing, back to Walden Pond, except Walden Pond, Alaska, has radically different creatures and much more severe challenges. Walden Pond, Massachusetts, has more in common with Club Med than Alaska. Ted explained that usually a city- or suburban-bred tenderfoot from outside Alaska only lasts about a year and a half. Sometimes they don't make it through one winter.

It was late fall. There had been a small salmon return, and the bears were looking in places other than the spawning streams for sustenance. This guy was doing the mushing thing, thought he'd have some sled dogs, he'd read Jack London's books. He also had a Dalmatian that ran outside in nice weather and lived inside with him at night and when it rained.

In a frantic voice, punctuated by hyper breathing, the tenderfoot said that something big and black, maybe dark brown and hairy, was chasing his Dalmatian around the outside of the house. The dog would try to leap high and crash through the door. The newly arrived pioneer didn't have a gun, didn't believe he needed one. If he needed help, as he did now, he would just call somebody. Often in Alaska there is no one to call, or by the time help arrives, it's too late. In some villages the nearest law, an Alaska state trooper, is more than a hundred miles away and must fly in on a bush plane when summoned. He wanted Ted to come over, catch his dog, and bring it inside, then "shoo off" the hairy thing. Ted told the man to open the door just a bit, turn on all the lights, and call for his dog. He followed Ted's instructions with Ted talking him through it as if he had been about to jump off a bridge. In a minute or two Ted heard the dog crash into the man, then a noise like something getting knocked over, and then the guy hung up. The man called back a bit later, thanking Ted, saying everything was fine.

Just when Ted thinks he has heard it all, an animal does something creative. There was the time a mother moose and her twin calves walked into someone's swimming pool, the kind with slick rubber sides. They could have been thirsty; maybe they just love water. The mama moose easily walked out, but the calves were stuck, almost drowned by the time Ted and his colleagues were alerted. The sides were too slick for their tiny hooves; they slipped every time they tried to walk out like their mother did. Ted pulled his truck up close to the edge of the pool, but when he'd try to get out of his truck, the mother would charge him. She'd lay back her long ears, the hair on the back of her neck would stand straight up, and she would attack, making a combination blowing, growling sound. A charging moose will run right over the top of you; Ted's seen one do it to a brown bear. And they strike with their potentially lethal front hooves, probably their most deadly weapon. Finally one of the other Fish and Game guys distracted her while Ted and another man put an old piece of carpet on the side of the pool, which the calves could climb up without slipping. They herded the calves toward the carpet; they got out, weak and hungry, but they lived.

"We get a bunch of terrified people calling in on those situations," Ted said.

And there are the ever-present waddling porcupines filling people's dogs with quills, using their awful darts to terrorize bear cubs who think the porcupines are so tempting, a free lunch. One time Ted had to rescue a pathetic black bear cub that had gone for such a slow-moving porcupine and filled his paws, lips, tongue, and nose with the barbed quills. Ted has been impressed with some creatures that in desperation come to human settlements, seemingly for help. This bear cub, who could have been helped by nothing else, even its mother, came and crawled under a car at the Ford dealer in Soldotna and would not leave. Ted sedated it, pulled out the quills, and released it to find its mother.

Ted must determine whether a call requires an instant response. There are plenty of calls where a bull moose in the rut has "attacked" someone's swing set and is completely tangled up in it. Apparently swing sets are attractive. The moose is now headed down the road with the whole swing set in its sixty-inch antlers, getting more tangled by the minute. Can you imagine driving home in the dark down a narrow, fog-coated back road in Alaska and seeing a swing set coming toward you? Then there are two glowing eyes in the middle of it, then horns five feet wide, then long, dark brown legs, and then huge ears. Then the moose gets frightened by the oncoming car and tries running through the tangled, jumbled, stunted spruce woods, the trees two or three feet apart. What a mess. Well, that kind of mess is the kind Ted and the others at Fish and Game get to handle.

When Ted gets a call at home, he has to get dressed, get his dart gun, and try to find the lovelorn bull moose. Fortunately many of the new swing sets are built cheap, so with each smack by the moose they lose another piece. It's the older swing sets built with better metal that really tangle them up, or the ones custom-built with stronger chain. One time Ted had to rescue a moose that had tangled with a swing set, then run for the middle of a marshy lake. Normally moose run into the middle of a lake when a major predator is chasing them, a pack of wolves or a brown bear. The swing set almost drowned the moose. By the time Ted got there with his boat, the moose was too weak to swim. Just his head and a bit of the swing set were sticking barely out of the water. Ted and his wife, feisty and blond Elaina, shot it with a dart, then had to hold its head above water and cut off the swing set. Elaina climbed into the water with it to get a better grip on its head. They were with that moose for over five hours, and finally it got strong enough to hold its head up by itself without fear of drowning, and they were able to leave.

Once a cross-country skier found a golden eagle that had lost its front talons on its right foot. It was so weak it could not take off from the small, dead tree it sat in. The skier caught it, wrapped it in a coat, risking freezing herself, and brought it to town. Ted met her and put the eagle in the truck with him. Ted shoots a moose every year, like many Alaskans; it is a large part of the meat he eats every year. The moose meat goes along with the salmon he and the family catch, the clams they dig, the halibut they haul in, and some caribou too. Well, that winter Ted fed a surprising amount of that moose to that recovering golden eagle that lived in his garage on the bad days and on the bright and sunny winter days in a perch in his backyard. He released her that spring as healthy as a golden eagle could be. She had gained so much weight eating at least 125 pounds of moose meat over that winter of recovery that she was a real armful, even for a strong man like Ted, who is six feet tall, 195 pounds.

In Alaska, more than most places on earth, the animals of the wild live out their dramatic daily existence haunted by the possibility of death. A bear or a wolverine, a lynx or a wolf, may find a dead moose. What a huge and thrilling pile of meat, but they may lose their life defending it. Every other predator wants it too. They may be crippled or have to kill something else to keep it. The wolves want the moose meat; the sly, shadowlike coyote wants it. So do the wolverines, the lynx, the eagles, and the black bears. The brown bears may want it the most—they have the largest need for it.

There is an order of dominance among bears; one brown bear may fight off every other predator only to be killed by a dominant member of its species. An orphaned set of twins might find the moose, the two cubs on the verge of starving, vicious to live, a gnawing in their stomachs so severe as to risk all for their prize. One big boar, though, can smell death from miles off if the wind is right and come to it. The orphans might growl a bit, the hair on their backs might stand up, but if they even attempt to fight the boar, they can easily be killed by just the physical force of the dominant male's nine-and-a-half-inch paws, his claws not even necessary.

Every minute of the day and night in Alaska these plays are acted out on the red- and blueberry-speckled tundra, in the rock- and snow-covered mountain passes, in the shadowed spruce woods, on top of the frozen lakes, up and down a once-gentle creek. Rarely do the few Alaskan humans see anything. But Ted has seen much as he has flown over the land that is home to the creatures he is charged to care for. Sometimes, Ted and his staff fly over the land looking to dart wolves; they give them shots to kill the horrible lice infestations they have gotten from dogs. In 1961, only one wolf was spotted on the 8,400 square miles of the Kenai Peninsula, where Ted is the state biologist. Today, twenty packs of wolves live on the peninsula.

Ted has a front-row seat, he and the hired bush pilot, to dramas where supreme predators lose their fight, their blood, their breath, their consciousness, to another, one more powerful, faster. He has seen the proof in the snow, a lengthy, drawn-out diagram that can easily be understood by those with his education, who can read the distance between tracks, the final body language of circling and confrontation.

He says that when they tranquilize the wolves to give them shots of Ivermectin to kill the destructive lice, it is amazing the severe injuries that they can see on almost every wolf, wounds that have mended. They've been kicked by moose before they've learned how to efficiently dodge and kill, bitten by members of their own pack, slashed with the claws of bears, embedded with porcupine quills, even scratched by ground squirrels that fight back.

THE NIGHTMARE BEGAN AT 2:30 A.M.

Tension-filled calls come during regular business hours at the office, which is in a metal-sided building off Kalifornsky Road in Soldotna. Alaska Fish and Game occupies the upstairs; Doors and Windows Unlimited is downstairs. Ted knows the various situations are of utmost importance to the caller, but sometimes it's all he can do to maintain his professional demeanor. He took one such call yesterday.

Yesterday's call was all about a building invasion by squirrels. First they got into the attic of the Woman's Resource and Crisis Center in Soldotna, and then they ate through the dryer vent. Once they got into the main living area, the rampaging squirrels took to running through the building at will. They chewed through electric lines; one electrocuted itself. The director was afraid there would be an electrical short and the place would burn to the ground. Ted came to the rescue; those little gray monsters were much harder to catch than the moose wrapped in the swing set in the middle of the lake.

Today's call was a different story. For the next call, when it came, was much more serious. It was June 16, 1999; it had not been dark for more than a couple of hours on the Kenai Peninsula when Ted was first called at home at 4:35 A.M. It was his coworker Larry Lewis on the line. Larry and a state trooper had responded at about 3:30 A.M. to a 911 call, "a defense of life and property shooting." It had been too dark to do any searching when Larry and the trooper had gone out there, especially once they learned from the callers that they were looking for marauding brown bears. Now it was later in the morning, and Ted had invited me along to answer the call in the light of day.

The original 911 call had come from a woman named Lisa; she is married to Brian. Ted knows them, as he does most longtime residents of the peninsula. He'd been called to their place once before, something about a suspected Sasquatch. When you see a very large male brown bear's tracks in powdery snow, I guess you could think they belonged to a Sasquatch, especially when they circled your horse corral. Maybe it was more comforting to think that something with feet that large was more human than giant male bear. This young couple has five small children; they live out in the woods by themselves. Brian's family are some of the original homesteaders in the area; they came here in the 1940s, when most were commercial fishermen. Brian and Lisa live right off the Sterling Highway at Mile 117, the major road that goes from Soldotna to Homer. Their homestead is just nineteen miles from Soldotna.

Soldotna is a bigger town, more like Anchorage. It has some wilderness surrounding it, but it also has Taco Bell, McDonald's, Kmart, Safeway, Fred Meyers (a twenty-four-hour superstore), car dealers, movie theaters, a sports bar, dentists and doctors, and much more. You can get your nails done, hear *All Things Considered*, and visit enough drive-in latte and espresso places on your routes through town to keep you wired. You just cannot say this about many places in Alaska. Some residents are delighted by this fact, some are horrified, and some don't know the difference. Around Soldotna and neighboring Kenai, it would be easy to get comfortable, to feel man has tamed Alaska. Stay in your car and house, plug into the Internet or your PlayStation, and you could believe that there is no harm that can come to you and your family from the surrounding woods and mountains. You could even become so disconnected from reality by never venturing into the wild that beckons from so close by that you really don't believe there is anything living in all those woods you drive by every day. Drink too many espressos in a day and you might think you were living in suburban Seattle.

This disorientation will never happen to Brian and Lisa or their five children, not after last night. Their nightmare began at about 2:30 A.M. It wasn't yet completely dark; many shades of gray light were still mixing with the night's black. Lisa heard something first; mothers sleep lightly when they have little ones. There was barking, some other noises. The family has several dogs, a couple sled dogs chained in the stunted spruce just beyond their front yard and their Great Pyrenees, which runs free and protects the place.

"In the last twenty years there have been more people killed by dogs than bears in Alaska," Ted mentioned to me matter-of-factly in the truck on the way there.

The road we drove down was modern, straight and smooth, with wide shoulders. It comfortably carried thousands of tourists and locals year-round. It appeared devoid of risk, almost boring. White spruce dotted the hillsides and the gently rolling land alongside, which had occasional muskeg swamps carpeted in golden grass. They looked like little pastures; they attracted the moose.

Ted carried in a padded case a bolt-action .338 Winchester magnum rifle with open iron sights. Many would think this gun would not be enough to stop a brown bear. He told me about the other sow in the area about which he has gotten complaints. He said her territory overlapped with that of the bad-behaving sow.

"I wonder, was this shooting due to this extremely dangerous sow, a sow that had been causing real problems for years, but always escaped," Ted said, trying to plan what our actions would be when we arrived at the site. "Will she ever cross the line from killing dogs, chickens, and goats and savaging property to destroying human life?" We were now just past Mile 100.

When the *good* sow entered human territory, she normally didn't come out of the brush, he told me. She stayed hidden, making loud blowing and woofing sounds, trying to call her cubs away from people's dogs, chickens, rabbits, and smokehouses. Ted said that she tried to teach her cubs that raiding human settlements is dangerous. This sow understood that her cubs could be killed if they began attacking someone's dogs or killing someone's goats. We drove by a homestead with a corral made of hand-cut spruce poles in front, holding a couple horses.

Ted said he had been dealing with the dangerous sow for years, cleaning up her attacks, her messes, but he'd never been able to trap and move her. He had never even seen her, he just knew her by her distinctive behavior and territory. She goes right into people's yards; she roars, letting everyone around know *she* is afraid of nothing, *she* is supreme to all living creatures and seemingly unafraid of their biggest, baddest bullets. Naturally, she scares the hell out of people and doesn't seem to care that her act is life-threatening.

"She is teaching her cubs the worst possible behavior," Ted said, sincerely concerned. "Larry said they saw a bear running away from the house, across the road, but it was still dark and it could have been an older cub."

Brown bear sows and their cubs on the Kenai Peninsula have home ranges of three hundred to four hundred square miles, males some five hundred to six hundred square miles. Keep in mind, Rhode Island is only 1,212 square miles. Ted clearly struggles with issues of problem bears and his official response. There had been shots fired. If she was severely wounded after her latest con-

Two brown bears after some easy pickings. Photo by Peter Jenkins

frontation with humans, would they find her? What if she lived, what if next time she broke into someone's cabin and killed a child or maimed an adult? There would be an intense public outcry, and if the public then found out that she had been terrorizing people for years, what would they say? Ted and his associates had to think about all of this. They usually made great efforts not to kill bears. They trapped problem animals, moved them a hundred miles away. Often of course, the bears came right back; as old and smart as this sow was, she would probably be too smart to enter a trap.

When their dogs had first started barking, Lisa hadn't thought much of anything. It could have been a slow-moving porcupine just out of reach of the dogs, or a moose browsing on the hillside. A lynx might have killed a snowshoe hare in sight of the dogs. But then Lisa heard the barking become more pronounced, more agitated, higher pitched, faster, until it was incessant. She surely hoped the dogs would stop or slow as they usually do after the animal passes from view. Surely she hoped they would stop, just like any mother with five small children yearning for more sleep, rest, and peace.

But these dogs were not barking out of curiosity, or plain intrigue, nor were they stopping or slowing down. Whatever was bothering them was getting closer, more threatening, more terrifying. Their Great Pyrenees, who was loose, was normally fearless. Lisa went through the possibilities. This time of the year it was not likely to be a moose, unless maybe a late calf had somehow got scared and wandered in between the dogs. A mother moose could kill all the chained dogs, maim them; it would be a disaster. And there was too much intensity in the barking for it to be a porcupine waddling on its self-involved way. Stray dogs almost never came out this far; stray dogs in the Alaska wilds are like Snickers bars sitting on a fourth-grader's desk—just waiting to be eaten. Wolves, coyotes, bears, love to eat them, so they are almost never a problem.

It just about had to be a major predator out in Lisa and Brian's yard. If it was black bears or brown bears, this was a bad time of the year for them because the salmon were not spawning in the creeks yet and therefore they would go hungry. If it was a brown bear sow with twin two-and-a-half-year-olds outside, that would be about the worst possible thing. The two-and-a-half-year-olds are the equivalents of human teenagers, capable of real damage, not as big as an adult but still strong enough to kill a human or anything else. They are fearless, the bear version of "ten feet tall and bulletproof." An old male could be a big problem, his teeth worn, his metabolism unable to convert meat and protein to muscle the way it used to, hungry, smelling dog food, or better yet, tasty dog. It could be the sow with year-and-a-half-old cubs. These young cubs, maybe 140 pounds if it was a male, 120 if it was a female, were more curious and rambunctious than dangerous, although if cornered, they could certainly kill a person. A 110-pound black bear cub had recently killed a grown woman in the Smoky Mountains. In this case, though, Ted said the "good" sow normally ended up getting a cub out of a jam with aggressive sled dogs. She was smart enough to realize that to keep her cubs and herself alive, they needed to avoid being too threatening to humans and their property.

What Lisa and Brian wanted most was for the barking to stop and for whatever was outside to go away, to leave their little clearing. They all wanted to go back to sleep and not have to bring their own conclusion to this rapidly escalating situation. It was incredible how loud it was inside. They usually lived in the deep silence that exists in few places other than Alaska. They prayed, if they were praying people, that these sounds would not wake their children. They hoped beyond hope that whatever was out there would not come any closer to their hand-hewn log cabin.

And there were other sounds that Lisa did not recognize. Finally, there was so much sound outside their log cabin that it did wake up the kids. When the noise became unbearable, they decided to call 911, and that's what had led to our morning drive.

Reacting to the initial 911 call was Larry Lewis, forty-two, a State of Alaska wildlife technician and often Ted's sidekick, and Alaska state trooper Jim Moen, Fish and Game Enforcement. They arrived at Mile 117 at around 3:30 A.M. Trooper Moen saw something run across the road and away from the house right as they arrived. Larry was there because Brian had fired his rifle and thought he had hit one of the bears. In Alaska, if you are being attacked or are in fear of your life, or your property is being destroyed—your dogs, your home, your boat—you can legally shoot a bear or moose. Then you must call the state, and if the animal is found dead, you must skin it and turn over the entire bear or moose to the state. These quintessentially Alaskan moments are called Defense of Property and Defense of Life Shootings. Because the hides and skulls and gallbladders and claws of bears are valuable, the shooter, regardless if the bear came within a hair of killing him, must turn over all parts of value to the state.

Larry and Trooper Moen were not going to follow a possibly wounded bear into the almost impenetrable underbrush and forest surrounding Brian and Lisa's in the dark. Even in bright daylight these woods, thickets, head-high wild grasses, and swamps have too many hiding places.

They'd gone home, and now it was 10:30 A.M. and I was with Ted and we were to meet them and another guy where the road to Clam Gulch dead-ends into Sterling Highway between Kasilof and Ninilchik. A bunch of dog mushers, commercial fisherman, partially retired hippies, and Ed Borden live in Kasilof.

Ed, in his mid-forties, wearing his salt-and-pepper hair pulled back in a pony-tail, has run the Iditarod but now supports himself by making exquisite racing sleds. He is also a seasonal employee of Fish and Game. Ted told me that Ed is an incredible craftsman and in great demand as a racing dog-sled maker. Tracking a wounded brown bear is one of the most dangerous things in the world anyone could possibly do; Ed is obviously not doing this for his state hourly wage.

Three trucks were waiting for us in the brown dirt parking lot that was our meeting place. Ed was out leaning against his.

"Ted, why am I here? I don't want to spend my time looking for another hairy female." Ed was rarely serious. After all, he lived in Kasilof, where Ted said poaching is considered a right, where moose season begins three days early so the locals can get their winter's meat. The logic is "Hey, man, we've been feeding the things all summer from our garden, why should somebody from Anchorage or Soldotna get it before we do?"

"Peter," Ted said, as he prepared to introduce us, "this guy Ed, here, he's got more girlfriends than anyone I know. They all love him, and look at him." Ed's irreverent charm dripped off him; he was not a looker.

One of the guys said that Ed lived in a place called North Coho, an area where to buy property you needed to have "at least fifteen outstanding warrants." It's a place, I was told, where curvy, skinny dirt roads empty into little clearings filled with little log cabins or shacks. "There are more hidden greenhouses back there than you could imagine," someone else said.

"Larry," Ed asked, "what does that brown bear look like, anyway?"

It seemed a perfectly serious question for Ed to ask, since he might soon be risking his life going after her. The three looked at each other and let Larry answer for them. This group obviously knew each other well.

"She looks just like the women you date. She's big and hairy and has a fat ass."

"Seriously, guys, I want to have some idea what we're looking for before I go off into the woods. I don't make a habit of running into the woods where there are females with bullets in them." Ed's serious tone seemed to catch the other men off guard.

Ted responded in kind, filling the others in on the theory he'd already shared with me about the cub they'd trapped at Lyle Winters's in 1994. He unzipped his coat as he talked, as it was warming up fast. I was as surprised as the others—what was I doing here? Certainly I hadn't realized we were going to be tracking a potentially wounded bear through the underbrush. I thought the bear had already been shot and killed.

But we all got back into our trucks and headed south to the site of the shooting at Mile 117. Ted's rifle had no scope. He said that he didn't use a scope because if there was to be any shooting, it would be at close range. The action would be fast and furious, and there would not be enough time for looking into a scope. He would more than likely have to shoot instinctively if we were charged or surprised.

The road was straight; it basically followed the west side of the peninsula, keeping away from the knife-sharp mountains and massive blue glaciers thirty or forty miles to the east, over where I lived. We could see them looming over us because the land between here and there was flat. The brown bears and the moose preferred this flatter country, which opened up periodically, usually around swamps and wetlands. Elsewhere, the peninsula was deeply forested with rivers, ponds, and creeks. Ted had told me that he and his fellow biologists and technicians felt there were somewhere between 250 and 300 brown bears on the peninsula and 2,500 to 3,000 black bears.

While we drove, Ted told me about another wildlife-disturbance call he'd gotten about two weeks before from a distraught woman. He felt that her problem could have been caused by this same bear. She told Ted that a huge bear was harassing her dogs, and that all the dogs had returned to the house but one, which was killed. Brown bears often come into a yard of chained-up sled dogs and eat some. But if the dogs are running free, it is rare for a bear to catch them.

Still, something perplexed Ted about this lady's dead dog. When Ted saw no marks on the dog, no blood, no bone breaks, he asked the woman how old the dog was. She told him that the dog was fourteen. Utilizing all of his twenty-plus years of experience, Ted felt every inch of the body to feel for internal injuries, hematomas like those made from moose kicks, and he felt nothing. Not one hair was out of place. Ted noticed when he'd arrived that the other dogs appeared incredibly happy to see him and came quickly out of the shed where they were hiding.

"You know," Ted had suggested to the understandably distraught woman, "I think it is possible that your dog was scared to death. Its old heart just couldn't take it." I was hoping my heart could take it if we had a confrontation of our own.

"After we check out what has happened at Mile 117, I will tell you if I think it is okay for you to track the bear with us, all right?" he said to me.

"Sure," I said. A dog scared to death?!

"In the last thirty years," Ted volunteered, answering a question I had not wanted to ask until we were done with this investigation, "only three people have been killed by brown bear attacks on the Kenai Peninsula and two of these have been in the last couple years. One was on February eighth, 1998, the other May twenty-fifth, 1999, just a few weeks ago. I knew the guy who died a couple weeks ago pretty well. Now, he was as experienced in the woods and with bears as you get around here. Both men were killed principally by the terrible bites they sustained to the head. A bear knows your head is a place of great vulnerability, and when they stand over you and bend down, it is the first place they bite." Ted stopped.

I let the conversation die—I mean, I didn't pursue any more details. I didn't want to hear anything else.

AT BRIAN AND LISA'S

Ted slowed down, put on his blinker, and took a slow left into a rough, partially eroded dirt driveway leading to where Brian and Lisa, their five small children, dogs, horses, and cats lived. Brian and Lisa had hacked out a clearing in the Alaskan jungle. Their house was two log cabins that were put together, the logs probably cut off their land. One cabin was newer, built attached to the other. The edges of the logs were not perfectly flat; I wondered how they kept it warm. The ragtag assortment of different-sized outbuildings included one with a fenced-in pen to keep their chickens and rabbits separated from their dogs and bobtailed cats. They also kept a horse or two in a rough-hewn corral. They must have been able to hear just about any sound made outside; no human neighbors were anywhere in sight.

"See that corral?" Ted pointed at it, beyond the house and to our left. "Several years ago I got a call from here. They thought there might have been a Sasquatch out here. Hey, this guy is a descendant of a homesteader; they don't get worried about much. Brian has a sound mind, he doesn't imagine footprints or roaring in the woods."

A few fifty-five-gallon oil drums were in the yard, most empty, a few filled with something. At a homestead out in the country almost nothing is thrown away. There will eventually be another use for whatever it is, even if it is five years from now. There were a couple piles of rough-cut corral pieces. Some car doors were lying in front of the corral, some old car engines on a rotting wood pallet. I also saw a couple long sections of fishing net hanging between two small spruce trees, and some salmon nets rolled up on racks.

In the partially cleared woods in front of the log cabin were patches, mostly round, of bare dirt where their sled dogs were chained. When they had dug too many burrows, they were moved to another patch of ground. The dogs had obviously started near the house and were now being kept closer to the road. Sometimes they dug burrows under large roots, not unlike wolves, to make safe places for their puppies. Brown bears are known to dig up several-hundred-pound boulders to get to a ground squirrel; no burrow, no matter how deep, would protect any puppies or dogs from a hungry bear.

"If I remember right, Brian and Lisa have one of the largest Great Pyrenees dogs I have ever seen. They let it run free, hoping that its guarding instincts would help against any invading bears, wolves, coyotes, wolverines, whatever. I don't see it; last time I was here, it came bounding up to our car. It could be hiding, shivering in some corner of one of the outbuildings," Ted said.

I could feel a slightly out-of-control aura around the grounds and the house. Some broken plastic children's toys were lying in grass that hadn't been cut in a while. On the right side of the house rose a slight hill covered with a thick stand of white spruce and alder. Old and new bicycles were lying around, and some slab lumber that would someday be used for something. Ted and the others pulled up to the south side of the cabin and we all got out.

Ted pointed out to me an outhouse-sized shed with a door built on the side of the cabin. "That's what we call an arctic entry. No heat in it, just a place to step into when its way below zero, so as not to lose too much heat, plus you can take off and store all your bulky winter clothes in there."

As we walked up to it, the door opened and out stepped a thin, tired-looking woman, maybe in her late twenties to midthirties, with black hair. She seemed shy; she went back inside, and through the door we could see that on the walls of the arctic entry were many large nails with snow-machine suits, heavy coats, and boots.

"You notice how their door swings out? You always want a door that swings out in bear country," Ted said to me. He had the patience of a gifted teacher.

Ted explained that normally if you surprised a bear on your front or back porch, say, eating your dog's food, and you're in close quarters, they will respond by either fighting or fleeing. Bear and moose will tolerate a human about thirty or forty yards away, but any closer and they will decide either to fight or flee. If a bear decides to fight and stands up and pushes on your door, as some will, if you have a door that opens in, then here comes the bear.

Lisa came back out. "I had to tell my kids what was going on. They are still scared after what happened last night."

"I see." Ted's calm and orderly demeanor was immediately comforting to this woman. He did not have his rifle in his hands yet.

"I need to keep an eye on the house and the kids. My husband had to go do something. None of us have ever experienced anything like last night. The sound that brown bear made, awful." Lisa didn't have much if any excess body fat. She shivered slightly at times, and it didn't seem to have anything to do with being chilled by the warming air.

Two broad-winged, black-black ravens soared over and spoke to each other. They circled over the woods near the dogs. Did they see something? It is uncanny how quickly ravens arrive at places of injury, death, and food.

"Last night was terrible and we still don't know what has happened. None of us was going out there after all that happened, after all we heard," she said.

As I looked over at a side window on the log cabin, two children's faces stared at us from behind a curtain.

"So what did happen?" Ted asked, speaking gently so as to not rekindle the emotions. Ted and all the men seemed quite serious. They knew this family and knew they had experienced something serious here last night.

"First our dogs woke us up barking. We had a couple sled dogs chained out there," she answered, pointing to the woods.

"The first barking, that was nothing too unusual. My Great Pyrenees, he runs loose, we want it that way. He can scare off most things, and he's smart, he won't let them draw him too far away from the house."

The official book of the American Kennel Club speaks glowingly of the Great Pyrenees: "Perhaps no other breed can boast such a colorful history of association with, and service to, mankind through as many centuries as can this breed. . . . Armed by nature with a long, heavy coat which rendered him invulnerable against attack except from the point of the chin and the base of the brain, the Pyrenees dog was an almost unbeatable foe which won such glory and fame as a vanquisher of wolves and bears that he became known as the Pyrenean wolf dog or hound, and the Pyrenean bearhound."

None of their dogs were making any sound now. Yet shouldn't they have been barking as we five strange men surrounded their female master?

"Were all your other dogs chained?" Ted asked.

"I think I see all the dogs but the Pyrenees," she replied haltingly.

I wondered how she could have had five children already, she looked so young.

"Before we go looking around, just tell me what else happened last night." Ted reached out his right hand toward her without touching her. She seemed to be having trouble getting the whole story out.

"The dogs' barking, they were all going nuts out here, and they wouldn't stop, that woke us all up. Usually our kids can sleep through anything. This woke them all up. Their fear made it all worse, that's for sure."

The shaded air was damp, so we stepped out into the sunlight.

"My husband, he went outside. I'm sure he was hoping it was something stupid like a porcupine too close. My Pyrenees is way too smart to mess with a porcupine, but not the huskies. Some of them don't have the greatest brainpower." She brushed her hair back from her dark eyes.

"And what happened then?" Ted asked.

"Well, right before he got out of the house, there was this awful noise, a different sound, coming from down in the dog yard." She pointed in front of us. "Brian said there were some bears out there. It was just getting the slightest bit light, so he couldn't see much but some shadows. The sound was so loud it was like they, the dogs and the bears, were in the house with us." One of the older kids opened the arctic entry door. She told him to get back inside.

"Anyway, Brian ran in and got his rifle [which we learned was a .444 Marlin lever action], didn't say anything, just ran back outside. Before he got to the front of the house, I heard something that . . . I didn't want to show how afraid it made me, the kids were looking at me." She appeared to be having a hard time standing out here with us while her kids were inside, yet she wouldn't call them outside, either.

"I heard my husband shoot—that gun of his is so loud—once, maybe twice. After that it got quiet; my husband ran back inside. He said he could not see much but dark shadows and some blurred movement. He said he thought one of the bears had been fighting with one of the huskies. *Fight* would be the wrong word, though, when they're chained." Her eyes grew sadder.

"Then, right when my husband got back inside, that's when the sounds I'd never heard before started coming through the walls of the house. This sound was something else. I guess it was one of the bears, but, man, was it intense and unusual." Lisa reached down to pick up one of her cats. Petting it seemed to soothe her nerves. The cat did not purr.

"This bear was alternating between growling, this terrifying growl, and then roaring, a sound I have never heard anywhere in all my years living in the wilderness of Alaska. Then the kids started; first one of the older ones began crying.

"My husband, he went back outside to see if he could scare the bear or bears off. As he rounded the front corner of the house, a bear charged him. It wasn't slowing down either. He ran back inside the house." A Steller's jay, a deep blue in the sunlight and colorless in the shade, flew harmlessly through the area of their yard where we were gathered.

"Did he shoot again, that time?" Ted wondered.

"No, he didn't have time. Then that bear began making this other awful moaning sound. It sounded like it was walking up the hill and down the hill back to the house, over and over again, filling the woods and all our ears with that terrible moaning roar."

I couldn't help but wonder what I would have done in their situation, especially knowing the couple of brown bear stories I did. I'd heard about one instance where a sow and her two cubs tore four-by-eight-foot sheets of the strongest plywood off the outside of a cabin to get in. These extremely tough plywood sheets had been screwed into the stud walls, not nailed, making them even harder to remove. And then there was the brown bear who climbed through a double-pane window, cut itself up, bled all over, tore apart everything in the cabin, crushing metal cans as if they were nothing, then went out another double-pane window, bleeding all the way. What pain tolerance and outrageous strength these animals must have.

"I have never *ever* heard anything like the sound that bear was making after my husband shot. It was not only the roar and the growling anymore. I can't tell you what it was like." Her body seemed to tighten and twist with memory of it.

"I'm not sure I have ever heard about a bear making all the kinds of sounds you're talking about. And the fact that it kept walking up the hill and coming back to your house and yard, that's unusual," Ted said.

"It seemed every time that bear came down the hill towards the house, that horrible sound was more intense, louder." She glanced back toward her house; now the whole bottom of one of the larger windows was filled with her children's faces.

"All right, we're going to see if we can figure out what happened here, see if your husband shot a bear or wounded one. Or, maybe the bears killed something," Ted said in the measured tones of law enforcement.

Ted pulled back the bolt of his rifle and put a bullet into the chamber. I wondered what would get him charged up. I was the only one without a weapon, so I decided to stay as close to Ted as I could without invading his space. I also remembered the joke about being in bear country: "Always be with someone who runs slower than you do." I doubted I could run faster than Ted, but hoped I could beat at least one of the others.

"I think you should go on inside with your kids and stay there until I, or one of us, comes back." She did as Ted asked, stepping quickly.

We walked across the yard down a slight incline; cut-off stumps were here and there and a couple of old dog water dishes. There was bare dirt when we got close to where the huskies were supposed to be chained. When we got within twenty yards, something with fur stood up. If I'd had a gun, I would have drawn down on it. It was one of the dogs, a thin husky. It slinked toward us. When I reached out to pet it, it looked up at me with what seemed to be intense fear, but not of being struck by a human. It *wanted* my attention, my hand.

"Look, over there," Larry Lewis said. In the dark shade was an old, dirty towel or some crumpled, light yellow blanket the kids had dragged out here while playing with the dogs. Lisa did say her kids loved all their dogs, that they were gentle. As we got closer, it looked like a big clump of lamb's wool. Oh, no, is it her Great Pyrenees? It was; it lay rigid, all four legs straight out. There was no doubt it was dead.

We walked over to it. The other four guys had their rifles ready, walking as if they were in a Vietnam movie, stalking through the jungle: eyes up, heads moving from side to side, gun moving from side to side, slowly, deliberately. One or two of them always kept their head up, looking, revolving, and watching for a possible charge of a bear.

There, stiffened by death, was the Great Pyrenees. The midpoint of its back was soaked with blood. This dog had to weigh 125 pounds, maybe close to 150. I'd never seen one larger.

Ted leaned down; at this, the other three turned to the outside facing all directions, ready. He ran his hand down the dog's backbone.

"What has happened here, I'm quite sure, is that a large adult bear, probably our sow, grabbed this dog by its back, picked it off the ground in its mouth, and with one bite, killed it."

The smell of several dogs living in close proximity was strong. I smelled for bear scent, not that I would know it. I was searching for any kind of warning.

"Probably, one of the sow's cubs or both came in here harassing these dogs, maybe thinking of trying to kill one, and the mama came in when this Great Pyrenees came over to protect his friends. These are some damn tough dogs, and this one was not even chained up. These bears are fearsome predators."

Ted stood up and began walking toward the hill; a trail went up it, maybe a moose trail. On either side of the trail grew patches of devil's club, dense brush, ferns, spruce whose branches grew all the way to the ground. Bears could be lying anywhere. The men walked slowly and deliberately, each trying to keep his own sphere of view and his own shooting lane. A bear could be on one of them in an instant.

We hadn't gone twenty-five yards when Larry stopped, ahead of Ted and me. He put his rifle to his shoulder and motioned to us. He was looking down. I saw some brown fur, medium brown, and some mosquitoes hovering around the still body. It was a year-and-a-half-old brown bear cub, maybe 125 pounds, dead. It looked at peace; there was no blood, but Brian's single bullet had found its mark in the shadows of a dark summer night. Among the men, there was no excited chest pounding, no glad-it-got-shot statement. Instead there was a heavy feeling, more of a sorrow for the two lives that had been taken last night.

Ted and Larry dragged the dead bear toward Brian and Lisa's cabin. Ted went over and knocked on the door, and Lisa came out with a baby in her arms. He said something to her; she went back inside and came out alone.

Ted took her to the dead bear first. She stood over it, silent, rubbed her tired eyes, and folded her thin arms over her chest.

"This is so sad. No wonder that sow was making those awful noises for so long after my husband shot. This is why she was running up the hill and then came back down, roaring and making that unreal noise. Maybe that's the sound a bear makes when it is crying."

Ted explained the state law to her, which she knew, but he had to say it anyway: "Have Brian skin out the bear and bring me the hide, claws attached, and the skull to the office as soon as he can. Sorry about your dog." He pointed to where her beloved dog lay. She shook her head; she couldn't look at it right now. She walked with us back to where our trucks were parked and stood by Ted's, looking off toward the woods, where so many creatures live. This family is surrounded by everything but other humans, and that's the way they liked it. Most of the time.

EXTREMELY RARE

Some believe that bears like this sow that come in and kill dogs or tear apart buildings and destroy property do it more than once. Ted investigated two of the three killings of humans by bears on the Kenai in the last thirty years. The following is a report done by Ted on the February 8, 1998, fatality.

From: Spraker, Ted
Sent: Tuesday, March 03, 1998, 1:47 P.M.
To: Bartley, Bruce
Cc: Del Frate, Gino
Subject: Feb. report

An extremely rare, fatal brown bear mauling occurred February 8, 1998, on Kenai Peninsula. The victim was a forty-year male employed by Northern Seismic Company from Anchorage. A second person, working on the same crew, was chased but avoided injury by climbing a tree. Reports from the two workers that witnessed the attack revealed there was no warning except one growl as the man was attacked, and that the mauling lasted less than one minute. The victim was the fourth man in the crew, spaced approximately two-hundred feet apart along the seismic line.

This incident occurred on a Sunday afternoon, and Ted Spraker was notified by staff from Kenai National Wildlife Refuge. Since this mauling resulted in a fatality, there were still ninety-plus employees working in the area, the bear could be identified by tracking, and a harvestable surplus of brown bear exists on the Kenai, the decision was made to shoot the bear as a public safety precaution if it could be found. An additional concern was the building local sentiment against this bear and a sense that the local public would shoot any bear they see this spring. The fury surrounding this incident will probably be gone before other bears emerge from their dens, but if not, it was believed that innocent bears may be killed if this bear was not. A thorough search, starting the following morning by Spraker and Kris Hundertmark, revealed that the bear moved at least three miles away from the site of the mauling. Tracks followed on Monday were not fresh and appeared to have been made the previous day. The last tracks found indicated the bear entered an undeveloped six to eight square miles of dense, mature spruce timber. Since the bear had moved away from the seismic work area, it was not tracked with the intention of killing it beyond this point.

Although the reason for this attack will never be fully understood, at least several logical assumptions exist. First, the bear had a nine-inch-wide front paw print, indicating it was a large animal, especially for the Kenai. The length of its stride and the fact that it broke through hard-crusted snow in a track made by a snow machine also suggest a large bear. From the indications of size it is reasonable to assume this was an adult male. The fact that it stayed in heavy cover from the mauling site to the last tracks also suggest an animal with learned experience rather than a juvenile. The bear's den was appropriately large, measuring three feet across a western-facing opening with a seven-foot-round chamber. The den was made in a good site for cover (primarily dense young birch) but the slope did not allow for a deep den. Because of the shallow slope and shallow snow cover, the den entrance caved in exposing the front edge of the chamber, and the bear. The bear had not been out of the den prior to the attack. The den site was revisited four days after the mauling and there was no evidence of the animal's return.

A great deal of speculation has focused on the level of disturbance caused by the seismic crew's activities and this event, and there should be. Although there had been no seismic blasting in the area, workers were drilling fifteen-to-twenty-five-feet-deep holes in preparation for blasting on a line two hundred yards away. They had walked past the den on at least two separate occasions when the lines were first established. Their trail was a measured fourteen yards from the den. The crew was transported to the area by helicopter. With several crews working in the area one can assume that human and helicopter disturbance was common.

Approximately one month prior to this fatal mauling a seismic worker stepped through the snow den entrance of a sow brown bear with cubs. The man and the bear reportedly both exited the den about the same time with the bear running one way and the worker running the other.

Since we have not received any reports of bears being out of their dens or problems, we have changed the initial decision to capture/collar any large bear found in the area. Since hair was collected at the site of the mauling, we will be able to make a positive identification if the bear responsible for this fatality is located. If the bear is captured, we will be able to monitor its activities in the event it establishes in a developed area.

What Ted did not write about in his report was that he had had to inspect the body of the fatally mauled man. Even after all his years in the field seeing what these animals can do, he said it was almost unbelievable what that bear did to that man so quickly.

PUNCTURED SKULL

As we drove back to Soldotna, we passed several large motor homes. The tourists were back. Some Alaskans are thrilled by their arrival; some can't wait until they leave again, usually sometime in September.

"Some of these folks will have some unforgettable run-ins," Ted said, but didn't finish his thought. He turned his head sharply to the right; a political sign had caught his attention.

"Now, that reminds me of one of the investigations I did back in 1994. Talk about a close call. Right now the guy is running for borough mayor. He's a local guy, born and raised around here, his name is Dale Bagley. He lived to tell his experience."

A few days later, back in Seward, I called Dale Bagley, told him I'd been talking to Ted, and arranged to meet him. If you met Dale at a national convention of Realtors, which he is, you would not be able to distinguish him from someone who grew up in New Jersey or Ohio or Oregon. Nothing about his look, his walk, his way of talking, or the way he looks at you would make you think he grew up in Alaska doing the things in the wilderness that he did. You would never dream that he was a marine.

He has no beard, no tattoos, no earrings, doesn't wear what people would call hip clothes, and for that matter, doesn't look terribly outdoorsy. He doesn't look like a macho hunter, or a homesteader or mountain man. He wears glasses. His personality is camouflaged by apparent normalcy. Looking at Dale tells you nothing much about who he is or what he has done. He probably represents the real white Alaskan far more than the ones that look the part.

When he was in the fifth grade, he and his best friend, now a doctor in Tok, took three- and four-day camping trips alone out through the mountains on the

Kenai Peninsula. Their parents thought it was good for them. Dale Bagley's father moved to Alaska when he was three, then their family moved to the Kenai Peninsula when he was twelve. Dale spent his summers working on his grandfather's farm in Palmer, north of Anchorage, where the state's few farmers live and where the Alaska State Fair is held every year. He spent from 1983 to 1987 in the marines.

In Alaska, as in every place in the world, at times of the year large numbers of people have traditional things that they do. In some places, families take their vacation at the beach in July; some families go to football games in the fall. Many families in Alaska go moose hunting in September. It is a tradition, a way to get all your red meat for the year. Alaskans take their vacations to moose hunt; they close down their business, even break up with this year's boyfriend if he's antihunting.

If you get a moose, you have four, five, or six hundred pounds of some of the best-tasting meat the world has ever known. Alaska moose are bigger than many cattle, and instead of going to the grocery store for your meat or raising your own, Alaskans get out on the land and hunt down their own. It is brutal work, packing out hindquarters that can weigh 130 pounds through muskeg and knee-deep bogs and swamps. Carrying out the four quarters, two hindquarters, and two fronts, could break just about anyone.

Every September as Dale Bagley grew up, his family and some of their friends would move to a place on the Kenai Peninsula called Hidden Lake and Skilak Lake. They'd set up army-surplus-style wall tents, stay a week the beginning of the season, and go out on the weekends after that. The Bagleys would hunt for moose in the mornings and afternoons and fish for salmon, rainbows, and lake trout in between.

All his life Dale had shared game trails with black bears and brown bears making their way through the woods. He'd seen them foraging on the sides of the mountains digging in the blueberries and tundra. He'd experienced plenty of them working high school summers at remote camps at fish weirs counting salmon as they returned to spawn. These places are bear and wolf magnets. As a kid out on a hiking trip, one time he had to climb a tree and wait for a brown bear to leave. One time he and a friend were charged by a black bear; his friend shot in the water in front of it and it turned away.

If he had run into serious trouble any of those times he was out in the wilderness alone or with his friend, he would not have been able to defend himself until he was in tenth grade. That year he got himself a .44. Most times bears smell you but you never see them. Most of the time when they see or scent you, their response is to run away. And that is good.

Being a Realtor, Dale has a flexible schedule, unlike many of his friends and family. So it is not unusual for him to take off a bit early from work, before the season. He drives by all of Soldotna's strip malls, an odd sight that can make a person too confident. In Anchorage, about two hours northeast of the Kenai, many people say, "From here you can be in Alaska in thirty minutes." A few years ago a mother, her son, and her teenage grandson were jogging together down a trail in an Anchorage park on the edge of the city. They were unaware a brown bear was in the brush near them as they ran. The bear ran down the woman and her son, killed them both; the teenager only survived by climbing a tree.

"The way I hunt, I don't like to compete with road hunters, so I explore the roadless country. All my life I had used my uncle's model 760 Remington pump-action 30/06. I'd been working on the North Slope and made good money, so I gave the gun back to him and bought me a new rifle, a Remington 742, with a three-by-nine Leopold scope."

Dale stopped, seemed to detect I was not visualizing the guns he described. "You know that rifle, right?"

"No, I can't say that I do. I don't know much about guns," I answered.

"Well, it's not the biggest gun that people use in Alaska, but it's the one I use," Dale explained. "That afternoon I was going out to walk through some creeks and swamps and I took it with me. I'd only shot a few times. It was April twenty-sixth, early spring. I was hiking near the end of Funny River Road."

"Isn't that near where the man was killed just a month ago?" I interrupted.

"Yes, it is six or seven miles from there. I was walking cross-country, planning on hitting Killey River. I made it to the river, turned around, and headed back to the road where my truck was parked. There were lots of open swamps and very dense young spruce, young birch, some tall aspen. There were no leaves on the trees yet." Dale didn't move at all as he talked, he didn't even blink.

"What did you have on?" I asked.

"I had on jeans, a T-shirt, a flannel shirt, baseball cap, hiking boots. I had my new 30/06 and my .44. Only reason I had the 30/06 was in case I saw a large black bear. Wasn't too far from the truck when something struck me, something told me I should pay more attention. There was, all of a sudden, quite a bit of bird noise, the kind that normally means a moose kill. Ravens, jays, they all gather around. Anytime there is a dead moose, there are birds feeding on it. They make lots of noise. For anyone in Alaska, hearing birds like that is as dangerous a sound as you can hear."

I thought to myself, why would hearing birds be anything to worry about?

"Quickly, the sounds got louder and the danger signals went off in me. I smelled something, just slightly. I knew somewhere close there was a moose kill or one had just died. In the spring quite a few moose die from the effects of winter starvation."

A cloud moved away from the front of the sun, and a shaft of light came through the window and hit Dale's face. The skin and muscles of his face appeared to be a bit misshapen, as if there had been some trauma and some repair. It was subtle and I did not want to stare.

"I immediately realized it was time to turn away and get out of there. I was basically retracing my steps. I didn't get far. I was quartering away, got about fifteen feet when I saw a bear sit up and look at me." Dale's eyes began to blink.

"The bear was about forty feet away. When it sat up, all I saw was its shoulders and head. The brush was very thick. My first thought was, you're never supposed to back away from a bear. So I held my ground and began to yell."

Even though Dale had come to tell me his story, I could only imagine how horrific it would be to relive such an experience.

"Then the brown bear got up on all four feet, facing me. Once I'd been much closer to a black bear—we actually ran into each other and it took off running, shocked. I had my rifle in my left hand. I pulled out my .44, a pistol, from its holster and fired a shot over its head. That shot, and it was loud, didn't faze it in the least."

Dale put his right hand in his pocket, then pulled it out again. He was sitting on a sofa and it appeared to be inhaling him, as if the retelling of this story were taking away his energy, making him smaller.

"After I shot and yelled more, the bear started running toward me. I slammed the .44 into the holster again and raised the rifle to my shoulder, and then took the safety off. By now it is running at me, full bore; there was no way I could see it in the scope. I didn't even try. That's one reason a lot of guys don't have scopes on their rifles in Alaska, so that you can do close-in shooting, shoot in the brush, shoot something charging you." Dale breathed; it sounded loud but it wasn't.

There were no trees to climb and the bear was coming at him at about thirty miles an hour, forty-four feet per second. A world-class sprinter running the hundred-meter dash in ten seconds is only traveling at thirty-three feet per second.

"Next I fired. The bear stopped from the shock of the bullet like it hit a wall, then it started coming again, as fast or faster than before. I squeezed off another shot, nothing happened. I had fired about twenty bullets through this new rifle, and twice it had not fired. I pulled the trigger again, nothing happened and for a split second it was sheer panic. Then I remembered my Marine Corps drill instructor used to say, if your gun jams, just pull the trigger again. That got me thinking again." Dale was looking off into the space in front of him.

"Now it was a few feet away. There was a small row of trees next to me on my left, the bear's right. I ran around the end of the trees. I pulled the .44 out and cocked it. As I turned around, I slipped on a root. I fell through the air. It was like I was in super slow motion, and then the bear was point-blank on top of me." Dale's voice was filled with emotion.

"Before I hit the ground, the bear had me by the chin. I fired my .44 into the bear's chest. I am on my back, my body is under the bear's and my face is under his. The bear is pressing me to the ground with his chest, pinning me."

Dale is five feet ten inches tall and about 180 pounds. A brown bear can kill an adult bull moose weighing sixteen hundred pounds with one bite or one twist of the neck. And that is a moose tough enough to live its life outdoors in Alaska, through every severe winter. Unarmed humans are not much more challenging to a brown bear than a bug.

"My head was immediately in its mouth. I could feel and hear bones in my face and jaw and skull breaking, being crushed. It bit me on my lower jaw area, then bit in the middle of my face and head, breaking through my temple, puncturing my skull. Then it bit down on the top of my head. I was on my back and pinned, both my hands were under its chest. I needed to get my right hand free, where I was holding my .44. I'm continuing to hear bones crunching, but I'm worried about shooting my left arm off. I've got my .44 in my right hand but it is pinned under the bear's chest, pointed right at my left arm." I try, but I cannot visualize Dale pinned under the bear, his head being crushed in this predator's jaws. The fantastic bite into his temple broke out a piece of his skull.

"First he was pinning me to the ground with his body so I could not move. The bear seemed to be concentrating on crushing my head and breaking my neck. I struggled, as I heard the bones breaking in my jaw and around my eyes, to get my .44 free. I finally did and I shot once more at an angle. Then it got me by the top of the head and was dragging me through its front legs out from under its body. It wanted to shake me violently and break my neck."

I did not want to move a muscle for fear of breaking his concentration. The brutal reality of this terrifying afternoon was brought so vividly to life by Dale's telling, the room actually felt as if it were getting colder.

"With a Smith and Wesson double-action revolver, you can just keep pulling the trigger. He was about to shake me violently, which most probably would have broken my neck, when I shot the bear three more times. It then dropped me and took off running." Dale moved to the corner of the sofa.

"How could anything be shot six times and run off, but it did. I had a speed loader, I put in another six rounds. I had now shot it once with the 30/06 and five times with the .44."

I was wearing a dark brown shirt and I noticed Dale was now staring at me. He told me the bear was about the color of my shirt.

"Blood, lots of blood, was flowing out from all over my head. My glasses were knocked off, one of my eyes wasn't working, the bear's tooth had punctured the back of my right eye socket, went right through. I just knew I was going to die, but I remember thinking I did not want to be eaten. I put my cap on, thinking that would slow the bleeding, and to tell you the truth, I wasn't sure, maybe there was some exposed brain." Dale was squeezing the couch's armrest. He has big hands.

"I remember thinking I wasn't too happy with my rifle. I tried to keep the sun at my back. If I could, I figured I would hit the road where my truck was. I could barely see, everything was blurred. I had no idea where the bear was; they are extremely dangerous when wounded." Dale spoke this quickly, as if by reliving it his metabolism had sped up.

I wondered how it must have felt knowing that the bear was somewhere close. How would all that adrenaline feel, how would it alter your behavior?

"My jaw was badly broken, all the skin was off my right ear, one of my cheekbones was broken, my temple was punctured. I now have metal plate in my forehead. I knew it had to have been a big bear because otherwise my head wouldn't have fit in its jaws. The most serious injury I'd ever had before this was a broken leg when I was fifteen." Dale took off his glasses to clean them; he explained that without his glasses that day he couldn't have seen much at all.

"I felt like if I could walk three-quarters of a mile, I would hit the road. Turns out I went over a mile and a half, got lost somehow." With his skull punctured, flesh torn off his face and ear, bones in his face crushed, how could he have gotten up and kept going? The will to survive must be strong in Dale Bagley.

"Finally, I hit the road and backtracked to my truck. I lost all track of time. The bleeding had slowed down some, though I was soaked in blood from the top of my head to below my chest. I'm Red Cross certified, but couldn't see myself. I got in my truck, couldn't really see, just tried to drive down the middle of the road." The surgeons must have done an outstanding job on Dale because the radical extent of the wounds he had just told me about were not evident, even when the sun shone directly on his face.

"After a couple miles—I have no idea how I drove that far—I was in the middle of the road, I saw another truck or some kind of vehicle, coming the other way. It is hard to say what the other driver thought when they saw the way I must have been driving. I wouldn't, I couldn't, let them by me. I stopped and got out and flagged the man over. I couldn't really talk the way my jaw and all was crushed and mangled. I asked him, it took almost all I had, to take me to the hospital." What would someone have thought seeing Dale so damaged, so soaked in blood, his face so misshapen, his voice gurgling or whatever it was doing, barely able to speak?

"This man, his name was Jerry, he had been out there looking at property. I am fortunate he was there, and he was an Alaskan." Dale comes across serious, sincere, and deliberate, under control.

"I don't remember much about getting to the hospital. Jerry was trying to ask me a lot of questions, but it was too painful to talk. He pulled up to the front door of the hospital in Soldotna and let me out. I told the young gal, the first one I saw at some desk or something, that I had been mauled by a bear. She ran away from me, didn't say anything. Everyone around me ran off. I thought, where did everyone go?" Surely Dale must have looked worse than anything they'd ever seen there. It turned out they went to get help.

Dale mentioned that he did remember seeing the infamous human mannequin at the hospital, the one where they hang all the fishing lures that the doctors have pulled out of the salmon and trout fishermen who have come to the Kenai for the world-famous fishing. They put the lures and hooks back into the mannequin in the same place the humans got them stuck.

"Dr. Steve Hileman came and took care of me, first. The Soldotna doctor decided my condition was more than should be handled there, so they had a jet fly down from Anchorage and I went there. Before I left, I talked to Fish and Game and told them where the attack occurred; they obviously could see what happened. There was now a very seriously wounded bear nearby. Ted Spraker and several guys went looking for the bear.

"I was in the hospital ten days. I don't do well in hospitals, don't do pain medication normally, don't take novocaine at the dentist. I don't know how much I slept, and after five days I was trying to leave. They had me on morphine for two days." The vast majority of people who are severely mauled, as Dale was, are treated at Providence Hospital.

"Brown bears like to age their meat. That was what the bear that attacked me was doing with that moose, letting it age. But black bears, now, they will eat you right now." I kept trying to force the image away of those huge white bear teeth tearing into my flesh, crushing my bones.

It appeared that now Dale was back in the present. There was more color in his face.

"Twenty days after it happened, my father and I went back to Funny River Road and found where I had been mauled. We followed the trail the bear took, found logs it crossed with blotches of blood on some of them. We found where it went into a swamp, and then we could not follow it any further." Dale's father is a respected man on the Kenai Peninsula. To say that Alaskans respect you is to have earned a high honor.

"The next year in that same general area I got my moose," Dale said with no extra facial expression, no comment on the irony of it. Dale stood up from the sofa. I noticed that while he did not fill the room with his physicality, he filled the room with his spirit.

He looked at a set of caribou antlers hanging on the wall. "You know, I don't hold any ill feelings towards that bear or any bear. It's awfully hard to survive here in Alaska. All it was doing was defending its food. And besides, I woke it up from a nap. All I was doing was defending my life. Thankfully my lifetime of outdoor experiences, my time in the marines, and some luck prepared me to fight back." Dale climbed back into his truck, which had a political banner on it advertising his run for borough mayor.

As we shook hands through the driver's side window, he said one last thing: "Ted Spraker, Fish and Game, the state troopers elite tracking unit, they never found the bear, dead or alive."

That was true. Ted and about eight other men went to the site of Dale Bagley's mauling off Funny River Road early the next morning. Already strong sentiment was building within the community about a killer bear on the loose; there was pressure to find it, dead, or find it and kill it. Ted wore jeans and hiking boots, and brought a Wildlife Enforcement trooper. The Alaska State Troopers sent their top tracking team, six of them, dressed from head to toe in camouflage. They wore earpieces, communication devices like those of the Secret Service, to talk with each other when they split up. Each one had an automatic rifle. They had assault knives attached to their chests. They were an Alaskan SWAT team about to track a living thing far superior in every way, even riddled with bullets, to any human criminal. With one bite this bear could bite the whole top of your skull off; it could smell you from far, far away; it could live in this wilderness understanding all it is, intimidated by none of it.

From Dale's description of the location they parked their vehicles and quickly pinpointed the birds that were on the kill. They walked slowly about a half mile into where it had all happened. Ted said that usually if you don't find the dead bear within a hundred yards, you don't find it, period.

Ted explained that bears know this country, it is their home. He is intensely respectful of them based on decades of experience. Mature ones know how to get away from humans; it is rather easy for them. They know to get in the water, enter swamps, backtrack, cover their tracks. They go over mountaintops like a set of stairs. They go down creeks, then come up again. They know to get into brush so impregnable that no man could follow except by crawling on his belly, and no man would want to do that. They are smart and they seem to know when they have done something that will cause people to come after them. They don't need a compass; you can fly them a hundred miles from their home territory, and the next week they are right back.

This high-powered, most-qualified search party found a place where a killing had taken place among the young and mature spruce. Little, inch-wide saplings were growing in this area too, several of which had been snapped off in a straight line. Moose hair was on the leftover portions of the inch-wide saplings, with a few small spots of blood on some of them. In some spots in these woods you couldn't see more than twenty, thirty feet, or even less. There were a few small muskeg openings. The bear had obviously been chasing the moose, probably grabbed it once and it got away, then the bear killed it.

Ted found the moose kill, completely covered with dirt and vegetation. You

Dale Bagley and his truck in Soldotna. Photo by Peter Jenkins

couldn't even see the moose; it looked more like a big beaver lodge in the middle of the dark woods. The bear had cleared away a wide circle of vegetation and dirt to cover the dead moose. Ted said it was always surprising to see how bears dug up the country to cover a kill. It was not a sight one wanted to see on foot, the sight of one of the most dangerous spots on earth.

"We found a big pool of blood on the ground at the edge of the place where the bear had covered the moose. We found his glasses, kind of ground into the dirt, and his rifle lying there too. The pool of blood was about three times the size of your fist." Ted's tone was deliberate.

The search party didn't expect to find the bear close by, although it would have been a relief. They split up into teams and walked in circles around the kill site. The State Troopers team was well trained; they would take a step, look, and listen, and the search was slow and methodical. They did finally find more bear blood, a faint trail that led them away from the kill site, away from the road.

"There was no real blood trail. Bears have thick, thick fur, a layer like an undercoat, and it tends to soak up their blood and so they tend not to bleed a great deal," Ted told me.

When they did find some bear blood, they got down on their hands and knees and searched for more.

"The next day we had a helicopter out there flying in concentric circles, looking for a dead bear. They saw no bear. Then we had a Super Cub fly the area; they found nothing." Ted was not surprised it had gotten away. He had not expected to find it.

"I have never found a wounded bear, ever; you just don't find them if they are not within the first hundred yards. They are the ultimate predators, and I guess you could say the ultimate survivor, I cannot tell you how much respect I have for them."

Dale recovered remarkably from his wounds, almost all of them to his head. He told me that every morning when he shaves, he sees the scars. He had over two hundred staples and stitches in his head and face, to minimize the scarring. On October 5, 1999, Dale ran in an election against the powerful incumbent Kenai borough mayor, Mike Navarre. Mike already represented the peninsula in the state house, he was well-connected in Juneau. Politicians running for borough mayor don't run as a member of any party. To win the regular election Mike Navarre would have had to get at least 50 percent of the vote. He got 44 percent, and Dale Bagley got 30 percent. Three other candidates were in the race. In the runoff on October 26, 1999, Mike Navarre got 48 percent and Dale Bagley got 52 percent. Dale Bagley was now mayor.

3

At Home with "The Police Log"

It's a lovely thing to feel at home. It doesn't matter where; to me and most of my family, anywhere will do. I felt at home, quickly, in Seward, Alaska. The second time I drove by Espresso Simpatico, Darien knew I wanted an Americano, a bit of milk, no sugar. His coffee place is housed inside a large metal coffee cup, just big enough for two to stand in. The coffee cup sits in a large gravel parking lot with the Seward Bus Line office. The Espresso Simpatico and the bus office are next to the graveyard.

The bus line office is in a small wooden building; Darien's parents, Dan and Shirley Seavey, run it. In the summer the place is lined with the backpacks of travelers who have tired of hitchhiking. Alaska is one place there are still plenty of hitchhikers. The Seaveys are dog mushers; Darien's brother, Mitch, has run the Iditarod six times, his best finish was fourth, in 1998. In 2001 Darien's father, Mitch, and Mitch's son, Danny, are all planning to run the Iditarod.

Living in Alaska means you are far away from big bunches of stuff that are usually instantly available. If you want to stay in Alaska, you figure out how to get the stuff you need whether it be the stuff to survive, stuff to entertain yourself, or stuff to feed your pet eel. Seward has some stores: a True Value; a couple auto parts stores; a couple places to get groceries, Eagle and Big Bear. There's a guy who sells some computer stuff; there are a few places to get gas. There's Terry, who does tires. When there is road construction, as now, the sharp shale rocks cut up your tires almost as bad as malicious slashers. There are several restaurants, the ones that are open for the tourist season and the ones that stay open year-round. Red's, in an old school bus, serves the best burgers in town; he opens in time for the tourists, although he's one of the locals' favorites.

In Alaska the top of the stuff chain is Anchorage, and Seward is only 125 miles from it—just around the block, as Alaska goes. We have to drive through Moose Pass to get there. Moose Pass is stuff-needy, and that's how most Moose Passians like it. They didn't move to "the Pass" to shop. There is one person in Moose Pass—other than the little general store—who has some things for sale. On nice days she puts a stuffed bear in her yard. The thing that elevates Moose Pass far above Tshayagagamut or Hydaburg or Adak or Deering on the stuff chain is that residents can drive from Moose Pass someplace bigger to buy things. Being able to drive somewhere else is a really big deal in Alaska. Many Alaskans cannot drive away from where they live. It's impossible. How shocking this must be to millions of Americans who stay in their cars to eat, bank, read, conduct business, have family time, apply makeup, find peace and quiet.

To keep from driving the 250-mile round-trip to Anchorage for necessities, there is the Seward Bus Line. If you need a rebuilt starter for your 1992, F-150, six-cylinder Ford pickup and can't find it in Seward, you can pay the bus driver a small fee, $10 for anything under ten pounds, and he will pick it up for you in Anchorage on that day's trip. Call by 1 P.M. and Shirley Seavey can call the driver and what you need can be back in Seward by 5 P.M. For most of the rest of Alaska, that kind of convenience would be considered living life easy. (If you need a tuxedo for Seward's high school prom, call Shirley, they pick up bunches of tuxedos.)

Need a difficult prescription, but it snowed eighteen inches last night and there are avalanche worries? Call Shirley. Maybe the bus will get through. Need a couple rare bolts without which the motor for your halibut fishing boat will not run and you must be fishing tomorrow? Call Shirley. Need a new washer and dryer, a set of studded tires? Call 224-3608. It rings at the bus lines' office, and at their home too. Alaskans are informal. You might hear the Seavey grandchildren in the background, or the phone may slide off the kitchen table and disconnect. Just call back. One guy in town had them pick up goldfish every week to feed his huge pet eel. If that hard-to-find toy just arrived at Toys "R" Us in Anchorage three days before Christmas, and your son Travis has to have it, no problem. Call Santa Seavey.

Like every other place, there is the public Seward and the private Seward.

Small-town people know so much more about each other than in cities. One big difference in small-town Seward is you get to read about the private Seward in the paper every week. It's called "The Police Log." Walk down the snow-covered street naked, beat up your boyfriend, steal a bowling ball and bowl for pedestrians down a city sidewalk and someone calls the police for help, it's in the paper. Steal $1.57 in gas from the gas station and the thin, dirty-blond attendant, originally from Maine, calls the police, you are nailed. Seward is the kind of place that takes stealing less than $2 seriously. How wonderful. Become obsessed with your neighbor's barking dogs, especially in the winter when the speck in your eye can become a mountain range, and call the police, boom, you and your neighbor have gone public. You and your two friends lift up your blouses to expose your own little mountain range on the main bridge coming into town and someone calls, you're in "The Police Log." Call 911 about a bear in your unprotected garbage (bad, bad, bad) and it will be in the log, too, your name included.

Sometimes "The Police Log" says, "Journal page missing." There is endless speculation about this. Did one of the policemen do something? Did one of the town's brightest stars get pulled over for the D-thing? Fortunately, for those of us who love to read it—until we're in it, of course—there aren't many "Journal page missing" entries. My appearance certainly did not come up missing.

Citizens read and sometimes fret over typical small-town newspaper headlines in the *Seward Phoenix Log*: "Local Property Taxes Up." "Sewardites Divided between Burners, Preservers." "Smith Skis Her Way to World Junior Championship, U.S. Ski Team." There are ads too, of course. "Shoreside Petroleum, Inc. Serving you with Heating Fuels. Marine Fuels. Propane Gas. Welding Gases. Serving Seward, Whittier and Valdez." There are notices of public hearings, such as one last winter that said, "Changes in Documentation in Order to Receive a Housing Preference from Domestic Violence."

If every town and city ran a police log, it would be a great way to learn about what really goes on, in case you were thinking of moving in or sending your son to college there. What if the *Washington Post* had its own police log, a composite of all calls and action taken by law enforcement? What if one section of this log was just for politicians, lawyers, lobbyists, and their family members? There would be so many "Journal page missing" entries there would be almost nothing printed. Imagine if New Orleans had "The Police Log"; or New York

City; Selawik, Alaska; Westerville, Ohio; Austin, Texas. But they don't, and Seward does.

"The Police Log" begins with an editor's note: "All charges brought against individuals listed below will be argued before a judge or magistrate. Individuals are presumed innocent until proven guilty in court proceedings. Entries are unverified police reports as they are written in the dispatcher's journals." You get your Seward community character details with entries like these, "1:55 P.M. Report of loud music on Alder Street; advised to turn it down." Notice that was P.M., not A.M. Seward is a community where many people value their personal sound-zone and where you can get something done about the invasion of it. "6:55 A.M. Caller dialed 911 and was asked to call back on the business line to report he had ridden in a taxi that had no seat belts in the back. He did not wish to make a formal complaint." Seward cabs have less need for seat belts than taxis in New York City.

The good humans of Seward have an abundance of wild animals as neighbors. "9:13 A.M. Report of a baby moose shaking and shivering on a river sandbar about 2.3 miles past blacktop on Exit Glacier Road. Fish/Wildlife Protection Officer advised." This call is just one example of the many observant and compassionate Seward animal lovers. After all, if the mother moose was gone, that baby moose could be killed by brown bears right in town. A local man was mauled by a brown bear at the edge of town, across from the infamous Pit Bar, in 1998. "10:51 A.M. Caller advised a black bear climbed onto his deck and was trying to push on the window to get in. Bear gone on officer's arrival." Proof that Seward's got black bears who know enough to split when the cops are coming.

"7:31 P.M. 911 call that two people on Mount Marathon [the mountain behind Seward where the famous up-and-down-the-mountain race takes place] were being chased by a bear; ambulance put on standby. Trooper found the people were hiking with a black dog." A tourist probably made that 911 call. "2:31 P.M. Horse running loose on the airport runway." Local pilots have dodged bigger obstacles in the runway than horses, such as bull moose in the rut, which are stupid like all males ready to breed. Fortunately there are not many horses in Seward. "5:01 P.M. Advised a porcupine in a tree the past couple of days; it tangled with dog who now owns some of the quills. Requested advice on how to get porcupine out of their yard." Police dispatchers in Seward become experts on porcupine behavior. "8:28 P.M. Advised there was a Steller's sea lion on B-float dock that looks sick; Sea Life Center will send someone to check." Most Seward people are concerned about the health of their nonhuman neighbors, unless they can be eaten. And then they are still concerned about them until the moment they can be harvested. You cannot eat Steller's sea lions; they are on the endangered species list. "8:32 P.M. Advised a sea otter at the culvert with a yellow tag on its flipper was sick and you could see its ribs; FWP officer contacted." Sea otters are on the list too. "9:29 P.M. Report of a fat porcupine on the front porch shooting quills at the door." Seward may have some overweight porcupines; Seward porcupines do not, however, shoot quills at your door. Caller may have been prone to exaggerate or just close to prone.

Seward has eight churches and one small hospital. Surely this man was not a local pastor or one of our beloved doctors: "7:45 A.M. Advised of a man in green surgical scrubs, surgical gloves, staggering along the road by Napa, carrying the Bible."

The area around Seward can be dangerous. "2:08 A.M. Earthquake, magnitude 6.8, near New Britain. No tsunami or damages reported. May be some sea level fluctuations." It shook so hard it woke us up. In 1964, Seward was almost wiped off the face of the earth by a severe earthquake and the resulting tsunami. I wonder what the man carrying the Bible thought of the earthquake?

Local and visiting boaters see and report all kinds of possibly life-threatening events: sinkings, "man overboard," fires. "3:17 P.M. Boater reported a hang glider out of control and heading toward the sea. Coast Guard cutter *Mustang* advised." Eight minutes later, another call. "3:25 P.M. Same caller advised the hang glider was a kite; no one is in danger."

Seward is a major sport and commercial fishing port. Resurrection Bay has one of the world's best silver salmon runs. Icicle Seafoods and others process huge amounts of halibut, salmon, and black cod. Plenty of fishing-related calls are recorded in "The Police Log." "12:20 A.M. Male removed from Yukon Bar, told not to go into any more bars tonight and go home. Dispute over a fishing pole." Does this mean the guy was bringing his favorite brand rod and reel into the bars and picking fights with other patrons over what was the best brand, or did someone try to steal his pole?

"8:17 P.M. Advised of people shooting fish in the 'Y' where Bear Creek and Salmon Creek come together." Obviously these weren't the same people at Yukon Bar fighting over the fishing pole, unless they were arguing the merits of

Me, Rita, Brooke, Jody, Luke, Aaron, Julianne, and Jed after one of our salmon fishing trips in Seward. PHOTO BY PETER JENKINS

shooting a fish with a gun, which is totally illegal. It was physically impossible for them to be shooting fish in the water from the Yukon Bar, the water's too far away from Main Street. Speaking of fishing, some of the best fish catchers around Seward are the bald eagles. They congregate around town in winter—I've seen seven on the top of one telephone pole crosspiece. But sometimes even our national bird is falsely accused in "The Police Log." "9:25 A.M. Two subjects advised eagles on Nash Road were eating what appeared to be a human; later revealed to be discarded parts of a small black bear."

During salmon season (when the salmon are in and entering the creeks that flow into the bay) people around Seward fish day and night. There are so many silver salmon at times that everywhere you look they are jumping out of the water. I've seen hundreds of people snagging them with a treble hook; the locals call it meat fishing. Good snaggers can catch over fifty pounds of ocean-fresh silver salmon in an hour and a half. One guy trying to meat fish made "The Police Log." "1:25 A.M. Warning issued to male for endangering the welfare of a child following report of male fishing in the surf at the waterfall with an infant in a backpack."

I got nailed for sport fishing with the wrong license. One June morning after I'd been in Alaska a month or so, I rushed down to the bait and fishing supply place, the Fish House, right across from the docks. I was going out on a charter, it was six something in the morning; I was still not used to the almost perpetual daylight and wasn't sleeping well. That night I'd gotten about three hours of sleep. I was rushing to buy my license. Eight or ten people were hovering around the counter doing the same, I was about to miss my boat. The teenager asked me my address; I gave her 1907 Dora Way, Seward, the address of the house we were renting. She wrote down my Alaska phone number, I told her I wanted a yearlong license. I paid what she asked for. Turned out she sold me a resident license, but I was no resident. To be one I would have had to be living in Alaska already for a year.

The trooper found out eight months later, somehow, and one short winter day I got a call. It was our local State of Alaska Fish and Wildlife Protection officer. He asked me to come down to his office in city hall. When I got there, some trappers were checking in some beaver and wolverine pelts. I paid my fine, and then this appeared in "The Police Log" under "Fish and Wildlife Protection": "The following has been cited by Seward Fish and Wildlife Protection officers. Peter G. Jenkins, of Seward, cited on charge of making a false statement on a resident sport license June 6. Bail set at $200." I'm sure just about everyone we knew saw it, but only two mentioned it to me.

The old saying about commercial fishermen hitting a port ready to fight is certainly proven true in the log. "1:18 A.M. Officers responded to Peking Restaurant for report of four males fighting. Subjects were advised not to enter any more bars tonight and return to their boat." "9:59 P.M. 911 caller said male going in and out of consciousness at the Yukon Bar had said he thought it was fish poisoning from out at sea: medics responded." Fish poisoning? Creative. The folks that work at the canneries in Alaska get in the most trouble. Hillary Clinton worked in one when she was still in college. "5:09 P.M. Caller advised he had just been involved in a fight with another subject who was making a lot of noise and urinated on his tent at Seward Fisheries tent city. Officer responded and restored peace."

Like people everywhere else, people in and around Seward pound on each other every so often. "4:17 P.M. Advised of a male and female arguing at the campground near Coast Guard housing. Officer brought the female, who allegedly assaulted the male, to the Seward jail." Rarely are people taken to jail. This man must have been seriously beat up by this female. "4:43 P.M. Advised a shot had been heard in 500 block of First Avenue; it was an accidental discharge when a pickup driver was putting his shotgun under the seat." I didn't know you could put a loaded shotgun under the seat of your vehicle.

"9:00 P.M. Report of two juveniles rolling bowling balls down Fourth Avenue." As creative as I was as a juvenile, this activity never occurred to me, probably because bowling wasn't hip back then. "9:30 P.M. Caller advised two bowling balls were taken from his vehicle while parked at AVTEC [a statewide technical school] last night." Those stolen bowling balls were never the same after their trip down the street. "12:08 P.M. Advised of two hitchhikers at Mile 3; the man was hitting the woman on the head. Contacted, all OK, playing around." Seward people do love to play around.

I'm not sure what was going on with this family: "5:17 P.M. Advised of white Mazda driving in Lost Lake subdivision and looking at empty cabins." "5:31 P.M. Caller asked if there had been a body found on Exit Glacier Road. His mom, driving a white Mazda (see previous entry), had been gone for a while and he was concerned."

And there was this one, called in by some thoughtful, law-abiding citizens: "7:44 P.M. Female called wanting to know if they would get in trouble and how much it would cost if someone wrote 'Bob' or 'Cindy' in the fresh cement in front of the Breeze Motel. Also, mentioned something about 'butt' and 'boob' prints. Not sure if they had already done it or if she just wanted to."

Does wet concrete stick to bare skin or hairy skin? How do you get it off? What if the fresh concrete was deeper than you thought it would be and you went to sit down to make your butt or boob print and slipped and couldn't get up? And then "Cindy" reached over to help remove you, butt first, and she fell in boob first, and you were both stuck and the cement was drying fast. Could the dispatcher advise Cindy and Bob how to escape the hardening grip of the concrete? At least you were in there together.

4

"Fly Through That Hole"

Most Alaskans hate standing in lines. This giant place is filled with people determined to live as free from others' intervention as possible. Alaska may have served as the incubator for the behavior now termed politically incorrect. They despise being herded; if they were sheep, they would never go off the cliff together. More than likely, they'd trample the shepherd.

Fortunately, Alaskans don't have to wait in line regularly, unless they're in certain places in Anchorage or their boats are lined up outside the cannery to off-load their catch of salmon. This summer day I was standing in line in the Ketchikan airport, about as far south in Alaska as I could be. Another fifty miles and I would have been in British Columbia. Just one other person was in this little line. She was in her twenties, dressed in blue jeans, frayed; a blue jean shirt, with holes; and a blue jean jacket, with two different Harley-Davidson patches. Her only luggage was an oil-stained, orange plastic case, and inside it was a chain saw. She was flying out to a fish camp to meet her boyfriend (in Alaska the word is often *partner*). I didn't ask her what she was doing with the chain saw.

Earlier she'd mentioned that she, but not her boyfriend, belonged to a bikers' club in town, the Ketchikan Harley Riders Association. She said her boyfriend, who was from California, did not own a Harley since the main road to ride was just twenty-something miles long and there was no road that could get you "the hell out." The road that leads out of town is only twenty-six miles, and then it ends. There is no way to drive away from Ketchikan, or from most Alaskan communities, even the capital city. This doesn't stop thirty or forty riders from getting on their Harleys and running out the road just so they can come back, screaming through town, those beautiful motors rumbling.

"There are forty bars and forty churches in Ketchikan," she said from out of nowhere. Her statement was thrown at me aggressively, like a punch.

That seemed to me to be about right for Alaska, keeping heaven and hell right across the street from each other, nothing hidden, one Alaskan convinced heaven is here and hell is there, the next Alaskan having the opposite opinion.

The girl and I had all kinds of time to talk because we were waiting for the fog to lift and the weather to improve, something Alaskans must be willing to wait for or to risk dying. The fog lay on the water and moved like liquid mercury; it sifted through the needles of the spruce trees; it hid killer mountainsides. The list of people who have died in small-plane crashes in Alaska is filled with far too many pilots who thought they could fly through, over, and around the low clouds, the fog, the curtains of gray.

Here the clouds in the sky and the fog blowing off glaciers, sea, and land merge and make landscapes deceptive, a world sugarcoated in soft-as-cotton-looking clouds. It becomes moisture-laden, seductive fluff hiding a cruel, hard death. The clouds and the fog are as much a part of southeast Alaska as sunshine is part of Arizona. Some pilots, with too little Alaska experience or too much, pilots who just *once* get a false sense of their abilities, are sometimes tricked by this shrouded world and end up running into unmovable mountains or the tundra. Some people I met won't fly with any pilot who doesn't have ten thousand hours of flying in Alaska.

Right before we stepped up to the counter, the chain-saw-toting biker woman stuck out her square jaw and said, "We get a hundred and seventy inches of rain a year here too, and that doesn't keep us from riding." The more intense the environment, the weather, and the wilderness get, the more some Alaskans enjoy not being intimidated by it all.

A cargo guy strained to push a cart by us; it was loaded to well above his head with Styrofoam boxes filled with vacuum-packed salmon from some sport-fishing lodge.

"Hi, where you headed?" the surprisingly young, black-haired woman asked me. She clearly worked for Taquan Air, though she wore no uniform.

"I'm going to Prince of Wales Island, to Craig."

"Okay," she said, "what's your name or are you just a number?" She had a playful personality.

"My name is 1 . . . 2 . . . 1 . . . 2."

In response she began doing jumping jacks behind the counter.

"What are you, some kind of aerobics instructor that doesn't believe in your own program?"

"All right my name begins with *P*, and the next letter is an *o* . . ."

"Come on, now . . . if you don't hurry, you can swim to the island."

"All right. My name is Polar Eskimo."

She lifted her eyebrows and frowned. "You're not even ready for my high school talent contest and my high school had twelve people in it."

I gave in. "Okay, my name's Peter Jenkins."

"How much do you weigh?"

"What'd you say?" I wasn't sure I'd heard her correctly.

"I said, how much do you weigh?" She stepped to the opening in the counter for the baggage and looked me over.

"Why do you want to know *that*?"

"Because this is a floatplane you're flying on."

"A floatplane, I don't want to—"

She interrupted me, "You'd have to tell me your weight no matter what plane of ours you're flying on." She sighed. "Come on, you can tell me, how much?"

She seemed almost flirtatious. I definitely wasn't happy about answering; I don't get on scales. Surely she wasn't serious. And if she was, I was beginning to wonder what else they might want to know.

"I weigh one hundred twenty-five pounds."

She started to write it down, then looked up and raised her eyebrows at me. "Your right leg weighs more than that! Be serious."

"All right, I weigh two ten."

She stepped back again so that she could see all of me. "Come on. You're leaving out body parts. Now, just add 'em all up: legs, arms, head—you know what there is under those fashionable clothes you have on, then subtract fifteen pounds, since you males are known to exaggerate."

I had on my favorite three-year-old blue jean shirt, some almost as old jeans, and a pair of scuffed Roper boots. She didn't appear to be in any hurry.

It had been years since I'd experienced an airline employee with a sense of humor, other than the folks at wacky and wonderful Southwest Airlines.

"By the way," she sighed, "when was the last time *you* stepped on a scale?"

"A couple years ago. You don't really need to know my weight."

"We really do," she replied, now with all seriousness. "We're trying to figure out how much food you've eaten since you've been in Alaska. It's a study we're conducting for the Alaska Department of Tourism. Now, how much do you weigh? We know what you weighed when you first got here. Ever see the movie *Enemy of the State?*"

The Harley-driving woman tapped me on the shoulder. "Listen, dude," she whispered, "they really need to know because these planes only carry so much weight, and if you don't tell them correctly, it could be dangerous. You know the plane can't take off overloaded. They haul mail, cargo, whatever, up to their capacity, *after* they figure in the weights of the passengers and pilot."

Behind the counter the young woman smiled and held up her pencil. I told her what I thought I weighed.

I couldn't help imagining: What if this was happening at LAX, the Los Angeles airport, and this same feisty counter worker was asking the same question of a fifty-plus-year-old woman who was overtanned, underfed, and so altered by plastic surgery that nothing original was left unchanged on her head but her skull. "I weighed myself this morning and I was one hundred and twelve and a half pounds, three pounds less than I weighed in high school." What if they asked passengers at La Guardia or Kennedy Airport how much *they* weighed?

About half an hour later we walked down a gangplank to a floatplane, tied up like a boat at a dock. This airport was on an island, across the water from Ketchikan. You can't even drive to their airport; you've got to take the ferry less than a half mile or fly in. Flat land in Southeast Alaska is rare.

Even if I hated flying, there were few other ways to get around much of Alaska. At least in Southeast you had two choices, flying or the ferry. If I were to take the state ferry all the way from Seward to Prince of Wales Island, just to avoid flying, it would take days, maybe longer than a week, to cover the six-hundred-plus miles.

Alaskans call this part of the state Southeast. It's a thin strip of some of the world's most wildly awesome mountain-and-ocean-dominated land. Southeast is about five hundred miles long and is attached to the giant part of the state by a glacier larger than Rhode Island. Alaskans who live north of Southeast condescendingly call this part of Alaska a suburb of Seattle. Even though they may never have been here, they think of it as a place with "some" yuppies. (I hadn't seen any yet.) It's supposed to be a part of Alaska where the living is too easy.

On a map, Southeast looks like nothing but islands. The only part of the land that isn't an island is a thin strip backed by Canada. Alaska's equivalent of the Great Wall of China, a nearly impregnable string of mountains and glaciers, barricades it in. Juneau, the capital of Alaska, is in Southeast, and there's no way to drive to it, no roads that reach there. There are only three roads out of Southeast, and unless you live in one of the small communities that boasts a road, you are out of luck. The only way to get out in a vehicle is to put it on the Alaska Marine Ferry and travel to one of these towns where a road starts. One road leaves from Haines, one from Skagway, and one from Hyder; none of them are connected to the others. They all lead into Canada.

I noticed a young man striding down the walkway toward us from the airport. Surely this was not our pilot. He wore jeans, a Denver Broncos cap, jogging shoes, and a navy blue windbreaker. How many times in his life had this guy shaved?

"You both ready to go?" he asked.

"I am," I said.

He opened the right-hand door of the plane.

"Now, who wants to ride in the front seat?"

Neither of us volunteered. I was confused. How do you sit in the front next to the pilot? Where does the copilot sit?

"Okay, then," the guy who couldn't be our pilot said, "you both can climb on in to the two backseats. Watch your step." This guy appeared to be in his twenties. I decided he must be a combination baggage-handler/steward.

I stepped onto one of the floats as waves lapped against it. One wave came over and got my foot wet. A colossal cruise ship had just passed by on its way north. I heard steps coming from the covered walkway and turned. A man in his mid-to-late thirties was running toward us.

As he reached the plane, the woman said, "Hey, Jerry."

"Oh, hi." He wasn't even out of breath.

"You been politicking?" she asked.

"Always," Jerry answered.

I got in, then the woman with the chain saw got in. She had not allowed the guy to load it in the luggage area; for some reason she seemed to want to be near it. What was really in there?

The young guy in the Broncos hat climbed into the pilot's seat, and then Jerry got into what I'd assumed was the "copilot's" seat. The young guy started the engine. The insides of this floatplane were scuffed and scratched; portions of my side window looked as if some child had worked it over with a nail. The floatplane had started bobbing up and down in the waves from passing boats.

"One time flying this same route to Prince of Wales Island I saw a pool of orcas attacking a humpback whale," the biker babe said. I could not really think about that, I was too consumed with who this guy was, acting like he was going to fly the plane.

The guy revved up the engine; I thought he must be warming up the motor for the still unseen pilot. It was now raining directly over us. A hundred yards to our left I couldn't see through the fog, yet a half mile behind us the sun was shining and it was clear blue skies.

Some guy, even younger, appeared beside us on the dock. He reached down and untied us from the dock's moorings. The young guy in the Broncos hat, who didn't look old enough to be a weatherman at the smallest TV station in Alaska, let the current take us, then powered up the motors and we headed out. He *was* the pilot. There were boats everywhere. I knew there was no way we were going to take off with this much boat traffic in our way. Right?

I glanced over at this guy in the copilot's seat, Jerry. He was looking out the window.

"Excuse me, what kind of plane is this?" I asked.

I had to speak loudly, in the direction of his ear.

"You ever flown on a floatplane?" he answered. I detected a strong energy in his voice.

"No, I haven't."

"Well, you're on a DeHavilland Beaver."

"Oh." We sped across the waves, through the pelting rain. I could feel the aluminum floats on the plane pounding so hard on the water it was as if we were taking off from a fresh-plowed, furrowed dirt field.

"They stopped building these planes in the fifties," Jerry volunteered.

"In the *what*?"

"In the fifties."

That's great. This plane could have been built the year I was born. I sure don't fly the way I did when I was younger.

When would we ever take off? Were we having some kind of trouble? Hopefully, I had guessed close to my actual weight, and so had everyone else. "Come on, plane, *come on, come on, plane, please lift off the water.*" I think I even spoke my hope out loud, though no one could have heard me. It was very noisy inside the cockpit by now.

For a time just as we began to lift, maybe three seconds, though it felt like much longer, it looked as if we might run into a slow-moving, black-hulled tugboat. Finally with the plane off the water, the pilot banked it hard to the right. The pilot upped the power dramatically to get us over the green mountains in front of us.

Ahead spread out before us was an ever-changing shutter of white-gray clouds dangling from the silver walls of rain. Would there be the holes in the clouds to fly through? If you had to wait for ideal weather to fly in Alaska, there wouldn't be much flying.

These planes were not flown using autopilots; the human pilot must be able to see. We climbed and climbed; the plane seemed to have plenty of power. I heard Jerry say something to the pilot about this plane having had a turbo conversion done to its engines, whatever that meant.

Without warning we hit something and the plane dropped, then slammed into some kind of fierce air. I don't understand much about air masses, but these didn't like each other. If I hadn't had my seat belt on, I would have popped up and hit the ceiling of the plane with my head. The plane had no windshield wipers, and the overwhelming rain blasting at us had to be pushed off the glass by the wind. It sounded as if machine guns were shooting BBs at us.

I pressed my face to my side window, but when I did, it fogged up. I could see nothing in front of us but banks of clouds. If I were just a spirit, capable of passing through physical reality, which is the way I felt in the clouds at times, this could be joyful. If we'd cleared Gravina Island, then we were supposed to be flying over Clarence Strait. I tried to look down; there was nothing but clouds and fog. Were we over a glacier? How would we know if we were headed left or right? Was the pilot disoriented?

There, below us—if that was below us—something dark appeared, then it was gone. There it was again. It looked like the ocean. Then it was gone, then it was back. I saw another hole in the clouds, and in it I saw something that was not the open ocean. It was the land, covered with evergreens, mature and tall. Then into the hole came large boulders, perched on the edge of the ocean. Then, as quickly, the gray hid everything again. I could feel my body tightening with every droning moment. The muscles in the back of my neck were strung so tight it felt as if they could pull my head back until my skull hit my back.

It seemed just a matter of time before we would hit something that would tear the plane and all of us apart. I'd always wondered about when a plane crashes. How much force is required to tear it into so many tiny pieces, with people actually missing body parts here and there? The impact must be unimaginable. Right now we could be headed straight into a mountain and wouldn't know it. Or what if we landed in the water? Would we hit so hard that I would be dead on contact? What if my legs or arms were broken? Was there any kind of life raft on board? Did the plane float? No one survives long in Alaskan salt water. Would the Coast Guard be upon us quickly enough? If we were trapped inside the plane, would the girl crank up her chain saw and cut us out? Damn my imagination. I wished I could turn it off.

Another large hole was below us. We were over the ocean; I spotted white-caps through the hole, even from this height. Had the pilot circled away from the island, was he turning around? I was totally disoriented; was he?

The young pilot seemed to be taking the floatplane higher. It did not respond as effortlessly, as powerfully, as before. Was something wrong with the engines? The next bit of reality I saw through the clouds was a slab of green mountainside right outside the window, not below us, but next to us. No wonder so many planes crash out here. Surely the pilot had a route he was following, but how did he know where he was, or if he had drifted off his route? There was no radar, no screens in front of him showing him where he was, where to go. For me, the worst thing about this dire situation was that I was completely powerless to do anything about it.

"Hey, see that hole in the clouds? I think you need to head through there," Jerry suddenly said to the pilot, but calmly, as if he were directing a blind grandfather to the bathroom at a restaurant.

To head where this guy Jerry had directed, the pilot would have to make an almost ninety-degree turn. Surely we weren't that far off course. And who was he to tell the pilot where to go? The pilot didn't say anything, but I could feel that he had slowed down, possibly as slow as the plane would go. I remembered hearing something about going too slow and stalling the plane out. For a moment it seemed we were standing still; then we hit another batch of rough air and lurched down like a rock falling off a cliff until we hit another batch of invisible air and bounced back up.

"Listen, I've flown here hundreds, probably thousands, of times. We need to be over Kasan Bay. I see too much ground below. Fly through that hole in the clouds." Jerry spoke with a calm assurance.

This conversation was beginning to remind me of what I'd heard on the news from recovered black boxes, when professional pilots are trying everything to avoid crashing, talking to each other as calmly as if they were out fishing on a warm summer afternoon. Why didn't they scream, raise their voices, lose control? I wished for a parachute so that I could take my chances floating to the ground or the water. The pilot still said nothing. He just looked around too much.

I felt like screaming out to him, "What do you think about what Jerry is saying!"

Jerry again pointed to the hole in the clouds, which was closing, and the pilot finally turned the plane and bolted through it. I'm not sure why, but I trusted this unknown Jerry more than I trusted the pilot.

Jerry pointed down and said, "There's Hollis, the ferry dock, okay, we're heading in the right direction now." The pilot never said a word.

Shortly afterward, we dropped over a medium-size mountain into a narrow valley. The pilot got close to the long spine of mountains on our right. More rough, up-flowing air hit us. At least we could see. Jerry pointed to some deer that were actually above us near the mountain ridge. Their golden hair stood out vividly in the Irish-green grass. Below us sat several homes, spaced far apart, built along a road. The land around the houses had been logged. The plane was now bouncing around like a Ping-Pong ball in a wind tunnel, but it was almost enjoyable compared to what we'd just come through.

Soon the pilot swung wide again. Why was he doing that?—Jerry hadn't said anything. I looked and found it was because we were headed for a gorgeous bay, surrounded by evergreen-covered outer islands. A sawmill was below us; several huge piles of sawdust stood around it. The pilot threaded his way between some anchored salmon-seining boats and landed right in front of the little village of Craig (pop. 2,043). It is the largest community on Prince of Wales Island, which is the third-largest island in the United States. Only Kodiak Island, north of here, and the island of Hawaii are bigger.

The pilot maneuvered the plane up to a floating dock. Most of the fog that had so imprisoned people earlier this morning was now evaporated. If you'd just woken up, you'd wonder why all the flights were coming in late this morning.

Rays of golden sun shot through the little bit of fog that still floated on the water. Slivers of clouds, highlighted by the deep yellow sunlight, poured down from the surrounding mountaintops like waterfalls. Our whole world was clearing up. The mysterious closed-in world of gray-white clouds and fogs was gradually being overtaken by a rich blue sky and a bronze sunlight that together colored everything regally. The world now seemed perfectly clear and evident.

While we squirmed out of the plane, a bald eagle screeched from the tall spruce trees that grew on a point across the bay. I was surprised the pilot didn't thank Jerry. The pilot said nothing. Maybe he was stunned, or maybe I was too new to Alaska to realize what I had just come through. Could that trip have been normal? We didn't crash, everyone survived—just another flight in Southeast Alaska.

THE LONE WASP

Sam Kito, sixty-two, the half-Tlingit, half-Japanese-American man who had summoned me here to Craig, was waiting at the dock. He is an influential Alaskan Native leader, a wise man, and an elder. He doesn't want to be called an elder, possibly the most respect-filled word in the Native world, because it is given to men and women who are the oldest in the community, usually in their seventies and eighties. I think Sam thinks he is in his thirties; sometimes he acts like he is still in his twenties.

Sam's hair is naturally coal black. He is stocky, short, kind of bowlegged, and he dresses fashionably. I'm not sure what I was expecting; you would think after all my years of traveling and living in other worlds that I would have stopped previsualizing people and places. Had I expected Sam and the others I would be fishing with to have Chilkat blankets draped over their shoulders, their heads protected from the rain by woven cedar hats painted with stylized ravens? No, but I hadn't expected them to be so universally stylish. These Native leaders dress in a uniform that allows them to be twenty-first-century warriors for their people. Sam wore black silk T-shirts, fine blue blazers, Italian sweaters, Dockers khakis, and Florsheim black loafers, with tassels. His assistant, Linda Sylvester, told me that he spends a large sum at the Juneau shoe shop having tassels put back on his loafers. This may be because Sam loves to dance and people keep stepping on his tassels. Almost no one steps on his toes, though.

In Alaska you don't hear the word *Indian* very often—the word is *Native*.

"Native politics." "Native musher." "Native women writers." "Native issues." "Native arts." Then several phrases are used all the time in Alaska that have paired *Native* with a word of the outside world. "Native corporation." "Native Olympics." "Native airline pilot." "Native orthopedic surgeon." "Native lawyer." "Native oil-field worker." "Native comedian."

Making up Alaska's Native population are five major groups. Starting with the top of Alaska and working down, there are the northern Eskimos, the Inupiats; the interior Indians, the Athabascans; the southern Eskimos, the Yupik; the Aleuts, whose place is on the Aleutian Islands and the Alaska Peninsula; and the Tlingits and the Haidas, the Southeast coastal Indians. Although not long ago some of these groups warred with each other, now they have banded together to fight for their piece of Alaska, which was once all theirs. Their organization is called AFN, Alaska Federation of Natives.

"Jerry, good to see you," Sam said first. "Have you and Peter met yet?" Sam's words were sort of clipped off at the end.

"In a way," Jerry answered.

"Hey, Sam," I said. "Whoever Jerry is, I think I owe him for guiding us in here through the fog. I wondered a few times if we were going to make it."

"Welcome to Alaska." Sam had an amused sense of calmness that made me wonder if anything could surprise him. "Peter, this is Jerry Mackie. He's from here, grew up here, he's Haida, he's the local state senator, he's going to fish with us."

We shook hands.

Sam's Native Alaskan side comes from his mother, who is Tlingit. The Tlingits settled in the farthest northern places, the land mass and islands of Southeast Alaska. They share more culturally with the Indians of British Columbia than they do other Alaska Natives.

"You lose any weight on the way over?" Jerry smiled at me.

The woman with the chain saw chimed in, "I about . . . Oh, never mind."

Then she spotted her partner, who had a red ponytail, and jogged toward him. When they met, she grabbed him and lifted him off the ground.

We walked up to a small wooden building that was used for ticketing and luggage and waited a few minutes for our bags. On the outside wall was a For Sale sign. It said, "For sale 100' x 35' float house. 30' x 30' full working woodshop. Located near Saltery Cove, POW Island. Wood stove. Propane refrigerator. Full-size gas range. Two generators. This is a legally permitted float house.

Fly or boat to house. $85,000." It listed the name of the man in Craig to contact.

A plump Native woman in jeans so tight she could barely bend her knees hauled our luggage up to us on a Yamaha four-wheeler. We jumped into a white van—there are lots of roads on Prince of Wales Island—and drove less than a mile to the lodge where we would stay. In less than an hour, two fiberglass fishing boats full of Native leaders and me were headed out to the fishing grounds. We had changed into rain suits and XtraTuf rubber boots. Local people call these boots "Southeast tennis shoes."

In our boat were Sam, Jerry, thirty-seven, Bill Thomas, Senator Al Adams, and me. Sam and I had met a few years before fishing for king salmon on the Kenai River. When I'd decided to explore Alaska, I knew that to have a "true" experience I would have to spend time in Native villages. I was sure it would be difficult, or even impossible, without some Native leaders who would be willing to speak for me, to open some doors.

I had read something revealing in J. Daniel Vaughan's dissertation, which was entitled "Alaska Haida and the New World Drama," that had concerned me while preparing to explore Alaska. Mr. Vaughan wrote about the difficulty in getting Native people to answer questions, to speak about their history, to open up, to trust outsiders. He wrote an account of a woman trying to interview an elderly Haida man. His anecdote ends:

"Satisfied with what she had learned, the woman soon left the house. 'Did you notice how she called me uncle?' the man asked me. 'She did that so that I would have to talk to her and answer her questions. . . . Now she has her story on tape, she'll go back . . . and write it down just the way she wants to, as though it is the real story. . . . Those people I told her about were not real people at all. . . . They weren't people, they were mind stuff! . . . Well, from now on, Dan, you can ask me anything you want about the Haidas. I'll tell you anything you want to know and you can write it down just the way you like."

Every year Sam invites some Native leaders here to Prince of Wales Island for an annual salmon fishing trip, and this year he'd asked me if I wanted to join them. He said it was one way for the leadership to get to know me—a bit—to determine if I could be trusted. Sam had explained that for hundreds of years whites and other non-Natives had been coming to Alaska, either trying to save them with their God or their different ways of life, resulting in a strong, deep-seated resentment and distrust of outsiders.

Over several decades Sam has become one of the most influential if behind-the-scenes Native leaders in Alaska. Alaska has so few people that little goes unknown. Sam makes a living as a lobbyist for certain Native organizations; he also represents the dentists of Alaska, the community-college federation of teachers, the Aleut community of St. George on the Pribilofs, and so on. Native Alaskans have had to fight hard to get where they are today. They have learned the hard way that getting represented fairly in the United States is still a war, but fought without guns or war canoes or whalebone clubs. Today, it is fought by lawyers, lobbyists, and politicians (or if you prefer, politicians, lobbyists, and lawyers).

Sam's Japanese father and uncle had come to the States to work in canneries, first in Seattle, then in Alaska. Their plan was to make some money and go back. They never did. Sam's father met and married a Tlingit. Sam grew up in Petersburg, Alaska, a mostly Norwegian-American fishing village not far from Prince of Wales Island. During World War II, Sam's family was put into an internment camp because his father was Japanese. In Sam's early days, when they would go to town to get ice cream, signs directed the whites to one place and nonwhites—Tlingits, Haidas, Japanese, whatever—to another. One of the bars in Petersburg is called Kito's Cave, a rough and rowdy fishermen's bar owned by one of Sam's cousins.

Al, another of our fishermen, is about Sam's age, and also has dark black hair, no gray yet. He's from Kotzebue, over twelve hundred miles northwest of here. Al is an Inupiat Eskimo and an elegant man. People love him immediately, a great trait for a politician to have. Some call him the Giorgio Armani of Kotzebue. To put these three words together only illustrates how extraordinary Al is. You may have a sense of Giorgio, and if you have been to "Kotz," as the locals call it, you know what I mean.

In Alaska, now, the Republicans rule, and since Jerry changed from the Democratic to the Republican Party in 1998, he has become a powerful young man. Jerry is majority leader of the Alaska State Senate. He's fiscally conservative but definitely not a part of the right-wing extreme social agenda. He is a natural leader and politician. For example, when he was sixteen, no one seemed to want to show up to fight the fires that broke out around Craig that year. So, Jerry organized the disorganized volunteer fire department and soon there were twenty-plus volunteers.

Bill Thomas could pass for a retired professional football player, a middle linebacker. He is a Tlingit; Vietnam vet; a professional halibut fisherman; CEO of Klukwan, Inc., his local Native corporation; and a lobbyist. He lobbies when he is not fishing. Bill lives in Haines with his wife, Joyce, a gifted artist of Tlingit-based designs.

The testing, the judging, of me, the lone WASP, began early on.

"Peter, you ever seen an Eskimo fish without a spear before?" Al asked.

I wasn't sure what to say, so I didn't say anything. I'm not sure I'd ever seen an Eskimo before.

Bill chimed in, "Don't worry, Pete, you can't tell them Eskimos apart from any other Native when they're not in their igloos."

Bill was not a man you would want to make angry. I could picture him in a raiding war canoe, the kind his ancestors used to stab fear into their adversaries. It would probably be a good idea to laugh at his jokes.

"Peter, you ever been with this many Natives before?" Al asked, his dark brown eyes dancing, I hoped, with mischief.

"No," I said faintly.

"You look nervous. You think we might be planning to have you for dinner?" Al began to laugh. "You know how much we like raw meat. You ever eat stink flipper?"

"Yeah, Al, I, uh, teethed on stink flipper back in Connecticut." Here's hoping Al has a good sense of humor.

At one time, when the Democrats controlled the Alaskan House and Senate, Al was chairman of the House Finance Committee and quite powerful. Now that the Republicans rule, it was frustrating for Al, and he would be retiring soon.

"What are we using for bait?" Sam asked me.

"How about Al," Bill replied quickly.

"Nah, I'm too skinny, we need to use Sam, we'll catch more," Al said.

Jerry, who was driving, didn't slow down as we made our way through a pass that went between two outer islands, west of Prince of Wales Island. We were close to Canadian waters. Once through the pass, which was edged by massive rocks, we came to the open Pacific Ocean. The Pacific was rolling under us, big rollers, white foam at the top of some of the waves. A rain came down on us that was really a mist. People around here call this mist "liquid sunshine."

When we stopped, the tiny drops felt cool and soothing on my face and beard. I love being on the ocean, sitting, riding waves with distances between them, in a small boat, feeling like a cork. We pulled along one island, steep-sided with bare rock at the ocean level. Jerry told me this was Cape Addington. The smashing, pounding waves on the ocean side of the island kept anything from growing wherever they crashed. Spruce trees grew above the rock, and elegant waterfalls were here and there just waiting to be seen, meant to be painted into nineteenth-century landscapes. The dramatic lighting would not need to be manipulated by the artist; everywhere I looked was like a classic painting. We pulled up next to a boulder about the size of a two-story home coming out from the shore. It was time to fish.

Because the pass was so narrow, the tidal currents were strong in the pass, and therefore the small fish, the herring, the needlefish, were funneled in here. This in turn brought all the local ocean predators to feed here; about twenty bald eagles sat on the boulder, and that was just the mature eagles with white heads and tails, the ones we could see. Immature eagles are brown and white and were hidden by the colors of the rock. Many more eagles were diving into the water here and there, too many to see or count. There were also Steller's sea lions lounging on the rocks, huge and brown, fat and warm, laid out on their beds of stone.

The halibut can weigh over three hundred pounds and be well over six feet long. They too come here where the herring and the salmon thrive. Hopefully, the king salmon were here, thrashing, dashing, and feeding, gaining weight and power. They needed all the pent-up strength they could gain in order to reach their spawning rivers and creeks where they would lay their eggs, or fertilize them, and then die. And now we were here, the human predators, inept compared to the others, but attempting to catch our share.

All I could hear were the loud, absolutely pure sounds all around us. The notes made by the world here were boisterous and overpowering. The sounds made me feel more powerful one moment and intimidated the next. Ocean waves broke on the sheer rock of the west-facing islands they met. Mature bald eagles fought and taught their young, both activities requiring different sounds. Our motor gurgled when the propeller was raised out of the water by a passing wave. But none of these sounds compared to the blasting, concentrated whoosh of air that overcame all the rest the instant it occurred, less than twenty feet from the boat.

One moment there was just the surface of the water, and the next there was the black, bumpy, glistening back of a humpback whale. It exhaled, then inhaled and dove back to be completely surrounded by the water of the ocean, where it is the most massive predator of all. Apparently the whales were here too.

I put a piece of herring on my hook and dropped it to the bottom. We were in about seventy-five feet of water. Once the weight hit the bottom, I began reeling it up; the king could hit the bait anytime. We did this over and over and over, not talking, concentrating intensely to feel the slightest nudge that would mean a salmon had been hooked. We all wanted to be the first to catch one. Then Sam's line went limp as he dropped to the bottom—the weight below the hook was no longer keeping the line tight. Bill had said that the kings would often hit the bait on the way down. Sam set the hook and—*zoom*—the fight was on. Line instantly began peeling off his reel. The king salmon swam straight toward Japan and didn't stop until Sam bore down enough to turn it, after it had stripped off a large bit of line. What astounding power for a fish that probably did not weigh more than thirty-five pounds.

Sam pumped and reeled and pulled and fought. Tourists have been known to have heart attacks fighting these Alaskan kings. Sam is tough, though, and has serious sea legs. Waves, six feet and higher, were rolling into our boat, occasionally hitting it on its side, making it hard to stand. We had to hold on with one hand or sometimes both for extra balance. Sam could not spare even a finger in this all-out battle. He fought the king to the surface.

In the pristine, dark blue and green ocean I caught occasional flashes of its bright silver side as it neared the top. It was thrilling to watch. Sam reeled in the line, then the salmon would answer and take back whatever line Sam had reeled in and more. Sam said nothing; he knew from over sixty years of living in Alaska that you should never lose your focus when fighting the life-and-death battle with a king salmon. They will somehow win the struggle with those who can't keep total concentration. Even with fantastic focus, the kings can break your equipment or wear you out—anything to win and regain their freedom.

Jerry had the net ready. The fish made another run, this time off the back of the boat, almost wrapping Sam's line in the motor. It took more line than at any time before. Sam's strong back worked and fought and brought the king back close enough again to where Jerry thought he could net it. Jerry, a longtime fishing guide before he got into politics, knows you don't net an ocean-run king too soon. When they see the net, they seem to get a new burst of energy, enough often to break the line, get tangled—somehow, some way, to get away. To net one takes precise, definitive moves. Strike with the net if the king is not close enough to the top or is still too energized, and there is possible ruin. There may be nothing worse than fighting a magnificent king salmon with great skill and expenditure of strength, only to have the person with the net lose your fish. Jerry came within a foot of netting it; it responded by heading straight down to the bottom.

"This is an exceptional king," Al said in awe, showing his deep-seated respect for the determined fish.

The reel screamed and the pole pumped as if it had its own heartbeat as the line went out. Sam probably wanted to scream too. I know what my forty-something back feels like when I fight one, but during the twenty minutes he fought the king, he never said a word, just pulled and pulled. The humpback surfaced again, this time behind us, and blew and breathed. There was some golden sunlight now and it lit the whale's exhaled spray of droplets. This time Sam would not allow the fish to make another run; he knew he could exert his will now. He brought it straight in and Jerry netted it.

I always regret it a little when a creature like this king salmon, one that will provide sustenance to me and my family, or to Sam's, has to die after a struggle, mighty or otherwise. I know the thrill of the hunt and the chase, but then sadness when the end comes. It is always, for me, a moment of the greatest respect for a life force that has ended its reign.

We all dropped our lines out again quickly. Next Al hooked one. Al had been talking about getting as much salmon as possible. He said it has been this way for his people for thousands of years, to put up fish and all other food to survive the deep dark winters. Sam and Bill started harassing Al all they could.

"Al, when will you be satisfied, when you get all our salmon too?"

Al responded, "It takes a village."

"We're no village," Bill said.

"All right then. Instead of 'it takes a village,' it takes *me* to feed the village." Al smiled his million-dollar smile, bright enough for any arctic night.

"We'd need a huge net to feed all of Kotzebue," Bill said. Kotzebue is the most populated Inupiat Eskimo community in Alaska.

"Never mind, just catch enough salmon to feed my own village, at home, get me through the winter. I'll even take any salmon Peter might catch."

Al's salmon did not protest his being caught, but came right in. When we got it in the boat, Al pointed to a large, bloodred gash in its silver side.

"A sea lion grabbed that one," Bill pointed out.

The light was perfect, as it often is in Alaska. There was no glare, and this was summer and just past noon. There was no pollution; this was as pristine and profound a marine coastal environment as exists in the whole world. What a joy. All around the colors were so richly exciting—the gemlike blue-green of the sea; the warm, angelic white of the breaking waves; the purified gold of the fog-filtered sunlight; the hundreds of varieties of light browns that colored the exposed rock that made up the islands near us.

Everyone else was getting ready to fish again. The salmon run must be harvested; it hasn't been long since a family, a village, lived or died on the outcome of the harvest. This intense need to catch during the season still flows through the systems of all the men I was with. We called it sportfishing, but it was not sport.

Bill, who has a deep voice and a deliberate style of talking, pointed to the west and said casually, "Look."

A flock of large birds hovered about fifteen feet over the water. The easy rolling waves were coated in silver-green light. There were at least twenty-five, maybe forty birds. They were huge, brown and white. Were they some kind of rare albatross blown in here by some advancing storm? Jerry pulled the boat toward them until I could see it was a flock of bald eagles. I thought I must be mistaken; there is no such thing as a flock of eagles. They were diving down to the tips of the waves, which were boiling and bubbling.

They were catching something, and whatever it was, there was enough for all of them to congregate. I couldn't believe what I was seeing. Then, what looked like a shiny black submarine came straight out of the water, rocketing up at ninety degrees. It was a humpback whale.

Bill explained to me what was happening. "That whale has made a 'net' of bubbles it has blown around a school of herring. This way they concentrate even more than they are usually. Then the humpy dives straight down and comes straight up, mouth wide open, right through the herring."

The upwelling power of the great white splash the humpback made when it landed threw a couple eagles higher into the air. Then a minute later the bubbles began to explode to the top of the water again.

"That's called bubble netting. We have seen it quite a bit, but for someone like you, not long in Alaska, that sight is pretty nice. Must be some reason you

Bill Thomas, Senator Al Adams, Sam Kito, and me, the lone WASP, in Craig. PHOTO BY JERRY MACKIE

get to see that," Bill said. "You sure you don't have any Native blood in you?" He was only half-joking.

"No, but three of my children do, they're part Cherokee."

"That explains it," Al added. He hadn't appeared to be paying attention to us.

Sam, Al, Jerry, and Bill were watching the eagles, soaking it in, silently, not overwhelmed the way I was, but moved all the same. Alaska was their home no matter how astounding, and they'd been here a collective two hundred years. I was stunned, practically on fire, by what I was seeing. The bald eagles continued diving from the sky into the ocean, and the whale rocketed into that same sky another three or four times. The herring, the source of their attention, their sustenance, could do nothing to escape but had to wait until the predators had eaten their fill. Even concentrating 100 percent, I could not get enough of this part of Alaska. I was having a holy experience, this place was too rare to close my tired eyes. I didn't want to miss anything. Al was asleep, so was Sam. Eventually Jerry steered the boat back to the lodge. Bill just sat. We'd caught our limit of kings, two each. Al could feed his imaginary village.

Back at the lodge, I took a hot shower. When I closed my eyes, I lost my balance and had to reach for the wall. The whole place was moving. My equilibrium had not yet readjusted to the stable ground. Dinner that night began with baked king-salmon heads; Sam couldn't wait to eat the eyes, all very traditional. I ate some—no eyes, though. While we ate, a middle-aged Native guy, who moved slowly and seemed shy, came in holding a couple hand-carved and hand-painted cedar paddles. He just stood there until Sam noticed, then Sam introduced him and his work. Haidas are renowned for their abilities to carve and work cedar and for their artistic abilities in general. Jerry mentioned that his sister-in-law, Tina, had painted the stylized, all-black traditional Haida designs on them. Both the carving and the designs were exquisite.

"Cedar paddles, like those but much bigger, and our oceangoing cedar canoes, some fifty feet long, were one reason all other Native people feared the Haidas. We could come from here, across large open water, raid their villages on the mainland, and they could not come after us. They did not have the canoes we did," Jerry said.

"Yeah, yeah," Bill, the Tlingit, said in sarcastic response.

Haidas and Tlingits now only make war on the basketball courts, during high school games and Southeast's extremely important Gold Medal Tournament, held every year in Juneau.

"Jerry, you gonna sing for Pete at the Hill Bar tonight?" Bill asked.

"Only if Pete gets up there with me."

The Hill Bar is just a half block down the street from the lodge where we were staying. It overlooks the dark harbor, the fishing boats that are tied together because there isn't enough dock space to handle all of them, and most of old town. JT Browns General Store and Ruth Ann's Restaurant, with their straight-up wood storefronts, the boat docks, and the fishing boats gave old town a look like a block off the San Francisco wharf during gold rush times. This night a new fog swam up at us from the ocean that surrounded the village, swirled around the streetlights, and hid other people as they walked through it. It gave me chills.

Jerry's mother, Marge, owns the Hill Bar, a combination bar, pool hall, and pull-tabs place. Pull tabs are a form of legal Alaska gambling; you buy a pile of cards and pull segmented tabs of paper off the front of them to see what you've won. Some people do nothing but sit at the bar and pull tabs and drink, pull tabs and drink and drink and drink, pull tabs and drink, lose all their money, leave. There is a liquor store downstairs, Hill Bar Liquors, and a convenience store next door. Marge owns these too; in fact she owns the building and all of the grocery stores on the island. She is a powerful, discreet woman.

As we walked into the Hill Bar, two raven-haired Native women ahead of us saw each other, ran to each other, hugged, yipped, swirled each other around.

"Where have you been?" one yelled, excited. I didn't hear the answer.

Jerry tapped me on the shoulder. "You know why that was such a big deal, Pete?"

"No."

"Because you can't lose someone on this island."

Jerry's brother-in-law was playing tonight, as he did a few nights a week, every week, and has for years. A light bank above his stage, controlled by foot pedals, shone on him and the dance floor. It had red, yellow, orange, blue, purple, and green lights. Another one rotated round and round like John Travolta's disco light. There was no real reason in the Hill Bar to get rid of the sixties or the seventies or the eighties, to worry about precisely what was hip this minute.

The interior of this bar was dark, the walls were smoke-stained cedar, there was a long, L-shaped, wood-topped bar. A stuffed king salmon hung behind the bar between the windows that looked out into the fog that now hid about half of everything. This bar had obviously been here for many decades and hadn't tried to change much with the times; then again, "the times" on this island have a very different way of passing. Sam told us he'd been to this bar when he was sixteen. He was a deckhand on a seining boat, and some strapping Norwegian fisherman had thrown him over the railing by the door. The shrub he had landed in is still here; he made sure to point it out.

Jerry's brother-in-law, a Mexican-American named Serafin Lara, has dark black hair, is in his forties, and has a medium build. His horn-rimmed glasses and air of restraint give him an oddly intellectual appearance. But in this place, colored with the patina of thousands of brawls, one-night regrets, a million smoked cigarettes, patrons who haven't left this island in a couple decades, and streetlights outside that couldn't overpower the gripping fog, this aloof music man was a welcome relief. It didn't seem to matter to anyone that he'd been playing here nonstop for years and years. It is a long, long way to any other live music, and you definitely don't leave this island in the dark looking for nightlife. Some people who have tried it ended up in eternal darkness.

We sat at the front two tables. Everyone knew Jerry, of course, but everyone also knew Sam. People treat Sam with an "I'd die for you" respect. Sam is known all over Alaska for his ability to entertain; there would be no way to count how many rounds of drinks he has bought. And Sam doesn't just buy drinks for people who can do him some good. He is known while entertaining to outlast men and women half to a third his age. On his black and gold Jeep Grand Cherokee is a bumper sticker that reads, "I'm a living legend at Kooteeya Bar, Hoonah, Alaska."

It appeared that everyone in the place, maybe one hundred people, knew who Sam was, and a good number of them came by during the night to say hello, timing their arrival so as not to interfere with what was going on at the table. There were fishing guides and three bartenders who came by, and a tug-boat captain and several people from Hydaburg. A trolling-boat owner about six feet six from Petersburg who had played basketball with Sam in high school bought Sam a Crown Royal on the rocks. Even someone's mother who looked to have spent too much time here stumbled up to Sam and asked him to dance. Everyone had been turning her down, but he didn't. No matter who you are or aren't, what you've done or not done, you feel accepted around Sam Kito.

Jerry leaned over to me and gestured to the far inside corner of the bar, near the partition that separated it from the pool hall and pull tabs. About fifteen people, about an equal number of men and women, most with black hair, were sitting together there, including one skinny lady with gray hair.

"Those people are from Hydaburg. That's their corner when they come here, nobody messes with people from Hydaburg. It's an all-Haida village. See that lady with them? She's ninety, comes here all the time, has a few glasses of wine, listens to my brother-in-law, dances a couple times. Them Haidas are something. I'm probably related to half of them."

"Yeah, yeah. Pete, come here, I need to tell you about the Tlingits, they never lost a war," Bill said, motioning with his large right hand.

A striking young woman who had occasionally been getting up to sing with the island's music man came to sit at our table. Someone said she was half-Haida, half-Tlingit. Someone else smirked that she was always at war with herself, you know, they joked, since the Tlingits and Haidas were always at war. She had a wide face and high cheekbones, very exotic looking. She sat next to one of the fishing captains who had come to buy drinks for Sam and Al.

"I wish there was someone in this boring place that knew how to dance," she said so everyone could hear.

The boat captain next to her, who smelled like fish, picked her up without any warning, threw her to his shoulder, and ran around the dance floor for half the song. No one, except me, seemed to notice the guy or the woman on his shoulder. I wondered what it would take to get the Hill Bar's attention.

The music man was playing "Sweet Home Alabama" by Lynyrd Skynyrd. I was surprised, this far from the Deep South, to see so many people singing this song as if it were their anthem. Some Alaskans relate to Southerners. Southerners lost their ancestral homes and land to a war with "outside aggressors." The ones that survived got some of it back, eventually. Alaskans also lost their ancestral homes and land to "outside aggressors," the Russians, who never bought it or fought a war over it, they just claimed it. Then the Russians sold it to the United States in 1867. The U.S. government could not have bought a home in Vermont at that time without proof of ownership, deed, survey, etc., but they had no problem buying Alaska.

I noticed Jerry was missing from the table and found him standing onstage. His brother-in-law was thumbing through a multipage list on his music stand. He punched in a track, and Jerry, holding the microphone sensitively, began to sing. Jerry is about six feet tall, weighs maybe 190. He was wearing faded jeans, Timberlands, and a navy blue, short-sleeve shirt. Jerry definitely doesn't have the outlaw look; he could be a thousand different people. Put him in the right suit and he could be walking down Wall Street. Put him in Carhart's and cover him with sawdust and he could be a logger. Meet him at the bar and he could be your best friend from high school. He could own your neighborhood hardware store. He could be the state trooper who stopped you for speeding, and you wouldn't get mad at him. He could be teaching your Sunday school class.

And since he is at least half-white, he could pass for a white man, something Sam, Bill, and Al could not do. This might be an advantage. But give Jerry a Haida deerskin drum and he could go to any Native village and beat that drum with intense passion.

First Jerry did "Achy Breaky Heart" by Billy Ray Cyrus, a former number one country hit, then three others. No one paid any special attention; it was just Jerry singing again, the same guy they all grew up with. In the middle of the third song it hit me—this guy, who started with "Achy, Breaky Heart" and is now singing "Celebration" by Kool and the Gang is majority leader of the Alaska Senate. If this were *The Gong Show*, I'm not sure how long Jerry would have lasted. He does not have the moves of Kool or the gang. The whole scene was oddly refreshing.

I thought I heard my name being called above the noise of a couple of women having a shouting match.

"Pete, come up here, now," Jerry was saying into the microphone.

"Get up there and let us have it," Sam said. "Tell him I want to hear some Rod Stewart." Some guy at the next table put a birth control device over his entire head. He didn't have a very big head.

I wove through the crowd on the dance floor and climbed up to stand next to Jerry. I had to dance for a few seconds with the mother of the woman the fisherman had thrown on his shoulder.

"What do you want to do?" Jerry asked, sounding sincere.

"I don't care."

Jerry said something I couldn't hear to Serafin, and they started the song "Tub Thumping," with its unforgettable chorus, "I get knocked down, and I get up again," repeated over and over. I grabbed the tambourine and backed up Jerry.

We got back to the table at close to midnight. The main door of the bar opened, and as they had done all night, people automatically looked to see who it was. In walked a stunning and stylish Native woman, someone who was used to being noticed. She had on a bright red sweater; faded jeans, not too tight; and she had perfectly thick, shoulder-length black hair. She weighed maybe 115, stood about five feet three inches. She looked to see who was at every table—apparently she knew everyone—then came straight to our table. The only empty chair was between me and Jerry. Before she got to us, Jerry whispered to me that this was his sister-in-law, the Haida artist who had done the paintings on the carved cedar paddles. Just while taking the short walk to our table, she lit up the place, many eyes on her. Whom was she here to see, whom would she throw her gaze on, whom would she talk to, and whose turn was it to get warmed by her obvious charisma? No one else in the bar that night had her candlepower.

She talked to Jerry for about five minutes. She had already noticed that I was the only person at the table she didn't know.

"Jerry, who is this guy?" She leaned toward me.

"Oh, that's Peter. He's a writer, he's going to be living in Alaska for a while. He's been fishing with us."

"He wants to get to know some real live Natives that will be nice to him," Bill added in an instigating tone.

"How well?" she asked, taking Bill's bait. She leaned into me again, her red sweater brushing against my arm. "Right over there in the Haida corner is about as real a bunch of Natives as you're going to find in Alaska. They are the least known of all Alaskan Natives, yet the most talented, most beautiful, most handsome, and most intelligent."

Bill coughed.

"Those people are Jerry's and my people. People are afraid of Haidas—are you afraid of Haidas?" She leaned even closer to me.

"I'm sitting next to Jerry, aren't I?"

"You come with me then." She grabbed my arm and tried to jerk me out of my chair. She was strong but not that strong. I stood up anyway.

Before we got to the corner, three or four people called out to her.

A couple of women, both under thirty and beautiful, jumped up and grabbed two chairs from an empty table nearby. These young ladies' faces showed combinations of genetic influences that I'd never seen before, a mix of Norwegian, Haida, Tlingit.

"Tina," they both said as they hugged her.

"This is my sister, Jody, and this is my soul sister, Laverne," Tina said, introducing them to me proudly. No wonder many of the early explorers and traders were quite cheerful about being in Alaska.

They nodded, but kept their arms around her and didn't say anything to me. No one did. I hung around for a half hour or so. They talked of their families and their lives in shorthand I did not understand. There were smiles all around, big two-hundred-watt smiles, loud talking, and dancing. Tina sat shoulder to shoulder with this person and that person, then she was dancing and then she disappeared. I went back and sat with Sam and Bill.

Right before we left, Tina showed up back at our table, as if she'd been around all along and the fog in the room had moved to reveal her.

"How long you going to be on Prince of Wales Island?"

"A few days," I answered.

"You need to come with me to Hydaburg, you got to know the Haidas." She winked toward Sam and Bill.

"I'd like to," I said.

Right then Al asked Sam where he thought we'd be fishing in the morning; after the answer, I looked and Tina was gone again.

We all caught our limit of king salmon the next day and were back at the lodge before lunch. I was sitting with Al, Sam, and Bill at a small table eating snacks when Al looked up at me.

"Hey, shithead, would you get me a coffee, since you're getting up," Al said aggressively.

Oh, no, what have I done? With these guys I had learned that it wasn't what you said but what you did that they cared about. They judge people the way the first violinist tunes an instrument: their interiors can accurately judge someone's intentions, his or her soul, as precisely as a violinist knows when one string is out of tune. But I must have failed them somehow, or why would Al, such a pleasant man, call me a name like that.

Plus, Al and I had been roommates at the lodge. His side of the room was immaculate, his clothes laid out, all pressed, a different set of clothes for each situation. His shaving-kit stuff was clean and tidy; everything, his tube of toothpaste, his toothbrush, his shaving cream, seemed to be new. I was more the opposite. I had tried to keep my stuff orderly. I felt awful as I walked over to the coffee machine. Besides, how had Al known I was going to get coffee?

Sam must have noticed my shock and disappointment. He got up to get a coffee too.

"Pete, how's it going?" Sam asked.

"Not too well. You heard what Al called me." I kept my head facing away from Al and Bill so they wouldn't hear.

"Oh, that. That's good. He calls you that, you can consider yourself one of the boys."

I got the coffees and went back to the table. Al left after lunch, he had some meetings in Anchorage. Before he left, taking with him a huge box filled with vacuum-packed salmon, he handed me his card and told me to call him if I needed anything in Alaska. On the card he had written his home phone number.

5

Tina

The next day, Sam was talking on his cell phone and Bill was telling me some chilling stories from his experiences fighting in the infantry in Vietnam. Bill usually stayed in the background, didn't say much, when Sam and Al were up front, observed the masters at work. I did not hear the door of the lodge open, but then standing in the doorway, like a pure spirit, was Tina. She did not glow quite the same in the light of day.

Everyone stopped talking. Even Sam held his hand over the tiny mike on his cell phone.

"Come on, let's go, we're headed to Hydaburg," Tina said to me, as if I had no choice. She looked much more vulnerable this morning.

I looked over at Sam; he nodded toward Tina. I took it to mean, go on. I grabbed my JanSport daypack, put my notebooks and cameras in it, and followed her out.

Tina's four-wheel-drive, black and silver Subaru was running outside the lodge. She opened the passenger side door and picked up some glass jars of canned sockeye salmon off the seat and put them in the back of the car. She held one up to the light so I could see it. The skin on the salmon was golden, the meat a dark, dark red.

"This is some of the best food in the world," she said. I had to remember to get some to send to people.

An Al Green tape was on in the car, playing "I'm Still in Love with You." Tina was married to Jerry's brother, Jimmy, though they had recently separated. They had four children: twenty-two-year-old Daniel, who was a student at the

University of Alaska at Anchorage; sixteen-year-old James; Kari, four; and Nicole, who was eleven months old. Pearl Jam and JJ Cale cassettes lay in the built-in cup holders.

"I need to run by the house real quick, tell the baby-sitter something," she said. I noticed again that she seemed smaller in the daylight.

We drove up a hill, then down it, and pulled up to a smallish house. Someone had exerted a great deal of effort to plant flowers, wild and otherwise, all around the cute little house. This lot with this view in Seattle would be worth at least a million dollars, maybe two.

"I planted all these flowers, did all this landscaping. I've let it go, lately," she said. "I love flowers, they are beauty."

Inside were two adorable, dark-eyed, black-haired girls, very Native, and the baby-sitter, who looked to be about fifteen. A Teletubbies video was on TV, and I could see an extralarge bag of Pampers in the open closet. The four-year-old had obviously been exploring closets and drawers, pulling things out into the middle of the living room floor, which was a beautiful light wood. On the counter—I couldn't miss it since I sat down right next to it—was a large prescription bottle of painkillers. On the walls were all kinds of Haida art.

The view out the picture window was alive with the sea, the islands, the kelp beds, the rocks. Everything in the window frame was constantly changed by the sun, fog, tides, storms, wind, and passing wildlife. I could see pink salmon jumping out of the water. A sea otter was lying on its back, floating, eating something out of a large shell. Tina said the otters ate large quantities of abalone. The otters, she said, competed with her sister's boyfriend, who dove for the abalone too. She told me she resents the sea otters because it is their fur, the most luxurious in the world, that had brought the outside world to Haida country. The sea otter had kept the Russians and the Yankee traders coming back. Then, she said, trying to restrain her anger since I was obviously a white man, then they just took this place, took Alaska.

She pointed, and her four-year-old walked over to us as if she was used to Tina showing her things outside this large picture window.

"There is a pod of killer whales that passes here all the time. It is so beautiful to watch them come through the narrow passes at low tide. I've seen them catch all kinds of stuff right out this window. This window brings me so much. Living on an island means things must come to you, and much of what comes to me, I first see from this window.

"My grandmother was a double-fin killer whale, a high-class killer whale, not many people are that. When she died, the killer whales came to the head of the bay." In Haida and Tlingit culture, each person belongs to a clan; you are a raven, a killer whale, and so on. The clan you belong to is as important as your last name, your first name. You married outside your clan; a raven married a killer whale, for example. Tina knows her grandmother had a great and power-filled spirit. Tina believes the killer whales came to the head of the bay to pay their respects to her grandmother and to welcome her spirit, which was now gone from her body.

We got in the car and took off, in more ways than one. She began talking to me as if we were best friends who had been apart for fifteen years. Why was she opening up so completely, so quickly? Did she feel that she could trust me because of seeing me with Jerry and Sam? A half-empty baby bottle rolled across the floor and hit my foot as we took a sharp corner. I picked it up and Tina said to put it in the backseat.

"This last year or so I've been trying to look backward instead of forward. I need to do that right now after living in Craig all these years. I thought that by coming here I would find what I needed. There has been a twenty-year stretch where I have lost something. I got lost in the influence of the lifestyle I was living with Jimmy. It was more the white lifestyle. I need to go back to when I was twelve, fourteen, still living in Hydaburg. I quit growing spiritually when I was sixteen. The spirit was always there, but I traded it in the seventies for sex, drugs, and rock and roll."

It took us less than a half minute to drive by old town. At the edge of it was the Hill Bar and across the street the competing Craig Inn, which was painted pink. A giant whale pelvis bone sat in front of it. We passed a town dock area, then got to the only place on the island where you might think you were in a tiny bit of suburbs, anywhere USA. It only lasts about a block, on the left; it consists of a Burger King; a bookstore; the main grocery store, with what must seem to the locals like a giant parking lot; a National Bank of Alaska. The difference with this little mall is that the people of Prince of Wales work in all the stores. So the teenager at the bookstore will stare at you, ask you when you got to town and where you are from, and remember exactly how you like your coffee after the first time you order it. Shopping for groceries is like a combination family and class reunion and banking requires no ID, unless you're a new-to-the-area fisherman. Once we drove past this block, we were back in the clouds

The totem park in Klawock on Prince of Wales Island. PHOTO BY PETER JENKINS

of mystery and intrigue that move all over the island through the dark shadows of the trees and the tangled clear-cuts. Some parts are so overgrown a hundred black bears could be scavenging in a hundred-acre chunk of it and you would not see them.

If you can imagine Seattle, its climate and look, as an island with 990 miles of coastline and only sixty-three hundred full-time residents, you can visualize this place. It's six hundred miles north of Seattle. Steep, forested mountains two thousand to three thousand feet high cover it. Glaciers carved this place, leaving deep, U-shaped valleys. I would soon find out from Tina about the other powerful forces at work here that had carved her into so many conflicting pieces.

The clouds today were not ethereal, mixing with the trees and rocks and hard world. They were high and heavy, well-defined. There was no wasted babbling between us in the car. From Tina came either silence or passionate conversation, each intense in its own way.

"My grandfather was an artist, like me, like many Haidas. The Tlingits liked to make slaves of Haidas because the Haidas carved better totems, better canoes. You mention that to Bill, see what he says. My grandfather would lie on his back in his boat and look at the clouds and the trees and the eagles and ravens. This is where our designs and patterns came from. I will show you some incredible totems in Hydaburg, right next to the Presbyterian church."

We drove by the school, the sawmill, and a lot where a construction company was busy clearing the forest to build some low-income government houses. There are not many jobs on the island. Some whole hillsides had been clear-cut, maybe five, ten years before, on Native land. The massive stumps had not yet rotted; a jungle of devil's club, spruce seedlings, ferns, and all kinds of green had grown up among them. Tina mentioned that all kinds of herbs and usable plants were in the clear-cuts. She seemed to know every car and truck we passed and who was inside each one. I guessed everyone knew that Tina was driving down the road with me, a man no one knew. In a place like Prince of Wales Island everyone knows which man should be in which car with which woman, who should be close to whom. She didn't care. Tina is bold and in your face; I heard her say several times, you let small-town people rule you, it will drive you crazy.

"I lost my grandmother, my mother, and my sister in Hydaburg. For years I couldn't go there much, the pain was too intense. I had to get away from there. You can't run far on this island, but Craig and Hydaburg are very far apart, much further apart than the forty-six miles we will be driving. You will see."

Tina pointed out a brand-new SUV driving by. She said large amounts of marijuana were grown on this island, in basements and on whole floors of some homes. That person knew where most of it was, she mentioned. There was some kind of history or connection between Tina and seemingly every man-made object, and man and woman, on this island.

"Lately, I've been able to go back. I cut fish again and gossip about everyone until they come around and then we talk about someone else. My grandmother's house was a typical old Haida lady's small wood house. Always smelled like fish and holigan grease [rendered from a small, oily fish and used for preserving everything]. There would be seaweed drying around, cases of canned berries and salmon and other gathered foods everywhere. Her favorite things were her smokehouse and her skiff."

Right before Klawock she pulled into a gas station and filled up. She didn't seem to mind pumping the gas herself, although after she put the hose in, she got back in the car and kept talking. It was if she didn't want to stop, take a chance things she wanted to say to me would stop coming to her.

"My childhood in Hydaburg, I just knew I was a princess, a black-haired Haida princess. My grandmothers told us all the time about our people. We didn't think of who we were and I wouldn't have except for my grandmother.

My grandmother Helen Sanderson, she was one of the very first Native teachers in Hydaburg. She was trained in Seattle. They even have named the elementary school after her. She was the biggest influence in my life. She had me reading encyclopedias, Tolstoy, *Gone with the Wind*, Faulkner in the ninth grade. I was real interested in Russian and southern writers." A tear, just one, fell down her cheek. She wiped it away as if it made her mad that she showed this emotion.

Outside Klawock, Tina stopped her car, got out, and motioned for me to follow her into a clear-cut. The ground was not clear anymore but jammed with growing things. She gathered some Hudson Bay tea, talking while she worked, then we got back in the car.

"I was a cheerleader when I lived in Hydaburg. We used to all pile on my uncle's seine boat and ride to the basketball games, be gone a few days. In 1970, Patty, my friend, she wouldn't be on the pep squad or be a cheerleader—she wanted to play basketball on the boys' team. So they had a meeting and let her play. These basketball games are each like a little war."

A woman passed us in a red Chevy; its rear fender was dented in the middle. Tina said the woman had a main squeeze in Hydaburg, even though she was Tlingit. A black bear appeared standing atop a tree that was felled but not used. As we watched, it hopped off and was gone.

"When I was small, there were only two cars in the whole town and no road to get here. There was an old green Ford and one of those chubby kinds of cars. The big thrill was all of us kids would pile on and we would get a ride out the one-and-a-half-mile road, then back. The boys used to play cowboys and Indians all the time. All the boys wanted to be cowboys until they figured out what was going on."

We passed a small sign stuck in the ground, which seemed out of place because there had not been much evidence of human life for a while. It said, "COHO for SALE $1.00 a pound. Prince of Wales Hatchery." Coho are silver salmon.

"Everyone around here that smokes sockeye and kings, they give cases and cases of it to their cousins and family that live in places they can't get it or can't smoke it. Early Haidas made villages where there were good sockeye streams. And certain families actually owned their own stream, where they would move every year when the salmon returned. Without the salmon there would never have been the Haidas on these islands."

The sky allowed enough light through the dense growth and tall trees to see about half of our surroundings. We turned off on State Road 913 and headed to Hydaburg (pop. 400). If we hadn't turned, we would have ended up in Hollis at the state ferry dock, the cheapest way for someone to get off the island. Local people call leaving "getting off the rock."

"There is a place on this road where Haida country begins and the rest of the world drops off. Just past the Natzahini River is where our country begins. You can take the Native out of the village, but you can't take the village out of the Native." Tina seemed strengthened just by the spirit of her people's land. She looked strong and clear now that we were nearing Hydaburg. Tina's face showed just where she was at any moment.

"This is what has been wrong with me: I've been living in the confused world of Craig too long, part white, part Native, too influenced by a material world and spiritual influences that are not my own. Yet, it is a world I feel I must have. I get lost unless I can kneel on the beach where three hundred years ago they knelt down and dug clams, where the women had babies, kneeling in the woods. I was born in 1958. I weighed four pounds eleven ounces, delivered by a midwife up there in Hydaburg."

Tina's personal power regenerated the closer we got to her home village. I could feel it inside her Subaru; it was a power source that she could harness. She said that lately she has felt that maybe what she needed to do is move to an island and just "put up" fish and seaweed, do her art, weave, smoke fish, and cut wood.

"You know death comes in threes." It was an abrupt statement, and I wondered where it came from, where she was headed, with such an observation.

"You know what my grandmother used to say about all the Yankee sea captains and other ships that first came through here in the late 1700s, early 1800s, trading with the Haidas and Tlingits?" Tina asked.

"No, what?" We had another ten miles to go.

"She used to say, 'If it wasn't for all those sea captains long ago that came from New England, the Yankee traders, us Haidas would all be ugly.' Haidas have always been bold towards outsiders, never afraid. Our best carvers who did the eighty-foot totems even carved what they called 'the Boston man' with the stovepipe hat into their totems." Back at her house she had said that she was sorry the Yankee traders had ever come to Alaska.

The road to Hydaburg is twenty-three miles long. As we went over bridges, I saw salmon fighting their way through the clear water. Bright red huckleberrys mingled with some dark hemlock and cedar left uncut. The land had an almost tropical look. A haunting spirit lingers over the land on either side of the road to Hydaburg, one that is compelling but also a bit frightening. Riding down it today was not just a way to get to Hydaburg but a spiritual quest, a haunting flashback. Fireweed grew six feet high and added its pink-purple to the overwhelming green. We drove by a second black bear; this one trotted along in the other lane, headed away from the village.

I struggled to understand these different sensations, this different spirit that wove in and out and on top of this Haida land we had entered. It wasn't just because it had been logged. It was as if the spirits of the Haida forefathers and those who had died too early of substance abuse or suicide or car wrecks had not left the area but lived out here. They guarded what was left of their land, their way of life, from people like me. Once this whole island had been theirs, as had the sea that surrounded it as far as their superior canoes would take them. This spirit had obviously taken hold of Tina.

"I will never forget my first trip to the outside world. I was so excited I couldn't sleep for days. My aunt and uncle took me to San Diego. I'm not sure why we were even going." She shook her head.

"I will never forget what I thought as I packed my prettiest dresses and holiday shoes, getting ready for California. It was in the early seventies and I just knew I would be considered beautiful and rare and smart down there. My grandmother told me this all the time, how special and smart and pretty I was. We were royalty, really, Haida royalty. I wondered if people in California would know without anyone telling them that I was a Native, one from a high-class clan." She gritted her teeth and held her chin up.

"We got there and it seemed that everyone was blond and tan. It was like we walked through a door and entered the Twilight Zone, everything, everyone, was so different. I'd never wanted to be blond or tan. There is no real way to be either in Haida country. Black hair is what is beautiful to Haidas. You try to lie in the sun around here, you will grow mold."

She was so overwhelmed thinking about that first trip to California, she pulled off the road, on a bridge. She said we were probably seeing so many bears because the salmon were this far up in the streams. The wolves would be working the streams too. This Hydaburg road allowed Tina to pull over, to go as fast or as slow as she wished, to just stop. How many places were there left in our world where someone could take a drive the way Tina was today and look over his or her life?

"The people that we saw driving the nicest cars, in the yards of the finest houses, all seemed to be blond and tan. We went through a Mexican neighborhood and they seemed to have little houses and old cars, lots of people in each car. They looked more like Haidas.

"I remember we went to a hamburger place, I was so excited, we didn't have anything like that on Prince of Wales then. Didn't even have a road to get out of Hydaburg. The waitress was Mexican. I was so in awe of all the people and the shiny cars and this restaurant. I guess I looked like someone who had just crossed the border. Anyway, she spoke to me in Spanish. When I obviously didn't understand, she asked me in English what country I was from." Tina reached out and turned off the music.

"See, our grandmothers told us our whole lives we were the first people in this country. We had our own world, creating beautiful art, hundreds of years before all the people's relatives I was seeing in San Diego got here. Our Grandma Helen told us Haida stories all our lives; she showed us rare Native artifacts and pictures she had collected. In California I felt like we were treated like second- or third-class people, not first-class people. It was like no one wanted to know who I was." Something ferocious rose up in Tina, remembering.

"It was confusing to me. It made me angry. I went home to Hydaburg feeling like maybe there was something wrong with us Haidas. After that I didn't feel like the world was waiting for me to see it. I didn't leave this rock much after that. That world was a shock."

It suddenly started to pour, gray rain overwhelming the windshield wipers, which were on high. Tina turned on the air-conditioning and defroster so we could see.

"I remember thinking back on all that happy sun in California and being around that happy world and thinking that maybe being Native was not what I needed to be. There was so much sadness sometimes. I wanted to be happy and bright like in California, I thought."

On both sides of the road now the trees had not been cut, so it was dark and dense. The farther we drove, the more this place seemed to me to have the same kind of spiritual qualities that the Navajo lands do, the feeling it had been lived in forever, unchanged, spirits everywhere, although the two places could not have looked more different. I kept expecting Carlos Castaneda to appear, standing in the middle of the road.

"It wasn't long after I got back from California that my mother left. When I was fourteen years old and my sister Jody was nine, my mother, explaining nothing to us, went to the ferry and a doctor's appointment in Ketchikan. She didn't come back for ten years. We found out later, she went through woman's counseling, got a job and another relationship. My father was postmaster then."

We passed another bear, this time a small one, lying in a ball on the side of the road. Tina slowed down; it lifted its head. She thought that the mother must have been run over and the Hydaburg people were dropping off food to the little one here.

"I don't know why I have had so much confusion in my life. I have tried so many ways to answer my questions, to solve my problems. There is no preacher or pill that has helped me figure it all out. I've tried them all: counselors; self-help books; *Oprah*; pastors. Seems like I've taken all the pills: Librium, Valium, amitriptyline, lorazepam. Nothing I've tried seems to help me as much as being Native does: cutting strips [salmon], picking berries, going hunting, walking on the beach, being in the village with my people, doing my art. All that other stuff I tried from the non-Native world just dulled the pain. It came back worse. I drive down this road and I can feel me coming back to life. There is a place just back there on this road where the rest of the world drops away. That spot is a place of peace for me. Why don't I come here more often!"

Tina was so consumed in the telling of her life, sometimes I felt that she didn't remember I was there. She'd be going forty-five, then slow down to fifteen miles per hour. Going that slow on this road felt bizarre. Physically we were traveling in slow motion when we should have been speeding; we had the road all to ourselves. Yet Tina could not make herself go any faster.

"A lot of my depression and my anxiety, and I think this every time I come back here, comes from my disconnection from my people and nature. I need to go back, or I try to go back to nature every day, because that is where God is every day, all the time."

I wasn't sure what Tina was fumbling around in her purse for; she again said she hoped we did not see any more bears. She pulled out a small, battered white envelope. She pulled the car over; we had only seen one other car the whole time we'd been on this road. She opened it and pulled out a black braid of hair.

"This is my sister's hair, my older sister. She committed suicide. She went through such a deep time of sadness and confusion; I spoke to her the day she died. I couldn't tell what she was planning to do. We believe that if you have someone's hair, their spirit is always there." The life seemed to go out of Tina's face for a moment, then returned, albeit weakened.

"This place has always had some kind of hold on my family. My grandfather ran away from Indian boarding school in Oregon when he was twelve, made his way to Seattle, then worked his way on a fishing boat from there to Hydaburg."

When we finally got to Hydaburg, there was no sign, just a couple of dirt streets. The main road, Main Street, ran along the water, Sukkwan Strait. On it were Tina's auntie Martha's house and the ANB (Alaska Native Brotherhood) community center, where they have memorial dinners for people who have died, play bingo, host traditional Native dances. Because of all the twists and turns of the bays, roads, and mountains on the collection of islands in this part of Southeast, if you didn't know exactly where you were, it would be impossible to tell from looking at the mountains or the coastline whether you were on the main island or one of the smaller surrounding islands. It seemed to me like an intricate maze. Suddenly, Tina stopped, not pulling over to the side; she just put the car into park right in the middle of the "busiest" road in Hydaburg.

"I have this amazing sense of smell, everyone who knows me knows that. I remember that in summer we were all barefoot, running right through here. I can still smell the dust and the way it mixed with the ocean smells. In summer, all us kids would be on the creek snagging salmon. There was only one little store, Grant's; they had chains for your chain saw, penny candy." About three young boys, followed by two mixed-collie dogs, ran in front of us. One carried a fishing pole with a snagging hook on it.

"My grandma Violet, I remember so well the smells of her perfume and smoked salmon. Sometimes one was stronger than the other. I never knew which one would win out when I opened her door. She was the one who lived to fish, catch, and put up the Native foods. I remember, she had her own skiff; one of my favorite things was to go out with her and gather driftwood. We could get almost everything we needed from the ocean. It even brought us our wood. In summertime, we'd get the best blueberries and thimbleberries, and then us kids, we'd go swimming. During the summer we ate lots of crab, salmon, all kinds of shellfish."

Across from Hydaburg are several large islands—Dall Island, Goat Island, Sukkwan Island, and Suemez Island—and hundreds of tiny islands: Lone Tree

Island, McFarland Island, and on and on. The summer has the most sun, and though there are sometimes large snowfalls in the winter, the dominant weather is rain. Haidas always built their villages to face the southwest to take as much advantage as possible of the sun's drying power.

"In the winter, snow could be deep sometimes, the creek would freeze up. We would get Nana's high-heel shoes and put 'em on. I'd zoom on top of the frozen creek. We would get in lots of trouble; they were her favorite shoes and she could not afford to get more. I think back now and I wonder where she wore those high heels around here."

The Haidas that live here order almost everything from catalogs. The world comes to them in catalogs on the mail plane. They get tired of explaining to the order-center people in Arizona or Nebraska that they don't live in igloos, that they aren't Eskimos, that there are no polar bears, and that they only get mail three times a week. The mail comes in on a floatplane, and it is not unusual for mail to be delayed by weather; sometimes they go four days without it. Always the people have to explain that everyone has a P.O. box in Hydaburg. When asked for a street address for something to be delivered, they just make up a street and number. Everyone knows where everyone lives. Tina and Jody are related to about a fourth of the town, and they are not one of the larger families. (The Edinshaws are.)

Most of the houses have been built a few at a time by some government agency. Few people plant gardens or flowers or have fences. Every few years there get to be so many free-ranging dogs that they have to hire someone special to come in and get rid of the ones that aren't registered. Black bears raid just about everybody's garbage, that's just part of it. Few people have decks; there are far more smokehouses in backyards to smoke the salmon. There is one store, the Haida Market, now owned by Jerry's mother, and two gas pumps, one for regular gas and one for diesel, run by the village Native corporation. There are two churches, one Presbyterian—which has a red neon cross and is next to a totem park, in front of the school—and an Assembly of God. The Presbyterians have more people as they were the first missionaries here. There are no places for the public to drink alcohol, but when you think of it, there is no "public" here at all—it is all personal.

The Haidas of Hydaburg let it be known that if you're not Haida, then don't think about moving here. You probably don't even want to come visit, unless you are related to someone. At least one Native village in Alaska does not allow whites to spend the night, though it is not Hydaburg. The Haidas have always been considered the fiercest of all coastal Natives. Now, they just want their own community, they want no one else coming here telling them how to live or what to believe. Some people are afraid of the place. When the village did not have a village public safety officer, a VPSO, and there was no one to keep the law, basketball teams, their fans, and the refs had state trooper escorts to get in and out of the village. Now since they have a VPSO, a white woman who worked in some prisons upstate, they only have to call the state troopers for serious crime.

On the way into town I had noticed a large sickle-shaped skid mark that began on the left side of the road and went across the centerline and then off the road. I could see where something had skidded through the dirt shoulder. Tina was in a trancelike flashback then; I'd hoped no deer or bear ran out in front of us. I thought about asking to drive a few times to free her up to concentrate on her stories.

We were headed for Jody's, Tina's younger sister's house. Both have black hair, but they look nothing alike. They're close, though, clearly—Jody had four or five of Tina's paintings hanging on her walls.

When we arrived, there was almost no time for any greeting or introductions.

"Tina," Jody said, "did you hear?"

"What?" Tina's voice could change whole octaves and get low.

"The other night when we were all at the Hill Bar, Lori, from here—you know, the one you always see in town taking her little kids for a walk—well, she died in a car crash."

"What?" Tina seemed spooked.

"She was rushing to catch the ferry, had her three kids in the car, they were going to Ketchikan to buy school clothes. One of the kids may have been squirming around, no one knows—she lost control of the car, anyway, and rolled it. She was the only one without a seat belt on, and she died."

"Oh, God, maybe this is why I was thinking of death on the way here. Is that why there are all the cars across the street?"

"Yeah, the body is over in the house."

Tina got up, walked across the dirt road, said she needed to go pay her respects.

Jody's boyfriend, Tony, came out from a back room. He is a massive young man, seven years younger than Jody. Tony was an Alaska state heavyweight wrestling champion; he has hands twice my size. He seemed like a gentle giant or just a man who knew he had nothing to fear and could always be relaxed. He is a gifted carver, Native-designs painter, drum-maker, hunter, fisherman. Tony can be standing in a river on the island and catch ten cohos while three tourists catch one between them. He can see the fish, while they see only rushing water. He can call deer to within fifteen feet of him using a piece of grass.

Tony explained that the Alaska State Troopers had already done their investigation and there was no foul play. Lori never hurt anyone, he said; she didn't drink or smoke dope. When you saw her, her kids were always with her. She took care of an elder, bathed her and cooked her meals. She was one of those uptight lady drivers, Tony said, always drove with both hands on the wheel. Her body would never leave the Hydaburg area. She would be laid out and never left alone in the house across the street.

According to Tony, village men, about ten to twelve guys, would go over in a boat to a small island across the bay and dig her grave by hand. Then after the church service, someone with a seine boat would put the casket and the family on the big boat and the rest of the town would go over for the service in their own skiffs. Sadness often visits Hydaburg, as it does every place; it's just that here everyone feels it.

Tina stayed visiting for a long time. When she returned, we went to her auntie Martha's. She sat at her kitchen table in her small wood home, with a cigarette in one hand and a beer in the other. She had a smoker's voice and a skinny, skinny body. She was taking care of one of her grandsons, who had just taken a bath. He had splashed around so much the water had run under the bathroom door. Auntie Martha was confrontational, the life of her own party that never seemed to end, and knew everything that was going on in Hydaburg. She and Tina spent some time catching up with each other while I sat quietly and listened.

Tina said it was time to drive the forty-six miles back to Craig. For the different world it was, it might as well be forty-six hundred miles. I don't know what I was expecting out of Hydaburg after all Tina had said coming over here, but as is often the case, that's not what I experienced. But then Hydaburg holds no part of my history, my heart; it's not the scene for any of my memories or nightmares. No one in Tina's family wanted her to leave. Her baby-sitter had been taking care of her girls all day and it was getting dark, she said. Time does not tick off at the same speed in Craig as in Hydaburg. Sometimes it seems that time does not pass at all in Hydaburg. It gets light and it gets dark, but the moment stays the same.

Tina was ready to leave, but first we stopped by Jody's house again to call the baby-sitter to let her know when we'd be there. Louise, sixteen, one of Jody's neighbors, was on the phone ordering school clothes from J. Crew. Finally, Tina got to use the phone. Someone she called before the baby-sitter mentioned that there was a house party tonight, at Laverne's mother and stepfather's house. Laverne's father had died years ago in one of Hydaburg's worst tragedies. It has cast an awful dark shadow over the people here for over fifteen years. There was no road then and five of Hydaburg's most handsome, athletic, and popular guys were partying. They decided they would get in one of their skiffs and run to Craig, forty dangerous miles in a large boat, much less a little skiff. No one knows what happened, but they all perished. This dark, cold death lay down a cloud of depression that will never completely leave. I could almost feel the wailing of the mothers and brothers and sisters and fathers and grandparents still.

"Peter, you want to go by this house party? I grew up with both these people; you met them at the Hill Bar. People are afraid to come to Hydaburg, there are very few whites that would ever go to a house party." Tina winked at Jody. I had been dared. Of course I wanted to go, I said.

Jody had just gotten out one of Tina's paintings, a woman growing out of a killer whale, and asked Tina how it should be framed. Jody also showed us a print she'd recently bought of some Haida men traveling several hundred years ago in the open ocean in one of their renowned cedar canoes. The canoe had magnificent carvings on the high bow and sides; it was a living, floating totem.

"Jody, what do you think about taking him to a house party?" Tina wondered aloud, perhaps second-guessing her invitation.

"I think he can handle it. They liked him the other night, but you know how things can get." Jody lifted her dark eyebrows, showing off a childlike quality to her personality.

The party was at the edge of town, where some of the newer houses are. They all looked to be about twelve hundred square feet, with three bedrooms, one bath, and no garage. Four or five young teenagers were standing outside; Tina said they were there to watch what went on; it was a local form of entertainment to see what adults did what, or to whom. Some early James Brown song was blasting out all the open windows and doors. Inside, the local people, about equally divided between men and women, sat and stood mainly in the kitchen. The host couple recognized me from the Hill Bar. After a half hour, six people were dancing in the living room, the rest were talking around the kitchen table or out on the steps. A half hour later I noticed I had to raise my voice to be heard. Outside, a woman about twenty was shouting to someone on the steps. She had gone home and changed clothes, changed into a dress. She said that her "boyfriend" was still talking to that other woman, he hadn't noticed she had changed clothes. She seemed ready to cross over into totally out of control. The teenagers in the yard were all ears. They certainly knew something about this young woman's past. She was yelling so loud at the person trying to calm her that she could be heard over the stereo playing "Lodi" by Creedence Clearwater Revival on about eight and everyone else talking as loud as they could.

Tina walked over to me. I half smiled and lifted my eyebrows. She said she thought it would be a good time to leave.

"There aren't many white people, or for that matter, any outsiders that can say they were at a house party in Hydaburg," Tina said to compliment me.

"All that drama, that girl yelling, it brings back too much. It reminds me what a tiny little world it is over here in Hydaburg. I love it here and I hate it here. Why can't I find the right place for me? It doesn't seem to be in Craig, and it doesn't seem to be in Hydaburg."

One of her cassettes was playing, but it was turned down so low I couldn't make it out. She turned it up; it was Lionel Ritchie and Diana Ross singing "Endless Love." The road and everything surrounding it was the blackest dark. Something ran across the road, far in front of us. Was it a black bear or a wolf or one of the many dogs running free?

"When our mother got on the ferry and didn't come back, I went to live with Jerry's family. That's how I met my present husband, Jimmy. I told you we're separated, right?"

"Yes," I answered.

"Well, my grandmother Helen, the teacher, who got me reading everything, she raised this man Foo, Alvin Young. He was orphaned. He married Jerry's mother, Margie. I was a good student, I loved to learn. My grandmother asked Margie and Foo if I could live with them and go to high school in Craig. They had four sons, some of the best-looking guys on the island. Jimmy was four and a half years older than I was, and Jerry was four or five years younger. I was young and impressionable when I first went to live with them. Man, Jimmy was good-looking.

"There wasn't any TV on the island then at all," Tina continued. "Margie's house is right across the street from the Hill Bar. Jerry and I, we would open the second-floor window and just watch people come and go. We knew just about everyone, and they didn't know us kids were watching them. It was better than any soap opera. Every weekend it was something different. And it got funny too. On real icy nights in the winter, people would come out, set foot on the street, and slip and slide, usually on their butts, all the way down the hill towards old town. We liked the fights the best. You could always tell when one was going to start. The people, guys and girls, would walk puffed up, usually around closing time. Some of the fights would be huge, twenty people. Some woman would say something to someone else's old lady. There were the rowdy ones, one family we called the James Gang. If we saw them there, we were almost positive there would be a fight. It was better than watching WWF. Foo would go down the next morning, pour Pine-Sol all over, and the place would be ready for another night."

We passed the place where Lori had run off the road and died. Someone had placed some flowers there since we'd passed.

"After Jimmy and I got married, I thought I was right where I wanted to be. Maybe my life would be happy, like I saw in California, just without the sun and the blondes. I became the Martha Stewart of Prince of Wales Island. All my Christmas ornaments matched. I changed my theme for Christmas every year." Tina now spoke in a different cadence; her words were coming out faster.

"I saw something in the Spiegel catalog, I ordered it. I had a J. Crew card, Nordstrom's card, Alaska Airlines card, Visa. I wore Lancôme makeup. Last thing I wanted was the smell of the life that I grew up with. We used to say my grandmother's perfume was the smell of salmon. I didn't want to smell like the smoke from the smokehouse or, for that matter, even smell it at all. I didn't want to smell stink eggs or kneel on the beach, gather driftwood and seaweed. I became a gourmet cook, cooking Martha Stewart recipes instead of my own people's foods."

Tina put the bright lights on, finally, something I had wanted to do for miles. I couldn't see the road because her low beams were incorrectly adjusted, and I'd wondered how she could.

"I thought if I lived more the white man's way with a man that wasn't so Native, I would have a better life. I married into this island's version of the Ewings, you know, from that TV show *Dallas*. I found that I could not only adapt but also excel doing their things. Jimmy's part Native, but really the white side is much stronger in him. I had so much more than I did growing up. We certainly didn't have to haul water like my father did. But, I lost myself with all those things. My heart almost died, like it was covered with a black blanket."

There was silence in the car for quite some time until we almost ran into a doe, blinded by the bright lights, frozen in the middle of the road.

"You know, Peter, the Haidas believe our spirits are from people that were here before. I wish I knew who mine came from. I feel pulled in so many directions. My life has been like the experience of giving birth: there is this lust involved, then this pain, then joy comes, and it goes on and on like that."

We made it to the end of the Hydaburg road, took a left, and had another twenty-something miles more of almost no streetlights. The headlights caught the glowing eyes of several deer feeding on the grass that grew on the side of the road. Driving down these roads on this part of the island, I felt as if Tina and I were the only ones in the world. When she spoke again, it startled me a little bit.

"I don't know what it is about you, but I feel like I could drive around this island for a week with you and never run out of things to talk about." I have noticed during my decades of traveling that people from every walk of life seem to trust me with their stories. I told Tina I knew how difficult it is to speak about yourself, your pains and joys, when you're in the midst of such change. I was honored she felt free to talk.

She spoke the next few sentences in almost a chant. "Someday I will, someday I really will be strong enough, someday. I can't believe I am already forty. I will . . . I will become an artist. . . . I will do what I need to do. I really will."

Then when it seemed that we would never see our surroundings again, we passed a couple of streetlights; it seemed bizarre to have light coming from something other than the car. We were back in Klawock. It was as if we had been flying around in outer space and were returning to the mother ship. Tina turned up a hill, and halfway up she slowed way down. On the right side of the road was a trailer with a light on the front porch and a small house next to it, with another light shining from the corner eave. The weak light couldn't overpower the night, but it did shine into the field across the street. Dimly lit by the feeble light, there were maybe twenty totems rising up from the ground, their faces barely discernible, eerie. Tina didn't say anything about why she had taken this detour but just drove on.

In another ten minutes or so, we were back to several streetlights; to Craig; the Burger King; Margie's main grocery store, Thompson House Grocery. Jimmy worked at this store. She pulled in to buy some diapers. Jimmy saw her and me, and she introduced us. Jimmy managed the store and was living somewhere else right now, but took care of the girls often. Tina had mentioned he was an excellent father, a really good friend. Jimmy was small, very fit; Tina said he worked out to stay in shape. There was a pained bubble around them, filled with history and conflict. I understood and felt awkward.

We left. The bookstore light went out as we drove by. We pulled into Tina and Jimmy's house. Tina walked into the house, paid the baby-sitter, and stood looking out the picture window. It should have been a big, black, shiny rectangle, but it wasn't. From every corner of it, from every part of the black ocean and the black sky, came twinkling lights, white lights mostly. Tina lingered, looking, and I walked over to her and looked too. The lights were moving, ever so slowly. At first I thought the lights were stars, but they were not. Tina, who had changed into the harried-mother mood the moment we walked inside, changed her mood again, radically. She spoke with intense excitement.

"You see those lights, those are the seine boats. They are all coming to Craig, coming to port, coming to off-load their catches. They have had an opener [a few days of legal fishing] and now it is ending. Do you realize there are seven men on each one of those boats? You watch, soon my girlfriends will be calling me, watch. Those fishermen are from all over the Northwest—Seattle, Oregon, all over Alaska, who cares where they're from, they're not from this island. Many of them will soon be at the Hill Bar. Even the married couples like to go out when all these new men are in. They like the energy, everyone laughing, loving, and fighting too. It's one time when I don't feel like I need to get off this rock."

As if she'd summoned it, the phone rang once, twice. Tina asked the baby-sitter if she could spend the night; after all, it was summer, she could make some more money. Tina and some of her friends were going to go to the Hill Bar. One of the best-selling drinks at the Hill Bar that night was a drink in a shot glass with vodka and lemon juice, the rim dipped in sugar. It's called the Panty Dropper. They wanted me to go with them, but I didn't. I thanked her for her time and told her I hoped she was able to sort through all her confusion, pain, and sense of responsibility to locate the way that would be best for her and her family.

Sam and Bill were still up, watching ESPN on the satellite TV, when I arrived back at the lodge. I felt that I had lived a part of an entire life today. I was exhausted, though I had done nothing physically.

"How was your trip to Hydaburg, Pete?" Bill asked. Sam looked up.

"It was something. It will probably take some time to figure out what I saw and heard," I answered. They didn't ask for details, they said nothing else about it.

I took home enough salmon and halibut to fill up a third of a chest freezer. I had not expected to take any fish home; I figured my fish would go to feed Al's "village." Sam, Bill, Al, and Jerry had other ideas. It seemed that I had been accepted into their world, and I was honored.

6

Bears on Dora Way

Jed and Luke were home from their summer jobs; they had three attractive young women visiting. Sabri and Teresa were sisters; their mother is the outspoken Mickey. They live across the street from us. The third girl, Jessica, lived one house down from them. Her mother, Rosie, manages the Hertz rent-a-car place. They were watching *Real World* on MTV. This was the third or fourth time I'd seen it, as they tended to control our only TV. The *Real World* character they focused on always seemed to be drunk, drugged up, picking a fight in a club, wanting to leap out a window, get back with her partner, deny everything, or if all else failed, accuse everyone else for what was going wrong in her life. Tonight her house members were telling her she had to go into rehab or get kicked off the show.

We had almost no furniture in our rented house in Seward. There was a good-size living room, which was carpeted. It had a great view to the street and to the homes where the girls lived. The picture window had no curtain. The $5 TV we had bought at the high school fund-raiser didn't have sound after the first week, so we'd picked up a new TV at the superstore in Soldotna. There wasn't a sofa, just some white plastic chairs we'd borrowed from Ben Ellis. Luke had already leaned back in one and shattered it. I sat on the rug, leaned against the wall, and watched these five people—my two sons and their three female friends—communicate, relate, and watch *Real World*. Luke just asked Jessica a question; Jed just touched Sabri's shoulder.

I didn't really want to be sitting here, I felt that I was intruding. But there was nowhere else to be except in our bedroom, and so far only a mattress and box spring were up there. Rita was making salmon dip; that's probably why I was hovering near her. Eventually Jed and Luke and the girls left, headed for Sabri's to watch a movie. Sabri had just announced that in the fall she was going to be an exchange student in South Africa, where she would live with a black African family.

It was July and about midnight. Eight-year-old Julianne had a friend over from the neighborhood, Leah, also eight, and they were still up. At the height of summer in Alaska, it is nothing to see young kids up late, very late. The farther north they live, the later they stay awake.

Leah walked over to the picture window. "Look, Julianne, look." Leah was pointing down, into the front yard. She was a freckle-faced, self-amused, low-key child.

Julianne ran over. "Dad, look, look, a bear. It's a brown bear."

There, strolling slowly across our tiny, bright green front yard was a medium-size brown bear. I called Rita. Jed and Luke and the girls were across the street, hopefully inside. The bear walked onto our street, Dora Way, crossed it, and headed right for Sabri and Teresa's house, where their mother Mickey's 1970s, brown Ford pickup was parked in the driveway. Two metal garbage cans sat in the pickup.

The bear stood up on its hind legs and shook the bed of the pickup until the two garbage cans slid toward it. It then grabbed on to one of the cans and tipped its contents out on the street. It snacked until the police came, when it ran into the darkly shadowed woods behind our houses. Our street was basically the only one on this mountain. Every house on our side of the road had a backyard that stretched into more than a million acres of at times almost vertical wilderness. Someone must have called 911, because I read about the bear and its activities in the next edition of "The Police Log."

Some government person went around the neighborhood and stapled up bright pink and green signs that said, "Caution [then a picture of a bear] bears in the area, be alert, removal of this sign may result in injury to others, USDA Forest Service." These signs were posted on all the telephone poles, on the post of our front porch, and those of all the other houses up and down the street.

The house we rented had a small entry on the street level. Then there was a flight of stairs down to where the kids had their rooms, three bedrooms. There was also a flight up to the living room and kitchen area, open to each other. Up another four stairs and there was Rita's and my room. That night Julianne and her little freckle-faced friend, Leah, were worried because the windows in their bedroom were right at ground level. What if the bear just jumped through the window? That bear had just been in our yard, they said in stereo. Could it fit in the window, it was so large? They wondered, could they bring their sleeping bags up and sleep in the living room? Of course they could. They fell asleep before the bear came back. Mickey's garbage would lie there until the safety of morning. Mickey, a former Dead Head, is now drama tech at the high school. Before the police came, she'd stepped out on her front steps and yelled at the bear to get away. It had looked up, then gone back to its easy meal.

The next night, at about the same time, Julianne and Luke came running upstairs. They said they had just seen some long brown legs walk right by their bedroom windows. They got upstairs to the living room window in time to see the same brown bear leaving our front yard and crossing the street. Our garage was filled with salmon and halibut, but it was in the freezer.

A friend of mine, Albert Kookesh, from Angoon on Admiralty Island, was awakened one night by his dog barking. He went out to his storage shed to see a large mother brown bear standing in front of his chest freezer, holding the top open with one paw, humanlike. It was sorting through the shrink-wrapped salmon, venison, and halibut for its favorite food. I hadn't told anybody that story, including Rita, nor the stories I'd heard of bears peeling away screwed-on four-by-eight-foot sheets of the strongest plywood to get into a cabin. It was clear to me that this bear, any bear, could easily pry open or tear apart the comparatively flimsy garage door on this house.

The next "Police Log" recorded the action around the neighborhood this way: "July 21—12:49 A.M. Extra patrols on Dora Way where there are reports of a black bear and a large brown bear getting into trash; callers were informed to secure their trash." About the only way to secure trash from a serious brown bear would be to build a large steel safe and then bolt it to a concrete slab.

"1:50 A.M. Two 911 calls of a brown bear on Dora Way; caller was advised to use the business phone line unless the bear was threatening life or property." Sounds like this dispatcher was a bit irritable that night. When a brown bear is one foot from the stairs that go up to your deck, which opens into your bedroom or your baby's room, or is standing two feet from your child's bedroom window, what's wrong with being nervous and calling 911? Does the bear have to be in your house and clicking its teeth before you call 911? In Seward it's acceptable to be crabby every so often. Sometimes the weather gets to you.

"2:39 A.M. Police spotted a grizzly on Dora Way [technically a brown bear] and directed it into the woods. Fish and Game will be contacted in the morning." This means they would be calling Ted Spraker. He'd call his sidekick Larry Lewis, and they'd come to our rescue. When our Seward police directed the bear into the woods, what technique did they use? Did they get out of the patrol car and wave their arms in the air and cowboy it? Did they inch toward it in their car?

The next night while on bear watch, Jed, Luke, their friend Warren, and their three girlfriends decided they'd sit in the middle of Dora Way, in front of our house, beginning around midnight, and dare the bear to join them. It didn't show until fifteen minutes after they left. It must have been watching them from the dark, dangerous woods.

After they dispersed, I was standing on the back deck, looking at the stars. I heard something walking in the damp, dark shadows under the limbs of the trees that grew everywhere in the woods behind our house.

I called inside to Rita and Julianne; everyone else was over at Mickey's. Julianne was wearing her white terry-cloth bathrobe and she was chilled, but not by the cool Alaskan night or the bluish white light of the moon. No, what made her shiver was the sound of something coming toward us in the three-to-four-foot-high weeds growing in the yard a few feet from us.

"Daddy," she whispered, grabbing ahold of my shirt and pointing in the direction of the approaching sounds. Her white-blond hair looked silver in this moonlight.

Below us, suddenly, was the head of a brown bear, walking toward us, its body hidden by the tall weeds. In two seconds it was in our yard; in another second it was under the deck we stood on. I heard it paw at some bottles; I later found someone had had a beer or two under there.

"I'm afraid," Julianne whispered.

"It's okay, honey. I think it will go over to Mickey's house again."

It walked under the deck, almost silent on the soft summer grass. I thought I heard it breathing, or was that me? It went by the stairs that would have led to us and then, as predicted, headed over to stand up and shake Mickey's truck again. This time, though, the truck contained no trash cans.

"The Police Log" in the Seward weekly newspaper reported, "July 22—11:19 P.M. Report of brown bear seen in the Dora Way and La Touche area." "July 23—12:51 A.M. Report of brown bear going through garbage in 1900 block

Dora Way for more than an hour in the same area." "1:15 A.M. Coast Guard Kodiak [the largest Coast Guard base in the United States is just 185 nautical miles from here on Kodiak Island] received report of vessel capsizing in vicinity of Resurrection Bay." A few things were happening around Seward other than the wandering, hungry bears. "1:52 A.M. Report of a black bear going through garbage at a residence at 2500 Cedar area; caller said their dog was stuck outside with the bear."

"2:35 A.M. Bear has returned to Dora Way area; dispatcher will make a 'bear log,' noting addresses and whether trash was secured for future citations." Uh-oh, now the garbage-creating humans are in trouble with the police too. Knowing how stiff-necked and tough-minded some of these Alaskans are, if I were a Seward policeman, I would rather deal with the bears.

At 11 P.M. during the summer, there were usually a fair number of children out playing in the front and backyards of our neighborhood. Julianne and her friend Nicole bounced on the trampoline in Rosie's backyard. Next door to Rosie, going uphill, were Mike and Sue. They had two black-haired sons who were constantly making jumps to run over with their skateboards or trick bikes. As July wore on, the brown bear was coming out earlier and earlier, overlapping into times when the children were out playing.

"July 23—3:18 A.M. 911 caller said brown bear at 2000 block Dora Way was tearing through trash in backyard." "4:28 A.M. Officer sighted brown bear at 1900 block of Dora Way."

The bears kept on getting bolder, coming into our yards, sniffing around our garages, harassing the neighbors' dogs. They were showing up now before it was fully dark.

"The Police Log" for the week of July 23, 1999, printed in the *Seward Phoenix Log,* was filled with bear calls along with some of the usual "Police Log" fare: "1:05 P.M. 911 call received of a woman stuck in trunk of vehicle. Out of vehicle 1:22 P.M." Did she call from inside the trunk? "4:40 P.M. Caller advised he gave ride on his bicycle to a subject who appeared to be intoxicated and thought it strange the subject has many T-shirts with tags still on them." I think it's a bit strange the guy on the bicycle picked up a hitchhiking drunk. Riding two on a bicycle requires real balance. "8:38 P.M. Manager at Burger King [the only fast food in town, unless you count Subway] advised that occupant of an older white vehicle blew marijuana smoke into drive-thru window and was drinking alcohol. Contact made. Driver passed field sobriety test."

And of course there was still report after report of the bear invasion of our street, which was now spreading to other parts of town. "July 23—6:31 P.M. Officer went door-to-door in Dora Way to advise of brown bear sighting." "July 24—2:17 P.M. Bear reported on patio of home on Wolfe Circle. Trooper scared bear off for now." "5:00 P.M. Bear trap will not be set tonight at Dora Way and La Touche due to the state not approving overtime for Fish and Game to do it. Trap will be set tomorrow." Budget cuts equal longer freedom for brown bears in human habitats.

The state surely hoped no one would be mauled or injured by the bear that night. One entry that week was appropriate, especially if this bear was not caught soon. "8:10 P.M. Adult male handing out pamphlets at the Kenai Fjords Tours parking lot, referring to the 'wrath of GOD.'" If something tragic happened, after all those calls, forget about the wrath of God for now; the wrath of the folks on Dora Way and throughout Seward would be more than enough for any mere mortal.

"July 25—12:15 A.M. Brown bear eating garbage at 1920 Dora Way." "12:50 A.M. Brown bear eating garbage at 1910 Dora Way." "4:15 P.M. Bear trap set near water tower." "7:57 P.M. Security check of bear trap." "10:27 P.M. Bear sighted at 1721 Phoenix." This last sighting was a few blocks down the hill from our house, below the old, deserted orphanage. This was either a new bear or "our" bear was broadening his range. "11:05 P.M. Security check on bear trap." Notice how often the trap was being checked.

"July 26—11:16 P.M. Brown bear sighted at 1905 Dora Way." This is next door to us; we saw it a few minutes before they did. This was the earliest anyone had seen it, so far. The bear was rapidly becoming habituated. "11:30 P.M. Very large brown bear sighted east of Gary's Gas." Gary's, where they also sell snow machines, was about six miles from our house. This was a new bear. A person could begin to feel surrounded.

"July 27—2:59 A.M. Brown bear reported at Second Avenue." Now they were getting close to downtown, close to Providence Hospital. One especially outspoken female neighbor said that at least if someone was mauled in that part of town, they'd be close enough to the hospital to crawl there. "6:26 A.M. Small black bear in the trap." No one had ever seen this bear. "8:38 P.M. Bear trap moved to 2025 Dora Way." The trap was moved to the yard of the wildlife officer who'd given me the ticket for having the wrong fishing license.

"July 28—3:12 A.M. Security check of bear trap." "5:29 P.M. Caller from Dora

Way concerned for children playing in area due to the brown bear sightings. Requested a poster be put on his door."

"July 29—4:36 A.M. Advised of brown bear eating trash in the 300 block of First Avenue. Caller did not have their trash secured." Here we go again. "2:55 P.M. Report of a brown bear chasing kids at Creekside Trailer Park. Trooper responded." Uh-oh. A brown bear in middaylight chasing children. The tension around town was growing. The fuse was not only lit, it was nearing an explosion if something wasn't trapped soon. Even after this entire series of events, not one person had fired a shot. "5:54 P.M. Caller advised she could hear a child screaming from the Bayview Apartments, yelling, 'No, no.' Officer patrolled area and no screaming was heard." Surely no bear had broken into the child's apartment. "11:23 P.M. Security check on bear trap."

"July 30—3:53 A.M. Security check on bear trap." "5:18 A.M. Security check on bear trap." "7:07 A.M. Report of brown bear in trap. Caller contacting someone to come over and dart it." Finally, the bear was caught—at least, hopefully this was the one. A few nights gone by would tell. Ted Spraker got the early-morning call; he was still at home having coffee with Elaina. He and Larry drove the ninety-plus miles from Soldotna to Seward to take care of our bear, to take care of our neighborhood.

After the trapped two-and-a-half-year-old female brown bear was tranquilized, they fitted her with a tracking collar, took samples of her blood and hair, pulled a tooth, and tattooed her ear. After that they moved her to a place far away called Mystery Creek. That day the children spread out across the neighborhood to be children, some even playing late into the night.

7

Can a Glacier Cry?

Our bright yellow, oceangoing kayaks were lashed to the roof of the boat. Hopefully on the way to our destination we wouldn't run into any rough ocean that would try to wash them away. My daughter Rebekah and I were catching a ride from Seward out of Resurrection Bay, a bay too open to the fast-tempered winds of the Gulf of Alaska to allow for a several-day journey for a kayaker like me. It will always blow my mind that the Aleuts used to travel all around the bay, even across the open ocean to Kodiak and many other places, in their skin kayaks. Along with a friend, Mark Lindstrom, we were going to spend the next couple of days and nights in Aialik Bay.

Aialik Bay (pronounced I-al-lick) was almost surrounded by the Harding Icefield. Nothing man-made can compare to the Harding Icefield. Several glaciers ease off of it directly into the sea. Some of these glaciers confronted the ocean, one of a few natural things powerful enough to dare to do this. The bay is about twenty-five miles long, and all sides are steep rock walls or even steeper glaciers. Black bears, some iceberg-white mountain goats, a few lone wolves, and occasional brown bears have eaten the few things that live on the mountainsides among the rocks and in the alders. Some small glacier-fed creeks with small salmon-spawning runs empty into this bay. As far as I knew, no one had ever died kayaking in Aialik Bay.

The boat ride to haul us and our kayaks and equipment to our drop-off near Lechner Glacier was about forty-five miles. If a person knew he was going to die in two weeks, just that forty-five-mile ride would be an ideal top lifetime inspiration. A couple and their son from somewhere in California were getting dropped off before us at a U.S. Park Service wilderness cabin. They had made reservations a year in advance. It was hard to tell if they knew just how isolated they would be. Even though Aialik Bay was just a bay west of Resurrection Bay, it might as well have been a hundred miles deeper into the wilderness. If we got into any trouble, we'd have to handle it ourselves. I didn't know Mark well, but I knew he had experience out here, and all over Alaska.

When we got to the cabin where the couple and their son were to stay, I watched them look around. The wife looked at her husband. Was that fear on her face? Mostly they could only look up and up higher to the steep, stone-mountain faces, hanging glaciers, and sharp mountaintops surrounding them. What if something happened to them? They had a couple kayaks; what if the father and the son went across the bay and one capsized? Little happenings in Alaska can turn out to be major catastrophes. This family appeared to like each other, though, and you certainly wouldn't want to be out in a cabin like this with no way out if you didn't get along. I wondered if the Park Service allowed alcohol.

We'd had a planning session with Mark a few weeks before. He'd asked us how much ocean-kayaking experience we had—a couple hours each—except Rebekah had done all that white-water wilderness canoe travel in southeastern Oregon on her monthlong NOLS (National Outdoor Leadership School) trip. Mark told us that it could be extremely dangerous kayaking anywhere here in the ocean, especially in the more remote bays, because the weather can quickly get severe, blow down off the Harding Icefield. Fog can float in and around un-movable objects and hide reality. He told us to get these waterproof bags to put out cameras and clothes and food in, just in case we flipped.

He was studying the couple and their son. The man sounded as if he knew what he was doing, but all kinds of people talk a good Alaska game. Mark said he knew how to read the ocean and waves, how to gauge the truck-size pieces of ice breaking off the glaciers. He claimed to know about advancing bears and severe tidal flows and to be able to discern confronting cloud fronts. He seemed as if he would know how to fix a hole in the kayak and where to get wood and how to start a quick fire onshore to warm someone who'd been immersed.

I'd heard the story of a couple guys catching a hundred-plus-pound halibut from a kayak. It pulled them around, they couldn't control it. I'd brought my fishing pole. Mark said we'd see all kinds of black bears. We couldn't bring a gun even if we wanted to because on the land where we'd be camping out in Kenai Fjords National Park, there were "no firearms allowed." The last time I'd seen him, Captain Bob, the local shark fisherman, had mentioned that a halibut long-liner who had been a few bays farther west, in Black Bay, had said the whole bay was full of sea otters and their babies.

We packed our stuff into our kayak; it took careful consideration. I would be in the back and Rebekah the front; loading us, especially me, called for precision. Rebekah leapt around the kayak like a butterfly; I was not like a butterfly. We barely squeezed in our clothes (we were prepared for squalling, wailing weather), then had to find room for our tent and fishing poles. I don't like to wear life preservers, but I wore mine out here. If one or both of us fell in halfway across the bay a mile from either shore and couldn't get back into the kayak, we'd have to be towed to shore by Mark. Surely he could climb back in his kayak in the middle of the bay, but what if the waves and wind shot up? A few people had told me that winds could blow off these glaciers or down from the rugged, uninhabitable wild around us as if they'd been shot out of a cannon. In winter, there was fifty feet of snow out here. There were many whales; orcas fed in this bay where the current pushed up feed fish. A local fishing guide and our neighbor on Dora Way, Eric Jackson, had seen some orcas attack a baby humpback whale out here somewhere. He said two humpbacks had eventually pushed the baby between them and saved it, but it got bloody before the killer whales left. Surely the orcas would never mistake a kayak for something to eat.

I'd just seen a TV show where someone was experimenting towing a surfboard around great-white-shark country because they surmised that great whites attack surfboards because they mistake them for seals or sea lions on the surface. I'd seen enough of orca behavior to believe they were much more aware and intelligent than great white sharks. Captain Bob said he'd been out exploring deep in these bays and fjords and had seen times in Three Hole Bay and others when salmon shark fins seemed to fill the bay. The sharks seemed uninterested in people entirely. They appeared to be lolling on the surface. Maybe they'd already eaten their fill.

This beginning of this trip reminded me of a movie that begins on this birdsinging, sun-shining, no-wind, everyone-smiling day, and there's only one way to go from there—way down. We pushed off from the rocky beach; the three people we were leaving behind waved good-bye. We paddled north, staying

Mark and me in front of Pedersen Glacier. Photo by Rebekah Jenkins

along the exceedingly rugged coastline almost completely untouched by human intervention. Mark said we were going to go to the end of the bay and then kayak across by Frazer Rock to Aialik Glacier.

Mark managed a seaside B&B in Lowell Point, Alaska Saltwater Lodge, in the summer and worked with sled dogs around Mount McKinley in the winter. At one time, he'd been a tour-boat captain. He was a trail official during the Iditarod, following the entire race and trained sled dogs and assisted top mushers in running their dog kennels. Like many Alaskans he did almost anything to keep living here. He was from Oregon. He said the right way to live in Alaska year-round was to live by the sea in the summer and in the deep, dry, bright, powdery interior in winter. The idea is to glide on the water in summer and glide on the powder in winter. He motioned us to his side and said we'd paddle into this little cove.

It seemed the past and the present and the future, three streams of my vision, were fighting inside my head to see which one would dominate. Scenes from our past seemed as real as this very moment. I saw Dr. Andonie of Metairie, Louisiana, holding Rebekah up by her ankles, red and creased, a few seconds after she'd been delivered by C-section. It was odd, as if that memory of her birth were more real to me right now than being here in the yellow kayak. Maybe it was being on the water together, or the isolated purity of this moment. I could feel Rebekah as a six-year-old clinging to my back in a cool lake, wanting to swim in water over her head, water as deep as the water we were in now. I swam underneath her and she was grabbing hold of my neck as the water got deeper and darker and more filled with the unknown. I finally had to release her grip, I thought I would choke. Rebekah has always surprised me with her physical strength, not to mention her strength of will. Before she could walk, before there were any brothers or sisters, she hated sleeping alone in her room in her crib. One night after apparently sitting in there fretting, upset, I heard something crash onto the floor. She had leapt out of her crib. It was the first but not the last brave, daring, rebellious leap she would take. I was surprised, thankful, she would even spend this time with me in Alaska.

"Dad, paddle," Rebekah reminded me, politely but with a tone that could be intimidating.

I was having trouble coming back into this moment, this scene; I was in the past yet still present enough to be paddling forward atop this brilliant ocean water.

In my mind I saw Rebekah when she was five running as fast as her fawnlike legs could move her, through an open gate on what was then our farm. It was a Tennessee spring, when the new grass, the new green leaves of the trees, and the darker little clover leaves are so intense as to be almost blinding. Yet the green is so welcome, like the new warmth in the sky. I always encouraged Rebekah to run as fast as she could. She was athletic from the start. This time, right before she went through the gate, she slipped abruptly on a fresh cowpatty. She adjusted her fall in midair but still fell partially into the green and brown of it. She jumped up, mad and sickened and furious and grossed out, and looked around for someone to vent to or even to blame. She began to shout. I quickly went up to her and, grabbing some dried, dead grass, wiped her off a little.

"Rebekah," I said as softly as I could, "congratulations, honey."

She looked at me, puzzled, quieter, still angry, red-faced. "Why do you say that, Daddy?" She was standing in the newborn light of spring.

"Because someone told me the other day that you're not a real cowgirl until you walk right through a cowpatty. Well, since you just fell in one, I guess that qualifies you as a genuine cowgirl."

The tears stopped. Her chin jutted higher and tilted slightly. "Really? Well, good."

We walked back to the house. She started to head inside still wearing all that green on her side, her shorts, her T-shirt, her shoes, like a ribbon won in a race. I suggested we hose off her shoes and leg first.

"Dad," Rebekah said now with a teasing tone. "Earth to Dad. Where are you, can you see this unbelievable waterfall?"

I was coming back slowly. Had I paid enough attention to each and every moment we'd spent together? Did I do all I could for her brothers and sisters? Even when we were together, like now, was I somewhere else some of the time? Much of the time.

"Yes, it's fantastic, isn't it?"

I remembered my mother, who, although she was blond and hadn't matched Rebekah in "fight back" strength, reminded me a great deal of Rebekah. One Saturday in a field at one of my college professors' farms, my mother had run from one wildflower to the other, filled with joy. I remembered being slightly embarrassed at her childlike expression.

"Dad, what's up, where are you?" Rebekah kept pulling me back.

"I'm thinking back on our life."

I watched the water running down the front of that unrelenting rock face, falling, falling, falling, never stopping until it froze again. I saw that water as my tears, tears of joy at being in this kayak with my little girl, who was now a woman. The glacier and the rock were me: too often frozen, seeming still, expressionless. But glaciers do cry in Alaska.

"Dad, this kayak is way heavier back there on your end, so paddle. Look, Mark's right up to the waterfall."

"All right, honey." For most of the rest of our journey together I paddled and was present with her, Mark, and our often truly unbelievable environment. But maybe its power was what had brought the memories welling up in me in the first place. When we got right up to where the waterfall hit the ocean, the mist was cool and cleansing, and it washed over me.

LIKE ANOTHER PLANET

I began to dig my oar into the glass-clear ocean with more energy. We headed west out of the cove and across the bay. Two or three miles in front of us was a wall, a wall that could enclose a contented people, a wall of white and blue ice, the face of Aialik Glacier. More than halfway across the water we began to see chunks of floating ice, like mini icebergs, some the size of our kayak above water. Occasionally crashing, cracking sounds, sudden and violent, came from the direction we were headed. In an irregular, puffy wind, we moved toward it, silently cutting the salt water, which was surely several hundred feet deep below us. Clouds hung on top of the peaks rising up behind the glacier. Was that a front? Would it overtake us before we made it to the other side?

We were now in the middle of this twenty-five-mile-long bay, and it was only us on the water as far as we could see. We were as insignificant as a dry spruce needle floating on a lake. Mark said there were bears all over but we would not see them unless they crossed the barren fields of boulders or we found them grazing on a just-melted patch of avalanched snow.

Floating in this place was more like being in another world than anyplace else I'd ever been. Photographs I'd seen of planets with rock mountains and no plant life almost seemed to have more in common with this place.

We made it to the other side and pulled our kayak out of a beach made of rounded, smooth rocks. We were now at the side of Aialik Glacier. From our little toehold on the beach at sea level to a little over three miles inland, this world rose over five thousand feet. The humbling sound of the glacier calving was intimidating. *Crack.* An ancient piece of glacier fell from the face of Aialik Glacier and hit the ocean. A resulting large ring of waves came toward us, some big enough to surf on. A few people in Alaska have been killed by kayaking up to the face of a glacier. Out here alone, the power of this magnificent structure creates a false sense of invincibility. Only those who know what can happen can force themselves to be wary and remember how quickly humans can be swatted by the power of even a little bit of it.

We pulled our kayaks far onto the beach. Ours was so heavy, Mark and I had to pull it together. People on an Alaska high may get careless. They don't pull their kayaks far enough onto the beach; a glacier calves or a salmon seiner goes by, sending a wave high on the beach. The kayakers are off hiking or distracted by some awesome sight. When they come back their kayak and all their supplies are floating away, there is no way to reach it. You don't swim out to get your kayak in glacier-cooled, numbing Alaskan salt water. A local might swim out a short way, but you get too far out and your arms and legs quit working and you're gone, sinking, though your brain is still functioning. Many Alaskans have watched loved ones, brothers, best friends, barely known crew members, strangers, drown, unable to do anything to save them. Some have tried, knowing better, and died too. No wonder people dive in; the pristine water doesn't look dangerous. It is so enticing, so seductive. But because of the temperature, it is deadly.

Dark sand dunes rose from the beach. We walked over them toward the face of the glacier. A fresh line of wide tracks led away from the beach up toward the steep rock mountains. Mark said they belonged to a large black bear, that he could have been there a half an hour ago, even fifteen minutes. When we got to the left edge of the face of Aialik Glacier, it seemed that the glacier could be the size of twenty five-story buildings, stacked side by side. Some large pieces of ice, some the size of a pickup truck, were floating in front of it. *Crack*. A piece the size of a house popped off the glacier without warning and fell like an ice guillotine. A couple of seals, laying on floating pieces of the glacier's ice that had already fallen, were given quite a ride.

A rushing, turbulent creek streamed out of the far left side of the glacier. You could almost do some white-water kayaking down it, if you were skilled enough. Rebekah and I stood together, not talking, being uplifted by what spread out before us, feeling the cold blasts of glacier air, hearing so much. Sound was now coming from all around us. *Bang* came the largest sound we'd heard yet, as if a third of a mountain peak had just broken off. Large pieces the size of small cars had fallen into a heap at the mysterious hole in the bottom of the glacier that was also the source of this creek. The water was a brownish gray, full of silt. Pieces of the glacier were being washed down the fast-moving creek as they fell, some too large to float. They were the most pure ice-blue color, bouncing, rolling over the rocky creek bottom and standing out vividly from the opaque silver-brown water.

Rebekah and I stood silent and overwhelmed; we shared this spectacular moment, just us. I realized we didn't need the "spectacular," just the moment, just the two of us. Mark was relaxing on top of one of the dunes.

Mark and I dragged the double kayak across the sand until about three-quarters of it was in the water. Rebekah waded in and spryly eased into her front spot. I climbed in and, to keep water from getting in the kayak, attached my spray skirt to the plastic lip around the hole I sat in, and then we were moving. Our plan, really Mark's plan, was to make it to another hard-to-reach glacier and camp there. We paddled along about a hundred yards offshore. There were pieces of a narrow beach, and then the land began to climb and climb. I saw a black bear feeding. We were so silent it didn't notice us at first, then it ran into the dense underbrush. All we could see was the movement of the brush as the bear made its way up the mountainside. Even the bear had to squeeze and maneuver in and around the seemingly impregnable alders that grew up from the oceanside until there was mostly just rock.

Ahead was a bit of land shaped like an eagle's head, jutting into the bay. We'd paddled ten miles or so. We hugged the beach, looking for an opening somewhere that Mark said led to a saltwater lake. He had pulled out away from the wilderness beach, farther into the calmer bay waters, and he motioned us to join him.

"We need to be careful here. The tide is coming out and the current in that passageway to the lake can be dangerous," Mark said. He was a gentle, sensitive soul with eyes like a mischievous boy. "Follow my kayak and keep your bow into the current; you don't want to get sideways and get flipped in that current, okay?"

"We will follow you," Rebekah answered.

I could see turbulence, almost like whirlpools, where the water coming from Pedersen Glacier and the tidal lake met the prevailing water currents of the bay. Once past the agitated waters near the mouth of the creeklike entry, the water got shallow and clear as empty space. I looked for salmon or seals, anything swimming, but I saw nothing. Inside the cove we steered right and pulled up to a place to camp. There was no way to hike into this area. Mark immediately found bear sign everywhere. There was a metal container to put our food in, and we had gotten some "unbreakable" plastic containers from the park headquarters in Seward. We pitched our tents in an island of spruce, choosing the only area that had not been dug up too recently by bears. What were they looking for in the dark, loamy soil?

When I saw the claw marks in the soil, though, I realized what made me feel as if I were on another planet. There was almost no soil out here at all. It was mostly glaciers and ice fields and bare rock mountains and ocean and melted snow falling here, running there. The few trees or grass or lichen that did grow appeared lonely, just barely welcome.

There was bear sign all over. They had used some of the spruce to sharpen their claws. The ground was so shaded that little grew, but something must have been in the ground, grubs or roots or something tasty. Otherwise, why would so much of this dark soil be dug up? Some relatively big holes were here and there. The other thing I was surprised at but didn't mention to Rebekah or Mark was the amount of bear crap. There were many piles, much of it fresh, as if a couple of big bears lived in this spot and slept here every night, whenever they were not out foraging for food. Some clearings in parts of this island-shaped woods appeared to have been cleared by bears, the ground raked clean with their long claws. Rebekah paid close attention to all this recent bear activity. From the look of some of the bear piles, the bears could have been here ten minutes before we landed. I wondered where they were; maybe in some tall marsh grass at the north end of where we camped?

We chose the least-disturbed place to set up our two tents. I had done such a careful job packing: my still camera, my video camera, my minidisc player, and shotgun mike—all so sensitive to water, especially salt water. Mark didn't feel that we could get in too much trouble out here, or get lost. He had a handheld radio that could communicate if we needed to with any charter fishing-boat captain or tour boat that might be around.

I put all my electronic gear in a corner of the tent in a pile. We put our food in the "bearproof" containers. Rebekah was clearly accustomed to living in the wilderness after her recent monthlong experience. She had every piece of her equipment in an orderly pile. I looked around—something of mine was missing. I knew there should be a purple stuff sack I'd bought at REI in Anchorage, along with the waterproof bags. Where was it? It had my sleeping bag in it. I went back to the kayak; surely the purple stuff sack and the sleeping bag were in one of its holds. I went through every one, stuck my arm down the bigger ones until it disappeared. No sleeping bag. Okay, no problem. I did have my sleeping mat and the warm fleece pants and JanSport parka I'd used when we had gone to Tibet and Everest in 1984. I had warm socks and even a wool hat.

Rebekah noticed I was looking around too much. She lifted her head up from writing in her black notebook.

"Dad, what are you looking for, anyway?" she asked, mostly consumed with her journaling.

"Oh, nothing," I answered, hoping for no follow-up question. I didn't want to confess my mistake and look foolish.

She went back to writing. I just laid down my head and curled up on my mat. Only the faintest sound of her Pilot Precise Extra Fine pen was audible.

"Dad, what did you forget, some food?"

"No, it's all here." I hoped she would leave this alone.

"Well, what then, Dad? Let me see, you lost your paddle and now I'm going to *really* have to paddle you everywhere."

"No, the paddles are safe."

"Well, then what's up?"

"Wass up den, Reee-BA-kah . . ."

I switched into one of our accents, something of an inside joke in our family. We were known to carry on lengthy conversations in a variety of accents gathered from some places we'd been like Appalachia, Mississippi, a northeast country club, an electronics store employee going out of business in New York City, *The Simpsons*. I was hoping to sidetrack her inquisitive mind.

"Dad, seriously, you must have lost something important. Will it endanger us?"

"No . . ."

"Well, then, what's the big deal about telling me. What is it?"

"I forgot my sleeping bag!" I answered meekly.

"Dad, you're kidding."

"No, I'm serious, and it's supposed to be in the forties, maybe colder, tonight." The incredibly dramatic Pedersen Glacier was directly west of us; it looked so white and wide. It would certainly cool the night.

"Dad, before I was born, you walked *where*?" She seemed serious, then smiled with her warm eyes.

"I walked across the street."

"I should let you have my sleeping bag," she said, more serious.

"No, no. I'll pile all my clothes on top of me, the ones I'm not wearing. No problem, I'll be fine."

That night I could never get warm. It seemed that I went to sleep after it was very dark, when it was already getting light again. Soon after I finally fell asleep, I heard something. Either Rebekah was yelling something or I was dreaming.

"Bears. Bears. Look . . ."

I opened my eyes. She was talking in her sleep, loudly. She opened her eyes to say she'd heard something walking around outside our tent.

"There *are* bears," she almost shouted. "Bears!"

Turned out it was only Mark walking around outside our tent, warming up or something. Somehow he'd forgotten his sleeping bag too. Since it was light, we all got up, packed everything into the kayaks, and decided to see if we could paddle to the edge of the tidal lake, enter a little river, and weave our way to the face of the glacier to see the iceberg. Mark said that the only way there was by kayak or canoe, and our problem was that the tide was going out. We risked getting stranded at the glacier if the water level dropped so low we couldn't back down this narrow, gravel-bottomed river or creek. We decided to take the chance; Mark said if we could make it, we would have one of the most amazing experiences anyone could have in Alaska. He also said few people have been where we hoped to go.

The paddling was relatively easy even as the current from the retreating water wanted to pull us back into the massive bay. Being in the bay was like being the only leaf left on a two-hundred-year-old oak. Traveling back through this mysterious passageway was like crawling through an ant colony. How fast Alaska can change what it shows you. After not much more than a half mile, we left the confines of the narrow drainage river and entered a small tidal lake. Small icebergs, the size of boats, were floating exotically here and there. Some bizarre and rare sea ducks shot up from the water, several of them surprised they were seeing humans.

As we went along, I would stop paddling to see how long it would take Rebekah to notice. Just as she would begin to turn her head, I would start paddling again.

She would exhale, then say, "Dad, you're not funny."

This new world we were entering created its own microclimate. Fog hid and revealed the landscape. The wildlife in this place of mystery and isolation seemed surprised that humans existed. We came across some seals lying on the small ice chunks. They opened their large, round eyes and blinked surprise at our materializing. Our kayaks made little sound; we crept on top of the water, sneaking up on them. One seal seemed shocked, as if we were actually odd-colored killer whales. Those silent stalkers would never be able to reach this place. It was probably one reason the seals had come here.

More exotic, large sea ducks were startled as we paddled into a bit of open water. They flew over us; their wings made the sound of a faint whistle. A seal dropped into the water. We glided past small icebergs as they moved so slowly in the slight current of water stemming from Pedersen Glacier. For it was the glacier's melting that was the source of this little river of ice-cold mystery. Every so often cold breaths of air hit our faces.

Mark found the continuation of the water passageway where it left this interior lake and went farther toward the face of the glacier, the sculptor that you couldn't see, no matter how hard you watched, still working. It crept forward ever so slowly, carving away at the land. This entryway into the glacier's kingdom was filled with pieces of floating white ice, some the size of a sofa, a few narrow and tall and unsteady. Did icebergs block our way? This was the start—or really the end—of this gigantic slab of ice and compacted snow that stretched for hundreds and thousands of square miles. Few have been here to see it, for all the time that has passed. Several huge pieces of ice had broken off the front of the glacier and floated in the water, blocking us. It required real effort to squeeze through, but they finally allowed us into the inner sanctum.

Now it was before us; its throne room was the lake we now floated in, its surface dark and still as a mirror. The reflective water made the glacier's face double in size. I was overwhelmed by the colors, hues I'd never seen this close in nature. There were variations of light blue and ocean blue, a green shade of gray and an opal color. Some of the ice was the color of turquoise in silver that had faded to a dull polish. The height of the ice wall and the colors and the stillness—the sight of it all silenced us.

A couple of icebergs in front of the main glacier wall stood the size of a three- or four-story building. One was shaped like the profile of a polar bear head. Mark paddled right up to it. He disappeared behind it, then reappeared in a hole that went through the entire iceberg. Rebekah and I just floated in front of the multicolored face. Here, it was quieter; there didn't seem to be as many ice chunks falling into the water. Mark called us over, and it was an odd perception to hear his voice in the silence. The closer we got, the more serene it became. As a kid, I had thought that heaven would be green fields of grass and vivid blue sky and clouds as warm and white as a cotton shirt coming out of the dryer; but here was the version for those who like it cool.

We lingered for some time, but then Mark said we needed to head back to the bay or we might be stranded. We paddled out with the current this time, and when we got to the tidal lake where we'd camped on the far beach in the tender green grass, we saw a black shape, a black bear. We watched it for a bit, then shot out the mouth of this drainage back into the ocean.

The bay was sun-bright; a strong wind blew through it freely. It did not seem possible that the secret kingdom we'd come from could be only about a mile from here, and a neighbor of this light, airy bay.

Rebekah was a paddling energy machine, ready to make a wake, see more of this ocean and sharp rock world. I really wanted to pop my paddle into the water and splash her, but she seemed too focused for obnoxious Dad humor. Instead I dug in and felt my chest and back and shoulder muscles activate and assisted in pulling us through the salt water. It seemed like just a few weeks earlier that she and I had gone for a bike ride down our curving, downhill gravel driveway in Tennessee, out onto the paved roads leading away from town. At our house, you can often hear more birds singing than anything else. She was in fifth grade. We had just turned onto the paved road when I noticed I had to pedal without lagging to keep up with her. I looked over, and her thin, springy legs seemed a foot and a half longer than they had just the week before. Her arms had long, defined muscles; her neck seemed elongated; her whole body had a different energy, her face a different glow. I didn't stare but I noticed, and I remember thinking that she was the most beautiful, most coordinated, elegant, energized eleven-year-old girl in the world. And then I thought, why couldn't I keep focused on the passing of time? I seemed to spend too much time wanting to make life speed up or slow down.

We pulled up to a narrow, round-rock beach with almost black sand and hauled our kayaks out of the water to have lunch. I could not stop imagining what it would have been like for the Native people who lived here hundreds of years earlier, making a life in these sometimes sublime and sometimes intensely extreme water worlds.

Several hours later, moving quietly south, we had almost reached the tip of Holgate Head. The contour lines showing elevation gain were so close together around here on the map that the land just appeared brown. If we kept traveling west and then north in these kayaks, it would be about 140 miles to Homer from here. If we could have flown over the mountains and glaciers, it would have been about 65 miles. Why does Alaska make me feel that I can fly?

Mark had said we'd like it when we got to Holgate Head, the north point of land that opened into a small, five-mile-long bay called Holgate Arm. There were pillars of rock coming out of the ocean and arches. The tide was falling; exposed on the rock were many starfish, overlapping, offering up unusual colors to this world of blues and grays and whites.

"Dad, where are we going from here?" Rebekah asked.

Mark was a hundred yards ahead of us at a point where he'd either have to turn right to stay close to the rock or go straight and make an ocean crossing of a few miles. If we flipped our kayaks, we wouldn't be able to crawl up on the land because much of it was too steep. You could tread water for a bit, maybe hold on with your hands, but then your extremities would go numb.

Mark waited for us. He laid his head back on the kayak, kind of squeezed himself farther down in the boat, and seemed to become deeply relaxed. He made me think of a sea otter on its back; they spent most of their lives floating on the water's surface. They floated so well because they have the most follicles of fur per square inch of any mammal, and the fur traps air. It's one reason they roll in the water, to replenish the air in their fur.

"We'll cross Holgate Arm, and on the other side of here is Quicksand Cove, where we will probably camp for tonight," Mark said, confident leader that he is.

"How far is it?" I asked.

"A couple miles. The water here is a bit rough; just ride the waves and keep going until we get there, okay?"

"O—" was all I got out before a booming breath-sound interrupted me and forced me to turn my head.

A humpback whale had surfaced not one hundred feet from us. Mark told us that out here where the bay and Aialik Bay merged, an underwater shelf went straight across from land to land; it was where Holgate Glacier's face had once been. Today the face of this glacier was about five miles away. Mark had said that the humpbacks, killer whales, salmon, and Dall porpoise liked to feed here because currents loaded with herring and other small fish came out of the deep and were pushed up along this shelf, where the water's depth goes abruptly from three hundred or four hundred feet to sixty feet.

Mark paddled with quick strokes toward the whale, as if he wanted to join it. Then two whales surfaced, one after the other, feeding aggressively and breathing in shorter intervals.

"Dad, how do the whales know what's on top of the water when they're coming up to breathe? How do they keep from hitting boats or driftwood?" Rebekah asked.

She had stopped paddling. I could tell that until she was confident in my answer, we'd be staying here.

"I would think the whale looks up before it breaks the surface, turns one eye up, wouldn't you?" At that moment, another whale came shooting out of the water, straight up like a missile. It was lunge feeding, diving down and coming straight up through a school of small fish. The water around us was strongly turbulent; the whales were feeding, surfacing quickly, moving fast.

"How about if we're not sure, we let these hungry whales pass by?" Rebekah suggested, tucking in her hair, which was tied back in a red scarf. "Have *you* ever seen a whale look up before it surfaced, Daaaad?"

"No, I haven't been that close."

I tried to visualize a humpback whale coming up directly underneath our kayak. What would that kind of force do to us? I could see that painting of Moby Dick, breaking apart the large oceangoing whaling ship. Are whales color-blind or would they be able to see the yellow of our little cork?

We floated by a rock spire. The mountains on either side of Holgate Glacier, about five miles from us, formed the sides of a stage. The clouds dripped down from high above and softened the hard rock sides of our private show. The backdrop for the stage was the face of the glacier, which was lit bright ice-blue, like a million fluorescent lights. The top of the sea was the floor, the hunting whales the actors with the biggest parts. We were the audience, just us three. Nothing I have ever seen, including Mount Everest; my first sight of the Pacific Ocean by Florence, Oregon, after taking five years to walk there; my farm pastures, ringed by red and yellow maples at the height of fall, lit by the late-day sun; the canyon land around Moab, Utah; nothing could compare to the sight made by this stage and these actors.

I did remember someone telling me that a young whale breached somewhere near Juneau and landed on a sport fishing boat. So I agreed we should probably play it safe and stay to the side of the bay until the whales moved on by.

The hunting whales traveled closer to the glacier. Their passionate lunge feeding leaps became more numerous. The sun broke through the clouds and shone upon the glacier, and the whales were backlit by it each time they broke out of the water.

SHE COULD NOT TOUCH THE BOTTOM

The whales were halfway to the glacier now, so Rebekah began paddling. Mark was at least a half mile ahead of us. We paddled and paddled across the two miles, and I kept waiting to hear the whales' breath again. There must have been much feed for them toward the glacier. Right in the middle of the bay we passed a small bunch of feeding, deep-diving puffins. Once across we rounded a rock point into Quicksand Cove. There a dampness was in the air, and not a ripple anywhere. It was completely different from Holgate Arm, though we were right beside it.

This part of the Alaskan coast reminded me of Maine, where I had spent a couple summers during college. The irregular rock coastline, the preponderance of evergreens, the numerous bays, all reminded me of that northernmost eastern state. But for each rock outcropping in Maine, you'd have to add a rock mountain on top of it to get an idea of the magnitude here in Alaska. Also, Alaska's almost twenty times larger in area and has about half the population. No offense meant, Maine.

How could this cove be so radically different from the bay we just crossed? Quicksand Cove was total tranquillity, with a smooth and comparatively wide beach. A narrow, rushing, powerful creek ran into the end of it. Mark told us there was a small salmon run here. We could see some of them jumping out of the water where the creek flowed into the cove. At the end of Quicksand Cove, where we would set up our tents, several large logs had washed up; the land rose slightly into forest, then rocketed almost straight up from sea level over four thousand feet. A couple of smaller hanging glaciers were on top of the mountain. Every place we had been on this kayak trip had overwhelmed us, being singularly spectacular, and in every place we were the only humans around. In fact, all of Alaska had reignited my love for life; my soul felt as it had when I was in my twenties.

So often in my life, when I saw something that inspired me or something good happened, I found myself reaching for a phone to call my parents, to let them know about something that would make them happy or proud. I knew they would have been thrilled to hear that Rebekah and I were together in such a place. Rebekah was their first grandchild; they knew my divorce from her mother had been most unsettling, saddest, most traumatic for her.

Why did the differences between Quicksand Cove and Holgate Arm bring my parents to the movie screen in my head? We'd pulled our kayaks far up onto the beach; as we unpacked in silence, I looked out beyond the driftwood to the protective horseshoe of land that outlined the polished peace of this little bay. It was so completely different from the larger bay we'd just paddled across. Holgate Arm's surface was agitated, big and brawny. The glacier met the ocean dramatically, violently, pieces of itself smashing, almost exploding, into the sea. That bay scared you with its forcefulness. That bay was like my father.

Quicksand Cove was perfect, still, like my mother. Even the water fell from the mountaintops gently. The surface of the ocean was the definition of tranquil. Even the glaciers, their forces almost supernatural, were not at the water's surface but high up in the mountaintops, not too loud or threatening, not overpowering. By the time their dangerous pieces broke off and reached the water where we were, there was basically no impact.

Mark had set up his tent, hung our food high up in a tree, and was fishing. Rebekah had set up our tent as well and was leaning against one of the largest driftwood logs, writing in her journal. She seemed at home for being in such a place. Was it her long neck, the perfect way she printed, her thin face, the way she loved taking care of little children—whatever it was, Rebekah constantly reminded me of my mother. Though there were also parts of Rebekah—her fire; her quick ability to defend; her wild, impenetrable head of hair—that had no relation to my blond mother. Maybe the passing on of our genes was a way for our loved ones to always be with us, their memory never fading.

The stillness and green color of the water here reminded me of a past vacation; it was the same color and the same calmness as the setting for a significant experience of Rebekah's and mine. It was the summer of her sixth year; we were in North Carolina, and for two days she had been "swimming" where she could not touch the bottom. It was a freshwater lake, so it was the kind of dark water that held so much mystery down deep where none of us could see. It was like trying to see into jade. At first she kicked a lot but tried to hold on to my neck, almost choking me. Late in the first afternoon, she moved her arms and legs and breathed and at times even let go of me as I swam underneath her. Every several seconds she touched my back with her hand or foot to make sure I was still there, even if the back of my head was right in front of her.

On the afternoon of the third day, Rebekah said she wanted to swim out to the float in the deepest part of the lake where the teenagers were diving off or lying in the sun. I asked her how she wanted to do it; she said she wanted me to swim next to her. She started out, then stopped where she knew she could still stand. She gazed for a moment across the deep, opaque water, then pushed off again. She swam slowly, always keeping her head out of the green water. I stayed close. Less than halfway there, she veered toward me as if she were going to ask me to help, but then she moved back. She would make it there on her own; I could see that on her face. She had realized that she could swim on top of the deep water. She sped up as she got closer to the little ladder. Reaching it, she climbed out, and a tanned fifteen-year-old god and goddess lifted up their heads to see who had invaded their heady world. When they saw it was a six-year-old, they shut their eyes again, returning to dreams of each other, or whatever. Rebekah didn't say any foolish words or make obnoxious gestures; she looked around to see where I was, climbed down, and swam back, not asking me to accompany her. Of course, I did. For the rest of our time there she swam back and forth, thinking at the end of another two days that maybe she could swim out there faster than I could. And she did, on the last swim before we left.

Mark had hooked a pink salmon; they were jumping where the stream they would die in emptied into our private bay. Mark had said that salmon mill around at the mouth in the salt water until they're ready to spawn. I got up from my place on the beach and began gathering driftwood for a fire. Some pieces were too heavy to lift, so I dragged them to the spot, along with some sun-dried seaweed that made excellent kindling. Soon we had an outstanding fire, giving off the rich odors of smoke and salt. A pair of oyster catchers whose nest was nearby cried out their piercing calls. This was their beach usually.

We ate and then crawled into our tents trying to keep any mosquitoes from getting in with us.

I was sleepy; I hadn't slept but a few hours the previous night and it was warmer here, possibly because of the cove's protection from the wind. Rebekah and I hadn't been this close to each other for a long time, and I had a feeling these few days would become moments that we would remember for a lifetime, moments shared by us alone. Why was it so difficult to make times like this happen? As I fell asleep, I vowed to do more with my children. Nodding off, I could hear the winds from far above in the kingdom of the hanging glaciers whooshing down to us and over toward Three Hole Bay.

When Rebekah and I are together, I tend to be more emotional and more reflective, I'm not sure why. But whatever the reason, I had a dream that night. The dream was actually a replay of a day we'd spent with my parents. Rita, Julianne, and I had gone to my hometown, Greenwich, Connecticut, to see my parents. It was in early July 1995. Julianne was almost five; looking at pictures of my mother when she was that age, she and Julianne could have been twins.

Mother had wanted to go for a ride around town. My father actually agreed to go along, which was a surprise. We had a rented car, something new, which was a delight for them, I'm sure. Mother normally drove a 1970s, blue Chevy Impala. A woman from their church had left it to Mother in her will, after

Mother had nursed her through the last months of her life. My mother, still naturally blond at sixty-nine years old, was actually telling me where she wanted to go. That was unusual, a rare moment of self-indulgence for her.

First she wanted to go to Bruce Park, where we'd had many family picnics on a certain hill with big boulders. The three of us boys, her sons, had made forts in the rocks, only briefly blowing through where my parents and sisters sat to eat. Then Mother wanted to go by the flower gardens in the park, a spot she loved but that we didn't normally stop to see. Everyone else except maybe my sister Winky wanted to feed the ducks.

Then Mom wanted to drive over to the Mianus River. She remembered we boys used to go over there in the summer to jump off the rope swing. She pointed just up the hill toward Old Greenwich; my youngest brother, Fred, had married Coleen at that Catholic church. Now Fred and Coleen had four children, and Mother had been baby-sitting for them lately. Mother asked me to head back toward town past the YWCA, right across from the Congregational church and the temple. She'd run the YWCA day-care center for years and was so beloved that they'd named a playground after her. I asked her if she wanted to turn in. She asked if I wanted to see the playground. So we turned in and saw the place where Mother had encouraged hundreds of children to have fun, to not fight, to love other living things. Six of her own children were not enough for all the pure love she had in her heart.

I pulled the Ford Taurus out onto the Post Road and drove out to Craig McAllister's old house. Craig had been one of my best friends, a prep school kid who sometimes drove his mother's two-door, white Mercedes down to our low-rent neighborhood. He took my mother for a ride once. He was always teasing her because she called him Craig when he wanted to be called Craze. When we got to the deeply shaded, dead-end street where the McAllisters used to live, Mother asked how Craig was doing. I told her we had recently reconnected; he was back to being Craig, with two beautiful daughters and a wife he loved, and he lived in California. Mother was happy to hear it. The whole situation felt a bit odd to me; Mother seemed so deliberate, lingering everywhere, much more emotional than usual. Maybe it was just that I hadn't seen her in too long. Maybe I'd changed and become more sensitive. Anyway, something was different.

She wanted to drive down Greenwich Avenue and told us about walking three of us in a stroller up the avenue to Woolworth's. I'd seen a black-and-white photo, her thin arms and narrow face like Rebekah's, her blond hair pulled back, wearing shorts even though she complained that having all those babies had given her varicose veins. We drove farther, by the Greenwich Police Department. She asked me if those really were our clothes and bikes the police had confiscated back in high school. The three of us brothers and a couple of friends were accused of skinny-dipping in four straight pools. We'd gotten nailed, and they'd taken our clothes and bikes. We'd had to walk the more than two miles home nude. Twenty-eight years later when I told her it was us, she laughed and laughed and laughed. I don't think I'd ever heard her laugh like that before. Maybe she was just getting more carefree. Maybe she'd taken a class at the YWCA; something about Mother was different.

We drove by where we used to board the Island Beach boat, our town's own "island beach" on Long Island Sound. She remembered how I learned to swim on my dad's back. She remembered how Dad used to be a lifeguard, a very handsome one at Rye Beach, where they'd met and married. Mother asked if there was anywhere we wanted to go, but we said no. Mother was directing us, and we were doing what she wanted. Dad didn't say much, if anything. He went along with it, even enjoyed it. That ride was a completely different time from any other I could ever remember with my mother and father.

When we got home to the house on Pemberwick Road, the one they had moved into the year I went off to college, I opened their red door and we all walked in. For my first eighteen years, we'd lived mostly in a federal housing project named Wilbur Peck Court. Inside, the old radio was playing "Wichita Lineman" by Glen Campbell. I went to the hall to look at a collage of pictures on the wall of our children that we'd given them last Christmas.

Mother told me she loved the pictures, then turned and said, "Let's dance."

It was something I never thought I'd hear my mother ask me. She grabbed my hands and tried to waltz or do some box step in that little space with me. I am her first child, the one they slipped up and still sometimes called "cowboy." Dad, Rita, and Julianne looked at us as if we were crazy. As we tried to dance, I thought of how we used to harass Mother because she loved this song by Lou Christie, something about "in the jungle, the mighty jungle." Being a loving son, ready to do any rare thing my mother asked, I danced with her, awkwardly, if that's what she wanted. Late that evening we caught our plane home from White Plains to Nashville.

A few days later we got a call at home in Tennessee. Something was wrong with Mother, my sister Winky said. Dad had said she'd had stomach pain for some time, but she'd kept it to herself. Mother was an RN, so she knew about the human body. Winky's husband, Randy, said something about the possibility of pancreatic cancer. None of us knew then that *pancreatic* in front of *cancer* was perhaps the worst combination of words in the world. Randy said he'd looked it up on the Internet and it was really bad.

By this point in the events of that time, I couldn't handle the dream and had awakened. It was quite dark and still in our tent.

After talking to Winky and Randy, I'd quickly arranged a trip back to Connecticut with Rebekah, Jed, and Luke. All her children and grandchildren gathered around Mother. She asked to speak to all of us and said she just wanted to ask one thing of us: "that you all love each other." Mother died a week or so later. When I stood in her room the last time I saw her, I looked at her and wanted to be strong and smile and be happy for her, but all I could do was cry and cry and cry. Mother was beyond crying; she was already somewhere else that I will someday know. She pulled me to her and whispered, "You don't worry about me, you love those kids." Rebekah, who had her spirit, was sitting by her side.

I fell back to sleep eventually, but had a hard time getting up the next morning. Rebekah and Mark were already sitting on the beach talking when I emerged from the tent. A fog hid everything but a small piece of the cove. Our boat was to pick us up in a few hours. Rebekah got into the single kayak and paddled steadily into the fog until she was gone, off to explore by herself. She returned when she heard the boat's diesel motor rumbling faintly in the fog.

8

No Road

The word *road* is so boring, so unappreciated, but so essential, even resonant. Some of my favorite songs are about hitting the road. Many of my life's most inspiring moments came from traveling down unknown roads until I found something that surprised me and I stopped for a bit. But in Alaska, so many places cannot be reached by a road. Cordova, Alaska, is one of them. Dominating barriers surround this picturesque fishing village. The Chugach Mountains and the Robinson Mountains rise up on one side, the Copper River delta on another. The ocean, which has taken so many lives, is on the other. Adding to the city's protection is glacier after glacier after glacier after glacier. They seem at first glance to be coming to crush the city, but actually they are retreating ever so slowly.

Beyond that first row of mountain, water, or glacier blockades lie even more. There are the Wrangell Mountains, which are part of the 13-million-acre Wrangell–St. Elias National Park and Preserve, the largest U.S. national park. There are also the Talkeetna Mountains, and beyond them, the Alaska Range. Seventeen of the twenty highest mountain peaks in the United States are in Alaska. Some of these, the majority of Cordovans think, help to guard Cordova. Many of the people in this fishing village are actually glad that cars, trucks, campers, and SUVs can't reach them. Of course this means they can't drive away, either. For restless people this would be awful. In Cordova you need to fulfill your need for movement in a boat, on a snowboard, in a float plane, on a snow machine, atop a surfboard, or on foot. You could drive out their main road until it ends, over fifty miles away. A fifty-mile trip in a place like Cordova on a road is practically a cross-country journey. You would cross some of the most inspiring country in the world on a journey like that.

Being able to drive away, to listen to great long and winding road songs, is not that big of a deal to Alaskans. You cannot even drive to Juneau, the capital of Alaska. Alaskan citizens who are tough on politicians say that the governor, state senators, and representatives like being isolated and hard to reach. They claim Alaskan politicians hide behind their mountains and glaciers. In Alaska it's difficult to get mad enough at what the politicos are doing to go to the capital and protest when you can't drive there.

Roads in general are difficult to build and maintain in much of Alaska, always have been. Just as you'd imagine, the state gets massive amounts of snow in many parts. In some passes they get over seventy-five *feet* per winter. Valdez, the community closest to Cordova to the northwest, but still really hard to reach from Cordova, has so much snow they have in the past used the resulting banks as movie screens. The abundant snow around Valdez is one of the main reasons they host the extreme-snowboarding championships every winter. Then there is permafrost, ground that never thaws completely. In some places in Alaska they only have roads *after* everything freezes. They build them on the frozen foundations of snow and ice. All in all, though, there aren't many roads in Alaska, and what roads do exist are deeply appreciated and even loved for the freedom of movement they allow, just as long as they don't bring too much interference too. Alaskans are a stubborn, strong people; they must be to survive. Please, don't get in their way.

Cordova is just up the coast from Seward, but there is no easy way to get there from our Alaska home. Cordova is considered one of Alaska's larger "cities," even though it has only twelve hundred residents in the winter and twenty-five hundred in the summer. It is a city where, so far, fishermen and the people whom they support rule. The local voters have had several opportunities to vote on whether to build a road to connect them to the outside world. The road has never passed, although the last vote was the closest ever. The voters who oppose the road say the reason the vote is getting too close is because too many nonfishermen are moving into town. Even if they had a road, it would only be open in the summer, the time when most people in this fishing village are involved one way or the other in catching fish. The summer is their harvest time, when the fishermen of Cordova attempt to catch enough salmon and halibut to make the majority of their money, enough to get them through the year until the salmon and halibut return. They wouldn't get to use the road much, anyway. More important than a road is a protected place for their boats, and Cordova does have a fine natural harbor.

That the road would only be open in the summer aggravates plenty of Cordovans. Such a road would be loaded with tourists. Many Alaskans don't like driving on the same road with tourists. It would be like putting NASCAR drivers on the same racetrack with thousands of drivers like my grandfather at eighty-five. Lots of Alaskans drive like they're on the last lap of the Daytona 500 and they're one one-hundredth of a second in the lead. Tourists, on the other hand, often drive like my grandfather did right before he couldn't drive anymore because he couldn't hear and his sight was failing. They tend to speed up, then slow down to fifteen miles per hour, cross the centerline, weave onto the shoulder, and stop when there's no stop sign in sight. They drive like this not because they can't hear or can't see, but because they can. All around them their eyes and ears are filled with sights and creatures they've never seen. A bald eagle just plucked a salmon from the river running along the road. Eight tourist vehicles pull over, though there's no place for them to get completely out of the way. I once stopped right in a curve in Cooper Landing on the way to Soldotna to watch two eagles fighting over a salmon squirming on the icy bank of the river. It was not smart—there was even ice and snow on the road—but Alaska can overwhelm you until you do dumb things.

But tourists' driving habits are not the main reason certain Cordovans don't want a road. What would happen if outsiders could reach their lovely town? Cordovans aren't sure, but they have seen what's happened to the ranchers and small-town folk in Colorado, Montana, and Wyoming. Their high desert, their mountain valleys, their inspiring lands, have been discovered and much of it has been bought up. Alaskan fishermen are intelligent as well as ornery. They read national commercial-fishing magazines. They've read about their fellow fishermen in Florida. First people arrived as tourists, then they moved in and tried to take over the world that belonged to the fishermen. In Florida, some of these newly arrived used vicious tactics against the unorganized fishermen to push through a net-fishing ban in a statewide vote.

Cordovans know what has happened along all U.S. coastlines, where everybody wants waterfront property. They've read about the lobstermen of Maine, about others who harvest the sea on the West Coast, on the Gulf Coast. People with more money and more lawyers discovered these quaint, scenic

Cordova. Photo by Rebekah Jenkins

fishing villages, where folks had been making a living at the world's second-oldest profession for generations. These Alaskan fishermen are worldly enough to understand what could happen to their quirky and attractive hometown if it was "discovered" by some Ted Turner type, who after making his hundreds and hundreds of millions decided to let everything go back to the bears or wolves or buffalo. One of these "know-it-all" people might try to buy up a chunk of the town as a personal retreat, have something to brag about at parties now that Aspen has been in the movie *Dumb and Dumber*.

These fishermen know these kinds of people can have inordinate power in Washington and with the media. Alaskan commercial fishermen have more political power than any other fishermen do in the United States, but mostly that influence is in Alaska. It is shrinking. Sport fishermen like me want our fish too. The commercial fishermen don't mind these kinds of people coming to visit or even getting a summer place, just as long as they respect what Cordova is and what they do. Just don't try to tell the fishermen how to make their living or where to store their boats. These fishermen and their families are ready to fight for their world, without surrender.

I imagine many people would side with the Cordovans who don't want a road. The slogan No Road sounds so cool. No Road sounds almost as good as Save the Rain Forest. Who could be against it? It's easy to be against roads and oil drilling and the harvesting of wood when you already have as much of them as you could possibly use. How many would be against a road if they had none? Most of us have never spent a second thinking about roads, because there are so many, enough to take us in every single direction our lusty hearts might desire.

Right now the only way out of Cordova is on the Alaskan State Ferry, on your own boat, or by plane. None of the options are cheap. The way out on the sea is real slow, and you're still on foot when you get where you're going. For those who don't want a road to Cordova, such as the people I was going to visit, it's not about the romance; it's about the desire to save their way of life.

If you live in Cordova, you can drive fifty-one miles without going around and around. In Alaska, that's a bunch of road. In Angoon, on Admiralty Island, they are proud to have just three miles of road, "all paved." Some Cordova locals think their mostly Mayberry police department should not have gone so Rambo and bought the used "high pursuit" police cars from that police department in Nevada. In Nevada it's dry and flat and people can try to outrun the police. In Cordova, all you can do to get away from the police is go out the road and past the airport before you have to come back. No one would even try to walk away from here but Wild Gene, and he would never have caused the police any trouble anyway. You could use the slowest police car in the country and just ease out the road past Lake Eyak, park, and wait. Technically, you could just wait in town until whomever you're chasing comes back. Besides, in a high-pursuit police car you could hit a nesting trumpeter swan if you ran off the road.

If Rebekah and I had been ready one day earlier, we could have taken the Alaska Marine Ferry over there from Seward. It takes eleven hours and covers 144 nautical miles, which is 164 "normal" miles for those of us road-addicted people. Many, many Alaskans gauge their travel more by nautical miles, air miles, or hours down the trail. The cost for the ferry was only $64.

HANGING BASKETS

Rebekah, my firstborn child, who is almost twenty, was sitting next to me on the milk run to Cordova. They call this Alaska Airlines flight the milk run because it stops so many times. Anchorage, Cordova, Yakutat, Juneau, Ketchikan, and finally Seattle. When the salmon are running into the Copper River delta, which is the main catch of Cordova fishermen, the jets on the milk run have large cargo sections loaded with fresh king, red, and silver salmon, high-dollar fresh fish, headed for the markets and best restaurants in Seattle and beyond. Reds and kings are worth more as cargo than any human per square foot. Rebekah was in the middle seat; a handsome, blond Scandinavian-looking guy with earrings in both ears was in the window seat next to her. She handed me her CD player and asked me if I'd heard of Dave Matthews. I wasn't sure, I said. I never thought I'd lose track of who made the best music, but I wasn't paying so much attention to popular trends anymore. She said I must have a listen, she just knew I'd like it. I was a Dave Matthews fan after hearing her two favorite songs. Responding so intently this quickly to new music was rare for me. I closed my eyes, laid my head back, and listened.

When I opened my eyes to tell Rebekah how awesome I thought her music was, she was lost in conversation with the strong blond. Turned out he was headed to Petersburg, Alaska, the fishing village they call "little Norway," to crew on his dad's long-line halibut boat. He was a sophomore at the University of Alaska at Fairbanks. Being with Rebekah was an almost constant replay of my younger life. I watched her relate to people; I remembered what it was like. I listened to her music, some of which was mine first—Van Morrison, the Allman Brothers. I was honored she would even go to Cordova with me, but I got the feeling sitting on the plane she would have liked to change her plans and head to Petersburg. There was no way I could have hung around with my mother when I was Rebekah's age.

Landing the 737 at Cordova, if that's what we were doing now, was at once frightening and otherworldly. As we made our approach, if that's what it was, I couldn't even see a runway or any airport buildings, just the many fingers of the Copper River delta. It looked almost like the Mississippi River delta, except it was surrounded by plane-humbling mountain ranges and glaciers. It was raining one second, sunny the next, foggy here and there, over this chunk of Alaska. The jet engines seemed to be making a noise I hadn't heard before, but then I've learned that flying experiences in other places have little to do with Alaska.

We landed. There was no fence around this runway, which appeared to be hacked out of the wilderness by renegade bulldozers; what if a moose or a bear had been standing in our way? We could see one small building. Everybody got off and walked down some stairs into the real world. Inside the building were plaques celebrating that 2 million pounds of wild salmon and halibut had passed out of Cordova's airport on their way to the outside world. Some mounted salmon were on one wall alongside a diagram of the Copper River delta, which is one of the world's most alive, productive, and clean wetland areas. How did they ever get bulldozers out here, not to mention gravel and asphalt to make a runway? All over the state, Alaskans land planes on surfaces you have to see to believe.

We had arranged to meet up with Per Nolan, a local salmon fisherman. His wife, Neva, had invited us to come stay with them after she had heard me interviewed by the guru of Spenard, Alaska, Steve Heimel of Alaska Public Radio. She said she had known me from my earlier writings, and they wanted to show us their slice of Alaska. Alaska is one big pizza. Neva said it would be good if I could go out with a gillnetter while I was here, but her husband was a big guy and there was only one small bunk on his boat. We'd have to see about that. I asked Neva if it would be all right if I brought my daughter Rebekah with me. Neva said, great, bring the whole family. That was a typical Alaskan response. They always seem ready to take you in, feed you, provide you with shelter. It's been that way forever up here. Imagine Per as a cross between John Candy and an offensive lineman for the University of Idaho. He is funny; large-framed, not cut like a bodybuilder, he is surprisingly spry on his feet when he needs to be. Until you experience Per in a bar, you wouldn't know he is also a pool shark and the life of the party. Per is an observer. He was in college in Hawaii when John Travolta and disco hit, and he told us he had had the "disco fever" shiny suit, the open-at-the-chest shirt, the gold chain, and the platform shoes. After being in Cordova only a half hour, I could not imagine him wearing anything like that. Cordova is a flannel-shirt, blue-jeans, and work-boots kind of place.

Driving in from the airport, the wind was either chilled blowing off the glaciers or warmer coming out of the wetlands. To the south was the Gulf of Alaska. Compared to Cordova, Seward was wide-open. Per told us that if we could walk to the nearest town, Valdez, which was west along the tide line, it would be 140 to 150 miles. By boat, it's only 55 to 60 miles. This illustrates why Alaska has more coastline than the whole lower forty-eight states combined, thanks to thousands and thousands of bays and countless islands. And Cordova has the fishing industry that goes along with this vast area. Some Cordova fishermen became "spill-ionaires," renting themselves and their fishing boats to Exxon during the cleanup.

Neva Nolan in Cordova. PHOTO BY REBEKAH JENKINS

Per pulled up in town next to a ladder set up by a hanging basket spilling over with vividly colored flowers halfway to the ground. Neva, who grew up in Wrangell, took care of all the many hanging baskets of growing flowers on Main Street in Cordova. She stood atop the ladder, watering the basket carefully. She'd attached a greenhouse to the side of their trailer that was more than half the size of their home. It was instantly obvious, the way she lifted up the flowers to water them, the way she finished her job before turning to us, that she found much inspiration in the beauty, rich color, and delicate petals of her charges. Neva had an exotic look, almost Mediterranean. She said she took care of thirty hanging baskets in Cordova.

Cordova was not what I expected. Alaskan communities are competitive with each other. Don't ask a person from Seward what he thinks of Cordova. If you are in Soldotna and you want to know what Seward's like, don't ask a long-time Soldotna resident. They'll tell you all it does is rain in Seward, that moss grows on everything. And so it goes all over Alaska. I'd ask some people I knew in Seward what they thought of Cordova. "It's badly in need of a paint job." "There are too many old hippies and eccentrics."

The four of us stood on Main Street by Laura's Liquors, next to a flower box. Neva explained that here on the Alaskan coast she had to plant flowers that could survive wind and lots of rain. Daisies, pansies, petunias, lobelias, grew nicely until the end of October. The town was also adorned with brightly colored banners with sea otters, red salmon, waves, and wildflowers on them, which were hung from the streetlights. Imprinted in the concrete sidewalks were drawings of octopuses, starfish, and salmon. The sun shone down on Cordova and made all things bright.

Neva told us, "One day of sunshine is worth a week of rain." I'd heard that at least ten times since I'd arrived in Alaska. People truly appreciate sunny weather in the summer. It's like a wonderful meal someone else cooked and left as a surprise at your house. The people who live here year-round earn their portions.

Around us, people were walking everywhere, living their lives here. Cordova was impressively set up for so small a town; after all, all this art and these banners and Neva's flowers were provided by the city and her neighbors just to inspire the locals. Visitors like us, newcomers, were welcome, but life in Cordova was not designed for them. The town's biggest yearly festival was the Iceworm Festival, held the first week of February, put on for the benefit of just the year-round folk. Cordova even held their Fourth of July fireworks in February because it didn't get dark enough in July until too late for the little ones.

Neva drove an eighties Nissan Sentra. It had few miles on it; how could anyone put many miles on any vehicle here? Rebekah was going to help Neva with the rest of her watering while Per and I walked down the street; the boat docks and Orca Inlet were on the block below us. Per said it was common to see two hundred or more sea otters just off the docks by St. Elias Ocean Products and North Pacific Processors in the winter. We headed to Orca Book and Sound and the Killer Whale Café. Inside, we could have been in Seattle in the late eighties. Kelly, the owner, was once a kayak guide; he used to be mayor, but he had lost the most recent election to Margie by one vote. Margie owns the restaurant and motel one block below called the Reluctant Fisherman and is a passionate supporter of the road and the tourism industry.

We got a couple of mochas from Scott and wandered out to the sidewalk. I began asking Per questions about passersby. Who is that coming out of that store, who's parking that truck? Who is that leaning against the front of the smaller grocery store in town—why does that lady seem too dressed up for an Alaskan fishing town? (Turns out it was Phyllis Blake, secretary of the Prince William Sound Aquaculture Association. She always dresses nice, Per told me.)

Per knew every single person who walked, bicycled, or rode by in a car, truck, motorcycle, or van. As I pressed him for information on each person, he could and did speak detail after detail about everyone we saw. He knew more about people in this town than a normal person would at their own family reunion. Then as a joke and I thought something of a challenge, I asked him to name everyone we saw from behind, without seeing faces. He did it. Mary, who ran Muscle Mary's, a workout place, was an easy ID. She had about 2 percent body fat. Few people I saw in Cordova looked like her, from any angle. Per said that if we hadn't spotted her from the rear, I would have noticed that she always smiled, was always happy. Mary always took part in Cordova's biggest adult-female event of the year held in late February or early March. The local women decided on a theme every year. One recent theme was Dressed to Thrill. Per served as a bartender for that one, and he remembered Mary's outfit because it consisted of paint. She painted on her Dress to Thrill costume. They'd had a disco theme, one with evening gowns, one to "dress as slutty as you could." Per remembered one woman went wrapped in Saran Wrap for that one. Because everyone in Cordova knows almost everything about everyone else, having these parties is more like playing dress-up with your sisters.

Per acted surprised when he saw one fisherman with a woman he thought was involved with someone else. It reminded him of the often-repeated Alaskan mantra: "In Alaska you don't lose your girlfriend, you lose your turn." If you're the type who can't live around someone you went out with or were married to, don't move to Alaska.

A red Ford F250 pickup pulled up in front of the bookstore, which was next to the office of the Cordova District Fishermen United. CDFU lobbied, followed political winds of change, and fought for the rights of local commercial fishermen. The guy who parked the truck was Mark King; in his mid-to-late forties, he was a second-generation Cordova gillnetter and seiner, like Per. Gillnet fishermen like Per and Mark are the cowboys of the Alaskan fleet, the fast runners. They are after the big-dollar fish, the kings and the reds.

Floatplanes often flew over downtown. All gillnetting for king and red salmon, which was the current season, is tightly controlled by Alaska Fish and Game and usually done in "openings" of twenty-four hours, sometimes only twelve hours. The Alaska Fish and Game office in Cordova is responsible for deciding when and for how long salmon fishing will take place. The openings were scheduled based on a sonar salmon counter fifty miles up the Copper River. A certain number of salmon had to be passing by to allow fishing in the ocean. When they're ready, they announce the time and duration of the opening, usually a day or so before the appointed hour.

All the Cordova fishermen, including Per and Mark, were trying to decide where to go next time Alaska Fish and Game announced an opening. The word was flying around town like a bag of money ripped open in a west wind that there would be an opening in the next few days. It took the fish nine days to get from the ocean to the Copper River sonar counter. Some of the Copper River fish went over two hundred miles upriver to spawn, and it's having to travel so far that makes these salmon so full of oils and good fat. Once salmon enter freshwater, they stop feeding and must survive from their own energy stores. The longer, more difficult, and swift a river they must swim up, the more body oil and fat they need. Some Alaskan salmon don't swim over five miles. Don't ask an Alaskan fisherman about the pen-raised salmon of Norway, the salmon most Americans eat. Pen-raised fish do not have to struggle to survive and to catch their prey; their meat is not as firm and rich. They do not spawn, they don't have the fat and oil that give Alaskan salmon such flavor. It is illegal in Alaska to pen-raise salmon, only the wild will do.

"Only the wild will do," my theme for Alaska salmon, should be the theme for the state, exempting some federal government employees. "Only the wild will do" could be added to the state flag as a motto. Only the wild salmon will do. Only the wild bears will do. Only the wild eagles will do. Only the wild rivers will do. Only the wild whales will do. Only the wild Alaskans will do. There would have to be a committee appointed with Native and non-Native representation. Members of this committee could be named based on percentages of how the people voted in the last presidential election. Then these Alaskans, along with a couple state lawyers, would write up the definition of what makes a "wild Alaskan human," what makes "a wild salmon," and so on.

WILD GENE

Down our side of the sidewalk came a man that Per explained had been in a terrible motorcycle accident. He is partially blind and moved slowly. My first reaction was to try to help him, but that would have been the wrong impulse toward such a determined person. Per said he was headed to shoot pool at the Alaskan Hotel and Bar, a block or two down toward where we'd first seen Neva.

Several people walked or drove by, but Per didn't say anything about who they were. When he noticed I was waiting, he quickly rattled off their identities: a teacher, one of his fishing partners from the state of Washington, one of the stars of the high school basketball team, one of his neighbors from the trailer park. Then he told me about someone we hadn't seen, a Cordova resident who had died several years ago.

"Watching the people with you reminded me that I hadn't thought about Wild Gene in a while. Seems like most towns in Alaska had someone like Wild Gene in the seventies and eighties, but you don't see people like him much anymore," Per said.

Neva and Rebekah were getting closer to us as they watered the hanging baskets.

Per explained that Gene just showed up in Cordova one day; Per didn't know why or how Gene had chosen their town. Some people just materialize in Alaska. When they choose a town like Cordova where most everyone knows each other, they are not really paid much attention at first. They could be a tourist who got off the ferry and stayed. They will usually leave in a day or a week or after the summer. If they make it through a winter, some people will begin to notice them and open up to them, perhaps not fully accept them as one of their own, but open the door.

Gene didn't look too different at first, especially since he got here sometime in the seventies. Per graduated as salutatorian from Cordova High School, class of 1979, one of nineteen in his class. He remembers Gene being around during his later high school years, even during the time Per drove off the dock with his girlfriend in the car. (That's another story.) After Gene had been around awhile, people began to find out things about him. He was from the Seattle area; his family members were important people in that state, wealthy people, and it turns out caring people too. People found out that Gene had been raised by nannies. He had grown up wearing blue blazers; he had graduated from an Ivy League–type college. People noticed that members of Gene's family would come to town and visit him; he didn't have a phone, so surely they got in touch with him through the mail. Per knew Gene got mail because Per's mother, a high school English and drama teacher, belonged to the Fruit of the Month club and so did Gene. Per's mother and Gene started having tea together, partly because they shared a Fruit of the Month club membership, and because, although he was odd, Gene and Per's mother were both very intelligent.

Gene would often disappear into the wilderness for long periods and live off the land. Around Cordova even the locals don't venture into its extremities very often. Mountain-goat hunters, some of the most extreme outdoorsmen in

Alaska as they have to hike up to the frigid mountain peaks, traveled as far out as just about any human ventured in Alaska. Gene would often surface more than seventy-five miles from Cordova. One time he just appeared, as if he could astral project, right after a couple hunters had shot a mountain goat. He cut the balls off and popped them in his mouth, unfried, fresh Alaskan mountain oysters. His appearances and his appearance shocked some, and Alaskans are the hardest people to shock that I've ever met.

People would see Gene out on the road, past the airport, thirty miles out of town, pulling a 150-pound log by some rope. He told people if they asked that he was training to walk across Russia. He would load his pack with rocks, shoulder it, and hike the mountains, cross the glaciers, and even wade the surging rivers filled with small icebergs.

Some locals thought Gene had told them that he was here to write his master's thesis, on what they were not sure. When his family would arrive to visit—Gene never left Cordova except to explore the surrounding wilderness—they would eat at the Reluctant Fisherman. They realized, surely, as many Cordovans did, that Gene had entered a place that most of us cannot or will not go. Although I'm sure they hoped to be able to find him there and help him return, they never did. Gene stayed the rest of his life in Cordova, and it became almost impossible near the end to find him, even when he sat right next to you on Main Street.

Per said he looked like someone from the movie *Quest for Fire*. He lived in a primitive shack in Hippie Cove, Cordova's tent city. Almost every place in Alaska that has a cannery, where young college students, adventurers, drifters and escapers work, has a place in the deep woods at the edge of town where people squat. Some like Gene squat in these camps for years. Per said Gene had a small woodstove but no pipe for the smoke to flow properly out of his shelter. His body was saturated by wood smoke because he didn't have a way to bathe regularly. Some said he didn't believe in washing off the skin's oils. Per, always a good swimmer and basketball player, swam laps to stay in shape; he said he always knew when Gene came to Cordova's public pool to swim. Per would be swimming laps, his head down, and suddenly he'd taste something odd in the water. It seemed to be the distinctive taste/smell of wood smoke. The first time he noticed it he dismissed it, but then the second and third and fourth times he'd stop swimming laps and look to see who was in the pool. There was Wild Gene. Per would just keep swimming; he's a fisherman—fish slime is money to him—and a little smoke is not going to bother him.

"People who came to visit Cordova would see him and ask me, *who is that?*" Per remembered. Even I knew that to stand out in Alaska enough that people asked about you suggests you are extraordinary.

Although Gene looked as if he could break you in half, he never hurt anyone. For the first few years Per said Gene was exceedingly dark and handsome and well built. You don't pull 150-pound logs down an Alaskan logging road for days without getting fantastically in shape. He also rarely said much of anything to anyone. In his journeys into the Alaskan wilds alone he certainly saw more of this rare wilderness world than almost everyone, maybe more than anyone else.

"He actually lived the life of a Neanderthal. He put himself through such tough conditions his body just wore down after several years of it," Per said.

We saw Neva and Rebekah lingering at one of the hanging baskets down the block; Neva was talking to someone she knew.

People around town began to notice Gene was getting thinner. His muscles were disappearing; he was not training anymore, not to walk across Russia nor for whatever reason he used when he'd first come to Cordova. By now, he was part of the town. People cared about him, wondered why he was the way he was, wondered why he wouldn't eat well. Wild Gene had earned the townspeople's respect; he could survive Alaska, in all its severity. Some said all he ate toward the end was Crisco, some bread, and crackers. Surely he had support from his family if he needed it, or a ticket out at any time. But he didn't use it.

One day, someone who knew his habits noticed he hadn't been around. Worried about him, the friend finally checked and found him in his shelter with a knife in his stomach, dead. Many people had come to respect Gene's wild ways, the ability that almost none of them had to survive in the wilderness and live amid its extremity and brilliance. He was not buried at the local graveyard past Nirvana Park; he was taken back to finally be among his family in Washington, who had missed him.

Rebekah had joined us on the sidewalk in the moss-drying sunlight. Across the street from Orca Book and Sound where we stood was Davis Super Foods. It was a smallish grocery store; amazingly, Cordova had two and the other one was quite large. A dark-haired, athletic-looking young man standing out front was wearing X *Games*–style sunglasses; he wasn't looking right at us, but beyond.

"That's Andy Johnson," Per said, continuing to ID every person we saw. "He's a third-generation fisherman. He's in his early twenties, and he's a snowboarder."

Per gestured high into the air above downtown Cordova, toward the east to one of several large mountains that surround Cordova in a semicircle completed by ocean.

"That mountain, that's Mount Eccles, it looks over the town. Andy's best friend, Teal, another top snowboarder, was the first to snowboard it." Per pointed out that this time of year, because of snowmelt, the side of this mountain was shaped like a lady in a flowing dress.

I couldn't imagine anyone flying down that mountain's face. It looked almost vertical from here, and mountains always appear less steep than they are when you're looking at them from below and far away.

"When Teal died in a car wreck, Andy snowboarded down it as a tribute to him," Per said.

Andy was crossing the street toward us. Either he could tell we were talking about him, recognized (like just about everyone else) we were new in town, or had noticed Rebekah.

A cab went by. Per said Cordova was the kind of town where if a cabdriver saw your dog running loose, he'd give your puppy a ride home if he could get it to obey him.

Andy had short hair and the calm assurance of a daredevil who has never been seriously injured. He could have been one of those models in an Armani ad, one of those fit Italians. He walked slowly, like someone used to doing things at speeds faster than just about anyone else can. Per introduced us; Andy shook my hand politely and lingered just a fraction saying hello to Rebekah. Per explained to Andy what we were doing. When he heard we were writers, he told us he was planning to take a screenwriting class in L.A. in the off-season.

"Hey, man, you want to talk about writing sometime while you're here, get in touch with me," Andy said. He looked down the road and strode away before I could answer, his step light and long.

I called out to him, "Yeah, if I have some time, sure."

"I always know Andy's boat—he has an older bow-picker he bought from his grandfather—because he almost always has a surfboard strapped to the roof," Per said. "Around here, Andy and I, in the beginning of the season, we fish with gill nets. You make a set and sit awhile, let the fish swim into the net. Well, Andy will put on his wet suit and fish the beach side. He'll catch a wave or two before pulling up and picking the fish out of the nets." Per remembered Andy had been on the Junior Olympic ski team in the sixth grade.

An exotic-looking and quick-stepping woman walked by. Per said she was

Hanna, one of the bartenders at the Alaskan Hotel and Bar. She's been here since the mideighties. She'd come from Africa, came here with a fisherman she'd met, but it didn't work out. Per thought Hanna was from northern Africa, and he said she worked out at Muscle Mary's.

When these fishermen have big earning years, when the salmon are thick and the price is good, some travel to far-off, hot, dry, sunny places to have some fun. Given the dangers of the way they make a living, exotic and dangerous travel locations don't faze them at all. Some return with almost no money left and accompanied by a different woman from the one they had when they left.

THE ANNOUNCEMENT

Neva had finished watering her hanging baskets. Per asked if we were hungry, and everyone was. We went to the café frequented by the fishermen and locals, in a back room of the Cordova Hotel and Bar. Next door, the Alaskan Hotel and Bar sign outside was purposefully hung upside down, had been for some time. These bars looked as if they had been floated here from the Wild West, though Alaska *is* the Wild West. You could either walk through the bar or through a dark hallway. The hallway back to the Cordova Café was barely lit; the carpet was old and worn and a popular style from a decade or two ago. It was obviously a local's place. It felt as if we were entering a speakeasy or some other place where illegal acts were perpetrated. Almost every table was full. There were pictures on the walls taken by local commercial fishermen, photos of the fantastic situations all fishermen dream about.

"One time I know of, I think it was the largest single set ever, this gillnetter had thirty-eight thousand pounds of reds. That was in Bristol Bay," Per said, reminding himself, getting himself psyched up. These fishermen try to forget the sets with zero fish or three fish or twelve fish.

I looked at the decorations on the walls. There were pictures of old gillnet boats, the slow boats before they began using fiberglass hulls and fast $40,000 diesel engines. There was a mounted king crab and a picture of a seine boat with its net so full of pink salmon the boat leaned over into the water. Most exciting to these cowboys of the gulf was the picture of a gill net in the water, white foam all across the top of the net. This happens, Per explained, when hundreds of red salmon hit the net at once. Even better is when it's a smashing hit of salmon. Then the whole top of the net foams and splashes, corks even disappear. The picture represents every fisherman's dream; it is why they take all the risks. It is why when there are only five fish in their net after an hour, they still hope for the set when they will fill their icebox. The picture, that dream come true, is why they spend so much time grunting it out, rushing here and there in the ocean.

As we finished at the Cordova Café, Per introduced us to a couple of his fishing partners, Pip and Butch. Many of these fishermen belong to small groups. During an opening they fan out and fish in different places that have been hot in the past and might be again. Per had been debating with himself for hours. "Should I go around Ester Island and pick chum salmon? I'd be about guaranteed there would be lots of them at forty cents a pound. Or should I gamble and risk an opening going for the much higher priced kings and reds?" They're called reds because of their bright, bright red flesh.

The buyers don't like to announce the price until an opening has begun; it's always highest in the beginning of the season, and if numbers caught are high, it can drop. The fishermen-talk at the tables underneath the pictures of full nets at the Cordova Café was that kings might be $2.50 a pound, and they were hoping $1.60 to $1.80 for reds. Kings are not plentiful, but a couple twenty-pound kings in the net is $100 worth of salmon. Reds weighing five, six pounds are more abundant. If reds average five pounds each, and the buyers are paying $1.75 a pound or $8.75 a fish, 15 reds are $131.25, 150 reds are $1,312.50. If there are 1,500 fish, the net is quaking and shaking and half-sunk and your dream is alive in the daytime, that's $13,125 in one full net. Per told me as we hit the street and headed back to their trailer park that he's made sets without one salmon, and sets when the Steller's sea lions had a chance to pick them out before he did.

On the Cordova sidewalk, standing on a piece imprinted with a sea otter, Neva started talking to an older gentleman named Guy Beedle. He is her flower-growing buddy, a retiree who has created the latest excitement in the Cordova flower-growing community. He'd begun growing native Alaskan iris from seed. Guy wore his ever-present brown Carhartts. All over Alaska they have Carhartt fashion shows, or would that be antifashion shows? Whichever, it would be the only fashion show I would ever have a chance to star in. Neva was asking Guy about planting flowers near her church. She's active in St. George's Episcopal Church, an enchanted sanctuary with a peaked roof surrounded by old spruce trees that do not let in much sunlight. About 75 percent of the time one of the few parishioners led the service because there was no permanent clergy, just a priest who served them as well as several other isolated congregations. Guy's inspiration, Neva thought, came more from flowers, their care and growing, than organized religion. But Guy said he'd help her plant his vibrant flowers, several of which he'd grown from seed, around her church.

We walked down to Council Street, then to Railroad Avenue. We were headed to the Alaska Department of Fish and Game office. They are the permission givers—they schedule the openings. Daniel Sharp, the area management biologist, was a powerful man around here. His decisions were debated, directly questioned, but generally respected in town, Per said. What a job: to have to live in the town, a town with no road in or out, with no way to avoid the fishermen whose lives you affect in so many ways. And if the fishermen didn't have enough money, they couldn't hire crews, boat cleaners, engine mechanics. They couldn't belong to Muscle Mary's, buy books at Orca Book and Sound. Per and Neva couldn't eat out too often at the Cordova Café. Boats had to be used for several more years, engines pampered, propellers repaired one more time. Houses went unpainted, church offering plates showed more bottom, school fund-raisers brought in less, sports trips that required hundreds of miles of air travel were curtailed. This city depends on the exquisite salmon: kings, reds, chum, pinks, and halibut. Daniel Sharp was like a god here, but he could also be like a strict parent, making you come home early or not allowing you to go out at all.

"It's for your own good," they'd say. And it is. Fishermen like Per Nolan and Andy Johnson, second- and third-generation fishermen, want their way of life to continue. It's why they don't want the road and why they respect the inexact yet demanding job their management biologist must do. They know that the creatures they catch in their nets are wild. Every year the salmon must be able to get upriver in numbers large enough to lay their eggs so that there will be a next generation. The fingerlings must grow strong and return to the ocean. They must be fast and sleek and magnificent. Per hopes at least one of his sons will be a fisherman; Seth, the oldest, is already a full share hand on the family's seine boat.

We walked into the AF&G office. There was a Fish and Game handout there; it appeared there would be an opening. The announcement said:

Commercial Fisheries Announcement, Alaska Dept. of Fish and Game. Prince William Sound Salmon, Announcement #15, 2:00 P.M., Wednesday, June 23, 1999. Copper/Bering River Districts. The closure on Monday, June 21, in the Copper and Bering River Districts is anticipated to have improved sockeye salmon escapement in the Copper River delta systems. [Escapement means fish not getting caught in nets and making it up the river to spawn.] An aerial survey is scheduled for Friday, June 25, the results of which will be used to help determine the management strategy for the coming week. Survey results will be provided in Saturday's announcement. With early timed upriver stocks past their peak run timing, wild stock sockeye salmon escapement into the Copper River delta becomes the primary management consideration in determining fishing time in the Copper and Bering River Districts. Through June 22, the actual cumulative escapement past the Miles Lake sonar counter is 284,928 fish versus an anticipated cumulative count of 296,311 fish. The Copper and Bering River Districts will open for a 24-hour period beginning 7:00 P.M. Thursday, June 24, and ending at 7:00 P.M. on Friday, June 25.

Even though lately fishing time had been cut back, any chance to fish was cause for a big energy boost, a shot of hope. There would be an immediate and palpable increase in energy around Cordova. Per read it; it was shorthand to him. He first shook his head slightly in disappointment. Twenty-four hours is not much time to chase down the elusive reds and kings. It's an immense ocean, who knows where they are and when they will be there. You could catch stragglers for the twenty-four hours, and an hour after you roll up your net the big school comes through. It's the gamble they all take, no fish, no money, no living. And then a glow came to his face. In the end, he lives to be on the water to fish, fishing is his life.

Several fishermen leave Cordova when the season is closed and work as carpenters in Washington State. Pip was a commercial painter in Arizona and with a few partners owned a smoked-and-processed-fish company called Copper River Fine Seafoods. Several also fish out in Bristol Bay. Per made Cordova his home year-round; gillnetting for reds and kings and seining are his living. It used to be he could support Neva and their two young sons, Seth and Keith, but the past few years the openings have been short and Neva's had to take a full-time job.

ON THE *TERMINAL HARVESTER*

"You want to come fishing with me for this opening?" Per asked me as we stood in the office. Every phone was busy, every person was answering questions about the opening.

"Of course I would," I answered. I had no idea how big his boat was or how rough the ocean might get or where we'd eat or sleep, but for the excitement of twenty-four hours of fishing, it couldn't matter too much.

"There's only one bunk in my boat, the cabin's not very large, and we're not small men, but it'll be fine. You don't think I'm beautiful, do you?" Per said. He started walking toward their trailer park, past the school off Whiteshed Road.

"No, you're ugly," I answered.

"Good. We'll be leaving tomorrow afternoon. I don't cook either," Per added, enjoying himself. "If I can't buy it at the grocery store, we can't eat it."

Their trailer was fourteen feet wide by sixty-two feet long, with an added-on room housing their TV and woodstove. Neva's greenhouse was built on the side. Inside their arctic entry were two bright red survival suits, hanging on hooks. If a fisherman's boat sinks and he can get into one of these, fasten all the buttons and zippers, and pull on the hood, he might live to be rescued. When disaster strikes these gillnet boats, they normally either flip over in the surf or catch on fire. Either event leaves little or no time to get the suit on.

Per mentioned that if they lived in any of the towns west of here on Prince William Sound, such as Valdez or Whittier, Neva's adjoining greenhouse would be crushed by the snow. Cordova gets "only" about 106 inches of snow per year, about nine feet, but Cordova's not between the mountains and the glaciers. It's set in front of them, in the open, so storms can blow through town rather than getting trapped. Hurricane- and gale-force winds are common here.

Inside, Neva was making her famous BBQ salmon for dinner. Rebekah said we'd been given their boys' room. On the bunk was a dinosaur quilt made by his grandmother. LEGOs were everywhere. I noticed again how adaptable Rebekah was to strange situations and how people seemed to like her immediately. She already had her stuff stored away and told me she'd take the top bunk.

"I don't like top bunks, Dad, but then I'm not sure if it is strong enough to hold you," she said. The bunk bed was so short I could not straighten out. Rebekah told me in the morning that I'd talked in my sleep loud enough to wake her up.

The inside of the trailer was popping and crackling with anticipation. When you count all the days in a year, there is little actual fishing going on. There are all the days and nights spent waiting for these openings, when Per and the other permit holders are allowed to fish. No wonder Neva fixed a special meal and Per brought home bags full of expensive groceries. Soon, for twenty-four hours, Per would be able to make money. His new $30,000 diesel engine could be put to use again. The nets could catch again. All Per's decades of fishing savvy could come alive. It was still possible that he could come back without enough fish to cover his expenses. Or, hopefully, he could spend hours and hours picking kings and reds from his net, returning triumphant from the sea, his face red from the weather and wind. More than likely the results would be somewhere in between.

"Man, this summer's going by fast," Per said from out of nowhere. It was the early evening of June 23, one of the longest days of the year. When the last of the fishermen emerged from the Alaskan Hotel and Bar at 2 A.M., it would not be dark yet. Soon these cowboys would be cut loose to ride and chase down their prey, the highest-priced salmon in Alaska. Their fast-riding, big-motored gill nets are their sleek horses, nine hundred feet of net their ropes to lasso the fish. The big difference between them and cowboys that ride horses, other than the killer ocean they ride, is they can't see what they're after.

Per's fishing began at exactly 7 P.M., June 24, and would end at exactly 7 P.M., June 25. The whole family came down to the docks to see off Per and me. There are planes and observation boats with the best binoculars watching for law-breakers. Gillnetters almost always fish alone out of Cordova. Per said his high-strung side comes out at these times. A couple of the boats had already started their engines. All of us, including Per's two small sons, carried something to the boat, the *Terminal Harvester,* which had been built in 1991 in the state of Washington. As we loaded our supplies, a fisherman named Gerald Kompkoff was on the dock mending his net. Per said he was part Aleut and part Russian. He worked on the boat the *Inseine.*

We loaded up the groceries and idled out to a cannery, Ocean Beauty, to load up the boat's built-in fish box with crushed ice. Boats were coming from every direction, like people on horseback and in wagons easing up to the starting line of the Oklahoma land rush. Neva, Rebekah, Keith, and Seth waved, as did wives and partners and lovers and children and grandparents and parents all over Cordova's docks. Bankers and merchants and mechanics and fiberglass repairers and boatbuilders and electronics suppliers had their fingers crossed.

The prime area targeted by Per and his fishing partners is in the Prince William Sound management area. "It includes all coastal waters and inland drainages entering the north central Gulf of Alaska between Cape Suckling and Cape Fairfield. The area includes the Bering River, the Copper River, and all of Prince William Sound with a total adjacent land area of approximately 38,000 square miles." A report from one of the first explorations of the Copper River area by the United States, headed by Lieutenant Henry T. Allen of the Second U.S. Cavalry, in 1885 had nothing to do with salmon stocks. "In view of the fact that so little is known of the interior of the Territory of Alaska, and that the conflicting interests between the white people and the Indians of that Territory may in the near future result in serious disturbances between the two races, the department commander authorizes you to proceed to that Territory for the purpose of obtaining all information which will be valuable and important, especially to the military branch of the Government."

From atop a mountain between twenty-five hundred and three thousand feet high, there was a clear vision of the formidable obstacles that lay before them: "We had gained a sufficient altitude to see, far to the northeast, a high wall of ice, visible as far back as the eye (aided with a field glass) could see. To the north and almost joining the glacier on the northeast, we saw another monster moving off to the northeast. In our front, or east, lay a collection of thousands of small islands, varying from one-sixteenth of an acre to fifty acres in size, surrounded by light gray liquid, varying in breadth from a mile to a small stream, and in depth being about three feet here and about eighteen inches further down. This was the Copper River, that we thought might be ascended in a steamer for 50 to 100 miles!"

Lieutenant Allen, in his report upon returning from their remarkable "reconnaissance in Alaska" concluded, "Should the natives of the Tanana or Copper River commit outrages upon the whites who may be making their way into the interior, of such a nature to justify the intervention of the military, many difficulties would be encountered before redress could be obtained. To stop the sale of ammunition and arms would be a sad blow to them, but a decidedly negative retaliation. . . . Once on the Copper River, food in the form of salmon would be abundant, and a severe retaliation could be inflicted by patrolling the river, thus preventing, if possible, the natives from taking fish during the summer. By this means a large number of them would perish the following winter."

A hundred and fifteen years later, some Cordova fishermen believe that there are many organizations, not just the U.S. government, trying to prevent them from fishing. Some believe these organizations would like to shut them down completely, by posting patrols to control them until eventually their lifestyle would perish. The fishermen will fight this vigorously, hoping too that it does not happen so subtly and incrementally that they do not fight until it's too late.

Once we were out of the "no wake" zone and into Orca Inlet, Per and all the other bow-pickers of the Gulf of Alaska let their motors roar. Some had larger boats than Per, made of aluminum, powered by twin diesels, and worth close to $150,000. But no boat seemed to be gaining on us. Inside the cabin, Per told me a few fishermen, like "that macrobiotic eating" Sully, still had the wooden, slow boats. Sully sometimes left a day before the rest, and still, if they had to run to Controller Bay, where the Bering River empties, or near Strawberry Point, the fast boats beat him there. Sully and his artist wife, Rocky, are originally from the Northeast. Sully, who sometimes wore his white hair in a ponytail, was a beatnik, before *hippie* was a word. He is sixty-two or so; when he was younger, he had a huge beard, and he had always been lean, Per said. Sully was an extreme skier before there was even a word for these snow maniacs. Sully has a run named after him in Telluride, Sully's Gully. Pip, an excellent skier and one of Per's fishing partners, skied Telluride once, saw the run, and decided to pass on it for another lifetime. Per's boat ran twenty to twenty-five knots; Sully's little white boat does six to eight knots. Sully began his fishing career as a crewman on Per's stepdad's seine boat. Per says Sully survives on beans and rice. Per would feel much more at home at the dinner table with ex–football coaches John Madden and Mike Ditka.

The sky was slate gray and peppered with slow-moving puffs of light gray clouds. It was about fifty degrees. The ocean was smooth and lime green; the spray splashing up on both sides of our boat was silver. I could see something in the water, which was so shallow with sandbars and even isolated rocks that Per had to keep the boat up on plane, at full speed, so it could run without hitting anything. At first I thought it was some old kelp washing in from the ocean, but I kept seeing it. Per directed me out onto the deck. The cabin was at the back of this boat, the working area on the front two-thirds. Floating on their backs everywhere in the water, so many I could not count them all, were sea otters. Here they were protected by Egg Island. Most had their babies on their bellies, where they nursed and napped, nursed and napped. The wakes the gillnetting boats left gave the otters a modest ride. Per said he'd seen "rafts" of over a hundred sea otters before.

We'd passed Mummy Island and squeezed through the dangerous Whiteshed Point. Some barrier islands—Cooper Sands, Grass Island Bar, Kokinhenik Bar and Strawberry Reef—shield the Copper River delta. We were headed there to claim our spot to be able to begin fishing at 7 P.M. exactly. Per said there would be about three hundred boats in this district. Some would fish inside the islands, some up the river a bit—wherever they thought the salmon were. Where were the "high-liners" going? everyone wondered. High-liners are those fishermen seeking salmon who consistently seem to find the fish and catch more than the other professionals.

We were now in the Gulf of Alaska. On the beach of the barrier island to our left, three bald eagles fed on some dead flesh. What I wondered was, how do these fishermen keep from being completely overwhelmed? Water surrounded us, its surface giving no hint to what lay below. Per had said that they look for jumpers, salmon that occasionally leapt from the sea. But that worked more for seiners, when the fish were in larger schools. How intimidating it seemed that there are so many spots to let your net out into the water.

Per chose a spot and let his net out. We watched the net for top water splashes, for signs that reds or, even better, kings were hitting the net. The top would move and buoys would pop down in the water when they hit at first. Our hopes would soar—we hoped it would happen again. Per let some sets last an hour, or even less; a few were for three hours, when he would just leave the net fishing without pulling it up. The net jutted straight out from the boat's bow, stretching nine hundred feet and sinking twenty-three or twenty-four feet down. There was time for storytelling and for chats with Per's fishing partners on the radio. Pip called and said that the opening price was set by Norquest at $1.80 per pound for reds and $2.50 for kings. Per felt that the price would go up because the take would be small. He was having second thoughts; maybe we should have gone to another place to catch netfulls of cheap pink salmon. The situation made him thoughtful.

"This life on the water runs in our family. My father, he was studying the information obtained by Gary Power's U-2 spy plane. He is a university-trained physicist, but he didn't want to work for the industrial war complex. So we moved to Alaska," Per said.

He kept the motor running and his thirty-foot-long bow-picker in gear to keep the net straight. Without the power of the engine, the current or the net could suck us toward the breakers, where several boats have been flipped and fishermen killed.

Per explained how his father, an adventurer on many levels, had taken a huge spruce log from the Northwest and put two axles underneath it. He then towed it from Washington to Monterey, California. There he hollowed it out and sailed it, as a trimaran, from California to the Marquesas and then to the Big Island of Hawaii. He took a sextant and a book on celestial navigation and learned how to guide himself on the way there. Per's dad, also an inventor, fishes Bristol Bay and winters in Fiji. Bristol Bay is believed to have the most abundant run of red salmon in the world.

A Steller's sea lion popped up right along the net. Per had already told me to look for them; he said they knew the sound of the gillnet boats; to them it was the sound of an all-you-can-eat buffet. It certainly was easier for them to just rip the fish from the net instead of speeding through the ocean, darting and cutting, to catch these quick, sleek silver-sided salmon. Occasionally, a seven-foot-long salmon shark would about tear the nets in half, leaving gaping, expensive holes. Dolphin and killer whales, normally, were too intelligent to mess with the nets. Even the salmon could sometimes see the net and avoid it.

Per noticed a fisherman whose boat he did not know making a set close to the beach. Fishermen are tempted to head inland because salmon often run close to the beach. How do the fish find their way for possibly several thousand miles back to the exact place they were born? There are no landmarks underwater to follow; surely they don't "smell" their home freshwaters diluted beyond recognition in ocean waters. The return of the salmon is one of the unknown miracles of nature.

"Last year we lost a fisherman who got too close to the breakers," Per remembered, his voice tinged with a sadness for the young family in Oregon and a knowledge that most serious accidents are a result of a seemingly small, inconsequential decision. He explained how the fisherman's boat got turned sideways in the breakers. Then the full power of the ocean hits the boat broadside, wanting to turn it over. It flipped this boat; it was upside down, the engine might still have been running. The cabin probably filled with fumes and it was totally black. The man struggled frantically to find air to breathe and became disoriented, knowing he must get out.

Fish and Game happened to be around. They responded and went into the shallow breakers after him in their inflatable. The breakers flipped them, also, into waist-deep water. They spotted gas leaking from the fisherman's flipped gas tanks. The Fish and Game guys got a chain saw and cut a hole in the upside-down hull. One spark could have caused the whole thing to blow up. The fisherman had probably broken bones from being slammed inside the dark cabin by the waves breaking on his capsized boat. And after his boat had rolled, his net had broken loose. Fish and Game could never get to him; he died, Per told me, with no indication that the story was part of the norm for an Alaskan fisherman's life. People died every year and many more came close.

"My sister's boat, a seiner, rolled and sank in deep water three years ago," Per said. She and her crew were rescued.

Often the gillnetters are hustling around, walking on decks and bows and side rails smeared with salmon slime and ocean water. There's even the simple risk of slipping and falling off your boat, hitting your head on the way into the ocean. Your boat's running, you're knocked out or dazed. The gillnetters often fish all night. I saw no one wearing a life preserver, much less a survival suit. The water is never warm enough so someone would be able to swim to safety unless he's right outside the breakers, like where Andy Johnson the surfer likes to catch a wave. I'd been looking for a gillnet boat with a surfboard strapped to the top but had not seen one.

THE ABUSED SECRET CODE

The brotherhood of Per, Pip, Art, and Marc didn't talk to each other much at first. Was it because the excitement and anticipation of netfuls of salmon, what keeps all fishermen coming back, turned to disappointment? Per checked in with Pip and he was doing worse than we were and that was bad. Neither Marc nor Art were catching much either, or so Per discerned from the code-speak over the marine radio. Marc, who was from Washington and a rabid Washington State football fan, found out I was from Tennessee. The big debate this year in college football was over who would be the better pro quarterback, his Ryan Leaf of WSU or Peyton Manning of the University of Tennessee. I offered up all my reasons why Peyton would smoke Ryan. Marc knew it would go the other way—Ryan was the man. The argument over the radio went Peyton, Ryan, Peyton, Ryan, PEYTON, RYAN, until Per had to step in and referee.

Per had made several sets, laying out the net, letting it set, reeling it in and picking out the salmon. The faster the net came in, the less picking, the smaller the amount of salmon, the less money to survive. And the twenty-four hours were ticking, ticking away. Who knew when the sonar god and biologist god would let them fish again?

We moved down by Strawberry Reef, southwest of the steep Ragged Mountains, which shot up right from the beach. We made a set and then moved east some more toward Kanak Island. To our north was a potent maze of rivers, lakes, deltas, bays, marshes, and wetlands channeling the running waters, the apparently still waters, the waters controlled by the tides, the waters coming out of the glaciers. One prophetic past Alaskan governor had realized the worldwide value of pure water. And he understood the billions of gallons stored up in the glaciers and running through Alaska's pure wilderness filters of rock and wetland. He proposed that Alaska ship supertankers full of pure water to the rest of the world. Some people thought he was crazy; more and more think it may happen someday.

Close to dinnertime, a conversation not in code came over Per's radio between Pip and Marc:

Marc: "Tell me a good story to improve my mood."

Pip: "One night I had seven fish in the boat. I was off certain islands where we've done bad and done good."

Marc: "Yeah. So far my mood hasn't improved."

Pip: "I woke up around 3 A.M. from a nap and there were three hundred fish in the net. I ended up by the end of that morning with twelve hundred fish on ice."

Marc: "That's like Santa Claus. You go to sleep and when you wake up, there are presents under the tree."

At 6 A.M. the morning of June 25, after fishing for eleven hours, Per delivered 502 pounds of salmon to the tender. Tenders are large boats that have holds filled with ice. They anchor near groups of gillnetters. After they harvest a decent amount of salmon, Per and other fishermen deliver a load to them to lighten their boats and keep the salmon as fresh as possible. Our last set before we delivered held only twelve fish, and six of those were dog salmon, called chum; they only brought between ten cents and forty cents a pound. The first set Per had made was forty-two fish, forty reds and two kings, a fine beginning. It was never better. Pip finished stronger than Per but had started slower.

All these humans with their nets and fast, sleek boats, putting themselves up against what the misinformed think are dumb, small-brained fish. Yet these salmon are able to make their way down from the cold creeks in which they hatched to places of mystery hundreds and hundreds of miles away in the Pacific Ocean, then orient their way back again. A human can't get from one airport to another in the protective metal skin of a plane without sophisticated electronic navigational devices, often assisted by multimillion-dollar satellites. How do these salmon do it? The humans pit themselves against these fish; if they make a good catch, they come back. If they don't, they find other, less demanding work such as, as I heard several fishermen say, working for the government or working by the hour.

This set of four fishermen could be a mash of moods, all depending on the fishing. They were grumpier than old men when the fishing was bad. They could be poetic; there was almost no way to ignore the fullness of the beauty and wildlife all around them. They were in survival mode from the ever-present death waiting behind one tired, overdaring, or stupid mistake. They could be funny as long as one of them responded. If they were tired, especially Per and Marc, the more verbal ones, they'd make jokes, amuse themselves. Pip, on the other hand, was a stickler for detail, all work and intensity until it was time to party.

Pip was especially concerned with the use of their secret code. It was important to speak over public airways without any excitement or depression in your voice. If one of them got into the fish, had two hundred fish in the net when most others were thrilled to have twenty, the last thing Pip wanted was to give that location away to anyone but themselves. The other fishermen pay attention to the high-liners, try to break their codes. That's another reason Pip changes their code often. Their group had been known at times to be "in the fish." When Art, who was maybe in his fifties and the oldest guy in the group, got into the fish, or one of the others got into the fish, he tended to get too excited.

Say Per made contact via the radio, speaking in code, where any word beginning with A meant 6 and any word with D meant 7. So Per would say, "Anywhere doggy," meaning he just got sixty-seven in a set. Breathlessly, with a thrill infusing each word, Art would repeat, "Anywhere doggy!" They had letters that stood for the depth they fished in, their location, and so on. Some fishermen did anything, legal or otherwise, to gain information, even used illegal cell phone scanners. If the technology existed and could be bought, some fishermen would stop at nothing to get into the fish.

At least two hundred of the fishermen wanted to keep their nets out until the last allowable moment. We were fishing a riptide outside Grass Island Bar, our last set of this opening. Every set, Per hoped for a net load, the splashing of caught fish all along the corkline, the dream of a full box of layers of salmon and ice, some of the best-tasting salmon in the world, Copper River reds and Copper River kings. The riptide created a long line in the sea, the brown water filled with glacial silt coming at us from the Copper River delta meeting and overcoming the retreating jade-green clarity of the sea. Fishing in the rip was known to produce. We were a couple miles offshore. A couple orcas were hunting here too. Until the last fifty feet of the net was rolled up, Per expected abundance and accepted two last fish. The last two reds were worth about $9 each, plus fifteen to twenty-five cents a pound because Per layered his fish in ice and rushed them straight to the fish house, Ocean Beauty.

Our twenty-four hours together on Per's *Terminal Harvester* were over. Now the horses, these gillnetters, were headed back to the barn. From everywhere around us, from the east, the south, and the west, came almost all the gillnet boats, their throttle levers pushed forward to drive the boats as fast as they'd go. Some tenders, lit up like a tiny city, waited to unload in Orca Inlet. Most went straight into Cordova. We raced past several boats to catch up with Pip. From the highest strung to the seemingly most laid-back, these fishermen are intensely competitive people. We sped part of the way home through the delta running full blast down Pete Dahl Channel. The channels are the main fingers that carry the most water; this water spreads far out into the mudflats but is exceedingly shallow. It's easy to get stuck.

Boats that lingered closer to Cordova had beat us to the cannery and fish-processing place. We lined up and waited our turn. Family, wives, and girlfriends, children and other dependents, gathered at the docks to see the hunter-gatherers return. The gold, the meat, was iced and hidden, waiting to be lifted up in metal baskets by small cranes and weighed. After unloading, we headed back to Per's dock space, where Neva, Rebekah, Seth, and Keith waited. I held up a fat, silver, twenty-five-pound king salmon. Per had said he wanted our family to have it. Seth and Keith were totally focused on their father. They knew he'd waited all winter and most of the spring to be fishing again. They knew his mood—the mood for all of them—and their town depended on catching salmon. The catch wasn't fantastic, not even really good. But some money was made, bills would be paid, with still a month or so of gillnetting to go. The fishermen of Cordova would take it one opening at a time, one throw of the net at a time, to gamble with the sea.

Per was jovial, joking, his face was a healthy red, and he was content and full

Per Nolan in Cordova. Photo by Peter Jenkins

of himself. Per lived in Alaska so he could go out into the unknown, his net ready to unroll, and come back with these exquisite-eating wild salmon on the *Terminal Harvester* on a dark-blue-sky day. He wondered why people wanted to live in other places. He knew of nowhere else in the world he would rather be. These moments hunting the unseen salmon made the isolation and frigid, gray winds and the lack of any other jobs and life in a trailer worth it. On this Alaskan summer evening, the sun shone on Per's triumphant moment. His gamble, their gamble, had paid off once more.

Rebekah, Per, and I took the king salmon down to the other end of Cordova where Per said he could have it smoked. Pip and Scott, a partner, smoke, can, and sell some salmon every season. Neva works for them. A few years back, Scott almost lost his life when he was thrown out of his boat. The breakers hit the stern and flipped it over bow first. The cold water can numb your body and hands and arms, depriving you of the strength to hold on. If he hadn't wrapped himself up in the corkline, he would have drowned. And he'd only wrapped himself in the corkline so his loved ones would find his body and not doubt what had happened. But he was rescued. We'd get the salmon smoked at their facility, in an old cannery building built over Orca Inlet, looking out toward Hawkins Island.

Neva had said there were few sights as inspiring as six killer whales coming through here on their way in or out of Prince William Sound, especially with the sun setting in the west and lighting up their exhaled breath and their dorsal fins in silver and gold. They swam through the channel slowly, unless they were hunting. Looking for whales, I spotted instead an older bow-picker coming toward Cordova with a surfboard strapped to the roof of the cabin. The surfboard was creamy white with orange striping—it was Andy Johnson, the fisherman, the world-class extreme snowboarder, the surfer returning from his place of worship, where the ocean and mountains and snow and ice and water all meet.

I told Per I'd had about all of him I could stand and that he needed to go be with his wife. I would hang out with Andy, if I could catch up with him. While we were gone Rebekah opened some of her own doors.

FROM REBEKAH

Hippie Cove

Cordova is the place, Alaska is the country. I am near twenty the first time I visit Cordova with my father, and out of all the places my father has taken me or sent me to visit, Cordova remains my favorite. I know picking favorites is absurd; perhaps the best way to put it is that Cordova is the place in which I would most want to live. Why? Because of the countryside, the peaks and skies under which it sits, the hollow little corner of the world that it claims, and the people that attract me so, because they live out their lives, day in and day out, in their own little corner of this magic land.

Cordova is both bitter and sweet, but more sweet than bitter, the more "offbeat" you are. I love its roads, the way they all seem to have a part that moves uphill. I love Cordova's houses; the big furry dogs tied up to their front porches that never bark. I love the Russians who live in that hole over past Per and Neva's trailer park, and how the Russian women keep their heads covered in white, probably hand-stitched bonnets, and how these women all drive the nicest Ford and GMC trucks in town. I never saw any of the other locals talk to the Russians. I did, though, drive into their hole on one of my many Cordovan drives. The hole was really a fenced-in cemented RV park housing expensive RV after expensive RV. Neva let me take her old beat-up Sentra around town a lot. I would drive the back roads and then get scared and turn around because all of a sudden I would realize that I was out by myself and I knew nothing about how to come face-to-face with men like Wild Gene or wild bears like I'd seen on TV.

I love Cordova's baseball field and the view from the bleachers. I wonder if Neva even notices the mountains in that view anymore, just as I hardly ever notice the rolling hills and green flavors of my own state anymore. When is it that we actually stop looking out the window—when our eyes see nothing but road and the endless yellow and white lines on the pavement? It's sad. I know that's why people move, for the views of mountains and hills or lakes, but once they settle in and the years start to roll by, the wonderment finally wears off. Where do all of these magnificent views go, when exactly is it that the damn road becomes the only object of our stares? Thank God people have kids and the world hasn't exploded yet because in those kids' eyes, hope exists for reclaiming the view.

Cordova has a certain "air" to it that I have not found in any other Alaskan town, or anywhere else, for that matter. This air seems to represent all things reflective and deep. The people carry this air, as does the view. It made me want to look as far into the water as I could and keep the feel of the breeze that blew on my forearms while I stood on Per's boat on my skin forever. It made me want to climb a nearby mountain despite my fear of encountering that one pesky bear that Neva and the boys kept reminding me about. This air of reflection made me want to sit in the Orca Café and drink endless cups of coffee and write, my colored pencils at hand, and plunge into these new people I'd met. It made me want to never stop looking out the windows of Cordova, no matter whether they were the windows of the café, the windows of Per and Neva's home, or the windows to the world that are my come-with-me-everywhere eyes, windows that lead to the very essence of my soul.

"Hooch" was his name, and Andrea was hers. I had encountered people like this before, the lone-wanderer types who can find a home no matter the weather or the town. She reminded me of Alanis Morissette, with her long, nearly black hair falling to her ass, and she had these hands that were perfectly traveled and beckoning to the next best thing. They were the kind of hands that were made for acoustic guitar playing. Andrea and Hooch had dated, been together, whatever you want to call it, and I met her at the Orca Café. She was working the deli and coffee counter hidden in the back of the store behind all the shelves filled with books and trinkets. I was alone and shy and new in town, and I guess that was written all over my freckled face. She was kind and sweet-spirited, and she reached out to me, inviting me down to her place—Hippie Cove.

Hippie Cove is a piece of land inhabited by old rusted vans and school buses and people who need nothing but food, love, and liquid for the day. Thus the name, I suppose. All around were tall pines, pebble streams that you could either hop over or walk through (nothing wrong with getting a little wet, right?). The sound of small w aterfalls, a sound that seemed to me to be the marriage of silence and searching, filled the air. It was about three acres of land with a dozen or so buses and vans and a banya, so to speak. The banya lay past all the buses and vans and was for steaming and scrubbing and getting naked.

Another important relic to Hippie Cove is its "birdhouse." It's really a tree house that was built long ago by some hippies. It has a stove, tall ceilings, a porch filled with bongo drums, guitars, torn upholstered chairs, and candles, and shelves and shelves of books from backpacks and knapsacks off the backs of the hippies who have visited this place. They were all books about adventure and dreaming and bums, all the things near and dear to these bearded and long-haired young people. Although there was an old man or two, as there always seems to be an old man or two. The one I was introduced to had a long gray beard and glazed blue eyes, and he talked about how the land they all lived off of was going to be taken away because the people who owned it were tired of all those "squatters." Andrea seemed to think of this old man as her father figure, her protector. But then again, she seemed comfortable, despite its lack of skyscrapers and suits. It was all about "love" and "listen to this song," and "hey, man, check out that eagle over there!"

In some of these people's eyes I could see desperation, addiction, longing. It looked as though some of them were on the run from something or from someone. But not everyone—in Andrea I saw a peace and in Hooch I saw energy. He had "that look." It seemed everywhere I turned in Alaska, whether it be the airport or some tourist-filled street in Anchorage, there were men who wore beards and who had "that look" about them, the same "look" my dad wore once upon a time, when he was their age and of their build and of their hope. Hooch had all this. He was lean and tall with a brown/blond beard that ran to the middle of his chest. He had dirt under his fingernails and holes in his clothes, but he always seemed to wear a smile through all the muff and gruff. He was in his twenties, like most of the people who made up Hippie Cove. They came, Andrea and Hooch and all the others, I suppose, for the view—the mountains, the water, the isolation, and the assurance that no one whom you didn't want to find you could, way up here in this little hollow corner of Alaska.

Andrea lived alone in an old, multicolored school bus equipped with a stove, sleeping space, books, and other stuff that seemed old and worn-out, as if it had been *dragged all over the world. Hooch lived in another bus with another girl. A new fling had begun for him, and he was riding it. Andrea didn't seem to mind that he was with someone else. Rather, she was working on "soul stuff." She was learning how to fight her fear. She told me about how she went on daily walks in the woods behind the cove, how she'd been scared to go "out there" because of bears. But in her fight she had come to a place where she could "trust the universe." She said, "If the universe wants to take me, then it will." It was such a strong, confident statement, I will never forget her saying it to me.*

THE SNOW GHOST

Andy lived alone somewhere off the road to Nirvana Park, where he rented the downstairs of a wooden, two-story house from a fellow fisherman. On a light trailer at the side of the house was Andy's flying machine, an ultralight. He's trying to figure out how to fly to the top of the local mountains that only he and one or two others dare to snowboard down. Once he figures out how to fly to the top, he'd like to have someone fly him up there. Then he could leap off into four feet of powder and snowboard down without having to spend three to four hours hiking up for a two-minute ride down. That's how long it takes to go up and come down Queens Chair, Andy's favorite mountain in the world. You can see the mountain face from town. There are fewer ways to die hiking up, such as getting swept away in avalanches, than by coming down, when at these incredible speeds you can hit a surface that once was powdery snow but has been melted by the sun and refrozen icy hard. At those speeds, you can slide off cliffs or skid into unmovable trees or boulders.

Andy understands he can't fish or fly all the time, so he would like to write screenplays someday, and be a stuntman. He told me about fishing and flying, and I talked to him about writing.

Hung on the front door of Andy's place is one of his old license plates: "Boardom." That was the name of the snowboard shop started by Andy and his best friend Teal Copeland when they were in high school. Small towns anywhere can breed boredom and give added meaning to the teenage mantra that there's nowhere to go and nothing to do. Especially places of deep snow with no road in or out. In Alaska's small, isolated communities, more or less all its towns except Anchorage and Fairbanks, making your own fun can take on a radical and sometimes extreme definition. Andy had just one comfortable-looking chair;

he offered it to me. Playing on his TV, in what seemed like endless loops, was a video of some outrageous snowboard runs down what appeared to be an almost vertical mountain face. I would later learn one of the people going off the mountaintop was Andy, at an event in New Zealand.

A poster for Glissade snowboards hangs on the outside of the front door and one of Laird Hamilton, famous megawave surfer riding a wave called Jaws, on the inside. Jaws was perfect, the one God would show under the word *wave* in a dictionary. Another poster that read "The Beauty of Gray" hung by a logo for Smith, a snowboarding goggles and glasses maker. There was also a poster of Andy snowboarding down some insane-looking run on Mount Baker, near Bellingham, Washington. In the winter of 2000 it took away from Mount Rainier the world record for a winter's snowfall, more than 1,133 inches, or 94 feet. For people like Andy who like to fly over and through the snow, Mount Baker is a "sick" place. (*Sick* means "really good.")

On the windowsill was a primitive carving from Costa Rica of a man carrying a surfboard. Last winter, Andy spent a couple months down there surfing right before fishing started. He surfed, did yoga, ate super healthy, and adjusted for the first time in his life to a tropical place with bugs, snakes, and lizards. When Andy surfs the breakers off the Copper River delta he's got to watch for salmon sharks, Steller's sea lions, and humpback whales. He said he preferred Alaska; he'd rather worry about big predators than bloodsucking insects.

Also on the sill was a hand-carved, deadly looking piece of curved wood. It looked at first like a horn from some animal. Andy told me it was a spike for killing vampires. He does not care for the "users" in this world who suck the life out of you, who take your heart or spill your blood. He doesn't think they deserve to "be around," he told me in a voice heavy with experience, so he's ready for them. Obviously, he had met more of these people than he would have wished, and this stake is symbolically about warding off anymore "injuries." Andy's life is about the heights of sensation found in the extreme natural world. He reaches those heights by surfing on top of the deep powder or riding the curls of the waves or flying through the sky on his ultralight. All the while, he fights to control his gifted body, to keep from being injured or wiped out, to keep feeling as alive as possible.

Andy is a salmon fisherman because his grandfather and grandmother and father and uncles were before him. His boat, a twenty-six-foot-long fiberglass bow-picker powered by a jet drive, is named *The Snow Ghost*. Jet drives are

motors that use jets of water to power them instead of propellers. It lets fishermen get into really shallow water. Permits to fish the Copper River delta and
Prince William Sound are hard to come by. The authorities issue only 560, only
about 350 to 400 of which are active in any given fish season. Andy got his permit when his grandfather retired.

Andy's twenty-four years old and part Aleut. The Aleuts originally traveled
these treacherous oceans in kayaks. They did venture this far south, but were
centered mostly on the Aleutian chain. Traveling the open water in an animal-
skin kayak, like a cork on a deadly ocean, seems almost unimaginable. They
were the ultimate water explorers. Andy's hair is dark, his spirit deeply sensitive
yet death-defying. His last name, Johnson, probably means he is part Norwegian. No wonder he is so comfortable on, in, and zooming over the icy cold water. Andy fishes so that he can make enough money to live the life of the
spartan warrior-snowboarder the rest of the year. His life is not fishing, like
Per's; he fishes so that he can afford to fly the way few people can.

At some point between when his father's fishing boat doubled as his crib,
rocking him to sleep, and when he went to high school, Andy developed a
problem with taking the regal lives of so many salmon, especially the king
salmon. As a sixth-grader, having fished his entire life, he would look into the
powerful eyes of the king salmon as they died on the deck of his father's boat.
He wanted to see them, really look into their eyes as they flopped, captured by
the net, drawn out of the salt water to the boat where fishermen stood atop the
salmon world. When he was at his most sensitive, Andy felt the kings were
looking at him as if to say, "Please throw me back, please throw me back." The
salmon these fishermen catch have not fulfilled their reason for being yet because they have not spawned. They have spent every day of their lives avoiding
the sea's predators, the sea lions and salmon sharks, the orca and Dall porpoise.
If they get past the humans, and then the bears, to deposit their eggs or sperm
and create more king salmon, then their kind will last forever.

People like Andy's father and Per want their sons to be fishermen like them.
They love the life, for the most part, and understand how someone could want
to throw a dying king or a flopping red or a high-leaping silver salmon back to
live a bit longer before dying for their species. Andy came to appreciate that
some of the salmon have to give themselves to some of the many predators, and
that he is one of those predators. He still deeply respects the taking of a salmon's
life, especially the king. It's a sacrificial moment, and it's not felt by everyone,

but Andy does not care about what others feel or do. He will not think of the lives of the salmon he takes so that he can live, as a dollar amount that trivializes what incredible creatures they are and what their flesh provides.

Andy keeps a sort of sculptural tribute to these salmon and their sacrificed flesh wherever he goes, wherever he lives. In his apartment in Cordova, piled in carefully built pyramids of gleaming gold cans stacked on top of the kitchen cabinets, is Andy's "home pack." For almost all Alaskans, "home pack" is one of the most important symbols of their reason for living. Home pack is an Alaskan's own personal pile of canned, vacuum-packed, and/or smoked strips of salmon. Eating it makes existence enjoyable, even blessed, with moments of great pleasure.

Andy said he liked to keep his golden cans of the salmon caught by him and canned by his neighbor out where he can see them all the time, not hidden in some dark pantry. It makes him feel like a king to see what he thinks is the greatest food in the world; the cans are his piles of gold. The Copper River kings and sockeye and silver salmon give him much of his power and energy, because the flesh of a salmon is so loaded with fish oils and healthy fat and eye-opening, muscle-powering protein. The salmon pass on to him the energy they would have used to fight their way up the Copper River, some two hundred miles.

In Andy's apartment stood an old Ping-Pong table. Bent in the middle from a tidy arrangement of outdoor equipment, the Ping-Pong table was a display of who Andy truly was. The centerpiece of the display was a collection of shoes to put his body and mind and spirit to different uses. There were running shoes and basketball shoes. There was also a pair of old snowboard boots. He'd finally bought some expensive Northwave boots, red and white Apollos. They are the most supportive of all boots, and Andy had wanted them for a couple of years. They cost $240. Counting all his snowboards and boots and surfboards and flying machine and specialized clothes, he had to catch a lot of salmon to pay for it all. Andy spends the majority of his income on equipment so that he can fly, in the snow, in the water, in the air. Andy told me he uses his old Jamie Lynn snowboarding boots to fly his flying machine. On the day I was there, a car battery sat on the table, only temporarily. Andy had left the dome light on in his old truck and worn out the battery. He *is* human.

There was a pair of white, tall boots for the Kawasaki X500 dirt bike he rides. There was a pair of snowshoes, the skis for his flying machine, some old ski poles, some Techtron waterproofing spray. There was a box with his wet suit for surfing. There were six different helmets to protect his head. From all the death-defying things Andy has done, he knows the body can more easily be repaired than the head. There were two helmets for flying his ultralight, a helmet for snowboarding, a helmet for use on his Jet Ski, a helmet for mountain biking, and a helmet for dirt biking. Every year, Andy said, it seems as if one of the three hundred or four hundred fishermen in Cordova dies. A few years before, three had died during the short season. Everyone he knew, I suppose including himself, had been in really bad situations, but most lived to fish again. So far, none of these Alaskan cowboys wear helmets to fish.

On Andy's refrigerator, the one place in North America where you can find out what lies dear to a person's heart, was a poster of a mountain peak advertising his friend's helicopter company. They flew extreme skiers and snowboarders with money to surrounding ultrafantastic extreme skiing and snowboarding locations. Andy said with a smile that he needed to marry a superrich woman who was also a helicopter pilot.

Last winter, he'd hiked up alone to snowboard down Queens Chair. Andy has done quite well in competitions in Valdez at the World Championship, in New Zealand, and all over the Northwest. The Queens Chair is his favorite place in the whole world to snowboard. The mountain looks like a throne. It's a technical ride; it offers an "intricate playing field" for him, a challenge. Well, during this ride the challenge almost ended in his solitary death.

He had left at 5 A.M. and told only his landlord where he was going. It took him three hours to hike to the top of Queens Chair, the last hour of which was severely steep climbing to get to the top. When he began, the powder was deep and fine—he was "dancing in the white room." "Dancing in the white room" is one way to come down the mountain. When the powder's dry and deep enough, three or four feet, by flying through it with all this force and speed and gravity, the way a boarder turns creates "the white room." As Andy made each turn, the snow flew out and about and everywhere. Making sharp turns deep and wide, the snow was sprayed up all over the place, surrounding him, like the walls of a white room. He couldn't see anything but white. When a boarder is dancing in the white room, he must know precisely where the trees and cliffs and boulders outside are located. It used to be Andy wore his Walkman, and when he created the white room, he was in there listening to CDs by Pennywise and Offspring. Now he listens to the sounds of the powder and his breathing and his board. Andy had been in the white room an infinite amount of times and was in it again coming down Queens Chair, except this time, he said, he had this premonition that he should come out.

When he came out and stopped, he immediately saw the danger he was in. The sun had hit one side of the mountain, the side he hadn't started on, and hardened the crust so that Andy could not break through, couldn't get his edge in. He had to stop. He was stuck, and below him was a hundred-foot sheer cliff. If he went off the cliff, he would land in a section of boulders. He had no ropes and no transceiver, which skiers use when caught in an avalanche. Earlier that winter he'd been snowboarding in Washington and watched his friend get swept away in an avalanche.

As he perched there on the smooth, icy snow surface, he thought about how he had to turn around. Just turning around took ten minutes. He had to leap up and twist around without sliding off the cliff. But he did it. Every move put him on the edge of death. Finally he was able to get his snowboard off and hike back up to where he could go down a different chute. Just hiking up took another half hour, because he had to dig in his snowboard with each movement up, barely being held from sliding to his death. He had to make all the decisions himself. So alone. As so often happens in Alaska, he returned to his home before noon, only one person ever knowing he had even gone anywhere. And he'd told no one how close he'd come to ending his life until he told me, and initially to me he even made it sound about as noteworthy as turning on a light switch.

Already this summer, Andy had been surfing. He found it more complicated. Everything is constantly moving: the water's moving and he is moving and his feet are moving. When the fishing is slow, Andy will put his net out and go surfing. Some of the locals see him and think he's lost his mind. Andy surfs in water where so many have been chilled so badly by immersion that their body parts failed and they drowned. When he's surfing in the Gulf of Alaska, Andy's got his dark dry suit on and only his hands and face are exposed. Some of the middle-aged fishermen tell him that one day some older fisherman with bad eyesight will mistake him for a sea lion and throw a seal bomb at him.

On one of the warmest days of the year last summer, not very warm as warm goes but warm for Cordova, Andy, who's always searching for the most freeing rush to be found in nature, decided to catch a couple waves completely naked. He didn't think any of the near- or farsighted fishermen saw him. He said it felt pure and exhilarating. A sea lion was nearby; Andy understands now how they feel as they surf the waves. He was so inspired that he has a plan for this coming winter. Sometimes he and a few of his friends snowboard during a full moon. Instead of dancing in a white room, it is a beautiful blue room, inside it the dancer's dark, flowing shadows. Someday soon Andy plans to make the ultimate full-moon snowboard run in the blue room—naked.

I walked back to Per and Neva's. Andy had given me a couple cans of his home pack. Rebekah was still out kayaking. Right about the same time Rebekah got back to the trailer park, Per and Seth pulled in from having done their chores in the seine boat. By mid-July they'd be living aboard it, fishing for their living. Neva was out with Keith in her boxy Sentra caring for her beloved flowers. She pampered them and admired them the way most humans wished they were. Per asked Rebekah if we'd like him to cook dinner. Rebekah, not having been around Per enough to know if he was kidding or not, looked at me to answer.

"Per, how about Rebekah and I take your truck and get us some pizza," I said.

If Neva had been here, she would have said, "Oh, Per, come on."

Rebekah and I went to get the pizzas down past Orca Book and Sound. I was impressed to see how quickly she made things happen, completely on her own. Her NOLS wilderness course had added several layers to her foundation of confidence. Being with her in the cab of Per's old pickup felt like being by myself, like being able to talk to a female version of me when I was twenty. Our spirits and minds seemed so similar, just in different places on the spiral of decisions and experience. We don't look much alike; our hair couldn't have been more different. Hers is curly and thick—to die for, I often overheard people say. I've never heard *curly* or *thick* used to describe my hair, and if I had to depend on it for warmth, I would die. I was awed at times by her ability to discern things in the world around her. She saw things I did not, and it inspired me. Sometimes she set me straight.

We turned left on Railroad Avenue to see the boat docks, fish-processing places, boat-repair shops, and net and boat parts graveyard. Pip had told me that he didn't think commercial fishermen in Alaska would be able to make their living much longer from the waters of the Copper River delta and surrounding sea, including Prince William Sound. He said a giant comet was coming to squash them but no one could see it clearly, yet. How much longer will they be able to pull their boats and store them in their yard like Andy Johnson?

How long will Per be able to pile old nets in the net graveyard to be recycled? Will Cordova ever vote yes to build a road? What will happen then?

I pointed to a slow-moving white, wooden boat chugging into its space in the docks. It was Sully, the fisherman, the one who has a run at Telluride named after him, a run too daring for most. Sully, the man who has lived his working life defying death on the sea so he could defy death on the slopes and the mountaintops, had returned cruising at his own pace, from another fishing trip and sold his salmon. Like Per, like Andy Johnson and Pip, these fishermen love the extreme demands of their lives. They are even willing to be reined in by Alaskan biologists and sonar-counting gods because this is a way of life where they can feel completely challenged and alive.

Per dropped us off at the airport. He was proud we'd come to see the Cordovans' world. He doesn't mind people visiting Cordova. He would just rather not see the ones who think there may be a better way to live than to go to sea with your nets and hooks and pull your living out of it.

When we got back home to Seward, it was 7 p.m. and still light. Rebekah asked Julianne if she wanted to camp out in Rebekah's tent down at the bay. In the summer the bay turned into a lively, separate summer town of hitchhikers with tents, campers on Harleys, campers with awnings and full-size cars in tow. You could meet people from all over the world living down there for the night, a week, their summer vacation.

They were eleven years apart and had different mothers, Rebekah and Julianne, yet the fires of competitiveness that burned inside them were similar. Although they didn't live together all the time, there is an obvious big-sister/little-sister love between them. Julianne wants to do everything Rebekah does, while Rebekah still likes being in the world of a little girl.

I walked down our hill with them, looking for "my" bike. Rita had been asked to prepare special health food for a local woman who'd had a mastectomy, mostly oriented around tofu. Rita had stayed home to make her a week's worth. Redheaded Luke was working; the bike was leaning up against the wooden wall of Captain Jack's. I harassed Luke and Aaron a bit, then went flying off down the road.

9

The Largest Member of the Congregation

Captain Bob Candopoulos was taking me through Eldorado Narrows, a stunning ocean passage. The mountains and glaciers on our left are on the mainland. On our right was a series of rock islands that shot up out of the ocean, Fox Island being the largest. We'd left the docks in Seward maybe forty-five minutes earlier. This early morning it was salty-cool; the sky and sun were as clear as anywhere on earth—not 99.44 percent clear, 100 percent clear. The rock on both sides narrowed, and on our left the cliffs were filled with several thousand nesting gulls that flew off in riotous flocks as we rode by.

Captain Bob, thirty-seven, a large, dark, brooding Greek-American, was born in New Jersey and grew up in Florida and Louisiana. When his mother died young, in 1978, he asked his dad, "What are we going to do now?" His father answered, "Move to Alaska." In 1979 they did. I'd met many people in my travels in Alaska who had moved here to be healed or to forget. Bob and a partner own Saltwater Safari, a charter fishing business based in Seward. Their steel-hulled boats are named *The Legacy* and *The Legend*. Their fast, smaller aluminum boats are *The Phantom* and *The Ghost*. Bob doesn't captain a boat every day anymore, but he loves to fish for the salmon shark. Today was one of those trips. We were on *The Legacy* and still had a voyage of two or three hours before we got to Montague Straits, an opening to the big, bad ocean and a passageway into the western portion of Prince William Sound.

Large schools of the intensely aggressive salmon sharks, a relative of the great white and mako sharks, come here this time of year chasing schools of salmon. Bob was an early pioneer of shark fishing in Alaska. I was surprised to learn that there are sharks in Alaska, in this cold water. Fortunately, the salmon shark may be the healthiest segment of the shark population, worldwide. Only a few are caught in Alaska each year.

This daylong trip aboard this steel-hulled charter boat was one of the advantages of living in a small town where life revolved, and things happened, around knowing each other. I'd met Bob because of my habit of going down to the docks every day when I was in town, where I loved to watch the unloading of the day's charter-fishing catch. The fishing guides would hang the fish on a hook under a plaque that said "Seward, Alaska." Everyone would take pictures. Three hundred pound halibut have been caught in the waters around here; I'd seen several picture sessions where people had caught fish, halibut or sharks, that were longer or heavier than they were.

Sitting on the seat of my borrowed bike, watching the day's catches unloaded, I got to know Bob. One day, he mentioned that if I ever had a day free, I'd be welcome to come along on a shark charter. He said there were salmon sharks out in the swift underwater currents by Montague that were over seven hundred pounds and talked about how sometimes they'd leap out of the water, bunches of them. A few times, he warned, they'd had to turn back; the weather could be totally different out there, as opposed to the protected, nestled-inside-the-mountain-range weather of Resurrection Bay.

Montague Island was northeast of Seward, not visible. The island is over fifty miles long and unpopulated by humans. It is the home of some massive brown bears. It serves as an effective buffer for Prince William Sound from the sometimes raging seas and destructive winds of the Gulf of Alaska.

Bob and First Mate Mark Theriault, twenty-seven, were two of possibly the most irreverent men in Alaska. Mark especially. He had a thick chip on his shoulder. While we chugged along the coast, they were, of all things, talking about religion.

Bob looked at me as if wondering whether to say what was on his mind, and then spoke up. "This out here is our church. You can't feel God, whoever that is, out here, I'm sorry." Bob's comments surprised me. I didn't respond.

We rumbled along for ten or fifteen miles. I stood outside breathing in deeply the vivid salt air. Most of the fishermen and women who had chartered this boat were waiting inside the cabin, hopeful.

Suddenly the boat made a sharp turn to the north, almost a ninety-degree angle. Bob must have avoided some huge floating log.

Rufus, the lowest ranking of the four crewmen, opened the sliding door of the cabin and told me Bob wanted me. Once I went up to him, he pointed to an area of ocean between the mountains.

"That, out there, is the reason we do this."

"What do you mean?" I couldn't see anything deserving of a ninety-degree turn.

"See that humpback whale jumping out of the water? Look, way out there." Bob was genuinely excited, standing up to steer instead of steering with his toe. The glare-reducing sunglasses wrapped around his dark features made him look like someone you wouldn't want to be trapped with in a dark alley.

My eyes scanned the water's surface and saw nothing. Bob wasn't very descriptive, I was just expected to see it. Plus, these guys don't have much patience. By now, the whole crew, Mark, Rufus, and blond Jake were all in the cabin. All four of them saw the whale leap again, except for me. All I saw this time was some splash, way off.

The first time I'd met Jake, I'd asked him where he spent the winter. He asked me if he looked smarter than a bird. I said he did, Mark said he didn't. Jake asked me if birds were smart enough to fly south to Mexico or California for the winter. I said yes, and he answered that he flew south too, to Hawaii or the Caribbean, where he stayed from October to sometime in May.

"How far away are we now from the whale?" I asked.

"A mile or so. They normally breach a few times, then stop," Bob said, not hiding his disgust with me for not being able to see this rare occurrence from afar. The easy normalcy of just getting to the shark-fishing grounds off Montague was being traded away with wide-eyed excitement, and these men have seen whales breaching hundreds of times.

"Typically, the whale would have stopped by now," Bob said, his gaze focused on the area where the whale had been performing for them. "And I would not attempt to go this far out of our way, but this humpback's been jumping quite a bit more than usual. Sometimes one will jump and jump, breach and breach, over and over." Bob pushed the shiny stainless-steel lever that controlled the speed of the engines forward.

"There it is," I said. Finally I could see the splash and some of the falling body of the whale.

Then a few minutes later there it was again. This time I saw the whole body but the fluke come out of the ocean. With these guys, I could never be sure if they were serious or setting me up. I moved onto the bow into the fullness of the wind, and the whale came out of the water twice in close succession.

"These humpbacks have the world's most powerful muscles. Can you imagine how strong they must be to propel their thirty tons or forty tons [sixty-thousand to eighty-thousand pounds] almost completely out of the water like this one's doing now." I tried to imagine me breaching. I doubt Greg Louganis could breach. Before this moment the word *whale* for me had always denoted fat, overweight, not coordinated or graceful.

We were now less than a half mile away from the whale; Bob slowed the boat to about half speed. The whale had returned to its underwater world. All five of us looking intently out to sea could not find the whale.

"He's done. Let's go find some sharks," Mark growled. At six foot two, 220, he was a muscled-up fishing machine who *liked* to fight with commercial fishermen. Mark, twenty-seven, had grown up in New Hampshire before moving to Florida.

The weather was doing things that seemed odd to me but were normal for Alaska. It was very localized. Offshore we could see blue skies and a drying sun, yet here in close to shore, the mountains and glaciers created a hanging fog blanket that lay atop the midranged, spruce-covered mountains. Where had the whale gone?

Bob slowed to an idle as everyone searched around us, hoping for more. The clients wanted more; a display like this was what most people dreamed of seeing in Alaska. We circled slowly when we reached where Bob thought the whale had been last, not far off Danger Island.

Then I heard a jolting splash, as if a plane had dropped a boulder the size of this boat out of the sky. *Bam,* the whale was back. It jumped and jumped and leaped again, a ton of water splashing up all around it. It did not enter cleanly headfirst back into the ocean; it landed on its ample side. This is what generated the splash, the noise—the impact of the whale on the water. I wondered if the humpback could arch and reenter headfirst. Was there any reason for it to land on its side? I recalled what a belly flop felt like off a diving board, how painful it was entering the water wrong. It sometimes took my breath away, left red marks on my skin. How about sixty-thousand pounds of whale landing on its side. Did it hurt? Why did whales do it?

Whale specialists are not sure why humpbacks breach. Some say breaching is some kind of message to other whales, or a warning, a dramatic type of body language to other whales or boats to stay away. Some have speculated that it's a way for whales to pop off irritating barnacles or get rid of sea lice on the humpback's skin. Officially, no one but the whale knows for sure. I doubt this breaching was any sort of message to us, or anyone. We had been three miles or more from it when Bob had first seen it rocket out of the water. This whale seemed to be all alone.

We sat and watched, and nothing. I'd loaded my camera with film. Maybe I should have turned on the motor drive, but I didn't.

Up again it came, whoosh, an immense sound generated by a combination of the whale thrusting up into the air and the water falling off. Then, less than a minute later, the whale breached again, then in about thirty seconds, again. What fantastic pictures I hoped I was getting. I had only tiny bits of time to turn and shoot.

These extraordinary moments of purity and pure power had created a silence among this crew of irreverent men. As we sat idling in neutral, the whale's long, white flipper, close to a third of its body length, went straight up in the air less than a hundred yards away. The whale flopped it to and fro, appearing to be deeply relaxed. Bob eased us up toward it slowly. This close to it, we could see some of its massive black body in the Coke-bottle-colored water. This whale had come to the Montague Strait for the same reason we had. The powerful incoming and outgoing currents carried massive amounts of aquatic life. This whale ate forty-five to fifty-five hundred pounds of living things every day.

While we watched, it lolled around, flapping its snow-white flipper for a few minutes in this new restful state, like me back-floating in a sun-warmed Vermont lake. Bob had turned off the motors; there was just an occasional breeze across the cheek, and almost no sound except from some distant waves crashing. Then the whale came back to the surface within seventy-five feet of the bow and started slapping its tail on the top of the ocean. Bam . . . bam . . . bang . . . bam . . . bam . . . bang. When its tail hit flat, it made the banging sound; at an angle, it bammed!

The whale moved closer to us, even closer. I kept thinking how rare this was, how essential it was to focus on everything that was happening. Bam. Salt water splashed high up into the sky. The whale's fluke was at least ten feet across and almost completely black, with just a few white edges. Some whales' flukes are almost completely white; like fingerprints, none are identical.

I was in prolonged, pronounced ecstasy thanks to this whale in the midst of the head of Prince William Sound. This location was only reachable by a substantial boat like *The Legacy*, by hard-core fishermen like these, willing to ride for a few hours and risk the erratic and dangerous maritime weather.

The whale's tail-slaps continued to send water through the air and shower those of us in the front of the bow. Mark was standing near me; he tapped me on the shoulder and pointed toward the whale. "Look at that brown color in the water. The whale's taking a dump."

He was right. The water directly around the tail was brick brown; the rest was perfectly blue-green. A whale relieving itself, excreting waste—how could that be happening, especially now? The vision before us that just moments before was the height of natural holiness now seemed, ah, wet and dirty.

The whale slapped its tail again and again. The brick-brown water coming directly from the back end of its tail was spreading with every slap. Because it was surrounded by the forever of the blue-green ocean, it was quite easy to see. Then it hit me. I am no marine biologist; I've been known to eat a lot but certainly not over two tons of food. The whale is a mammal, I'm a mammal; we do some things the same.

Could it be possible that when whales are breaching, it is not always just to celebrate being alive? It may not always be because they are feeling good. What if this humpback, while gulping down part of a school of herring, accidentally swallowed a couple silver salmon? What if the whales have learned that by breaching and landing on their side, they can release blockages, built-up gases? What if breaching can give some relief for whale constipation? The whale slaps its tail on the water to further assist in the release of whale waste. Imagine a hundred-and-fifty-plus feet of intestine, processing four or five thousand pounds of seafood in a day. Thank God humans don't drink salt water.

The whale settled on its side, seeming happy, if *happy* is a word that relates to whale behavior. There was no doubt the whale was contented. There was no more leaping. Then it sank back into the depths and did not return. It was probably feeding time again. Another meal, another ton or two of herring.

Bob started up the engines and we headed east toward San Juan Bay, looking for the salmon shark.

10

Termination Dust

It was just late September and the season's creeping had begun. It was coming to take most of our colors away. Termination dust had already come to the top of the highest mountain peaks. Termination dust is what the first snowfalls are called, and it's a sign that enormous changes are coming. It seemed to take much of the summer to clear off last year's snow from the high rock faces around us. Then the termination dust creeps down the mountain slowly toward where people live. Half of it might melt off, but it is always replaced and added to. Not long from now almost everything would be void of color; at times our whole world would seem white.

Oddly, now was the most brilliantly colored time of year. Wild blueberry bushes that seemed to cover whole mountainsides were bright shades of red. Sometimes, as if to exclaim the brilliance, a cone-shaped, blue-green spruce would rise from the fields of red. Living in Alaska is in some ways like being a manic-depressive. You have a couple months of almost perpetual daylight, when every bit of your world is alive and breeding and blooming and offering itself up. There is no time to sleep. People and animals who have adapted to Alaska know that is the time to gather sustenance for the coming dark and cold, the hibernation time. You run here, run there, exhaust yourself; live, laugh, so many possibilities. In Barrow, as far to the north as I would go in Alaska, the sun comes up around May 10 and doesn't set again until around August 2. That's eighty-five straight days of light. Talk about light therapy. Then the trade-off comes; in winter they have seventy-seven days without sunlight.

On June 15 in Seward we had nineteen hours of daylight. On December 15 we would have nine hours. Then, no matter how hard you try, your jaw yawns, it seems to stretch and fall, your eyes seem to close involuntarily. Sometimes you feel like going to bed at 7 P.M. After an entire winter you feel your face is melting into a sleeping blob. Didn't I feel that I had too much energy three months ago? A triple shot of espresso in your Americano only keeps you wired for a half hour.

The termination dust crept down Paradise Peak first and had now appeared for the first time on Mount Benson, which we could see from our new home in the nearly empty fourplex. At the end of August, we had moved from the Tougases' old house to this apartment about a block down the hill. It was just Rita, Julianne, and I now, until next summer. Rebekah had returned to Nashville to start her sophomore year in the honors program at Belmont University. Aaron was going to live in our house in Tennessee and feed the cows over the winter. He was a full-time student at Middle Tennessee State University, studying criminal justice. Our farmer neighbor Hubert Ward, who was retired from construction but had grown up raising cattle, was going to make sure that our cow herd did well. I told him he could cut the hay off our place. He said he was doing it for "no reason other than to be neighborly." Brooke was going to get a new job and attempt to juggle the demands of single motherhood and self-sufficiency. Luke was going to be in the eighth grade, and Jed was going to be a junior in high school. They live with their mother. They had all made a big bunch of money in Alaska and had had a summer filled with thrills and challenges.

We moved to an upstairs apartment. Heat rises. I had not lived in a place this small, other than a tent, since college. There were two tiny bedrooms, a bathroom, and combined kitchen/living area. In the summer, it was used to house tour-boat captains, like Mike and Joe, and boat-crew members all who took people to see the orcas and humpbacks and puffins and glaciers. All summer we'd all burnt our own candles from both ends, lighting up our own skies with all of our own activities and time spent together. Now my candle was flickering—I missed the kids, and they seemed so far away.

When I met Alaskans and told them that I'd been here for the summer, the reaction was often "Yeah, so what?" Most would give me this look, which I didn't at first understand, until Darien at Espresso Simpatico handed me my usual one morning the first week of October and seemed surprised I was still in town. A dog could lie down in some streets, the Bardarsons' horses could graze on the corner, and there wouldn't be enough traffic to worry about now. The ravens' voices were the dominant sound again at the bottom of our hill.

"When are you leaving Alaska?" Darien asked. He looked up from his serving window in the coffee-cup-shaped structure toward Mount Alice. A fresh dash of termination dust was on it, like a light dose of powdered sugar on a well-done pound cake.

"We're not," I said.

"You're *staying* the winter?" he said, sounding surprised.

"Yeah, how could you understand this place and not live here for a winter?"

"You know, winter is many Alaskans' favorite time of the year. We just don't advertise it."

Darien looked at me differently from then on, as if I were one of them instead of one of those just passing through.

When you ask people who live in Alaska how long they've lived here, many answer with the number of winters they've lived through. I heard plenty of people say, "Fifteen winters" . . . "Eight winters" . . . "I came up for the summer, been here four winters."

I was leaving town. I had an eventual destination, a musher's place near Denali, but first I thought I would take a road trip and see what the coming of winter felt like. It was the first week of October. I would drive the road triangle. It was small for Alaska, big for anywhere else. This triangle is what almost everyone who drives anywhere in Alaska must ride on. Not that many people actually drive all the way to Alaska anymore. They either take a cruise ship through the island passage and never make it out of Southeast Alaska or take a longer cruise and end or begin in Seward. Before the road through Canada, the main way into Alaska for people other than Natives was to take a ship to Seward and the train into the interior.

The triangle is made up of Route 1, Route 2, and Route 3. Route 1 actually goes from Homer 554 miles northeast to the town of Tok. I'd take the road out of Seward until I connected with Route 1 at Tern Lake, then head up to Tok. Just about everyone who comes to Alaska and doesn't stay in the southern strip of the state comes through Anchorage. Until June 2001, U.S. senator Ted Stevens was head of the Appropriations Committee; they pass out all the money. Some say he is the second or third most powerful person in the U.S. Alaska has more federal money spent on its roads per person than any other state. I'm sure that's because it's so expensive to build and maintain roads in

Alaska. I heard more people call him Uncle Ted than anything else. I'm surprised there are not statues built in his honor everywhere.

It only took me a couple hours and a few spare minutes to get to Anchorage. From there, it was 328 miles to Tok (pop. 935). (Tok's not a community established by hippies.) It is almost always the first Alaskan town anyone driving to Alaska comes to. When it's fifty below zero in winter, the children of Tok don't have to go to school, but most do anyway. It's one of those kinds of towns where the school is the center of the community. From Tok, I was going to go to Fairbanks, 206 miles, then down the third leg of the road triangle back to Anchorage. That stretch, passing Mount McKinley and Denali Park, is 358 miles.

I was discovering the truth to the adage that Alaska, although the most formidable and intimidating place I've ever been, was really like a small town. A week before Rita and I had been having lunch at Resurrection Road House. It's on the road to Exit Glacier. I thought I saw a couple mountain goats across the Resurrection River, pure white specks moving among the hard rock. Maggie Kelley, who worked there and had become a friend, came over to say hello. She asked how our Alaskan experience was going. She was one of the Alaskans who had come up to fulfill a dream and work for the summer but never went back home, in her case upstate New York. Maggie asked if we were finding everything we were looking for. I told her that we were finding so much more than we could ever have imagined. But I also mentioned that I was trying to find someone who was going to run the Iditarod, so that maybe I could train with him, follow him around, just absorb his world.

Maggie, whose eyes and whole face sparkle, but who is kind of quiet, said she knew a musher. Her first summer in Alaska, she dug ditches at a hotel around Denali Park, and her boss, who was doing maintenance, plumbing, and electrical, was a guy from California named Jeff King. Maggie said she'd call him; she did. He invited me, through Maggie, whom he trusted implicitly, to stop off at his place near Denali on the last leg of my October road trip.

Some said that fall in Alaska only lasted a week, and if I stayed gone that long, I'd see it all. Some said fall only lasted a day. Maybe for those overwhelmed by winter, it felt that way. I have always been able to sense group spirits, the combination of personalities that is a place. Some people think it's weird, but when I was walking across America, I could feel the spirit of a place, say Dallas, before I got inside the city limits, within sixty, seventy-five miles of the place. I thought I could feel a sense of foreboding in the air blowing through the storefronts in tourist-centered towns that were already closed or would soon be. What must it be like for those who dread winter, who fear its influence and dark, cold powers? Especially for those who have no way out? It might be like knowing that a hostile army of one hundred thousand was advancing on your town, marching forward, knowing you would be powerless once they arrived.

I was on the Glen Highway section of Route 1, which went through Glennallen, on the way from Anchorage to Tok. I'd heard a few Alaskans trash the area around Palmer and Glennallen as being filled with Christian fundamentalists and gun owners who had several weapons each. Being "filled" is a relative term since on the roadway between Anchorage and Tok, 328 miles, the only town that shows up on my road atlas is Glennallen (pop. 451). This area north and east of Anchorage is "supposed" to be the home of survivalists and anti-government types, but I've quit judging people by groups.

I'd just come into Glennallen, which is over halfway to Tok. It is in an enclosed valley about one hundred miles wide by seventy-five miles long. Mountain ranges enclose it, the Chugach Mountains to the south, the Talkeetna Mountains to the west, the Alaska Range to the north, and the Wrangell Mountains to the east. If you draw a circle two hundred miles in diameter around Glennallen, you would enclose most of the highest mountains in the United States. The chorus in Tom Petty's spare, energy-laced song "Into the Great Wide Open," sounded like the perfect sound track for this chilling land during this lonely time of the year.

Somewhere in front of Mount Drum I saw something amazing. There were two V's in the sky, headed down the valley toward McCarthy. I pulled over and turned off the Explorer and got out. The flying V's were white and stood out because a high layer of dark clouds was behind them. It was a flock of rare and elegant trumpeter swans leaving with this year's hatchlings, finally feathered and keeping up. It was so silent and there was so much space, I could hear them. Their wings passing over the land were like a flying magic wand giving warning that soon the world would be as white as they are. It could be tonight.

There isn't a great deal of color in the landscape other than green after the fireweed is gone. But the green doesn't last long. The first show of white down here where humans live are these departing flocks of trumpeter swans and the seeds from the cottonwood soaring in the cooling air. I was feeling a bit intimidated by the empty spaces all around me.

The swans honked sporadically to each other, getting farther away from me with each strong wing flap. It was so silent out here that the sounds came to me even from so far off. I was startled when four swans flew right overhead; the sound of their wings passing through the air is what first alerted me. Maybe they were a family trying to hook up somewhere with the rest of their kind.

The trumpeter swans were actually some of the last to leave. Several of the charter-fishing guys I'd gotten to know in Seward had already flown south, and many other seasonal residents had left. The summer was over. Why did so many people look at me as if I were nuts for wanting to spend the winter here? Then again, why did so many show us no respect until we said we *would* spend the whole winter?

It was October 6. Today was, statewide, the happiest day of the year. It's good timing to tell every permanent resident in Alaska how much money he or she will get from the state fund, right at the start of these postsummer blues. Let all those part-time Alaskans leave first, head for Hawaii or Mexico or Arizona. The Permanent Fund is what it's called, and it's supplied by Alaska's share of the oil money, plus the interest it makes. This year, each Alaskan citizen would get a check for $1,768.84. If you were a family in Glennallen with a mother and father and three children you got checks totaling $8,844.20. Don't even think about moving to Alaska just to get a check, you definitely earn it—you must live there one full calendar year, from January to December. So, for example, if you arrive in February, you will have to live there for almost two years.

In 2000, the Permanent Fund dividend was $1,963.86 each and was received by an estimated 585,800 Alaskans. These Alaskans evenly divided up about $1.15 billion, every citizen, no matter whether he or she is a street person in Anchorage or a multimillionaire in Sitka. Many disciplined Alaskans plunk their kid's check into mutual funds each year. By the time the kid is eighteen and ready to go to college or buy her first boat, she has a nice chunk of money.

Every Alaskan newspaper is full of ads when the dividend is sent out across the state, around the end of December, to promote spending, which usually occurs in January.

Alaska Newspapers, Inc., owns seven local newspapers: *The Arctic Sounder, The Tundra Drums, The Valdez Vanguard, The Dutch Harbor Fisherman, The Seward Phoenix Log, The Cordova Times,* and *The Bristol Bay Times.* When the Permanent Fund dividend is paid, they run an insert called "The Alaska Bushmaster, a Shopping Guide for Rural Alaska." The "What's Inside" index gives a succinct list of what is essential to survive in the Alaska bush. Some of the items listed: "Air Cargo." (You've got to get stuff to you, and as you know by now, there is often no road.) "Beds." (They take up too much space in air cargo; better to send them on a barge when the ice leaves.) "Cargo Sleds." (The ad said, "I even haul my eggs in it . . . and don't break any. S.B., customer.") A cargo sled, perhaps with options like a "rear gas-can rack," is of major importance when you live, say, in the village of Akiak, on the Kuskokwim River, and you've just made a run on your snow machine to Bethel to buy gas, eggs, cases of Coke, and other necessities. "Caskets." (The ad said, "Alaska Casket Co. caskets ½ price of Funeral Home cost. $700–$850 wood and cloth covered. $3,000 Copper. Shipped anywhere in Alaska.") "Chain saws." (Used for cutting wood for heat and logs for your cabin, it's one of the most important tools anyone in Alaska owns.) "Four-wheelers." (In many busy communities in Alaska, people don't have cars or trucks, they have four-wheelers.) "Generators." (For plenty of people, their own generator is the only electricity they will ever have.)

A highway sign let me know I was getting close to my destination: "Tok 10 miles. Canada 100 miles." I'd done an Internet search before I left and planned to stay for the night at a B&B named Winter Cabin, which had a nice Web site. I was to turn left at the intersection of Highway 1 and Highway 2, driving northwest toward Fairbanks. The B&B was just a couple miles more, somewhere off this road.

I pulled down a gravel side street back into some woods and saw a sign for Winter Cabin. As I pulled in farther, I could see four or five log cabins in the shadows, a large garage, and stacks and stacks of cut firewood. A powerful-looking woman, with long red hair and freckles who looked to be connected strongly to the earth, yet gentle, walked out of the oldest-looking log cabin. I learned this was the owner, Donna Blasor-Bernhardt, a widow who was born and had lived the first six years of her life in Kansas. She told me later that she never wears sleeveless shirts because her arms are so muscled. Her husband, who died young from a heart attack, was named Dick, and everyone called him Big Dick because he was six feet tall and 280 pounds; Donna could beat Dick arm wrestling. She invited me into her cabin to show me around. I was the only guest at the B&B—there aren't many travelers coming through Tok in October. I would get my first snow in Alaska in Tok, a mild, quick-melting, wet snow.

DONNA'S LIST

On Donna's refrigerator was a "Before Winter" list, with all the things Donna needed to do every year to get ready for winter. Winter in Tok needs to be spelled in all capital letters, WINTER. Once it got really cold, which could be soon, Donna could not leave her cabin again overnight until spring. Her "Before Winter" list was not just the list of a compulsively organized person, it was a matter of survival.

Most of her list had already been done and crossed off by the time I arrived. Winter in the interior of Alaska is an intensely serious property- and life-threatening experience. The silent, invading severe cold can wreak havoc, drive its victims insane. It can crush and kill the weak, people who would not be called weak anywhere else. Imagine having plumbing, water and sewer pipes, in places where it gets fifty below zero. When the temperature drops to zero degrees Fahrenheit or below, she turns *off* her freezers. When it is below zero, especially way below zero, the motors have to work too hard to "warm" the freezer up to the proper temperature. The consequences of not respecting winter in Alaska can be extreme. Consider not being able to leave your shelter from sometime in October until the end of March, even April if you heat your home with wood. It's the reason the dreamers who come to Alaska to live in the wilderness don't make it through the winter unless they are extraordinarily prepared or living in southern coastal places. It's the reason Donna spends months carefully carrying out and crossing off the "to dos" on her list.

Donna Blasor-Bernhardt "Before Winter" List

1. Gas in gas barrel. (*She couldn't afford it this year.*)
2. Firewood, need 10 cords. (*Donna cuts it herself.*)
3. Fill propane tank. (*It runs the cooking stove and propane lights.*)
4. Caulk B&B logs. (*It's a never-ending job, keeping the spaces between logs sealed in the three cabins.*)
5. Sand B&B logs. (*To accept the oil that preserves the logs.*)
6. Oil B&B logs. (*To keep logs from rotting.*)
7. 1,000 gallons of diesel fuel in bathhouse tank. (*The fuel Donna, her son, and his family need to heat hot water for showers, laundry, etc.*)
8. Get Pea's medicine. (*Pea is Donna's old neutered male cat.*)
9. Make wildberry jelly from rose hips, cranberries, raspberries, and blueberries.

(She made plenty of jelly, using everything except blueberries, because the bears beat her to her favorite patch.)

10. Clean out freezers. *(Of old moose and caribou. It's two years old, Donna will can it.)*
11. Stop my roof leaks. *(This wasn't done yet.)*
12. Stop B&B roof leaks. *(Done.)*
13. Replace stovepipe. *(Done. One of the most dangerous things in an Alaskan winter is for a rusted-out stovepipe to catch a cabin on fire on some ten-dog night.)*
14. Get monitor heater. *(No, she can't afford it this year, very popular in Alaska, and also quite expensive.)*
15. Cut wildflowers and weeds on roof. *(There are two inches of self-hardening foam on top of her cabin roof. I've seen entire trailers coated in the stuff. Then on top of that there are six inches of dirt, where Donna has planted poppies, fireweed, and other wildflowers. The fireweed grows six feet tall. One winter she thought she'd leave them, like a huge dried-weed arrangement, but then a spark from the woodstove started a wildfire on her roof.)*
16. Get cat food and litter. *(She got eight fifty-pound bags of each.)*
17. Clean out floor fridge. *(In the middle of Donna's kitchen is a trapdoor, which opens to a naturally cold food-storage place.)*
18. Pick all veggies in the greenhouse.
19. Stack firewood. *(There seemed to be a woodsful of neatly stacked wood.)*
20. Get studded tires put on van.
21. Put new block heater on van. *(You must keep your engine warm or it will never start. In Fairbanks, where Donna goes for shopping and medical attention, people either leave their vehicles on or plug them in.)*
22. Stock up on groceries, toilet paper, etc. *(The "etc." cost hundreds and hundreds and hundreds of dollars.)*
23. Get winter supply of computer ink, paper, etc. *(Donna's a writer, too.)*

Donna's survival depends on her ability to do much of the work herself, but to afford all the fuel and supplies, she must do well with her B&B in the summer, Alaska's harvest time. It takes all her income from her B&B, her Permanent Fund check, and more to keep her world going. She would have it no other way.

After Donna had shown me around her place, she invited me into her small cabin for tea. She sat like the mother of the earth in the corner surrounded by her collection of books and told me about moving to Alaska. She remembers it

Donna and her largest chain saw in Tok.
PHOTO BY PETER JENKINS

as if it were last night, though she was only six years old. One of her favorite people in the furnace that Kansas can be in summer was the iceman. He came once a week to deliver ice to her granddad. She'd sit on the brick front porch waiting for the iceman as heat came off the road in waves big enough for an imaginary surfer. When he opened the back door of his truck, she would rush around to feel that blast of cold air.

"I was six years old, and I ran out to my granddad's carpentry shop and said as excited as a six-year-old could get, 'Granddad, guess what? We're moving to Alaska!'" Donna's green eyes seemed to open as wide as they must have then.

"Grandpa let out a terrible sigh and said, so very slowly, his voice lowered, 'You . . . are . . . going . . . to . . . the . . . end . . . of . . . the . . . world.'"

Donna's big cat, Sweet Pea, climbed up in her lap.

"I wanted to go to the end of the world, although that scared me just a bit— only until I saw my first northern lights and mountains. It took us seventeen days to get from Pittsburg, Kansas, to Anchorage. I was in love with Alaska before we ever got here." Donna's voice contained wisdom and warmth in equal measures.

Their old truck, which her dad had bought out of a farmer's field, had holes in the floorboard and the heater didn't work. Her feet were the only ones in the family that stayed warm, because the family dog lay on hers. They left right after Christmas 1950 and arrived in January 1951. The road to Alaska hadn't been open long, and she remembered that the grades and curves were wicked. A couple hills were so steep that they had to get out of the truck and walk partway up.

Donna met her husband while both worked at the post office in Anchorage, and in 1964 they married and subsequently had two children. In 1977, while Donna was out exercising, some weirdo tried to grab her and pull her into his car. She and her husband had wanted to live out by themselves; that incident gave them the reason. That whole summer of 1977, they traveled like gypsies, looking for a place to settle. They loved the area around the Taylor Highway toward Dawson, in the Yukon, but no land was available. They didn't want to go back to Anchorage; the idea of living out in the wilderness had captured them. Somehow they found out land was for sale around Tok. They drove there and discovered that land cost $50 down and $50 a month. They bought a plot, just off Route 2 in some flat land covered in cold-stunted spruce.

They cut some trees, made a clearing, and set up an army surplus canvas tent that measured sixteen feet by thirty-two feet, just like in the TV series M*A*S*H. It had no liner. They were kidding themselves that it would be warm enough, but while they were building their log cabin to live in, it was the only choice they had. Alaska in the summer in the interior can be so warm, so sunny, so blue-skyed, and so perfect it can seem like a time of ease and relaxation. Even some Alaskans who should know better become seduced. How could it be seventy-five or eighty-five degrees in Tok in July and be minus forty degrees three or four months later? Somehow, they survived the winter.

Donna and Dick loved their new land and life even if the only income they had was cutting firewood. They put up a paper plate at the local grocery store, a few miles away, that said, "Firewood for sale. Cut, split, delivered, and stacked. $65 a cord." Interested people would write down their names, and Donna would call them from the store's pay phone.

One night in January, it was sixty below zero outside the tent. They had down sleeping bags and a roaring fire, but the heat didn't last. Dick had been to the outhouse; now that's an experience, especially if you have to sit down at sixty below zero. They got their first outhouse from the government, a "worn-out" one with a metal seat. No one wants to imagine a metal seat and bare buttocks at forty below, much less sixty below. Two-hundred-eighty pound Dick came back into the tent overwhelmed. Donna wondered if something had happened outside.

"Dick told me to come outside. I thought something was wrong. Our bunny boots crunched real loud on that snow. He pointed up, but he didn't need to. The northern lights were unbelievable. There was a big moon too. The northern lights are usually green, but these had pink shooting through them. It was magic looking up through the black outlines of the spruce to the dancing, darting lights. They washed across the top of the sky like wave after wave. I could feel the hair on my arms stand straight up. Dick grabbed me and we danced under those lights. I cried, it was all so wonderful." Donna's eyes teared up all over again.

"I never danced. I just didn't. I'm not the type. But Dick was so strong; he had hands the size of bear paws. He just took me in those tattooed arms of his and we waltzed or something under the lights of magic and awe. We had single cots and somehow we ended up in the snowbank. Let's just say the next morning the indentation in the snow was not a snow angel. Or was it?"

Her story finished, Donna got up from her chair. The chair's arms were covered with little brown muskrat furs. She spent much of the winter in this chair, reading, or in her chair at her computer. Outside her little cabin window, she feeds the chickadees, magpies, three different kinds of woodpeckers, red squirrels, and flying squirrels. Also outside that window this time of the year is Marigold, the mama moose, who has come around Donna's cabins eight winters in a row. She stays till spring, when she's had her calf. One time Marigold had triplets. Some of the largest wolves in Alaska live around Tok, and they do major damage to moose in the winter that are not as smart as Marigold. Being this close to Donna, she has never lost a calf to predators.

Donna stoked the woodstove. It should snow soon, she said. Normally—though really, there is no such thing—by Halloween the temperature is usually steady at twenty to thirty below zero. Donna said she was ready to turn in. She reminded me I could use the bathhouse or the outhouse. She wanted to be sure I knew about her outhouse. The outhouse was surrounded with glowing, little tiny Christmas lights, and it gave off a faint red, yellow, blue, and white glow to the black-dark woods around it. Once she made a fur cover for the toilet seat, but it is the big award of which she is the most proud. A few months after Dick, the love of her life, died too young in February 1987, she entered a statewide contest: the First Annual Alaska Outhouse Contest, put on by *The Cordova Times*. Entries were accepted from all over the state. Categories included the "Prettiest Outhouse," "Outhouse with the Best View," "Outhouse Detrimental to Human Health" (built on the edge of a cliff, say), and the "Governor's Award." The Cordova folk chose all the winners except the Governor's Award, which was selected by Governor Steve Cowper. Donna wrote a poem about hers called "The Saga of One Great Alaskan Outhouse." She sent along a series of pictures showing its progression from hole in the ground, to A-frame, to a larger house built around it, to their Christmas picture, where it is outlined in Christmas lights with two candy canes on the door. Governor Cowper chose Donna and Dick's outhouse as top Alaska outhouse. She's left the Christmas lights up permanently since Dick passed away.

When I got up the next morning, I saw we'd had a surprise snow that had come in from the direction of Sixty-Mile Butte. It was my first Alaskan snow. I said good-bye to Donna. She'd put up her long red hair and was going to cut up and stack some more firewood with her two chain saws. She had a feeling the winter would be a demanding one. When Alaska has an extratough winter, it is like a two-year-old child you can't take your eyes off, even for a second, unless he's asleep, and sadly he doesn't sleep much. Winters like this wear you down, Donna said; they require all your attention, they cannot be ignored.

I headed northwest on Route 2. Luke, my only redheaded child, not my only one with freckles, had left his Creed CD here after the summer, and I'd gotten into listening to it. Luke and I have a talent for leaving things everywhere. The haunting power of Creed's music seemed small in Alaska. I listened to them with the windows down all the way through Delta Junction and Moose Creek. I was almost to North Pole. Then came Fairbanks. It's the home of the University of Alaska, which you'd better not confuse with the University of Alaska at Anchorage. That would be almost as bad as getting the University of Michigan and Michigan State, or UCLA and USC, confused. Past Fairbanks, I blew through Nenana, the home of several excellent Iditarod-class mushers, including Jerry Riley, Rick Mackey, and Bill Cotter. Another fifty miles or so, somewhere between Healy and Cantwell, past the entrance to Denali Park, I would be getting close to Jeff King's home.

11

Howls of Glee

I found the hidden entry through some thick spruce and figured I must be on the right driveway because there were a few yellow signs on a couple trees, one showing a team of sled dogs. I could hear dogs barking. At the top of the hill were the most sled dogs I'd ever seen in one place, each with its own wooden house. The young ones, the ones that were slim and hyper, moved around the most and so were farthest from the big house. A construction project was under way, with lots of workmen around. It looked like a garage and a few rooms over it were being built to connect to the older house. The front door, an arctic entry, was open, and I could see a step or two up into the kitchen.

I would come back to spend some time with Jeff King several times over the next several months to watch him train his dogs for the 2000 Iditarod. This first time, I don't know what I was expecting; my friend Maggie had known him and his wife for years and thought enough of them to encourage me to meet them. I knew he'd won the Iditarod three times. I'd heard from a couple people that he was a hard-ass, but I disregarded that. People in Alaska have strong feelings about Iditarod mushers. Everyone has a favorite. It is their Super Bowl, World Series, U.S. Open, Final Four, Stanley Cup, Daytona 500. The musher must be the coach, the trainer, the breeder, an intense athlete, and team spokesman. The dogs don't do interviews—too bad, because they'd have so much to say and probably notice more than some mushers do. In Alaska you choose your musher, and if you're an impassioned fan, you don't like your rivals. Families are divided, couples disagree. Mushing dogs, especially for the Iditarod, is so all-consuming in Alaska that when you walk into superstores in Alaska, you won't see a life-size cutout of some NFL or WWF or NBA superstar, you'll see one of a musher.

At Jeff King's, I could hear loud music coming from a stereo inside, Marshall Tucker. My knock went unheard; I knocked again. Nothing. I stepped inside, where I could see a small, thin guy with messed-up hair and a mustache sitting at the kitchen table. He was looking at some newspaper articles and wiping tears from his eyes. He didn't see me at first. When he did, he pushed the newspaper clippings into a pile, handed them to me, and stood up. He seemed embarrassed, as I'm sure I would have been.

"You must be Peter. I was looking over these family pictures, these newspaper stories from way back when I first married Donna, when I started mushing dogs taking loads up McKinley. When I first won the Yukon Quest and realized I might be able to be a musher. Donna and I looked so young. It just got to me. Here, I got these for you to look at. I'll be back in a minute." Their parakeet stood on top of its cage making some odd sound, and their only non–sled dog, a Border collie, came over and introduced herself.

Jeff has the tightened energy of a wolverine. People who have seen wolverines in Alaska say they are always moving, working, running, thinking, calculating, hunting, plotting their next move. Jeff is that way. He naturally searches for your weakness, it's the inborn competitor in him. He's always been this way and it's made him a kind of loner too. He warns everyone, because he is so aware of this intense trait, that he has little patience. He played a team sport in California where he grew up—football. As a 140-pound quarterback at Shasta Junior College, Jeff would take on at full speed a 230-pound linebacker. He would rather pit himself and a dog team against anything in primeval Alaska.

Jeff moved to Alaska to be a bushman, to draw his living from nature, to build and gather and hunt what he needed. He never planned or dreamed about becoming one of the best dog mushers of our day. He first tried mushing not as a race but to haul equipment up Mount McKinley for mountain climbers. Knowing Jeff, I think he found it a major rush coming down the highest mountain in North America empty, holding on to that long sled as it whipped back and forth, powder flying in his face. He probably let out one of his howls of glee.

When he first decided to try racing, his analytical, practical mind crunched the facts. He had two choices. He knew these long-distance races take years of experience for the dogs and the humans to succeed. He could start out with the Iditarod, already ten years old in 1984, or run the Yukon Quest and get in on the ground floor. Virtually the whole route of the Yukon Quest is accessible by road. Dog food and other supplies needed for the thousand-mile race are much easier to get to supply points, therefore the race is quite a bit cheaper to run. About half of the Yukon Quest is not only run through Canada but on the frozen Yukon River. Jeff felt running on the wide ice was boring, but it made the race feel shorter.

Late one night on the Yukon River, during the 1989 Yukon Quest, Jeff and his dogs got as close to a major catastrophe as he's ever been.

Jeff has cat-quick physical reactions and yet also the ability to keep analyzing future possibilities in a kind of slow motion. I've seen him fall off a sled in training going over a frozen spring, roll in the air, and hit the snowy ground on his side so he can grab hold of the sled with his good hand and pull himself back aboard. One thing I didn't realize in dog mushing: you fall off the sled, your dogs often don't stop. They leave you where you land, and that can mean frostbitten body parts or freezing to death, depending on where you're training. He did not foresee what would befall him this thirty-eight-degrees-below-zero night. On the trail, where Jeff and his team of athletes were in the lead, they ran into one of the hidden frozen black-nightmare dangers that lie in wait for those who move across the supposedly frozen far north.

"It was the year after I froze my hand and had had to withdraw. The Yukon Quest is run in February; our house caught on fire that year in January. After all that, I was determined to run the race," Jeff told me.

What he didn't tell me until later was that a couple years before this night, he'd been cutting out some stair risers with a circular saw at a construction site, and somehow the saw slipped. He almost cut off his left hand. He knew enough first aid to grip the wound in a kind of death grip with his other hand. The saw had cut everything in his wrist except the bones. He knew he had to hold that grip to keep from bleeding to death. One of the most powerful memories he has of this accident is that when they checked him into the clinic in Healy, they wrote down "musher" as his occupation. This was well before he knew if he was going to be able to make a living mushing. In the 1988 Yukon Quest, not long after the accident, he and his team had crossed a high, open part of the trail. The windchills were one hundred degrees below zero, and because of his considerable nerve damage and circulation problems, he couldn't feel his left hand and it froze. Jeff said it looked like something on a frozen corpse.

We were sitting in the living room one evening, talking about the night in the 1989 Yukon Quest. "I was first team into Dawson City, which is in the Yukon Territory of Canada," he continued. Above Jeff's head was the tanned hide, including the head, of an interior grizzly. They are significantly smaller than the coastal brown bears, as there is not nearly as much to eat up here around McKinley. And they are more aggressive. This bear made the mistake of thinking Jeff's dogs would make an easy meal. Eating one of Jeff and Donna's dogs would be about as risky for a bear as trying to eat one of their daughters. Although they have eighty dogs, each one is part of the family. Without them Jeff couldn't race and, therefore, support his family.

"At Dawson City, there is a mandatory thirty-six-hour stop. When it's done, you leave. At that point in the race I was ahead maybe a couple hours. It was cold and clear, the team had been doing some excellent running. My time to leave was eleven P.M. I was thankful to go out alone."

Jeff picked up a guitar that was on the floor and leaned it against the wall.

"I knew there were a number of open leads on the river," he said.

"An open lead is a place where there is no ice on the river. When it's as cold as it was, thirty-eight below zero, the open water creates a heavy fog. It makes it hard to see how to get around the lead. Obviously, getting wet at thirty-eight below could be a big problem."

Most people I know would not be able to deal with what Jeff King considers a big problem.

"I was in a hyper state of awareness. I wound my way down the trail until we finally came out of the fog. I could see the stars; it was a brilliant night. The aurora borealis was bouncing in the sky. I knew up ahead there were a couple cabins; the mushers always wanted to know if there would be anyone at Forty Mile Cabin or Trout Creek or Woodchoppers Cabin."

It must have been warm and rewarding to come upon a little log cabin with an orange glow in the window and smoke coming out of the chimney at 2 A.M. on a bank above the frozen Yukon River.

"The cabins got their names when the paddle wheelers used to come up the Yukon during the short summers. They would resupply them with wood that they burned as fuel. I knew there would be a warm cabin. I planned to go non-stop into the night about thirty miles until I got to this cabin."

Jeff looked out the picture window. A frozen lake, where I'd seen a small group of caribou, was in front of a frozen-blue spine of mountains.

"I would give the dogs a fifty percent break. If it took us four hours to get there, I would rest them four hours. Once I got past the open water, it's one A.M. I'm sleepy, on autopilot. I would mostly keep my headlight off. There was a bright sky," Jeff said, reminding me.

I'd seen these bright skies late at night in Alaska. It was as if a blue light shined on everything.

"I allowed myself to doze off. I remember thinking I could quit paying attention and doze off, there would be no chance of going by the cabin. My eyes would close for a few seconds at a time. You can tell by the sounds of the dogs and the feel of the handlebar what's happening. The first ten years I ran dogs, when I fell asleep, I fell off the sled. Now I don't. I've gone so far on those runners that I can be asleep and balanced." Jeff was rubbing one of his hands.

"Then I felt the dogs surge forward. The handlebar tightened in my grip. I hit the switch, my headlight came on—I have a push button on my chest which by squeezing my right arm to my chest, it turns on the light. The first thing I noticed, the dogs were bolting away from something, which meant it was not a moose." Moose in the trail is one of the worst things that can happen, but not as bad as what was about to happen.

"The dogs had inadvertently come too close to an open lead. The snow is on top of the ice. I saw this black spot, water that wasn't frozen. That seems strange, I know, at thirty-eight below zero. I wanted to get away from this black spot. I let the dogs surge forward about twenty yards and I hit the brake. I could tell the team was on thin ice because it was undulating under them like a water bed."

Jeff's retired lead dog Falcon, one of two huskies allowed to roam free, came into the room and leaned against Jeff. Falcon had fur like a wolf. He was the only husky that would come in the house. The other one Jeff allowed to be loose was Kitty, the black-and-white queen of the lead dogs. Crippled and so old, she walked around and around the dog yard, keeping watch. As far as she was concerned, it was hers.

"I could tell by the dogs' body language they were scared. They were not wet, any of them. I took a step to walk up to them. The minute I stepped off the sled, I broke through into a foot of overflow water. It had frozen on top an inch. I immediately recoiled and stood back on the sled."

Now Falcon lay down on Jeff's feet. Donna told me later that when Falcon was one of the world's great lead dogs, his "problem" was that he concerned himself too much with what all the other dogs were doing. And he worried about what lay ahead. He was a worrier. Jeff scratched Falcon's ears.

"The dogs are looking back at me with a look that says, what are we supposed to do now? I could see the frost circles around their feet. That meant their bootees were now freezing to the ice."

Jeff went silent. I couldn't tell if he was trying to remember or did not want to continue. As I got to know Jeff, sometimes he would begin telling me some amazing story and then act as if he didn't want to finish, as if talking and sitting took up too much time that could be used for something else.

"I figured I would have to get off the sled, stay as far as I could from them, and go along beside them. My weight could have been all it took to break the sheet of ice we were on and drop us all into the water. I did have to get the bootees off their paws so they wouldn't be frozen there. I had to stay far enough from them so that we would not all fall through."

Jeff paused. Falcon looked up. He seemed to read the dynamics of every situation. Did he want to hear more? You could tell that anything Jeff had to say, Falcon wanted to hear it.

"The leader I had then was Tommy. He did not like this situation. I had another leader named Hickey; she would have been better around water. Sometimes I extend the lead dog an extra length so that they will have plenty of room to pick the trail. When I got their bootees off, I switched and put Hickey into the lead. She was one smart and self-contained leader."

The blue parakeet flew over and landed on my shoulder. Jeff said he was surprised, normally the bird didn't relate to strangers this soon. It seemed odd to see a parakeet in a place that got to fifty below outside.

"It's so hard to give them direction on the ice. I left the team and walked about fifty yards ahead, trying to scout a route. Right on the edge of this trail there was fast-moving water. Even though there is water so close to where we'd be going, and remember it's thirty-eight below zero, I felt Hickey could negotiate this place I'd just walked through."

On the wall was a watercolor of Jeff and his team running through a large herd of caribou. The caribou weren't spooked, just trotting along. If they had been, they'd leave a dog team, even one of Jeff's, in a cloud of snow. I asked Jeff about the painting, if it had really happened. He said it had, several times, and that Donna had done the painting. She was quite talented.

"There ahead of us was an open lead. Imagine a rushing stream, in the middle of the huge Yukon River, which is frozen hard. This stream could have broken out of the ice and now is running on top of the ice. The water could be a foot deep, it could be much deeper. The deeper it is, the more dangerous at this temperature."

We were interrupted by some workmen who were hanging and taping Sheetrock upstairs. They were looking for some coffee; Jeff made them a pot. When he got back, his face tightened up, as if he were feeling the stress of this situation all over again, facing possible permanent injury or death for him or some of his dogs. Getting sucked up by the current of the Yukon River, after 1 A.M., alone, when it's almost forty below, has got to be about as risky a moment as possible in Alaska. Sometimes reliving a situation like this, without the surging adrenaline to help you overcome it, can be more intense than the original experience.

"I walked back to the sled. I scratched Hickey's ears and explained to her how much I needed her to do this. I told her she would have to confidently leap into the water and swim across it aggressively without panicking. Her actions as leader would set the tone. Believe me, these dogs, all twelve of them, knew what a bad situation we were in."

Jeff had so much energy it almost sparked off his small frame.

"Hickey was not afraid of water, she kind of liked it, but more than that, I believe she wanted to be in that leadership position where it all relied on her. I fully expected her to be able to touch the bottom ice. Maybe the water was only a foot, foot and a half deep, deep enough to do some damage, especially to a human's bare skin. I walked back to the sled. I pulled the anchor [a stainless-steel double hook mushers use to secure their teams by placing it into the hard-packed snow or on a smallish tree]. I said, 'Hike.'"

I tried to visualize that blue dark night. What movements did the nervous dogs make? Which dogs were not fearful? The beam of light from Jeff's headlamp bounced here and there, not wanting to focus too much on the running water. Then there were the sounds of the running danger, "warm" compared to the thirty-eight-below-zero air temperature. And above, on the steep banks of the Yukon, were the dark shadows of the dense tree growth in which almost nothing lived this time of winter. Were any of the dogs whining? They were Jeff's closest friends, his team; his life depended on them and he would never reveal their moments of weakness or fear to anyone.

"Hickey, she followed my directions perfectly. First she followed my footprints. I was saying, 'Good girl, good girl.' I knew when she saw the open lead— only I'd seen it so far—she could not want to enter the water. This was the worst situation, the highest risk we could have been in. I was well aware that if Hickey and the two swing dogs balked and didn't dive right into that ice and water, it could be catastrophic. If she stopped and the rest of the team, who couldn't see what was ahead, kept going and pushed her and the swing dogs in, then they all could get tangled in the water."

The look of intense concern returned to Jeff's face.

"I'd taken Hickey through water before, that's why I picked her. As she came up on the edge where the solid river ice gave way to overflow, she balked. The swing dogs came up on her. I'm encouraging her. Telling her she can do it. Suddenly, she launches herself with all four feet like a Labrador retriever right into the flow. Then the swing dogs balked. At that exact second, I could tell she wasn't touching, it was deeper than she is, a bad situation now made much worse." Jeff began opening and closing, opening and closing, the hand he'd almost cut off with the saw.

"Then her momentum pulls the swing dogs in. I still figured it was water on top of the ice. The more dogs that got in the water, the more they pull the others in. The next good thing I saw was Hickey getting out on the other side. But there was still much bad that could happen with the other eleven dogs. Remember, every dog is tied together. We still had to get the sled and me through it. Now the dogs are like lemmings off a cliff, no dog is touching, they're all swimming. It wasn't really water as most people think of it, it was like a giant, rushing margarita." Ellen, the youngest of Jeff and Donna's three daughters, came in the room, her homework done, and told her dad he had to help review her spelling words. He sat her down in his lap and asked her to hold on until he finished this story.

"The seconds that all this takes slow way, way down. I'm evaluating. Okay, I should be able to touch bottom, get across in two or three big leaps. You try to take splashing giant steps. By now enough dogs are on the other side, I'm encouraging them like hell. I remember saying really loud, 'Hike, hike.' There are six dogs still in the water. I'm continuing to give them verbal commands, I give the sled a huge push and . . ." Jeff rearranged the way he was sitting on the sofa.

"I jump in next to the sled, and it's lying over on its side. The water is moving pretty fast. I instinctively tried to crawl on top of the side of the sled. I gasped as I felt the water and ice going into my suit. Four dogs were treading water in front of me trying like hell to pull me and the sled to the other side. Eight dogs were on the other side shaking off." Jeff looked to see if I was focused.

"I knew if I didn't get out of the frozen, rushing water, it would be over. It still might be. What if my matches fell out of the sled and washed away? I launched myself on top of the wheel dogs, the ones closest to the sled, then launched myself on top of the next two, then went hand over hand up the rope and dragged myself out on the other side."

Jeff seemed to turn pale, remembering getting through the water, so frozen, so deadly. Plenty of people have died in Alaska in the water in the summer. Outside that night, it was seventy degrees below the freezing temperature of water. Imagine immersing yourself in that behind a twelve-dog team, all tangled, some of your best friends howling and possibly drowning and frantic. All you can think about is making sure you make it across.

"There were four dogs still in the water. I tried to get the other eight to pull them and the sled out, but they were rolling around trying to get the water and ice off their fur. I hollered at them in this tone of voice that almost shocked me. They bolted to attention and they pulled out the first two. I yelled, 'Hike.' They pulled out the next two and so on, until they pulled the sled out, which was by now fully soaked." My adrenaline was flowing in the extreme. I heard what sounded like a wolf howling. It was a couple of Jeff's dogs outside. They must have heard something, because then it seemed that all eighty joined in. Some of them had to be part wolf.

"I immediately worried about my hand. I'd almost cut it off, and then in this same race, in 1988, frozen it when it was one hundred below zero. The hand was in serious jeopardy now that my mittens were wet. I tore through the sled for the waterproof bag which has dry gloves and dry mittens." Jeff didn't have to reach for these memories, they flooded up instantly. Situations where the outcome of your life is unknown never seem to fade far away.

At this point in his story, Jeff encouraged Ellen to go find her mom, maybe this time she could help with the spelling review. He put some water in the kettle for tea and came back and sat in a chair instead of on the sofa.

"It's a very long way from out here to the nearest hospital . . . you know the only two mushers I know who have died, died in situations where there was open water or breaking through the ice. One of my fiercest and nicest competitors, Bruce Johnson, from British Columbia, was doing a training run. His leaders didn't take his command and steered him out onto a lake. The middle wasn't frozen yet. Instead of abandoning the team, he stayed with them and they all drowned. So sad . . ."

Someone knocked on the front door. With three daughters, eighty dogs, and three handlers working for them, there was always something happening at the Kings'. Plus, Jeff was chief of the Volunteer Fire Department and Rescue Squad. A guy with a warm hat with earflaps walked in, needed to ask about some new piece of equipment. After he left, Jeff picked up the story again.

"As I stood there, soaked to the bone, I was no longer in danger of drowning—I was in danger of freezing to death. I evaluated how I could help myself and the dogs. Remember, put yourself in the place I was: twelve wet huskies and me, two hours ahead of the nearest team. I scanned the riverbank with my headlamp. It was twelve feet high. There were some large trees up there, but it would be almost impossible to get up that bank. I figured my best bet was to find a pile of driftwood."

Jeff planned to light this driftwood on fire. He had a hatchet, some dry matches, and a can of fire starter. He said he could not stop thinking about his favorite Jack London story, "To Build a Fire." In it a man traveling alone along the Yukon gets about half as wet as Jeff was that night, gets a fire going, but snow from the trees above blows down on top of it. The fire goes out, and his dog, with a warm body mass, watches the man freeze to death.

"After a trauma like that you never know what your dogs will do, how they will be affected. I gave them the forward command, they took off like a bolt, like if a moose jumped out in front of them and began running away. Their response to the dunking was jubilance and energy. They took off like it was the start of the race."

When Jeff talks of his dogs, his voice changes. It warms up and becomes lined with the emotion that comes from profound appreciation. You wouldn't want to be one of his competitors, but you would want to be one of his dogs.

"I couldn't at first stop thinking about my competitors. The dogs follow the trail of the team that is ahead. When we cannot see any trail, say in a blizzard, they can smell it. What if they followed me and someone died, or some dogs died? But right then, I still had to be concerned about my own life. I remember taking stock of my body, something I know well. I measured each square inch, my neck, my rib cage, my biceps, my stomach, all of it. Where was I completely soaked, where was I not wet? I had a suit on, one custom-made by a neighbor before Cabela's began making them. The suit was completely frozen stiff, rigid. It became like a suit of iron."

I could see Jeff was missing the tips of a few fingers on his left hand. "I had never been all-over wet before in a race. I remember moving my arms and fingers, trying to keep my dexterity so that when I came to the firewood, I would be able to grasp the match."

Donna walked through with Ellen to take her downstairs and tuck her in to bed.

"I was really taken by the energy of the dogs. I was having difficulty moving. Time passed, a half hour, then an hour. I was getting discouraged, seeing no firewood. We came around a bend in the river. There in the distance was a little red dot. The dogs saw that light. They took off like a streak of lightning. There is a custom on the Yukon: trappers and others will hang out a lantern on a branch for anyone coming through." By now the kettle had been whistling for quite some time, but Jeff ignored it.

"On this part of the river there were protruding blocks of ice the size of refrigerators. We bang into them, and they'd about throw me off the back. If I had been thrown off, I don't think the dogs would have stopped until they got to the cabin. I was still, immobile, shivering. I would try to run, holding on, to warm up and couldn't. I knew now I would live, but it seemed to take forever." Jeff talked as if this short run to the red lantern had taken place last week. He is the kind of human who needs a challenge, a test. He actually enjoys being challenged in extraordinary ways, just not when it involves getting soaked at close to forty below.

"Finally we got to the light. The dogs just peeled out; I got off the sled to try to lessen their load and run up the bank. I was a frozen cylinder. I could not run; they dragged me up the bank. I took off their harnesses, fed them, and went inside. The trapper inside, a Cree, had his head laid on the table. Four-fifths of a bottle of rum was gone. A pot of moose stew was on the woodstove. Inside the cabin was a real strong smell of rutabagas. This guy, a Canadian, was a musher sometimes. He had a thin, black beard and is very powerfully built. From out of nowhere, he lifts up his head and says twice, 'I killed a moose with a tomahawk yesterday. I killed a moose with a tomahawk yesterday. I ran it down through the deep snow.' Then his head hit the table."

What a treasure that warmth inside those four walls was. And to be able to eat warm moose stew.

"It took me the better part of an hour to get out of my clothes because I had to thaw the zippers. When I woke up, there were several teams parked at the bank of the river. I asked them if anyone had problems at the water. They said everyone did—everyone got wet. I was dry again, the dogs were rested. We took off, and that was the first big race we won, the 1989 Yukon Quest."

At the end of the story, Jeff jumped up as if he'd been asleep for a week. That was the longest I would ever see him sit still, though I spent several days with him, his family, and their dogs.

YOU READY?

During my second trip to see Jeff, we were training not far from Mount McKinley. I had been on a snow machine following Jeff and Morten, one of the handlers. Morten, twenty-three, from Denmark, and the other two handlers, Helge and Shawn, lived in a tiny log cabin off in the woods apart from the main dog yard. They kept the newly weaned puppies around them. Shawn Sidelinger was originally from Maine. Morten and Helge, twenty-two, from Norway, were enrolled in a Norwegian college similar to the monthlong wilderness programs run in this country by the National Outdoor Leadership School except theirs was a several-year program. Today Morten ran one team, Jeff another. Training is about determining which dogs that have already run the Iditarod will make the "varsity" again, have no nagging injuries or lagging competitive spirits, and then too, which of the young guns are pushing to make the team. More females finish the Iditarod than male dogs, although probably more males start out.

The thin trail wove through dense evergreen woods. It is so cold around McKinley, here on the outside edge of Denali Park, that trees grow slowly. I had seen instantly that if the dogs went the wrong way, you could crash into trees. I was following them slowly on one of Jeff's well-used snow machines. I'd seen Helge on this snow machine running the trails with the young puppies already, getting them to love running in the snow. They were already evaluating the pups' spirits, their minds, their physical prowess.

The trail broke out of the woods, and the two teams emerged into the middle of open, softly rolling country. Was this tundra on frozen wetlands? Jeff stopped, Morten stopped, and then I stopped. Jeff motioned me over to them.

"You ready?" he asked.

The dogs were barking and pulling on their harnesses, they hadn't even warmed up yet.

"Am I ready for what?" I answered, my eyes widening.

"To take over Morten's team."

Jeff looked at me sometimes the way an eagle would a wounded rabbit.

"I don't know, what do I do?"

The dogs, all of them, were barking even more excitedly. They wanted to take off. Come on, they were saying, let's hit the trail. They live to zoom across these snow-covered wilds.

"Just hold on, stand on the runners, and watch me. I don't suggest that you stop, but if you need to, push down on this." Jeff stepped on a metal bar equipped with long teeth. "Morten, you ride the snow machine, okay?"

I was more than a bit surprised, though I always try to be ready for surprises. We hadn't talked about me actually taking over a sled. I felt that I should have had some training, education, or at least more time to psych myself up. What if I made a fool of myself while being hauled through the snow by some of the greatest athletes in the world, these refined long-distance runners? But I couldn't say no. I knew Jeff was testing me. I knew he'd been watching me just to see if I could keep up on the snow machine, following the unmarked trails through this maze of their fierce winter world. I had already taken the wrong trail once and gotten stuck in the deep snow trying to turn the snow machine around. I had come to a fork in the trail, going downhill, and I could see sled trails and dog prints, but the trail split and the prints went both ways. They'd been on this segment maybe a few days before. I wasn't far down one fork when I realized I'd gone the wrong way. It made me understand why Jeff had waited until we got out into open country before allowing me the chance to ride. Running into an unmovable tree could be really damaging to my health.

Jeff will observe something astutely, whether human or dog. I'm not sure which he prefers or respects more; it probably depends on the individual. Then, if he can, he will push you—again, human or dog—into places within yourself you didn't know existed. As a trainer of world-champion long-distance racing dogs, dogs that can accomplish feats that are unmatched by any other athlete in the world, Jeff knows what to do. He observes, then makes a highly specific analysis. He then attempts to put the subject of his attention, whether it be a potential lead dog or me, someone who said he wanted to understand what Jeff does, through a system of greater and greater stresses. How will the dog—or the writer—respond, learn, and retain what he has learned. This was my first test; I was caught by surprise and that was part of it.

I gave Morten my camera bag, stepped onto the runners, and grabbed hold of the handlebar on the small, light wooden sled. Morten pulled the hook out of the packed snow, said "Hold on" to me in his Danish accent, and then we were zooming. The dogs were fluid and thrilled. I was stiff, unsure, but trying to let the thrill in. Morten stayed fairly far back, I could not hear him. He was probably thinking that when I fell off, he didn't want to run over me with the snow machine.

The dogs made little noise as they trotted as fast as their long legs would go. Though the pace allowed larger dogs to keep up an even trot, a couple of the smallest dogs actually ran the whole way. Jeff told me that one of his top all-time leaders, Jenna, was only thirty-nine pounds. She had already guided him to a win in the Iditarod. Although I probably knew a bit more than some about sled dogs, I was astounded at how small and slender these dogs were. And they looked this way with fur, deep, dense hair capable of keeping them warm at way below zero. These races are not weight-pulling events; they are long-distance marathons that happen to pass through some of the most demanding, isolated, frigid, brutal country in the world. It felt as if I had grabbed hold of the rope on the back of a powerful waterskiing boat and the throttle was stuck on.

Some of the best mushers believe that the kind of genetics they want in their dogs are those from animals that have survived the rigors of Alaska for hundreds, even a few thousand, years. Before electricity, planes, boats, trains, cars, government assistance, before it was called Alaska, it was the Eskimo people and the Athabascans that relied on dogs. Really the names don't work—let's just say it was the Natives' dogs, the ones whose lives were even more difficult than people's. They only got food when there was enough food for all the humans. They had no medicines, they had to fight off each other to keep their food. The dogs that did live were the ones able to convert whatever food they got into sustenance. They could use efficiently however little they got and turn it into energy. They made the best use of available body heat and white blood cells and the pads on their paws. They could travel great distances without food, not really caring if they received human attention. Over hundreds and hundreds of years in arctic conditions, dogs were the only beasts of burden until a relatively few years ago when someone introduced snow machines. Truly, only the dogs with the rarest combination of traits survived the environment and their demanding masters. They had to have great stamina, superior strength, pound for pound—hopefully the fewer pounds the better—the best disease resistance, the best use of instincts and senses, the most unassailable

Jeff and Donna King's dog yard near Denali Park. Photo by Peter Jenkins

minds, the ability to adjust, the fastest recovery time. Then the best of these dogs were bred to each other by the Native people, who had survived with many of the same traits.

This is why mushers who know have searched the isolated Native villages, where distinct gene pools could develop relatively unhampered by someone in the village bringing home a collie, say. They want Native dog genetics in their bloodlines. They understand hybrid vigor. They like to get a superior bitch leader from an Athabascan village in the superfrozen interior and cross her with a long-legged Eskimo dog from a famous line of windswept Arctic Ocean–area dogs. Breed these dogs whose gene pools have never merged and you might get some superdogs.

Natives say that many white men want "a picture dog," a dog that looks good in a photo. Look at the ads on TV for Subaru. They use a matched set of identical-looking Siberian huskies. If you hooked them up to a sled and raced them against Jeff's team, they wouldn't have a chance. The picture has absolutely nothing to do with how capable, sound, and tough a sled dog is. How you look as a dog has nothing to do with how you can handle an open lead on the Yukon River at 2 A.M. when it's February and thirty-eight below.

I rode for a mile or so, though it seemed to last for an hour, or for just a few seconds. The creaking of the runners over the bumps in the snow was loud at times. I was fully alive, and more. The padding of the team's feet on the semi-hard trail of snow, the dry kind that falls all around Denali, was a clean sound. Everything was so deeply quiet in winter. It was amazing how the dogs were so jointly focused on just moving fast, covering trail. The occasional smell of dog mingled with the dry, cold, blue air.

I was glad I'd followed Jeff's suggestion and ordered from Cabela's a special zip-up bodysuit with a major hood and special rubber boots rated to keep you warm to one hundred below. Your feet don't move much when you're on the runners. Plus I was probably holding my body as stiff as a scared child who just had the training wheels taken off his bike. Jeff looked relaxed. Suddenly, he stopped, right before we were to go down a different trail and enter some spruce woods. I lifted my right foot off the right runner and pressed down on the metal brake. To my surprise, the team stopped, though they clearly didn't want to.

"Let Morten take the team home. There might be some tough turns and bumps and things through here," Jeff said. One of his dogs, then two and three, began barking; they wanted to crank it back up.

I waited for Morten to catch up on the snow machine. I got off the sled and he took off following Jeff. The trail on the way back had some sharp, severe turns, just about wide enough for the sled alone. Even Morten had to lean way over, as the sled's left-side runners came off the ground. He almost spilled the sled on its side. And there were bumps and sharp, skidding turns because the dogs sped up as they got closer to home. I didn't get the feeling they sped up because like a horse they just wanted to go to the barn, they sped up because they liked burning energy, of which they seemed to have an endless supply. They knew where they were, and it was like a runner sprinting the last hundred yards. The dogs are experts at energy use and know how much they can pump through their fantastic motors.

When you think about life before machines, which in the great scheme of things was not that long ago, and how important animals were to man's survival, you realize that few other animals could handle the work in the Arctic. Mules, horses, ox, require too much fuel because there is too much body to keep warm. Alaskan huskies can dig burrows into the snow to escape the predator winds and storms. They can dig a burrow in the ground to keep their young alive—from whatever might eat them—and keep the species going. Like the camel who is suited to the rigors of the anvil of the desert, so are these dogs to their frozen world.

The two teams roared up the hill to the Kings' compound. They call it Husky Homestead, as there are about ten times more dogs here than people. Once this was a Native land allotment, owned by an Athabascan woman from Cantwell. At one time individual Native Alaskans could get their own one-hundred-sixty-plus-acre chunks of land in specified areas. The woman used it as a hunting camp, but decided to sell it to Jeff. He bought it before he was a musher, before he was married; he had to borrow money from his family to afford it. Long before any huskies were in Jeff's life, there was this homestead, quite a ways off the road.

KITTY

The dog yard at the Kings' is where the "front yard" of a house in the suburbs would be. We pulled in and Jeff and Morten took off the harnesses one by one and brought each dog back to its area. Each was chained to its doghouse via a metal stake that rotated so the chain wouldn't get tangled. Every dog is different, with its own personality and distinct appearance. Red, a long-legged lead dog, is dark strawberry blond in color. He sits or lies there, holding his pointed snout at a regal angle, his sharp, oversize ears alert. When he is hooked up and standing ready to go, he looks awkward, painfully shy, almost scared. But when Jeff says "Mush," Red is a trail-eating intimidator, an unrelenting leader who will sacrifice his body. He even pulls too hard sometimes.

Jenna is one of Jeff's favorites, probably because of her eyes. She has large, dark eyes that seem rounder than the other dogs', bigger, as if they are better adapted for seeing in the dark. If you saw her on the street, you'd *know* she was a plain mutt, maybe even a stray having trouble scrounging dinner. She has the coloring of a gray wolf, but her hair isn't deep. She watches your every move, listens to your every sound, figures out your body language. Then if she loves you, she will do anything you wish, often before you ask. If you love her and she is smart enough to tell, she knows you would never ask her to do something too dangerous. She is discerning and intelligent enough to trust your judgment and know that you will trust hers. She knows you'll know how to comprehend her way of communicating. Jenna's run the Iditarod three times, won once, come in third twice. She knows the trail better than Jeff, and they both know that.

Yuksi is a dog Jeff believes will be a superstar. He belongs to Bryan Imus and will be running his first Iditarod in 2000. Bryan's mother was an outstanding sprint musher, and Bryan used to work for Jeff the way Morten does now. Jeff wants to buy Yuksi, but Bryan isn't sure. It's expensive to run the Iditarod—all the dogs, all the equipment, the months and months of training yourself and the dogs. Imagine feeding twenty, thirty dogs, much less eighty-plus puppies. Imagine the vet bills. Bryan, as tough as they come, wants to be like Jeff, a professional, but he must do well enough to get some sponsors, and soon. Bryan's girlfriend is an officer in training at National Bank of Alaska. How long will she want to live in the bush? Even in Alaska it's not easy on your neighbors if you have fifty dogs in your yard. So most mushers, like Jeff and Donna, live far enough out that they don't have close human neighbors. Although Bryan was running the Iditarod, he was renting or "renting to own" Yuksi to Jeff. Yuksi looked to have plenty of "Native village dog" blood, with some wolf mixed in. His legs are long, like those of the best human eight-hundred-meter runners, and he is never still. He prances, he walks around and around his doghouse at the maximum length his chain will allow, having worn a circle in the bare dirt. There is no other dog in this yard with his internal engine, one that could or would not shut off. The only conceivable comparison is to Jeff. It seems that mushers would prefer dogs like Yuksi. Or would they rather have dogs like Red that conserve their energy, that are languid until training or the race?

As I followed Jeff and the dogs through that fall, winter, and early spring, the retired dog Kitty roamed and watched. She was stiff and moved like any creature that has pushed its body as far as it would go, then pushed it further. She was also clearly a former champion of the world. She reminded me of videos I've seen of an older Joe Louis or Muhammad Ali. She was definitely not spry or fast anymore; it was all she could do to walk. But she still had that aura. "I should be revered." "I should be respected for what I've done." She has always been detached from humans. As Donna put it, "Kitty did not show love or affection for humans, even for me or Jeff. She recognized us and tolerated us, but she lived to run, to race, and especially to lead."

When the other dogs are being harnessed and unhooked from their doghouses, which are lined with straw in winter, Kitty seems again to feel the excitement of the run. She knows they are training for the last great race, the Iditarod, or the Kuskokwim 300, or one of the others. Kitty, oddly colored, black-and-white like a sheepdog except with shorter denser hair, never raced for the fame; she did not know what that was. Her eyes were almost the color of icy snow, her nose and ears black. She didn't run for the adulation of fans or for

Jeff and Kitty. PHOTO BY PETER JENKINS

food or prize money. She could have cared less about interviews and TV news. She needed the challenges and she needed to be in charge, to use her superior senses and stamina. She even seemed to be aware of her superiority. Some of her blood came from great Native dogs bred in the villages to help their people survive. Long ago people probably used her ancestors to chase moose into the openings in the ten-mile brush fences her people used.

She can no longer do what she once loved so much to do. Jeff and Donna let her roam the dog yard free to keep her blue eyes on everyone, possibly to communicate her strength to the young ones, the rowdy ones. I never saw Kitty stop walking and looking and observing the other dogs. It was all she could do to power herself up the walkway between the dog-food-mixing room with its outside puppy enclosure and the storage building with a guest apartment upstairs. The walkway has a slight incline and it leads to the house. She would look at the house but never go to it. Kitty does not concern herself with humans. It was as if she were making sure they, Jeff and Donna, knew she was still on the job. No dog dared growl or bother her as she checked on them all. She would pace around the yard all day looking at the other dogs. It was impossible to tell what she was thinking; she has always been aloof. She pays close attention to the end of the yard closest to the house, where the best dogs had their houses, including the leaders that have taken over from her. Kitty is now fourteen. She goes into anyone's doghouse and no one bothers her. Even if she sleeps in there, they'll sleep on top of their house or on the ground until she leaves. She just has that much influence, somehow all the dogs know it.

Kitty ran in six Iditarods as a main leader from 1991 to 1996. She led Jeff to two wins, in 1993 and 1996. In 1991 they finished twelfth; in 1992, sixth; in 1994, third; in 1995, seventh. In 1993, Kitty led Jeff to a win with only thirty-two minutes separating him from DeDe Janrowe, the powder-blue-dressed favorite of many Alaskans. In 1996, Jeff's team ran one of the fastest races in history, nine days, five hours, and forty-three minutes. Kitty was nine that time, old for a world-class long-distance racer, and she stumbled just out of Nome. Jeff said he knew she was tired, but the rest of the team, which was much younger, picked up the pace, knowing the end was near. After all those years of pulling Jeff over the finish, Jeff stopped long enough to put an exhausted Kitty in the sled, and she traveled the last few miles as a passenger. She certainly didn't like it, but Jeff wouldn't risk hurting her, even if it was tough on her monumental pride as a racer, as a leader, as a winner. Jeff knew she wouldn't ever wish to be a passenger, she was the captain. She was not only the head of their ship, she was the brains and the muscle and the heart.

When I think about how Donna described Kitty, saying that she was aloof and tolerated others but lived to run, lived to race, and lived to lead, well, that pretty well describes Donna's husband too.

"TRAVEL BEYOND THIS POINT NOT RECOMMENDED"

Before I left at the end of my first visit to go back to Seward, Jeff grabbed a blank Post-it note off the refrigerator and found a pen.

"Peter," he said, and I was surprised to hear him say my name. "I'm going to write down a list of clothing you will need when you come back. You do want to come back, make a few long training runs with us?"

"Yes, I really do." Maybe I'd passed Test #1. Though I got the feeling the tests never ended around Jeff.

"You have the Internet in Seward?"

"Yes, we do."

"Well, you click onto the Cabela's site, then put the Trans-Alaska suit in the search engine. Order one of those. Where we will be going, it could get extremely cold, at least forty below. Also get a pair of the Trans-Alaska boots, they're rated at one hundred below. The problem with mushing, your feet don't move around much." Jeff wrote down the two items.

"Oh, and get a couple pairs of Polartec gloves."

As he wrote, I looked at what was tacked on the front of the King refrigerator. The fronts of refrigerators are some of my favorite reads. There was an Algebra I, Chapter 3, test by Tessa, the middle daughter. She had got an A, a 96 out of a possible 100. There was a chart, with a pink heart for each day, Monday through Sunday, in which Ellen, their second-grader, writes in how many minutes she has read each day. Monday she marked in fifteen minutes. There was a card someone had sent them with a quote on the front: "If you're not happy with what you have, how could you be happier with more?" There was a picture of Cali, their oldest, her latest school picture from Healy. She looked twenty years old, and sophisticated, though she was in the ninth grade. And there were four pictures made into one from the family orthodontist in Fairbanks showing Tessa's shining grin. There was a close-up of her bite, a shot of her uppers, and lowers, all straight and white—no braces anymore!

Jeff said that I would be welcome back when I got my cold-weather clothes, just to call a few days in advance to warn them. So I packed up and headed back to Seward. When I got home, I ordered my equipment, then Rita, Julianne, and I went back to the Kings' around the end of November. They had invited our family, and other friends, to share their Thanksgiving. The night we arrived, Jeff said the next morning we were going to take a forty-something-mile run down the Denali Highway. It is closed in winter but offers an unusually smooth, wide trail for early long-distance training. We would come across a large sign in glowing orange and yellow a few miles down the road, east out of Cantwell, that would offer us a chilling warning, a warning totally unheeded by Jeff and another musher, Bruce Lee, who were on the road for training this day.

The sign said, "Travel beyond this point not recommended. If you must use this road expect extreme cold/heavy snow. Carry cold weather survival gear. Tell someone where you are going."

I had been to a few out-of-the-way places in Alaska by now on my trip but hadn't seen any such signs. Jeff told me about the road while he and his head assistant, Shawn, harnessed up the dogs. Shawn would be running a team of young dogs for Jeff, call them the junior varsity, in this year's Iditarod. They were scouting for the team of tomorrow, and this run would be a little workout.

Jeff said that a few years ago a couple and their grandchildren had driven down this road during an extremely cold winter. They had run off the road and got stuck, and eventually their gas ran out. They didn't have survival gear, and all four of them perished. They had traveled too far down the road to walk out. I wondered if we were going farther down the road than they had. But with Jeff and Shawn, I felt supremely confident, especially in my new clothing. I had the feeling I could sleep out in this black Trans-Alaska suit and not ever need a sleeping bag. The trails these guys go down in races and even in training would never have a sign this dramatic, though those trails are far more dangerous.

We drove out to the road, parked, and got ready to go. It was maybe ten below zero and perfectly still. Golden sunlight was shining down on us with a dark blue sky above. Jeff's dogs, I'd already noticed, didn't jump around much. But as always, they were ready to rock. Jeff had brought an extra sled for me to ride and attached it to the end of his. He told me we would go through this big valley; the frozen Nenana River would be on our left.

The first few miles I was a bit uptight. Jeff acted like an athletic six-year-old on a jungle gym, hyper and invincible. I remember he'd said that he'd traveled one hundred thousand miles on a sled in the last twenty-plus years of mushing. Jeff mentioned we'd probably see caribou, then a minute later, we came upon a small herd in the snow-covered roadbed. They ran at us, then turned off. The most dramatic group was about fifty animals down in a small area below a lone hill. When they finally saw us, they all leapt up and ran, powder snow swirling around their legs and hiding them, as if they were just bodies sliding surprisingly fast atop the snow. The sun turned the outlines of their beautiful hides to gold. Jeff turned around, stood on one foot, and pointed to some large tracks on our left in some fresh powder. He said the tracks were a couple of wolves following the caribou, and their food, as they wandered and dug up nourishment with their wide hooves.

We got to a hill, quite an incline, where the weight of Jeff and especially me slowed down our progress. Jeff got off and ran beside the sled. I thought it looked easy, and hadn't Jeff told me last time to watch him, to do what he did? So I jumped off, but we must have been moving faster than it appeared. My boots seemed to weigh twenty-five pounds each. I tried to run, stumbled, tried to regain my balance, but fell. I hit the snow, rolled, and was up. Jeff and Shawn both stopped their teams but didn't laugh or say anything. We went up hills, rode the brake hard coming down, then turned around and came back. This time most of the caribou were gone. The temperature was dropping; the dogs seemed just warmed up after our forty-two-mile run. I could see how this occupation could capture a person, ignite his passion. Moving silently through the wilderness with a team of willing, sleek, intelligent dogs as your companions, your extra eyes and ears and nose and feet and fur, was exhilarating.

The dogs were unharnessed and put in their compartments in the camper-type kennel built into the red Dodge truck Jeff had won by winning the Iditarod in 1998. The sleds went on top. When we got home, Donna, who was from Connecticut, was sitting at their kitchen table talking with Rita. Donna, originally trained in the intricately demanding field of medical illustration, was getting a couple of her prints ready to ship. She now paints wildlife from around Denali and other places in Alaska. My favorite is one she did in 1993 of a blond grizzly bear mother lying on her back in just-sprouted green grass and fireweed. She's just finished nursing. Looking at this sweet scene between a mother and her babies, you would never think this grizzly could ever be deadly—though observing humans at our gentlest would never warn anyone of our own vicious abilities to defend what's ours.

One of the Kings' daughters was surfing the Internet. Jeff was talking to someone in Norway about some kind of special dog food. These mushers are always searching for every competitive edge. They read Pat Riley's motivational book and study the effects of various temperatures on the performance of plastic, which they slip over their runners. They experiment with supernutrition. Jeff hired a woman from Kodiak who has a set-net site in the summer to work for him in the winter. One of her duties was to be a masseuse for the dogs. Jeff told me he had a new idea, a secret weapon he might try in this year's Iditarod. He told me he might tell me about it after he'd tried it.

Jeff excused himself to go down to their little village's Volunteer Fire Department and EMT building, which doubled as a community meeting hall. He remembered an atrocious car wreck from last year at Thanksgiving when a small car filled with people had crunched into one of the bridges that cross the Nenana River. Donna appeared as Jeff left and sat down with me at the kitchen table. Their parakeet skidded to a landing on top of my head. The family had at different times commented that maybe their bird had special feelings for me. Donna was holding a piece of tracing paper; she was working on a public arts project to be submitted to the school in Healy that their daughters attended.

She and another artist from Fairbanks who did ceramic murals proposed to work on it together. In Alaska 10 percent of school construction budgets are spent on art for the school. The local people decide on the art.

Something, the page with her design inspired by nature sketched out on it, a gust of wind, that the woodstove did not need to be stoked, made her think of the past.

"You know, since Jeff and I married," Donna said, "and moved out to this land on this little lake, we have lived the whole last hundred years of technological advancement, but we've done it in the last twenty years."

"What do you mean?" I asked.

"Well, we've gone from homesteading this land, building our house from the logs on the place. We used generators for our only electricity. We hauled our water, heated with wood. We were hunter-gatherers. Now we have electrical lines, phone lines, the Internet, computers, a hot tub, even bright lights that will come on and illuminate our dog yard in case a bear wants to think about eating some dog. Still, sometimes it gets fifty below, but we can handle it." Donna is as strong as Jeff is, and that's what made it possible to live this life they had constructed together.

That night, the night before Thanksgiving, I heard someone coming up the stairs from the basement where the girls were staying while the addition was finished. That someone was running, so it had to be Jeff. He sat down with me for a brief moment, as a courtesy. You got the idea that sleeping was sometimes an intrusion into Jeff's world. Already today he'd made the long run up the Denali Highway. Then he had made a shorter run beginning in the dog yard with a couple puppy teams. Helge, red-cheeked, thin-faced, and a natural comedian, took one team, Jeff the other.

It was 8 P.M. Since we'd gotten home from the Denali Park run, Jeff had made several calls to the contractors doing the addition. He'd also just gotten a call from a Native guy in a village near Bethel. Jeff had told him he had a few dogs for sale and gave him advice on setting up a breeding program on a small budget. Natives are increasingly wanting to get back into a prominent position in what was once their exclusive world of dog mushing. In the 2000 Iditarod race, the 1976 Iditarod winner, Jerry Riley, an Athabascan, would race, as well as Mike Williams, the Yupik from Akiak, an evangelical Christian and Native leader, who would be returning after two twenty-third-place finishes. Emitt Peters, the 1975 winner as a rookie, was running again. And there were the two

Inupiat Eskimo young guns, John Baker of Kotzebue, who had finished fifth in 1998, and whaler Russell Lane of Point Hope. Native Alaskans are now getting some sponsors. It costs more and more to devote your life to long-distance racing—across the toughest field in sports.

Jeff is a favorite around Bethel, the "capital city" of the Kuskokwim delta, because he has won their race, the Kuskokwim 300, several times. He told me that if I wanted to see what a hard-core, old-time Alaska dog race was like, often run in some of the most brutal conditions (i.e., lots of overflow), I should go to the K-300. I did and saw Jeff come in second to the gray-bearded Charlie Boulding.

Jeff made smoothies for his girls and for us and hugged and kissed his daughters good-night. He asked if we had everything we needed at our log cabin up on the hill, and we left. Before we did, he told Donna that they should jump in the hot tub, talk about their respective days. After that, maybe they could paint some trim in the new addition? We really appreciated being a part of Jeff and Donna's extended family on this moon so far away from our orbit.

"THESE ATHLETES EAT RAW MEAT, RUN NAKED, AND SLEEP IN THE SNOW"

The next time, I came back alone to go with Jeff, Helge, and Morten on an almost-one-hundred-mile, two-day training run. A couple lived out by Gold King Creek, a large Alaskan wetlands between the Wood and Totatlanika Rivers, who occasionally let long-distance mushers, a few snow machiners, and people from foreign countries craving the true wilderness stay the night with them. It would be forty-eight miles out there and forty-eight miles back. Jeff would take three teams, two filled with experienced dogs that could make his Iditarod team and one with young dogs, rookies wanting to make the team. When we left their dog yard, the forty dogs that couldn't come howled and leaped at the ends of their chains. They barked and yipped and hated being left behind. All but Kitty, who tried to sniff each dog that was leaving. She seemed to be trying to think through each of Jeff's decisions, why had he taken this dog and not that one. Falcon, the other retired lead dog who's free to roam unchained, sat and watched from atop Red's doghouse.

Jeff told me as we loaded up all the dogs that Kitty had been a significantly better leader than his present leaders, Red and Jenna, the pair who had led him to his 1998 win. Kitty was unrivaled as far as Jeff was concerned in her commitment, drive, and resiliency. She weighed fifty-four pounds in her prime. Jeff said Kitty never looked sideways, never looked back, was always looking intensely at what was around the next corner. Nothing he ever encountered was too tough for her; her superbly adapted genes still flow in his dog yard. Jeff uses the males Persian and Rhombus, her direct offspring, and he hopes to get a litter from one of her daughters, Cheyenne. Cheyenne no longer belongs to Jeff, but mushers wheel and deal dogs; they will let their supermale breed with your superfemale for a price, or let you keep this litter so they can keep the next, or any kind of trade or deal that can be arranged.

On the way to the trail we drove through Healy and headed toward Fairbanks. A good bunch of caribou that had been spooked by something stood in the road. There was almost no traffic now, though in the summer this road carried many Alaskan travelers. It was fifteen below on the truck's thermometer as we left Jeff's place; it rose to twelve above in Healy, then dropped back to fifteen below as we went down toward our starting place. Near Healy I saw an old blue pickup with a homemade dog box in back. It was owned by a beginning musher, or perhaps someone who had little money to put into motorized transportation, someone who spent most of his or her money on dogs, a fairly common addiction. Hand-painted on the back, it said, "These athletes eat raw meat, run naked, and sleep in the snow."

We pulled in behind a lonesome roadhouse; everything everywhere seemed frozen, brittle, and isolated. Jeff handed me a ten-dollar bill and told me to go inside and give it to the owner for allowing us to park the truck and trailer in their parking lot, and for plugging the truck in too. Kate Wood and Larry Mead's log cabins, where we were headed, were almost fifty miles from here. I knew it was possible to cross what was ahead, even though I had no idea what awaited. I never worried about anything thanks to Jeff. He exuded confidence that oozed out to all around him. When we left the roadhouse, the thermometer in Jeff's truck said minus twenty-eight.

I found an unexpected spirituality associated with Alaska's winter. It made me feel purified, high, strong, and intense. I'd been around Jeff enough now that I was feeling quite relaxed. I had no idea what test he had in store for me. Would I be taking my body and mind to its limits? I was sure he wouldn't push me too hard. While my forty-something-mile jaunt had been a gliding, relaxing run on a snow-covered flat and wide road, this was like being dragged through miles and miles of a war zone that had been bombed for a month behind a jeep going as fast as it could. The jeep would have much worse traction than the sled we'd used before; these thirteen dogs pulled each sled with fifty-two paws, and the traction was provided by their tough pads and their strong claws. There would be no stopping quickly, even if I did fall off.

Jeff yelled out for all of us to be really careful because in the first few hundred yards we'd cross a road with possible speeding vehicles. Every dog was barking with high anticipation. He didn't mention what it would be like to come up on the road at a right angle at full blast-off speed before the dogs settled down. The road, which did have a pickup on it a second before we crossed, served as a jump, not quite high enough to prepare you to fly over a couple parked buses, though it felt like that. Somehow I held on. Jeff glanced back quickly when we were in midair, as if to say he had forgotten to mention hitting the road and he was glad I had hung on. Then, without warning—which is how all the seemingly hundreds of obstacles in the trail appeared—the dogs, who knew where they were going, made a full-out ninety-degree turn to the right. My sled was tied to Jeff's, so at times it acted like the end of a whip. The sled dropped into ruts, frozen as hard as concrete, and flew on top of them, and then I flew off. Boom, thud, roll, stop. My breath was almost knocked out of me. There was no give in the snow on the beginning of this trail to Gold King. The frost heaves were dramatic, as they came up in the most uncomfortable, unruly ways. The team stopped, but they didn't want to. They wanted to burn this icehouse down. I got back on the sled, and we took off again.

About a mile or so later, nothing had smoothed out. We were running through an area that was all frozen wetlands, beaver ponds, muskrat trails, little streams, rivers, bog. The banks of these frozen slabs of ice served as catapults on the way down and immovable walls for us to hit on the way out.

Watching Jeff from behind was like skiing behind a champion slalom skier. He shifted his weight with the contours of the snow-covered earth we mushed over, from the left runner to the right. When it came time to turn, he bore down on the edge. The sled's runners were narrower than I had thought, with a piece of rubber on top to stand on.

We crashed, though that's not the word Jeff would use, up and over little mounds; the dogs would be over and going down while I was just coming up the front side. The mounds were like frozen heads in the trail. Occasionally, the lines holding my sled to Jeff's would grow slack, then snap forward when

How would you like to be hooked up to this? The Tustamena 200. Photo by Peter Jenkins

the force of the pulling dogs caught up to it. I could tell from Jeff's voice that this upset him. He explained to me that during a long-distance race, loose lines without the proper amount of pressure on them put great stress on the dogs. Every time the lines that connected to the sled went slack and then "caught up," it stressed the dogs' joints and legs and muscles, especially those of the wheel dogs, the two closest to the sled. There was a way to bend over the bumps to keep the pressure on the lines equal, and there was a way to drag your heel on the snow when going downhill to keep the sled from running too fast. Riding the sled required much more concentration than I could ever have imagined.

After maybe five miles I was somewhat relaxed on the runners. I was practicing adjusting to all the undulations on the surface of the ground, and I could see that if it was done right, over several days it would demand less energy of the dogs and certainly put less stress on them. Then, without warning, we came to a steep creekbank; the dogs never slowed; they even sped up. It seemed to head almost straight down, then we hit the ice of the creek, blown clear of snow. When we hit the ice, my sled began sliding sideways at a runaway speed. Plus my sled pulled Jeff's a bit to the side too. I was now sliding at a ninety-degree angle to the long, straight line of these thirteen blazing dogs. Half of them had already begun zooming out of the other side of the creek. I could tell this was not going to be elegant. I hit the creekbank, *bang,* and it sounded as though the sled would shatter, but it didn't. I smashed into the bank, came off the sled, which turned over sideways. The impact threw Jeff off his feet, but he did not release his grip even though his sled too was knocked on its side. Jeff held on with both hands. The dogs pulled him and the sleds up and out of the creek and across the bumpy, frozen ground. He was telling the dogs to stop, and they finally did. I ran out of the creek the best I could. I knew the way I'd hit I would have some bruises and knots, and I did.

"That was a pretty good fall. Those second sleds really whip on the ice. You all right?" Jeff asked me.

"Yeah, I'm fine. I wasn't ready for that one, though I'm not sure even if I was I could have hung on."

"And can you imagine, after running the Iditarod for five days or seven days, and you hit something like that. People fall off their sleds, it's a good way to lose your team. Sometimes they don't stop until they get to the next checkpoint or get tangled in something."

That crash illustrates what makes dogs and mushers such performers at the most extreme levels. It shows why they must be so qualified. They don't play out their game in a climate-controlled dome or stadium. They don't run across a place like California or Pennsylvania that has a comparatively mellow climate. Besides California and Pennsylvania are not large enough playing fields for the Iditarod. They need almost twelve hundred miles. They don't play out their game on a smooth wood floor where there is no concern about running full speed into a steep riverbank you couldn't see or were so sleep-deprived you forgot it was there. How many baseball games have been played in a whiteout, on top of the frozen Bering Sea, with winds blowing forty miles per hour? How many extreme sports events have contestants swim across an open lead in a frozen river near the arctic circle when the air temperature is thirty-eight below? And if they did, imagine the hype, the breathless announcer. The Iditarod, the Kuskokwim 300, represent what is Alaska. They pit people and Alaska's beloved sled dogs against all that Alaska can offer up. They race across and through whatever comes. They don't brag about where they've been or how they got there. They don't want comfort or luxury. They don't whine. They are all as tough as they come, they have to be—Alaska requires it.

The Iditarod captures the essence of Alaska. The most populated town the Iditarod travels through is the mostly Eskimo village of Unalakleet (pop. 714). To race eleven hundred–plus miles, pulled by dogs while standing behind them on the runners of a sled, from Anchorage to Nome—it's like racing from Dallas to beyond Aberdeen, South Dakota. Or from Atlanta to past Albany, New York, or from Los Angeles to Portland, Oregon. Imagine taking off from Chicago in the dead of winter and mushing to Casper, Wyoming. Nowhere Outside could you travel that far without encountering farm and ranch fences, towns, cities, traffic. You can run the Iditarod without running into any man-made obstacles. Though nature certainly has much in store.

Nowhere else I've ever been has nature and the environment been so dominant, the most powerful force. Man has created his own worlds in so many places; he seldom even has to enter what's left of nature. A few trees here, some squared-off grass "lawn" there. Alaskans have so much respect for Mother Earth that it would not be right to stage their biggest "event" on a man-made playing field. Alaskans don't live out their lives in controlled environments; they want to see who among them can handle and move through their real world, not just to survive but to cover one hundred–plus miles a day.

"For the first ten years of mushing, when I fell asleep, I fell off the sled. Now I fall asleep, my body is used to the movements and I stay on," Jeff said.

There off to our right sitting on a stump surrounded by white was a great horned owl. Moose tracks were everywhere, crossing the trail we ran on.

Jeff's long mustache was covered in frozen condensation from his breathing; he figured it was thirty below, at least. Jeff was so comfortable on the sled he would stand sideways on one runner with both feet and talk to me. I saw him change clothes going down the trail, search for things inside the sled. He pointed out Red, his long-legged leader. Jeff said when Red was on the move, he had a high-stepping gait and slanted slightly to the side at times. Several of the dogs would occasionally reach out and grab some snow in their mouth.

A gust of wind blew down from the mountains on our right. Jeff explained that some mushers are understandably afraid of the wind when they first feel its strength. The wind is alive, a being, it must be understood, used, not feared like all mighty powers. A famous Eskimo rescue team from Shaktoolik wears a patch on their jackets and hats that reads, "The wind is the Eskimo's friend."

Mystic Mountain was somewhere to our right. There was nothing south of us but the mountainous and the mystical. Being in a place this cold and silent and empty of human clutter had a spiritually powerful impact on me that I had not expected. I thought I'd be freezing and feeling lonely, but it wasn't so.

Back in Jeff and Donna's kitchen there's a rusted, well-used metal cookie tray. On it are many small, white rectangles with magnets on the back. Each dog being considered for the 2000 racing season has a magnet with its name on it. As the training continues, some of the second stringers, such as maybe Nickel or Pumba, may even make the top team. There may be injuries to the big dogs, the number one team, or the ravages of age may begin to show up, as compared to the unrelenting hunger that shows in the younger dogs. Some dogs want not only to push themselves but will demand the highest levels from those in the team with them. On our team today were the best of this early season, Red and Jenna, proven Iditarod leaders. There were Hanky and Whitney and Chip, Zazu and Beta, Conan and Hump, Paris, Raven, Deer, and Boogles. Jeff would watch them move as one, and you just knew he was thinking, "These dogs are the most beautiful, powerful, unbeatable team there is." He also knew that all mushers thought this sometimes while they trained their teams in splendid isolation. Jeff was trying some of Joe Garnie's dogs; he had leased Joe's team from last year's Iditarod. One of Joe's dogs was in the wheel and was fussing with the other: two males, an antagonistic look, a growl, some stiff-legged posturing. Joe's dog was attempting to exert his dominance over Jeff's dog. The wheel dogs, closest to the sled, are often the strongest, largest, and therefore most resistant to the physical punishment of long-distance running.

Their different characters prompted Jeff to think about the analogies he finds, and studies, between professional human athletes and professional dog athletes.

"Look at those dogs." Jeff pointed out from the sled while we sped along. He was always concentrating, always learning, always the teacher. He was his own most important pupil.

"I think about the NFL quarterbacks, Joe Montana and Jim McMahon, or Peyton Manning and Ryan Leaf. With Montana and McMahon, you had Montana, polite, shy, unthreatening, until he's on the field with the ultimate champion's heart. With McMahon, you had the outspoken, controversial human who refused to lose, sacrificed himself to win no matter how bleak it looked. I've had dogs I'd compare to both of them. I'd rather have the self-contained Montana-type model, but I'll take a champion's heart any day I can get one."

We popped unexpectedly into a frozen swamp area. I adjusted and stayed on the sled, though it was rough and jolting. Jeff stood on one runner. He spoke for several minutes about his feelings on this year's team in the making. His dogs Bryan and Dude had just been demoted to the "puppy" team that Shawn would run in the Iditarod. The idea of the puppy team, I heard Shawn and Jeff say, was to not push them, but run somewhere in the middle to back third of the pack. Let the young dogs have fun their first Iditarod, see which ones shine, strive to lead. Give them all kinds of rest, then if they make the varsity, they already know the trail. Once they've run it, I've heard mushers say, the dogs always remember the trail. They even know it during whiteouts and wicked storms when the wind can be their enemy.

Storms that smash through a race can cause inactivity, passive panic, even tragedy. They also create opportunities for the best leaders, the daring and the able, to pull away and win. It's how Libby Riddles became the first female musher to win. At that time she was Joe Garnie's partner, living in Teller. Leaders smell the trail when they can't see it. They smell dogs that have passed and snow machines that have gone by. Jeff remembered one storm so bad that some dogs tried to hide from their musher. Red and Jenna, however, got more aggressive because they knew how terrible this storm was, and they knew they had to get through it or continue to suffer in it.

We'd just passed a bull moose who'd lost his antlers. Jeff at first thought the moose was not going to leave the trail, which is another major potential catastrophe, but it finally moved off in time that we didn't have to stop. It is impossible to back up, and it is extremely difficult to get off the established trail, especially if the snow is deep. Jeff told me about a time one year a week before the big race when a moose was in the trail and attacked him and his team. It wouldn't give up its space on the trail. Moose become vulnerable to wolf attack when they get in the deep snow, so they prefer packed trails. Jeff had to dive off the sled into a hollow area beneath a spruce tree where the snow had not collected because of low branches. The moose slashed at one of his dogs with its lethal hoof, and the wound required seventy stitches.

"You know," Jeff said after our moose strutted into the willows, "leaders of lesser constitution will let the wind, after being buffeted by it for some time, blow them off course. Their will is weakened. Great leaders will stay on course and push through it. Like in the '98 Iditarod, big ol' Red and little Jenna did just that. Generally two great leaders are better than one, they give each other confidence."

FLYING FACE-FIRST THROUGH THE AIR

We had climbed in altitude and were traveling in some deeper powder. I was listening to Jeff, then lost some of my concentration on the sled, and we hit something and I was flying face-first through the air. I landed in some soft powder. Jeff stopped the sled; as I jogged back, he smiled slightly and said, "Outstanding landing, sir." I took it as a compliment, and we got going again.

One of Joe Garnie's dogs, Jazz, who was supposed to be one of the best, wasn't enjoying himself—he just wasn't having fun. Jeff demoted the dog but never gave up on him. Who knew, maybe Jazz missed the Eskimo village of Teller, his home on the Bering Sea, above Nome and so different from here in the interior. Walt, another of Joe's dogs, had a hitch in his gait. Jeff was letting him rest, putting him in the barn at night. Now Jeff was noticing a two-year-old named Kanga. He seemed to be the only rookie who could keep up with the veterans.

Jeff stopped. Even though Jeff's top team was pulling an extra sled and me, we were well ahead of Morten and Helge, who each had a team. Jeff was always racing, racing himself, racing anyone around. He wanted to make sure the apprentices were doing fine; this was their longest trip so far on a dog sled too. In about ten minutes they appeared, running smoothly, no problems. Jeff wanted a report. Morten and Helge were athletes themselves and gaining significant confidence as mushers.

A few miles across the trail, we came to a long incline; I stepped off the runners and ran a bit. That radically helped the circulation in my feet. Jeff looked back when he heard my heavy footsteps, and I thought I saw a slight smile through all the ice that covered his blond-brown mustache. About halfway up the hill, about half the team turned and looked back. Then fifty yards later, two-thirds of the team looked back. It seemed to me they were looking past Jeff at me. What kind of a load is back there anyway, the look seemed to say. We slowed down. I got off and ran again, and we sped up. I got back on when we were almost to the top, and the whole team but Jenna looked back.

We'd been on the trail three hours. Jeff said the team was running in excellent form. Their gait was a really fast walk, except for Jenna and another small female, who ran sometimes and fast-walked when we slowed just slightly. Jeff said he was getting a positive feeling about this year's racing, but he would know more after some shorter races. Jeff said he might run the Copper Basin 300 the second week in January, he wasn't sure yet. He planned to run the Knik 200 on

New Year's Eve; he always did, as it was near their home. That race did give him confidence; that week there was a slight cold snap at Jeff and Donna's and it got down to fifty-seven below. One of their daughters was having a slumber party and Jeff had to stay and fix the plumbing. Morten ran the team instead and won. Jeff would race in the Kuskokwim 300, one of the toughest races and one of his favorites, on the last weekend in January. Then just before the Iditarod, which begins the first Saturday in March, he wanted to run the Tustamena 200 on the Kenai Peninsula. It too would go well; he would win. Paul Gephardt, a musher many people thought was a future star, came in second. People around Alaska were talking knowledgeably about Paul's amazing lead dog with the awe that comes when a superstar is in your midst.

Right before we got to Kate and Larry's cabins, a bit over four hours after starting, we reached the top of a big hill. The trail ran through a stand of evergreens, a healthy, dense cluster. The dogs were not tired, they were speeding up. The trail was level and the powder up here was deep. Jeff let out a holler of joy based on the thrill he must have felt moving so effortlessly through the clean, cold spirits of winter. He yelled out some command; the dogs could clearly feel his thrill, it's transmitted to them. I was holding on tight, hyperalert because we were traveling so fast. The dogs and us, as a single unit, were soaring through the powder.

We came out of the wilderness to a little open runway for a Super Cub. Jeff told us to get ready, we were about to make almost a ninety-degree turn and then we'd be there. He obviously didn't want to slow down the dogs. I didn't slow down, my sled whipped out in the brush, I bent down, leaned left, and made it. Whoa, what a rush. Jeff told me as we both braked, easing toward the log cabin we'd sleep in, that last summer a grizzly had come around here. A Super Cub was parked out on the grass strip. The bear liked red, the color of the plane, or didn't like planes, whatever—it stood up on it hind legs and tore up the wing fabric covering, did $15,000 in damage. Alaska insurance agents get these kinds of "animals and equipment meet" calls more than you might think. The guy who owned the plane taped up the wings with duct tape and flew it to Fairbanks to be repaired.

Kate Wood and Larry Mead had their own kingdom out here near Gold King Creek. In some way, that whole concept of your own kingdom is why people love living in Alaska. You can carve out your own world and be completely (or however completely you want) surrounded by the natural world. Kate came to Alaska from Maine to go fishing for grayling. Her boat broke down, she had this feeling that she didn't care if she went back to Maine or not. No offense to Maine or anyplace else, but there is no comparison when it comes to Alaska, she told me. A year later, Kate, a registered nurse, sold her farm in midcoast Maine and moved up. Kate and Larry became partners and have had this place for several years. You can't call it a B&B; it would have to be a B&B&L&D, plus. Kate served us a dinner that night made on her woodstove, just Jeff, Morten, Helge, Larry, and me. It was exquisite food. There were homemade breads and cakes and pies and jellies and relishes and meats. Here was a place where there was time to cook, to bless your creations, to share them with strangers who don't stay so long. I remember Jeff saying this would be the best of both worlds, the thirty-five below and the potential brutality of the trip, and then the pampering of Kate's homemade food and Larry's sawmill, where he milled his own lumber and had used it to build their sauna. Jeff said he had nothing to prove anymore, he could tough it out enough in the races, he didn't have to beat up himself or his dogs anymore in training with Kate and Larry's place available as a halfway point. Amen, brother.

Before we ate, before we even met Kate, the dogs were all unhooked from the sled and bedded with fresh straw. Larry had water heated so their food could be mixed. Our cabin with four bunk beds had a woodstove going; it had heated the water. There was a wire "clothesline" for our frozen mittens and damp felt boot liners and wool hats. There was a place to hang our Trans-Alaska suits to dry; we could dress just in fleece pants and vests and coats. This cold is filled with clean spirits and dry landings; there is almost no way to get wet and cold unless you run into the dreaded overflow. It was warm and cozy inside their kitchen with Kate's big-mama cooking stove, and the living room and dining area had its own woodstove too. We sat up for hours after our meal, telling each other story after story. Larry told one about the time thirteen wolves surrounded the cabins and came down to the creek and out on the ridge. I don't quite remember how they knew there were thirteen, but they did, and Kate and Larry have no reason to exaggerate. When you're flushed by racing across the wild and filled with Kate's food and wine and herbal tea, there comes a state where the moment, the stories, the company, are just appreciated for their existence. The details are not stored in the memory. Jeff, Morten, Helge, and I took a sauna.

My bumps, bruises, and sore muscles were warmed, toasty and sweaty. Morten and Helge jumped into the snow nude. Little thirty-nine-pound Jenna, who watched Jeff's every move, was allowed into the cabin with us. She was probably as close to Jeff as any of his dogs. She slept in the bottom bunk with him.

Jeff was forty-four years old. It had been a long trail for him, starting in northern California where he had grown up, even played quarterback at Shasta Junior College at five feet eight, 140 pounds. He'd bought his first land bordering Denali Park in 1977. He did not dream of being a professional sled-dog racer, one of the greatest winners ever. His plan was simply to live in Alaska, and to do whatever it took to stay. But watching him today hollering to no one but himself and his dogs, expressing his feelings of pure joy at running through spruce and powder, was to see why he loved this life. Put him in a race and he and his dogs want to beat you. But between the beginning of the race and the end he loves what he's doing, he draws great inspiration from the act itself. He will never regret the life he has chosen because once he found it, it is what he wanted more than anything else. Even if he gets as old as Kitty and he's limping around, he will remember. He will hear the excitement of the dogs. He may watch one of his daughters cross the finish line in Nome someday.

I wished we could have stayed longer with Kate and Larry at their kingdom with the hundred-mile view, but we made the run back to the road. We got back and the dogs acted as if they wanted more. That's okay—Jeff and these dogs had a couple thousand miles to go before the winter of 2000 was over.

THE RACE

March 4 arrived. It was a day of excitement all over Alaska. The "last great race" would have its ceremonial start in Anchorage. Sometimes crews actually had to haul snow into Anchorage if there wasn't enough snow on the main streets so the eighty-one mushers could begin. Most of the mushers were from Alaska; places like Point Hope, Seward, Fairbanks, Two Rivers, Big Lake, Willow, Moose Pass, Kasilof, Nenana, Trapper Creek, Healy, and Kotzebue. There was a wild-looking guy named Fedor Konyukhov from Moscow, and others from Outside: Germany, England, Michigan, Australia, Canada, Colorado, even a former professional wrestler from Minnesota. There was Charlie Boulding, with his chest-length gray beard and long gray braids, a former southern country boy who had the aw-shucks aura of a southerner at Woodstock. People said he had

An equipment and food drop in Unalakleet along the Iditarod Trail during the 2000 Iditarod Race. Photo by Peter Jenkins

been Special Forces or an army Ranger, he was as tough as a frigid hell. Some said this was Charlie's year to win. He'd beaten Jeff in the Kuskokwim 300; his best finish at the Iditarod was third in 1998, when Jeff had last won. In 1999, he had beaten Jeff; Charlie had come in fifth, Jeff seventh. Knowing Jeff, if I had a million dollars to bet, I would have bet he did better than seventh this year. Although seven is a special number, it's too far from number one for Jeff.

Even though he was from far away, South Carolina to be exact, veterinarian Sonny King was back. He was well liked by Alaskans because he had paid his dues working as a veterinarian on the Iditarod and he smiles, yet steadily improves. Doug Swingley, the gunslinger from Montana, had ridden in on his black horse, in his black hat and black chaps. In one breath he is talking humbly about being the seventeenth member of his dog team (everyone begins with sixteen dogs—no substitutions are allowed, but injured or exhausted dogs are dropped along the way at checkpoints and flown back to Anchorage), while in another breath Doug is predicting a win and a race speed record, Joe Namath–style. Doug won last year; so far he's run the Iditarod eight times and won twice. He holds the record for the fastest time, nine days, two hours, and forty-two minutes. I'm sure there are people in Alaska who root for Swingley, but since he's the only musher from a state other than Alaska to have won, you won't find many fans. People who know dogs say he has an incredible team and that he has pioneered long-distance training, some days running 150 miles. Even the president of the Anchorage Rotary Club was running the race. Jeff would never say anything publicly or to me, but I know Doug was one of his main motivations for wanting to win, to have an Alaskan, preferably himself, take back the mantle of the winner of the last great race.

On Sunday, March 5, the real race began in Wasilla. The eighty-one mushers would depart every two minutes, headed to Knik, where there was the Knik Bar. Every year Alaska folksinger and my friend Hobo Jim sang the Iditarod song he had written, "I did, I did, I did the Iditarod Trail," for the rowdy crowd there. We saw Jeff start thirty-sixth, while Shawn Sidelinger, running the puppy team, started thirty-fifth. Bryan Imus, a rookie who had loaned Jeff his superdog, Yuksi, started fifty-fourth. Doug Swingley started one behind Paul Gephardt, the carpenter from the Kenai Peninsula. Jerry Riley, the 1976 champion, an Athabascan from the interior, was telling people he was back. He was around sixty years old and tough enough to whip up on the twenty-somethings. Twenty-somethings don't win the Iditarod. Middle-aged humans excel; it seems to take experience to master it. The gray-pigtailed, happy-eyed Charlie Boulding, the sly fox, began last. The weather was considered warm today, in the thirties; Jeff took it slow, didn't care who passed him.

This year, an even year, the race went from Wasilla to Knik. After Knik there would be no way to drive to any place on the Iditarod Trail, and Knik was only fourteen miles from Wasilla. From there it is eighty-six miles to Skwentna, then through Finger Lake, a checkpoint in a tent. Then over Rainy Pass, at 3,160 feet the highest place on the mushers' trail, unless they started hallucinating several days into the race. Then to Rohn, which is a steep downhill that leaves behind the Alaska Range, of which Mount McKinley is a part. The trail from Rohn to Nikolai, a Native village of a hundred or so, is one of the toughest stretches. It's ninety-three miles through an area where there was once a large wildfire; they call it Farewell Bunn. Then it's west toward the Kuskokwim Mountains and McGrath. Racers must take a twenty-four-hour break; many take theirs at the checkpoint in McGrath. McGrath has been having problems with wolves coming around town and eating its dogs.

The musher from Montana has introduced a new tactic. Among the elite fifteen or twenty mushers, this race is like a radical form of chess. Teams that want to win try to make surprising moves to weaken their competitors and suck away their fighting spirit. One adage is, never let your competitors see you. Play every head game you can, even just enough to be a pinprick in their balloon of fight. In the last few years, Doug Swingley has been pushing and pushing. His team are such extraordinary athletes, so well trained. He tries to get so far ahead before he takes his twenty-four-hour break that few feel they can catch up.

From McGrath, it's on to Takotna, then Ophir, a ghost town. Cripple is the halfway point and the first one there collects some money, $3,000. From Cripple it's a long route to Ruby. First dog team to Ruby, the musher gets a gourmet meal prepared by one of Alaska's best chefs.

All along the route, at every checkpoint there are vets and race officials, making sure the dogs are fine and that no musher is in trouble. Before the Iditarod every dog must get an EKG and have blood work done by race-hired technicians. I went with Jeff when he had all his dogs tested in Healy. From Ruby they go to Galena, then Nulato, then to Kaltag. These 150 miles are run on the Yukon River.

Jeff said he had been preparing a secret weapon for this flat, boring stretch. The dogs and he need inspiration at about that point, close to six hundred miles into the race. Everyone needs to stay motivated. Jeff had been experimenting with hooking up some speakers on his sled and playing music for the dogs. Jeff studies every angle. Pavlov, a noted animal behaviorist, who played music to milk cows to improve their milk output, discovered animals respond favorably to good music. Jeff wanted to play his dogs some Marshall Tucker Band, among others, to pick up their steps, fire up their high-performing spirits.

People all over Alaska followed the intricate details of each day, some checking in for several updates a day. The *Anchorage Daily News*, the *Fairbanks News Miner*, provided daily details of each musher. There were features on the unusual, the inspirational. One guy running the race was HIV-positive. There were citizens analyzing the difference between run times between Rohn and Nikolai. You can overhear someone in Barnes & Noble in Anchorage buying a book on yoga saying to the person making a mocha, "Can you believe Rick Swenson [a five-time champion] was less than an hour behind Swingley into Ophir?" The high school student with long blond hair making the mocha might respond, "I don't know about that, but Ramy Brooks sure is hot."

Following the Iditarod becomes a ten-day addiction, even two weeks if you know someone back in the pack. You want every source you can find. The Iditarod Web site has times and departures. You keep your map of the route handy, preferably on your refrigerator. You click on Cabela's Web site and read columns from the outstanding Joe Runyan, the John Madden of mushing commentators. Reading Joe Runyan's pieces on Cabela's daily race coverage was an excellent way to get a feel for the ever-changing dynamics of the leaders. Joe is an Iditarod winner and comments with an authenticity that only comes from having raised dogs, mushed, competed, and won. Plus, the mushers, a tough, sometimes stoic group, trust Joe far more than most media types. For example, here's an excerpt about the Yukon River: "The Yukon River is big, expansive, and complicated with dead-end oxbow sloughs and wide channels that divert for miles in endless excursions from the main channel. A musher should heed the warning 'Follow the markers.' 'Just follow the river, you can't get lost' is the worst piece of advice that you could take under your hat. From the surface of the Yukon, it is immense, like a lake. Hidden behind islands, one could never imagine that an entirely different part of the braided system of channels comprising the Yukon exists quite apart from the reality you envision. It is not inconceivable at all, in the moonless dark, to be entirely turned around. Great stories of adventurers traveling the river and finding themselves at a previous village several days later are not uncommon."

One night Joe's "Evening Appraisal" read, "Jeff King is still driving a very fast team and will depart almost arm in arm with Rick Swenson. When I talked with Jeff, he conceded that Swingley held a significant lead but pointed out that he had leaders that could travel even in the winds purported to be developing on the Bering Sea coast."

And since Alaska is the world's largest small town, Alaskans not only follow their top choice, but several other mushers they know, dislike, have dated, or been married to (keeping track of their prize money), and perhaps some of their uncle's or neighbor's or friend's dogs.

From Kaltag the trail veers off the Yukon River through mountains and valleys to the coast and Unalakleet. The first one to Unalakleet receives gold from the National Bank of Alaska. Next comes the Eskimo village of Shaktoolik, where the trail goes out onto the frozen ocean. There are still 229 miles to Nome and the finish line.

After all this racing across the totally unpredictable Alaskan wilderness, there could be only minutes separating the top teams. The race at this point calls for every racer's all-out push. Thousands of dollars in prize money separates first from second from third. The champions' hearts are showing, refusing to give. The word from the knowledgeable was that Paul Gephardt's lead dog was such a competitor that he refused even to lie down when the team stopped to rest. He just sat up, powerful chest and front legs supporting his huge heart. He would be named top lead dog at the awards banquet in Nome.

From Shaktoolik it's down the windswept trail of sea ice to Koyuk, then Elim, Golovin, and White Mountain. Mushers must take an eight-hour break here, seventy-seven miles from the finish. Then it's on to Safety and Nome. Every time a musher comes down Main Street in Nome the fire sirens go off all over town, whether it's noon, 2:31 A.M., or 4:44 A.M.

Doug Swingley won the 2000 Iditarod with the fastest time ever, nine days, fifty-eight minutes, and six seconds. He won $60,000 and another new Dodge truck. Jeff's team got some flu bug early on, which caused him to stop and take his twenty-four-hour layover much sooner than he had hoped. After almost twelve hundred miles of some of the most radical landscape in the world, Paul Gephardt was just five hours and two minutes behind Doug for second. His prize money was $52,500. Jeff and his team came in seven hours and forty-two minutes behind Doug, just two hours and forty minutes behind Paul. Ramy Brooks, 1999's Yukon Quest champion, a young charger, was just thirty-six minutes behind Jeff. Charlie, his long gray beard flying in the wind, came in fifth. Every musher and every dog that ran, raced, covered so much of Alaska, will never forget his or her own accomplishment. Running the 2000 Iditarod will become one of his or her most powerful memories, quietly recalled, drawn upon for inspiration.

After the racing season of 2000 ended, later that year, before the short Alaskan summer, Kitty just couldn't go on any longer. She passed away, having faded slowly, a supreme creature who had lived a life any racing dog would have loved.

12

Maximum Security

I never thought we could get trapped in Seward by avalanches, but in January, we did. It showed us what can happen when there is just one road out. An avalanche occurs, blanketing that road with piles and piles of snow; the one road gets closed down, and you're a prisoner. Although we had been stranded now four or five days, we had power most of the time; Seward has its own power generators. Just knowing we absolutely could not leave Seward, though, got to me. I was on edge and so was Rita; we are people who need to move.

Several communities between here and Anchorage—Hope, Moose Pass, and Girdwood—were in worse shape than we were. They had lost their electricity, and people with private generators were running out of gas. A group of women had driven to Girdwood, a ski resort community not far from Anchorage, for one of their birthdays and had been unable to get out. One of them kissed the chartered helicopter that finally came to get them. In Seward we'd gotten maybe four feet of snow in the past four days, maybe more. Alaska has plenty of outrageous weather that never makes the news, but after the whole Kenai Peninsula was blocked by avalanches for a couple of days, we even made some national newscasts.

Alaska is such a surprising place. Many of the things I thought about Alaska before I got here turned out in reality to be the opposite of what I'd expected. I thought summer would be a time for soaring, easy travel, for going all over the place. But the opposite was true. Summer was a time to let the sunlight soak into your life-giving batteries, to warm your face, to stay around the home place. It is the time to gather your fish and berries and earn your living wage.

It is when Alaska changes its relationship with sun, when winter comes and things freeze, that true freedom comes. It is a freedom of movement and a freedom from fear. As the sun gets farther away, it grows colder and darker. There is so much water flowing or standing still in Alaska, over 3 million lakes of over twenty acres each and more than three thousand rivers, not counting the ponds and small lakes and creeks and springs and swamps and other wetlands. All of these things make travel difficult when the water is not frozen. But the cold freezes the water, even the salt water.

Before Alaska freezes, the bears are not hibernating. Who knows when you might run into one in the dense undergrowth, lying around a kill site, waiting for its moose meat to age. Unfortunately, though, sometimes, when just the right conditions occur, winter traps us.

Out in a neighborhood called Questa Woods, where Julianne's friend Danielle lived, there looked to be seven feet of snow on some of the roofs. People stood on the roofs shoveling off the snow; it was taller than they were. I had heard someone call it Snow Acres. Whether you were up against our mountainside or out in the middle of the valley could make a drastic difference in the snowfall you received. In the valley, they may have had a third as much snow as we did even though they were only five miles from us.

We were told that this year the millions and billions of tons of snow that had floated to earth were resting on a slippery, icy base. What had not avalanched already could go at any time. Still we were unafraid. I had never known anyone who had been affected by an avalanche until this week. Like an unending snowfall, the avalanches kept falling. Workers would clean them up with dozers and other heavy equipment, and more snow would take its place. Avalanches would cover the road in places where no one could remember them coming down before or right next to where they'd cleaned up the last one.

If we rode about twenty miles or so out of town, we could see what had us walled in. Although I knew all this avalanche stuff was true—it was in the *Anchorage Daily News*—I wanted to see it. I called the local State Troopers office often and asked for updates. The woman in the office was relaxed and witty. She told me one day early on that someone had called in to report that some vehicle tracks went into one side of the avalanche that did not come out the other end. Could there be a car and people trapped under all that? A state trooper checked it out; I guess he had to walk up and over it and look on foot. Turned out the wind had blown the tracks clear on the far side. The heavy equipment whose task it was to free us could only remove one snow pile at a time. There were hundreds of avalanches in the 125 miles between here and Anchorage; several had made it to the road, leaving behind anywhere from a few feet to sixteen feet of snow.

Avalanches give no warning sounds; they destroy almost everything in their path, splintering trees two feet thick, demolishing power lines, everything. When the fallen trees are caught up in the wet snow and the whole mess crashes down the slopes until it comes to rest, it becomes like concrete with metal bars in it for strength. Avalanches are most frequent on slope angles between thirty and forty-five degrees; they're called slab avalanches and can travel at speeds approaching ninety miles per hour.

This season, the base under all this heavy, unstable snowpack formed around Christmas. After that, it warmed up into the forties and those twenty inches compressed, melted, and condensed into an icy base of about five inches. Then it got cold and the base froze. This base was somewhat like a hockey-rink ice surface, most unstable to the snow above on the moderate slopes. The steepest slopes did not allow the snow to build up; the flatter ones were not steep enough to create an avalanche. Then some loose and dry snow fell, and on top of that a slab of heavy snow, the type we had been getting night after day after night recently.

It seemed as if we had gotten a couple more feet since Julianne had gone to school this morning. Now, around lunchtime, it was storming wickedly. We could not see past three feet in front of the window of the fourplex. Where we live in middle Tennessee, if they see snowflakes in the air just blowing around, they have been known to close school, let the kids go early.

Earlier, the snowflakes floated peacefully to the ground or to rest on slanted spruce boughs. Now winds blew from a maniacal place and were smashing Seward. The ravens on the dead trees at the bottom of the hill would have to seek shelter. The windows that took the strongest bursts of wind popped against their frames. As we "walked" on the ice-covered sidewalks toward the Marina Café for a late breakfast and were blown backward, I told Rita that no doubt school would get out early.

We decided to drive over to Julianne's school. Maybe we could beat the buses, whose drivers could barely see the road. The winds were blowing so strong and unruly and were filled with snow. A moose walked out of the willows, crossing into some deep cover. We might have hit it if not for our four-wheel drive. I am not sure what wind system this was related to, but parts of Anchorage had been punched with winds over one hundred miles an hour. A part of town called the Lower Hillside had gotten it the worst. Cordova had been slapped too, but nothing too unusual, with winds over eighty-five miles per hour. Our storm was not comparable to these; our mountains protected us yet still we were blasted.

We got to the parking lot. On a clear day, this school has one of the most spectacular backdrops of any school in the world, a section of flat-faced high mountains on the edge of the Harding Icefield. But today neither the mountains nor the school was visible. I did not see any buses lined up either. I spotted the school as the storm let up momentarily, then to its right I thought I saw something colorful in the field next to the school. Several classes were having recess, including Julianne's. I thought I saw her yellow and blue parka. The children, some in snow up past their waists, were running, sliding down slides, making snow angels, disappearing in the snow. Julianne and three of her girlfriends came over when they saw us and said hello. Avalanche-producing weather, blizzards, and power-packed winds just add to the possibilities for fun when you are in third grade in Alaska.

Before we left the apartment, I had called the Alaska Department of Transportation road system number, 800-478-7675. Each day they update the recording. The road from Seward to Anchorage was closed, the recorded lady said, blocked by avalanches in several places. I felt that this lady was my friend. That is when I knew I had been walled into Seward way too long. State officials urged citizens to stay off the roads and definitely not to go into the backcountry. The year before just off the Seward-to-Anchorage road several snow machiners who were high-marking were killed by avalanches. High-marking is the dangerous practice of riding a snow machine straight up the incline of a mountain, seeing how high up the peak you can get before you have to swoop back down, and it's named for the tracks you can see from below.

In the *Anchorage Daily News*, which we could get at times on the Internet when the phone lines were not down, they quoted David Liebershach of the Alaska Division of Emergency Services: "We really want to caution folks. If they don't have to be out, if there's any way they can avoid traveling, they really shouldn't do it." When anyone cautions Alaskans and they listen, you know it is a serious situation. On one seven-mile stretch just west of Girdwood, over seventy miles from us, seven avalanches were in the road or across it, some ten feet deep. Just twenty-one miles out of Seward, by Kenai Lake, another avalanche blocked the road. This stretch of the Seward Highway is one of the most dangerous avalanche zones in the world. Just this week a bulldozer operator who had been clearing the road in this area was hit by an avalanche, swept off the road, and killed.

That afternoon, Rita and I were bored. But at least now we were feeling alive—we had just been to see Darien. We had ordered a coffee to share; Darien had come up with some milk, though he had been running low. Locals, including one of our school bus drivers, had been bringing him their milk. We depended on Darien to keep a sizable chunk of town from getting grumpy, zooming on caffeine and his restrained wit. While we were there, Skip, the man who owns and runs our little movie theater, came by. Darien asked him if the new movie had made it in. He said no; he was expecting *Snow Falling on Cedars*, except it should probably be called *Snow Falling on Seward*. We laughed as if this were hysterically funny. The whole town was getting slaphappy.

We needed something different to do, something other than driving in the deep snow on our few miles of road. We decided to head toward Anchorage. We'd heard people were trapped on the road between two avalanches up ahead. They would run their engines a few minutes every hour to keep warm. The troopers were trying to rescue them with a helicopter. A woman and her two daughters driving in a 1994 Suburban were swept off the road by Cooper Landing, between Seward and Soldotna. Most of the windows were broken and the car was hidden upside down under the killer snow. The mom hung by her seat belt, and her twelve-year-old daughter's legs were covered in snow, as she was crammed between the seat and the door. Her husband had been following in a car behind but had not seen his family disappear. The mom called 911 on her cell, but it did not connect. She then succeeded in getting through to a friend who lived nearby, and the friend summoned emergency crews to the scene.

No vehicles were heading north but us. For the first few miles there was no steep land on either side of us. Then we reached the beginning of a tight pass, with mountainsides on our right and left. Even knowing we were headed into a barricade of snow, it felt freeing to be going out of our snowbound town. I looked up at the snow on both sides of us. If even the drifts immediately surrounding us fell, it would bury our vehicle. Quite a few trees were on both sides, large, old trees, which meant no avalanche had come through as long as they had been growing. But the news about the avalanches on the Seward Highway had been that they were crashing down from places that had not had avalanches in decades. Looking at the seven or eight feet of snow above us, all the way up to the top of the mountain, I thought about how the middle layer was powder, and how the heavy, wet top portion put pressure on the icy base. What exactly did it take to break the snow loose and begin a trip down the mountain? There would be no warning. I'd heard about how if we were to be covered by snow, there would be no way to open the car doors. How long would the oxygen inside the vehicle last? And of course, it was still snowing, and snowing. How many more flakes had to land before it would all come down on us, before us, behind us, above us. We were in an area where cell phones didn't work. If an avalanche came down behind us and kept us from getting back, we would be stuck. I was about to tell Rita that we should turn around and go back to Seward, but before I could, Rita asked how far we were going to go. Soon it would be time for Julianne to get home from school. So far, I have never seen Rita afraid of anything.

Whittier, not far from us on Prince William Sound, hadn't had full power for a week. The city manager was quoted in the newspaper saying that people in her town were sleeping with their snow shovels because they didn't want their shovels to disappear. They had gotten almost five feet of fresh snow this week. The whole of the Kenai Peninsula was trapped, unable to drive to Anchorage. Seward was without a link to the outside, no railroad, no road, no airplanes. Sometimes our telephone lines worked, but more often than not there was brain-frying static. We'd been able to go nowhere but around town for a week. A reporter from Nashville's newspaper, *The Tennessean*, did a small piece about us being trapped by the avalanches. Jerry House, a Nashville morning DJ, got the story and began the "rumor" that we were trapped by an avalanche in a sewer in Alaska. Some people actually believed Jerry.

Our friends in the other upstairs apartment, Dawn Starke and Juanita O'Shea, said Seward would be all right as long as the town didn't run out of beer. Neighbors were socializing, since sometimes you could not talk on the telephone, E-mail anyone, feed your Internet addiction, or fax anybody.

One black night Dawn and I read to each other from "The Police Log." Several entries were avalanche-related. "4:12 A.M. Several avalanches on Lowell Point Road in areas where they've never seen avalanches before. Will not clear until daylight." That's the only road to Lowell Point. We hoped there wouldn't be any medical emergencies out there. "5:31 A.M. Caller advised the mail truck

Driving around Seward after a monster snowstorm. PHOTO BY PETER JENKINS

was stuck in an avalanche at mile 38.5 Seward Highway. No injuries reported. Advised there are two avalanches across the road." "10:36 A.M. Mother moose and calf seen on Adams near First. Children in area." We'd been seeing a moose out our kitchen window every few days. "11:10 A.M. Winter storm warning. Up to two feet of snow. Travel highly discouraged."

"11:31 A.M. Man wanted information about how to get a restraining order against his wife because she was getting drunk and breast-feeding their child. Advised to call DFYS." "8:20 P.M. Report of a man lying on the side of the road, motionless. Ambulance responded but trooper advised to cancel. Subject was extremely intoxicated. Given ride." "10:15 P.M. A mother, her daughter, and another female juvenile reported there were two blue cars following them. Stated this has been going on for several months."

"12:25 A.M. Advised of man lying in trunk of a car and not moving. All okay, car being worked on." "12:36 A.M. Ambulance requested for male, 43, at the prison having a possible heartache." They probably meant *heart attack*. "3:10 A.M. Male advised he had given the victory sign to a cabdriver who apparently took it for a different kind of gesture and stopped and yelled at the individual."

Our apartment at times seemed the size of my underwear drawer. But being snowed in by the heavy white quilt of snow did have a cozy quality. Our apartment was like a cave; Rita and I kept each other warmer than usual. In about nine months there will probably be a mini population explosion in all the places that were closed in by the sliding masses of snow. I loved looking out the window at the snow as it came down and down and down; lying on my back watching the big floating flakes put me to sleep. Every day I called the state 800 number waiting to be freed. Every day the message was the same: "The road conditions on this recording are divided into main highway areas and topics. Listen for the"—I pressed my phone keypad, beep—"current conditions." The woman at the state Department of Transportation who recorded the messages sounded stressed out to the point of not wanting to say anything. Or was that my stress?

Her message continued, "I'm just letting you know that the Seward Highway is closed at Mile 21 due to a natural avalanche."

The word *natural* was crucial because the state was shooting cannons at the mountaintops and dropping bombs from helicopters to create "unnatural" avalanches to hurry the process of clearing the mountains.

One morning we decided to drive out past where we had turned around before. The perky, feisty woman who worked at Darien's coffee place told us that her husband, who was handling DOT work, was bringing in a helicopter to the area around Mile 21 to drop bombs as they flew over the high mountain ridges, breaking loose avalanches.

We drove to Kenai Lake, where we could go no farther. I heard the helicopter far off, high above, then the bomb went off. The snow broke loose and roared down the mountain. We could hear trees snap like bone-dry twigs, boulders smashing against other boulders. The side of the mountain was being cleared off. Now I understood how the clear pathways through the forests on the sides of Alaskan mountains were made. It was not because trees could not grow there, but because snow had washed the life away and mangled any man-made stuff in its way. They dropped many bombs out of the helicopter; watching it was the most diversion we had had in a week. And it was so good to be traveling more than a few miles again.

The days ran together. A few times a day, I called the 800 number at DOT. Then one day when I called, it said something different: "Menu: Alaska and Dalton Highways, press *one*. [Beep] Avalanche and emergency information, press *two*. [Beep] Avalanche conditions along the Seward Highway, uh . . ." Oh, no—damn it to hell, she's pausing, the stress of telling us we're still prisoners by the white, frozen walls is finally getting to her. "We are glad to report the Seward Highway is open from Anchorage all the way to Seward." If she had been standing anywhere near me, I would have hugged her.

What a difference it made just knowing we could leave. Not that we had anywhere to go this moment. But it didn't matter—we were free again.

Mark in front of Pedersen Glacier in Aialik Bay. *Photo by Peter Jenkins*

A humpback whale, the largest member of the congregation, near Montague Island. *Photo by Peter Jenkins*

At the Y, coming back from Anchorage, one way leads home to Seward and the other goes to Soldotna and Homer. *Photo by Peter Jenkins*

Mark and Rebekah and I are about to take off up into the narrow passageway to Pedersen Glacier in Aialik Bay. *Photo by Peter Jenkins*

Tina stands in front of the school named after her grandmother in Hydaburg.
Photo by Peter Jenkins

Left: A bald eagle waits out a storm at the bottom of our hill in Seward.
Photo by Peter Jenkins

Bottom: Winter light on the mountains bordering Resurrection Bay in Seward.
Photo by Peter Jenkins

Close-up of a fishing boat at the docks in Cordova. *Photo by Peter Jenkins*

Per Nolan with a large sockeye salmon aboard the *Terminal Harvester* in Cordova. *Photo by Peter Jenkins*

Andy Johnson holds his surfboard at the edge of the Cordova harbor. *Photo by Peter Jenkins*

Jeff King trains for the Iditarod on a frozen river near Mount McKinley. *Photo by Peter Jenkins*

The Denali Highway is closed in winter, as this sign warns. We mushed down the road anyway.
Photo by Peter Jenkins

Paul Gephardt's unrelenting lead dog refused to lie down and rest during the Iditarod in Unalakleet. *Photo by Peter Jenkins*

Grog's transportation and cold-weather gear for the Bachelors Auction in Talkeetna. *Photo by Peter Jenkins*

Rita, Julianne, Vicky, Elizabeth, and Eric resting about halfway to Chandalar Lake on the winter trail in the Brooks Range. *Photo by Peter Jenkins*

Pete and Julianne mushing on Chandalar Lake in the Brooks Range. *Photo by Peter Jenkins*

Oliver Leavitt's whaling crew is ready to launch, near Barrow. *Photo by Peter Jenkins*

Watching for the bowhead whales at the neighboring whaling camp, near Barrow. *Photo by Peter Jenkins*

A small portion of the massive Western Arctic Herd of caribou between Deering and Shishmaref.
Photo by Peter Jenkins

Two musk ox bulls that have been driven from the herd by the dominant bull, near Deering.
Photo by Peter Jenkins

Hobo Jim on the table at the Yukon Bar in Seward. *Photo by Peter Jenkins*

Dean Cummings and Eric Smith standing with some of their students in front of the school where they teach in Deering. *Photo by Peter Jenkins*

The Fields's two horses, Rocket and Winddancer, on Harvester Island, looking back into Uyak Bay.
Photo by Rebekah Jenkins

Rebekah and Naphtali Fields picking salmon at one of the Fields's set-net sites in Uyak Bay.
Photo by Peter Jenkins

One of the Fields's set-nets with two work boats in Uyak Bay. *Photo by Rebekah Jenkins*

Eva Ryan's salmon-drying racks and work gloves in Unalakleet. *Photo by Peter Jenkins*

Eleanor and Johnny Sarren at their cabin up the Unalakleet River. *Photo by Peter Jenkins*

Our guide, Larry Fiedler, carries Jerry's antlers out of the valley to our campsite in Grizzly Flats.
Photo by Peter Jenkins

Jim Harrower's float plane anchored in the Stony River with the Alaska Range in the background.
Photo by Peter Jenkins

13

Bingo Anger

A large dog, part Saint Bernard, part husky, lay in the middle of the main road into Talkeetna. Was it dead? It was curled into a perfect ball, its nose covered with its fluffed-out tail. Dead dogs are not usually observed in such alive-looking positions. Had it frozen solid? I thought I saw the gray-white of exhaled breath coming from underneath the fur of its tail. A snow machine—don't call them snowmobiles in Alaska—came toward the dog and me from the direction of Talkeetna, the town I am headed for. The guy running it, dressed in oil-stained Carhartts, stopped, got off, and started talking to the dog, who was not only alive but lifted its nose up from the cozy warmth of fur.

The guy has a beard about the same color as the dog's fur; his beard falls to the middle of his chest. They appear to know each other, the dog and the man. He gets the dog to stand up, but when he turns to slow down a Jeep coming up too fast behind him, the dog lies back down, turns over on its back, and begins to shimmy around on the road, where some pavement is visible. It is snowing—huge, dry flakes. It was 4 P.M. and almost dark, with a gray light around everything.

This Talkeetna traffic-flow volunteer kneels down, again, and pleads with the dog. The dog returns to rubbing his backbone on the street. The bearded guy then bends over his snow machine and unhooks his snowshoes from the backseat. He kneels down and lifts the big dog onto the front of the seat where he'd been riding, the dog straddling the snow machine. Its legs are long enough to bounce on the road if he doesn't hold them up. The dog has obviously ridden like this before; he actually puts all four paws on the metal tracks made for the rider's feet. The guy plops down behind the dog and props his snowshoes between them. He pulls a power U-turn right in front of me—for a second I think they will hit me as they skid—then heads back into Talkeetna (pop. 330), driving really fast.

On any winter weekend except this one, that dog could have slept in the road and the local folks would just have driven around it. But for the next few days several fresh people will be in town. No place I have ever been recognizes someone new in town as quickly as they do in Alaska. The communities are so few, so spread out, so hard to reach. At least you can *drive* to funky Talkeetna.

Talkeetna is located in the part of Alaska where the sun rises and sets all year, not like above the Arctic Circle in Barrow where it sets and stays gone for several months. I parked in front of a rough-hewn place called The Roadhouse. Inside were several tables full of women, mostly middle-aged women. Everyone in the place looked up at me; was I a local, a bachelor, a what?

I overheard the three women at the table next to me saying that they would be playing bingo tonight, the night before the bachelor auction. They didn't look like bingo players, not that I know any. One had short, dark hair; she looked like an aging hippie from the seventies. One looked carefully put together, more like a suburban housewife, not a common look in Alaska. Her hair looked professionally colored, maybe to hide a few early gray hairs. The other, a reporter for the *Anchorage Daily News*, asked me if I was going to play bingo. I said I never had; she said I didn't know what I was missing. I mentioned that I might give it a try. She directed me to the VFW hall a few blocks west of downtown. She seemed aggressive, for Alaska. Many Alaskans just want to be left alone, not an easy thing for a reporter.

Five more women walked in and sat down. Obviously, some fresh women would be in town with money to burn, to bid on some of the men at the nineteenth annual Bachelors Auction. Or they might be here to enter the Wilderness Woman's Contest. Supposedly some of the toughest and most attractive women in Alaska take part. This weekend was Winterfest, one of the two big Talkeetna festivals. (The other is the Moose Dropping Festival.)

These women were here in town mainly to see what was displayed in the "Male Order Catalog," a hand-stapled, twenty-two-page, black-and-white, home-computer-produced pass-out done by the Talkeetna Bachelors Society, Inc. Not one man displayed inside is wearing a suit or a tie; thirteen had shoulder-length hair. Surely there were a few more ponytail types. Three of them are shown wearing fur hats, giving them the mountain-man look. Twenty-four of the thirty-four have beards. A few of the beards are so dense, so untamed, that a snake could survive inside.

The only auction I've ever been to that had a catalog and living things for sale was the University of Tennessee Annual Bull Sale. It is held twice a year near my farm. The bulls can't answer any questions, although they are measured and tested. "Scrotal circumference," which has a bearing on sperm production, is an important number. The higher the number, the more sperm. Also in the catalog are the bulls' height at the shoulder, birth weight, and daily weight gain while on feed. In cattle, many traits are inherited. It is important to know how much weight per day a bull can gain in a few months; he passes this trait on to his offspring.

I don't think weight-gain tests would be good for these bachelors. First, they would be put into rooms, then fed all the beer and food they could eat while watching TV. How much weight would they gain per day? Who cares? They weren't going to be slaughtered after this auction. No measurements were given by the bachelors. Interested bidders would have to get what they needed by looking them over on the auction block. From what I'd heard, some of the bachelors might become more visible as they were being auctioned.

Some of the guys did provide telling answers to a series of the catalog questions.

1. Name?
2. Bachelor number?
3. Address?
4. Age?
5. Birthplace?
6. How long have you lived in Talkeetna (or Alaska)?
7. Where did you live before you came to Talkeetna (or Alaska)?
8. What do you do for a living?
9. What do you like best about Alaska?
10. What was your most exciting Alaskan adventure?
11. What do you do for entertainment?
12. What are you looking for in a woman?

The president of the society, Robert, forty-eight, originally from Iceland, who is a guide, pilot, surveyor, and construction worker, answered "What do you do for entertainment?" with "I entertain myself."

I overheard two women in their twenties looking over the catalog while I was at the local grocery store getting a strong espresso. The shorter, redheaded one, whose clothes were too tight-fitting for winter, said, "Look here, that guy's president of the bachelors and he's standing there with some kind of big gun. He says he entertains himself, usually, but he's auctioning himself off tomorrow night for charity. Nice, not very demanding guy. He can take care of himself, you can tell by the way he holds his gun. I think I may bid on him. He's my kind of man, low maintenance."

Under the "What do you do for a living?" question the answers were classic Alaskan. Some of them were "own and produce building lumber," "pilot, teacher, writer, musher, retired air force," "refuse hauler," "eighth-grade teacher," "snowplow driver," "chef," "helicopter mechanic," "just about everything," "custom knife maker," "welder, mechanic," "commercial fisherman," "owner, rafting company," "bartender," "bridgeman for Alaska Railroad," "make pictures," "whatever is needed," "carpenter," "fishing charters," "as little as possible," "I receive checks."

Several bachelors were in their late twenties and early thirties. This group appeared more clean-cut, with trimmed beards. Their answers were laced with clichés. Their answers to "What are you looking for in a woman?" sounded copied from any personal ad, except for one. A thirty-five-year-old bachelor originally from Georgia, who had a brown goatee, long hair, and bandanna, explained precisely what he was looking for in a woman: "Deaf, dumb, blind, owns her own liquor store."

The guys in their forties, mostly with long beards just getting a few gray hairs, were more original. Under the "Age?" question, John "Dancing Bear" Sally, the custom knife maker and artist, put down, "Old enough to know my limits, but young enough to overstep them (49 and holding)." Forty-five-year-old "Free Trapper Rick" was looking for someone with "a cute smile and honest—likes to cook moose a thousand ways." A fellow nicknamed Grog, who rode into town from his remote cabin dressed in moose-skin clothes, wanted a woman who "wants to live remote for more than one night." What Grog likes best about Alaska is "wide-open spaces and crazy people."

Gary, the mellow-eyed bachelor with the longest beard, wanted a woman

*Gary Hermes, the director of the auction and
bachelor No. 17, answered the question "What was
your most exciting Alaskan experience?" by saying,
"Rescuing women in need."* PHOTO BY PETER JENKINS

"self-sufficient, determined, loving, caring, giving, and who cooks and cleans."
His answer to "What was your most exciting Alaskan experience?": "Rescuing
woman in need." Forty-five-year-old Dave from California had one simple request for the woman he was looking for: "One that will go home on New
Year's." That confused me. Did he want a woman that would go out with him
on New Year's Eve and then come home with him too?

The oldest bachelor, Clarence L. Wells, sixty-three, originally from Brent-
wood, California, answered "What are you looking for in a woman?" with
"Who's looking." Carl, the forty-two-year-old owner of a rafting company who
put just the word "Freedom" as the answer to the question "What do you like
best about Alaska?" got more specific when answering "What was your most exciting Alaskan experience?" His answer: "Making love on a catwalk under a
windy bridge five hundred feet up, on a ten-foot beam." Carl may have hurt his

chances to be bid upon when he answered "What are you looking for in a woman?" with "Someone who knows how to live, isn't a bitch, scoops dog shit, and isn't afraid to explore each other honestly, openly."

It was Friday night, the night before the men went for sale, a lovely night for bingo. I found the Veterans of Foreign Wars building, VFW Post 3836. Many cars were parked out front on this crisp night. Stars vibrated in the black, clear sky, unpolluted to infinity, and the glowing lights inside the frosted windows attracted me. To get here, I had turned left by a pair of caribou horns wrapped in tiny, blinking Christmas lights nailed to the outside of a building. My waitress said that if I went by a stuffed Dall sheep, entwined in lights, standing on a float, I'd gone too far. The snow squeaked loudly under the rubber soles of my insulated boots.

The VFW hall was a log building, and the central entry hallway had all the bachelors' bios and color pictures displayed on the walls. To the right was a bar and on the left a large room filled with tables and the bingo players. I sat down in perhaps the only open seat. The room was filled with a real cross section of people: a couple long-bearded guys, a man with a Santa Claus hat, some folks in their seventies, a couple in horn-rimmed glasses, a couple that had not yet given up on finding nirvana.

I sat across from a talkative, small, black-haired woman who immediately sensed I knew nothing about bingo. She introduced herself, said her name was Gina. She appeared to be sizing up the competition.

"When was the last time you played?" She stared at me aggressively. Alaskans seem to have a habit of looking you in the eye.

"Never have," I answered with a half smile. I couldn't believe I was doing this.

"Well, here, you need to buy some cards and do exactly as I tell you. Never fails, first-time players win. Understand?"

She seemed used to getting her way. There were eight tables of twelve, ninety-six people, plus the caller and some groupies. Almost one-third the town was here for bingo? Wow.

Gina pointed to the pile of prizes: a reindeer that lit up, smoked salmon fillets, a ham. A large, stuffed caribou head looked down at us all from the wall. Gina was serious in instructing me on how to play the game. She said I should play four cards at a time. Some Anchorage women here had once played nine cards, she exclaimed.

"Some of those Anchorage people, all they do is play bingo," Gina spat out disdainfully.

As the game began, and the man called out the numbers, the atmosphere changed radically. Number 75. Number 51. Number 49. On and on it went. So many numbers, so little time.

"Bingo is not for the weak of heart," Gina said, raising her voice, trash-talking.

Another lady across from me who was playing six cards mentioned that she was amazed I was playing four cards for my first time. I began to feel the pressure of missing a number, so many numbers, called out so quickly, and so few prizes. A couple games came and went and no one at our table won. Gina mentioned that she didn't care if she won one game because the prize was an electric blanket and she doesn't have electricity in her cabin.

After another game of no one winning at our table Gina asked me if I noticed the vibe changing in this crowded room, the most happening spot for miles in all frigid directions.

"Just feel it rising. That is bingo anger."

Someone Gina knew won at the table next to ours. The passions inside this room were becoming noticeably more intense.

"Dammit!" Gina punched the word out from inside her little, usually self-controlled body. "Sorry, you don't say *dammit* when someone else wins, dammit."

Then with no warning, two of Gina's cards were filling up. The right numbers were called and colored in. She was about to win. Her porcelain-white skin was flushed, a glowing pink color. Her eyes almost seemed to roll back in her head. I thought the thought but can't bring myself to complete it, she seemed almost . . . no, no. My mind left the bingo hall for a second; haven't some people reached great heights of ecstasy at Beatles, Luther Vandross, and Elvis concerts? Well? But not here, certainly not.

Gina's joyous squeal brought me back to the moment as she gushed, "I love this game." She was now fanning herself. "I don't know what happens to me when I am winning. What makes it even more exciting is that I have to go to the bathroom and I can't leave. I might get my number . . .

"Oh, my god."

Only she and a guy named Jason were still in the running for this win.

The caller alerted us all, "Now hold on, I'm running out of balls."

The white-haired ladies at the corner table giggled. I didn't get it at first; I was so hoping that Gina would get what she needed. One more number was called out, one more big chance for Gina. Her face was now turning red, and she was fanning herself faster and faster and faster. But then the *wrong* number was called out, Gina lost, and long-haired, tattooed Jason won.

"I hate bingo!" she blurted out.

Jason, the guy with the flowing beard and suspenders who Gina said directs traffic at the Moose Dropping Festival, won the big, fat ham. He had a huge and colorful tattoo on his arm visible to all as he strutted slowly and victoriously up to grab his prize. After it's all over and Gina's breathing had calmed, she told me that she thought I was a natural bingo player. That is until she grabbed my mostly colored-in cards and found three different numbers I had missed marking.

"What happened to you, bingo boy? I should have watched you closer, I told you beginners have good luck." She began to fan herself again. People were gathering up their cards, putting on their coats.

Abruptly, Gina walked away into the frozen night, headed back to her little cabin with no electricity in the moonlit woods. The snow was now falling in even bigger, fatter flakes.

After the surprising thrills of bingo, but feeling unfulfilled because I lost, I had to do something. So I went over to the Fairview Inn. A sled dog team was parked outside, along with several snow machines and a couple pickups. The local newspaper, *The Talkeetna Good Times*, free to all, was in a small, just-read pile on a free table. I smoothed it out, put it back together, and read it. I love small-town newspapers. This one appeared to be a monthly. You can tell so much about a place by the ads. In this week's were many ads, hoping to get the attention of the people in town for the Bachelors Auction and Wilderness Woman Contest. One said, "McKinley Snowmobile Adventures. Remote lodge with Alaskan atmosphere. . . . Access by snow machine, dog sled, snowshoe, or cross-country ski."

Out of all fifty states, Alaska must have the highest percentage of population that does not own cars. Many Alaskans travel by four-wheeler, in all kinds of boats, in bush planes, on snow machines, by foot, by ferry. Though oddly, taxis are a big deal, even in some of the smallest Eskimo villages. The local taxi ad said, "Talkeetna Taxi & Tours, Inc. Weekly Wasilla shopping [Wasilla's the closest place with a big grocery store, north of Anchorage]. Every Friday throughout winter. $25 per person. Minimum 4, maximum 10. 733-TAXI."

For any winter tourists there was "Talkeetna Air Taxi * McKinley Scenic Flights * Land on a glacier * Visit McKinley base camp * Since 1947." And for those who "Can't bear to be inside. Cross-country ski rentals. Skis, boots, poles, $15/day. Carhartts. Insulated bibs. Mountain hardware. Thick fleece jackets and pants."

For those Christmas shopping, there was this ad: "What your Santa wants for Christmas! A Stihl 018c chain saw. $199.95. At Talkeetna Arctic Cat." Under John "Dancing Bear" Sally's ad for his custom knives, antler carving, and scrimshaw was this one: "THE MOSQUITO NET. Sign up before the year 2000 and get 2 MONTHS FREE. Internet Access Service 357-8967."

Underneath the newspaper was an invitation on hot-pink paper. It said, "The Talkeetna Bachelors Society cordially invites ALL SINGLE LADIES (and other interested parties) to the Fourteenth Annual WILDERNESS WOMAN CONTEST. The Wilderness Woman Contest was added in 1986 to select the lady who best exemplified the traits most desired by a Wilderness Man. Single ladies demonstrate their proficiency at fire stoking, water fetching, snow machining, fish catching, moose dispatching, ptarmigan hunting, sandwich making, beverage opening, and other vital skills for daily living on the Last Frontier. . . . Saturday, December 4, 1999, in the Village Park, Talkeetna, Alaska."

December 4 dawned a mild twenty-two degrees and windy. The Olympian contests soon to begin would pit some of the world's most beautiful and least politically correct women against each other. The winner would get a gold nugget and a handcrafted fur hat. First came the "fifty-yard dash to a simulated creek to fill water buckets, in full winter gear, returning with them full." Each pail filled with cold, sloshing water weighed thirty to forty pounds. Many, many people in Alaska still haul their water from holes chopped in the ice of the neighboring lake or creek or river. This contest would weed the women down to five or six, based on their times. Event number one had the wilderness women panting and straining. There was no goofing around; these events were all about the serious, difficult, and essential skills required to survive in the Last Frontier.

Then came the wilderness woman obstacle course, a combining of normal winter duties. This included "driving a snow machine around a short course."

The hustling wilderness women in this event, either real ones who lived the life or wanna-bes, would "gather firewood and deposit it on a fire," all on snowshoes. They would catch a simulated fish, then use a pellet gun to shoot a simulated ptarmigan, which were balloons on a piece of painted plywood. A twenty-something dirty blonde from San Francisco who had never shot a gun or driven a snow machine was doing amazingly well; she was athletic and had a sense of humor. It took her more than fifteen tries to hit the required balloons. "What would my friends think if they could see me now?" she was overheard saying.

Then the ladies would climb a tree to escape a simulated enraged moose, after which she had to dispatch the angry moose with a simulated rifle, a cutout piece of wood. Real Alaska women shoot 375s, 300 magnums, 30/06s. One of the bachelors, a guy born in New York City, now a local eighth-grade teacher, played the enraged and then dying moose, falling into the snow every time he was shot by a wilderness woman. After the charismatic, short-haired, very feminine contestant from San Francisco "shot and killed" the male in the moose suit, she leapt on top of him and kissed him right on his big moose lips. I heard a few locals say the bachelor in the moose suit should bring a high price at the auction because he was "cute." Hearing the word *cute* in Alaska had the same impact on me as smelling rotted roadkill.

The best event for the young woman from San Francisco was the one in which she had to run across Main Street, make a sandwich, and grab a beer at a table laden with fixings, then sprint back to the deserving bachelor. The happily reclining man watched Sunday-afternoon football on a simulated TV. Points were not given for neatness, so most bachelors wore the largest black garbage bags they could find over their bodies to keep them from drowning in beer and being gagged by the sandwiches accidentally smashed into their faces.

This year a tall, stunning young woman, Hillary Schaefer from Ester, a hip, kind-of-artist community near Fairbanks, won for the third time. The woman from San Francisco came in fourth.

MALE ORDER CATALOG

When I walked into the VFW hall, people were everywhere, cleaned up and smelling of more cologne and perfume than I had experienced in months. The hall was filled with attractive women from their midtwenties to their fifties. A few had on sequined evening dresses, their hair teased and makeup applied artfully. There were three tall blondes, fashionably outdoorsy looking. None had been natural blondes since they were about six. They had on short, black, tight dresses; black stockings; they could have been at some art gallery opening in L.A. All kinds of ladies were here, some in jeans, some in custom-made fur coats made of mink, beaver, marten.

A woman with thick, wavy brown hair wondered aloud as she gazed at one of the bachelor bios and pictures on the wall, "Can we use our credit cards on some of these guys?"

One of the tall, outdoorsy-looking women in the black dresses answered, "Girl, you should hope so, because I brought a pile of cash and that one you're looking at is mine!"

It was body to body in the hall. I was one of the only men around; the bachelors were hidden somewhere, which aided in building great anticipation. One woman pressed herself against me. She seemed aroused by the feeding frenzy that was building fast in here.

She asked, "Do you know what they call a ten in Talkeetna?" But she didn't wait for me to answer. "A four with a six-pack."

She put her arm around me and got her face just a bit too close to mine. "Where is your picture and bio?"

"I'm not for sale."

"So what are you doing here then?" She didn't seem disappointed at all; she was a player.

"I'm writing a book about Alaska, traveling all over the place. I get to observe all this."

"Really." She squeezed my waist. "Well, I'm from around here, just became available again last month when my boyfriend moved back to California." She leaned her head on my shoulder. I didn't say anything. "Okay, then; well, answer this: What does a Talkeetna bachelor use for birth control?"

"I have no idea."

"Personality."

If in the middle of the United States you were a woman who was considered average on the physically attractive scale, in Alaska you would, if you wanted, have long lines vying for your attention, your companionship. You could feel like a goddess. There is a major shortage of available women in Alaska, especially in the bush. Alaska actually has a magazine whose whole purpose is to promote available Alaskan men. There are unfulfilled, masculine males loaded with testosterone, bouncing off every snowbank and mountain peak, howling from every remote village and fishing port. For all these lonesome men, though, most women who have taken advantage of their amazing Alaskan popularity seem to come to the same conclusion. I heard this saying at least fifty times, referring to Alaskan males: "The odds are good but the goods are odd."

Tonight, all this rational thinking about the odd goods, and good odds, would be thrown into the closest yellow-stained pile of snow. Hope, among other things, filled the air.

A different blond woman, her hair short, her gaze intense, opened the door into the auction room and said, "Okay, you all can begin to come on in and be seated." The place was decorated with cutout snowflakes. On the stage were a podium and the flags of Alaska and the USA.

Two men, original members of the Talkeetna Bachelor Society, walked up onstage. One was the bachelor called Grog, the other was Gary. Grog had long hair with natural blond highlights and a long brown beard. He had on a clean, fringed suit made of moose hide and looked as if he could run out into the wilderness anywhere in Alaska with a hatchet and survive for a year. His face had a glow, either natural or induced. If a person could have stayed at Woodstock since 1969 and kept the festival going, that person might have the same expression as Grog. He was handsome if you liked the mountain-man look, and he was obviously a character, used to living his own way.

Gary, who said he was fifty-plus, has those eyes that stare into you and want to bring something back with each look. He was bear-size and slow-moving. His beard was so thick that it could only be trimmed with hedge trimmers. He answered the question "What do you do for entertainment?" with "Love, listen, and rescue women."

Grog and Gary were here to tell the story of how the auction had come into being. They had been sitting in the bar together in 1981, and after a while, someone looked around and asked, where are all the women? Someone suggested they should have a party or maybe even an auction to bring some fresh females to town. Grog flashed way back to that instant and said, "Wow, man, it was like we suddenly realized maybe we could actually get some woman to pay money for us. Whoa, man. That was cool."

A few rows of women behind me suddenly howled, clapped, and whistled. Longtime bachelors Grog and Gary instinctively knew not to waste the desire as it rose.

"Hey, let's get this party started, huh, Gary?" Big-bearded, sad-eyed Gary nodded and they both walked off the stage.

The president of the society, Robert, the guy originally from Iceland who entertains himself, and Ed, the vice president, who had been in the moose suit during the Wilderness Woman Contest, came out dressed in tuxes. They were trim and classically handsome. The way these two looked they could have been walking out on any stage anywhere in the world to accept their awards for being leading corporate managers. That they were here at Talkeetna's Bachelor's Auction in Alaska showed how really deceiving looks and first impressions can be.

A woman in a red-sequined, tight-fitting dress in the row behind me told her friend loudly, "Ed's mine."

Robert and Ed delivered some polite official greetings. They both appeared shy, and Robert stuttered slightly. Before they could get out from behind the podium, some female yelled out, "Wow!" from the back.

Someone turned on a song, a tune that would give even Al Gore the flexibility and rhythm of James Brown.

"My son is going to kill me for being here," said a lady, at least fifty-five, sitting directly behind me.

I turned to see one of the bachelors, dark-haired Daryl, thirty-two, covered only by tattoos and foxtails, making his way—no, snaking his way—into the room. His tattoos were Native American designs, his foxtails from a gray fox. He weaved through the women; some petted his foxtail. They were ready to bid, but he was just the first of this entertainment meant to raise as much money as possible for charity.

A local folksinger named Steve Derr wore a once-preppy sports coat. Instead of leather as elbow patches, there was gray duct tape. He came out and sang a few songs. One was "Wilderness Woman," which went something like this:

She leaves man-sized tracks. She has a double-bit ax.
She has a house of logs. She has thirty-six dogs.
She's rough and ready and safe and clean.
Don't mess around no more, she's got a .44.

Most Alaskan men want their women to be good with firearms. One never knows in Alaska when a whole year of meat—a moose—might become available or when a bear might break into your cabin or try to eat your dogs.

*Daryl attempts to stimulate the auction crowd
in Talkeetna.* PHOTO BY PETER JENKINS

After Daryl's shimmy, the women wanted the bachelors brought to the auction block as quickly as possible. A hundred women seemed to be in this room.

The auctioneer was Robert Forgit, the weatherman for an Anchorage TV station. A weatherman?

"Let's get it on," someone with money to spend yelled out.

The president of the club, even in his tuxedo, went for only $35. Maybe he came across as too shy.

The next guy went for $38. A man with a gray beard, the local refuse collector, went for $65. The woman next to me said, "Oh, he is such a nice man."

I was surprised at the low prices these men were bringing, based on the lusty bragging I'd heard from women as they looked at the pictures and read the answers of the bachelors. Especially since all the money goes to the Valley Women's Resource Center. But I suppose it was like any auction where flesh is for sale—get what you can for as cheap as possible.

The eighth-grade teacher, the cute one from New York, walked out to whistles. I would not have been surprised if he'd brought this tux with him from a past life. But he stalled at $45.

The weatherman, a fine auctioneer, pointed out to the ladies, "Listen, now, this guy is worth more than forty-five dollars. I don't know for sure, I'm just guessing."

Two women, on either side of the hall, the one in the red sequins and one of the three in the tight black dresses, bid him up to $69, where he stalled again. But this guy was the type who always has something planned. He opened the shirt on his tux to reveal a T-shirt underneath that said, "I like hot . . ." I couldn't see the last word.

The woman in red sequins bid $75.

The next guy was young and obviously strong, able to handle any wilderness moment.

The weatherman shouted, "Look, ladies, at this strapping lad. He can haul your wood. He can haul you all winter."

He brought a few whistles and $50. I'd been hearing since we'd moved to Alaska that the economy was slow. Based on these prices, I guess it was true.

Something was going to have to happen to raise the prices. The something did— call it chest hair. Some guy revealed a thick crop on his muscular chest. A gray-haired lady bid him up to $200. Someone said she was a doctor from Anchorage.

Daryl, back in clothes, his foxtail not even stuffed in his pants, sold for only $40 to the young Wilderness Woman contestant from San Francisco.

"Look here," said the auctioneer, "this guy's a master mechanic on the North Slope, he makes all kinds of money! Bid high for him, he just bought a new Ford truck!" He went for $35, cheap, especially considering the new Ford.

The rowdy, all-powerful women were calling out the names of men they wanted to bid on. None of the real rugged, older guys, the ones who probably needed the attention most, were being summoned.

One of the other young guys was brought out. He was only twenty-nine and was the one who answered "What do you do for a living?" with "as little as possible."

The bidding did not even begin before the lady who was running the show stepped up to the microphone.

"Listen now, see this guy. This summer we were having trouble with birds flying into windows all over town. I saw Doug, here, pick up a pretty little songbird that was knocked out and give it mouth-to-mouth. He brought it back to life. Now, ladies, come on! He must be worth at least twenty dollars."

He went for under $50.

Then came a guy named Mark. I recognized him from bingo. He appeared nervous, almost ready to run. This apparent fear, or something about him, I couldn't tell, seemed to excite some of the bidders; he shot up to $115.

The auctioneer, sensing some possible competition, put his hand on Mark's shoulder and yelled out, "This is USDA Choice!"

Mark then unbuttoned three buttons on his shirt and began making his ample chest muscles move. A woman twice his age came out of her chair and bid $150.

Someone whispered, "She lives in Hawaii and Alaska. She's loaded."

She then walked up to Mark and took off his shirt. The place went wild.

"If he will take off more, I will up my bid to three hundred dollars."

Mark, now so bold he might have been a dancer sometime, looked as if the fearful look was only for effect. He took off his shoes. He then stepped behind the podium, bent over, and off came his jeans. Nothing was really visible but his head and neck above the podium. She put her arm around him, back there. He smiled a contented smile and then looked tired, as if he needed a nap.

The auctioneer asked if there was anyone else the ladies wanted to bid on.

"Come on, ladies, there are many more big-time men back there just waiting for you to want them. Who will it be?"

There is a stillness, a waning of interest; it must have been a sad silence for the bachelors in waiting. The auction appeared to be over.

Then someone says, "What about bachelor number thirteen?" I quickly opened my catalog. Number thirteen was Grog. His birth name is Robert Petersen, born in Milwaukee. He's forty-four. How do you get the name Grog?

His hair flowed to his ears, obviously specially washed and combed out for tonight, his nineteenth year on the auction block. His dress-up moose-hide, pullover shirt and pants had no stains. He looked as if he could snowshoe for fifty miles without stopping. But there was something about his eyes; they seemed closed, almost swollen shut.

As he walked to the stage, he began to talk. "I've been livin' around here twenty-two years. . . . I'm nervous, this is late in the show, are there a couple shekels left for the Grog?"

He walked up onstage, where the log walls are covered with a deep blue fabric and hand-cut snowflakes. Sparkly little Christmas lights blink.

The bachelors in the tuxedos seemed able to come to this Alaskan world, yet step right back into the other, more detached outside world. Grog probably couldn't go back there anymore, or wouldn't.

The auction was all supposed to be funny, ha, ha, yet it was sad that Grog had to auction himself off. He'd been doing this for almost twenty years.

What was he looking for in a woman? "Someone that wants to live remote for more than one night." Obviously, for all the partying and beer and bars, his love was living in the bush and he wanted someone to share that with. Now, he was hoping that someone would bid something, anything. And too, there were all his old-time friends, the guys with the longest beards, the men considered real Alaskans, who would not even get bid on.

Maybe the bachelors who waited expectantly and would not be bid on were now joking about getting too old for this, that their gut was too big. This rejection had to hurt. And besides, the several women here their age were bidding on the younger men.

The auctioneer was working hard to get a bid on Grog. Whoever called Grog's number was either mistaken or upon seeing him in person had decided not to bid.

"Look at this Alaskan man. Just look at him. He is everything any woman could want."

No one said anything. Grog hung his head, then regained his pride and just stared out at all of us.

"Remember the great cause your money goes for here, ladies. All that you've got to do is buy this man a drink, and if you want, a dance. Come on, who will give me twenty dollars? Twenty dollars."

I'd seen great Tennessee auctioneers keep a silent audience going until you thought your brain would explode, but then the bidding would begin, with ferocity, for something like an old woodstove. But how long could he stretch this out for a man? There was nothing tongue-in-cheek about this. It was painful. In those brief moments I relived the times I had been chosen last for some sports team, or not chosen at all when the girls could choose a dancing partner.

I yelled out, "Fifty dollars."

Grog jerked his head up at the sound of my voice and head-butted the wall.

The whole place was stunned. There was a bulging silence, then a roar of whispering. What had I done? Surely no one thought I was bidding on Grog because I was gay. But then again, no one knew me here. Who cares, anyway? I've got $75, I'll get it started, and the women will take over.

The whispering and the stares to the back of my head intensified. Grog walked back and forth, shaking his head, his long hair flying. "Oh, man what the . . ."

An almost overly polite little female voice said, "Sixty dollars."

I looked back; she was a slight woman in the row behind me. She looked as if she ran marathons.

"Oh, *great,* we have sixty dollars," the hard-to-stun weatherman said.

Stop now, I told myself, that's enough. But it quieted again. I'll give all my cash to the cause and stop, I decided.

"Seventy-five dollars," I yelled. Grog stared at me and kind of smiled. Uh-oh, what's he thinking?

The little lady behind me immediately countered, "Eighty-five dollars!"

The weatherman looked at me and shrugged, as if to say, it's a free world. I shrugged back; I had no money left. Then someone tapped me on the back and handed me $20.

I looked back and the generous lady directly behind me gave me a thumbs-up sign.

"Ninety-five dollars!" I said, loud and clear.

I looked back to my competition, winked, and smiled a you-ain't-gonna-out-bid-me grin.

She was talking to the woman behind her, counting her money now.

"One hundred and fifty dollars!"

There was a gasp from the audience; she was trying to smash me into submission.

Suddenly, hands filled with five- and ten- and twenty-dollar bills came at me from all over; one of the tall beauties in the short black dresses actually stood up and came across the aisle with a twenty for my next bid. The last guy who brought that much had had to take off his clothes. So far, Grog had not removed any of his moose hide. I counted the money; I had $75 more.

"Two hundred and twenty-five dollars," I said.

"We have two hundred and twenty-five dollars from the gentle—uh, man in the third row," said the weatherman.

My competition shot back almost instantly, "Two hundred and fifty dollars."

More hands reached out with more money. I told them to keep it, let's let the little lady get Grog. And she did.

I stood up and saw the reporter, Donna, from the *Anchorage Daily News* jotting down words as fast as she could write. Oh, man, what if this somehow makes it into the paper, which we subscribed to, and Rita read it before I got home.

"Ah, Donna, I'm a happily married man, okay?"

"Sure." What did she mean by that inflection?

"You understand, right?"

"Sure, I do."

I walked over to my competing bidder and thanked her. Then I tracked down Grog, who was surrounded by bewildered friends and curious women.

"Hey, Grog, you don't know me but, ah, I didn't mean to embarrass you or anything, hope you understand."

"Yeah, when it first happened, I was shocked, look at my head." There was a scrape where he had head-butted the wall. "But after a minute when the shock wore off, I looked you over and you looked like you were all right, no problem."

The story and some flashy pictures did make the paper. I called Rita and alerted her to what I'd done, which was accurately reported in the Anchorage paper the next morning before I got home. One of the main pictures in the piece was of Grog. Rita knows I love auctions and I sometimes get so carried away I buy things I would never use.

14

On the Way to Coldfoot

It was one of those superdark winter nights in Seward. The seeping darkness had a power over the people because it stayed so long this time of year. I was reading *Fifty Years Below Zero*, a book about an early white man who lived among the Eskimo. I felt someone near me and noticed Julianne standing behind the borrowed chair that I had claimed and now sat in. The chair rocked.

"Daddy, where are we going?" she asked.

The sweet and completely trusting tone of her voice made me want to change my answer. Should we really be going where I'd planned? Maybe I should take this risk without them? Rita had told Julianne when she got home from school that afternoon that we were going to spend her spring break in the wilderness of the Brooks Range. I'd certainly heard of this place, but until I'd looked at a map, I had had no idea how far it was from here. Julianne liked to plan and pack days in advance, just like her mother. Did I really want to take her, even Rita, to live with some eccentric family I didn't even know, sixty miles off the nearest road in one of the most isolated, coldest places on earth?

"Juge, we're supposed to drive north about eight hundred and twenty-five miles from here to a bunch of mountains called the Brooks Range," I answered.

She'd driven a couple thousand miles before—she'd driven from Miramar Naval Base in southern California to Tennessee after visiting her brother Aaron. The females of the family did that trip, Rita, Brooke, Rebekah, and Julianne. But driving from California to Tennessee in the summer and driving from Seward to above the Arctic Circle on the last day of winter might be a bit different sort of road trip.

The Weather Channel was on; as usual they showed nothing about Alaska. We had weather here that we considered just a "fun winter storm" that would have made headlines and specials on the Weather Channel, CNN, and all the networks for days if it were happening somewhere else. A few days ago the Weather Channel had one of their traveling reporters standing beside an interstate in the middle of a nor'easter that had fizzled and dropped only an inch and a half of snow.

"Why the Brooks Range, Dad?" Julianne asked.

"Oh, because it's good"—I gave her the thumbs-up sign—"and because a man named Eric Jayne invited me, you, and your mother to visit them there."

Julianne and I had a little thing going because every time I asked her how school was or how her first attempt at skiing went, she would just say, "Good." When I started teasing her about using the word *good* too much, she would just give me a thumbs-up sign.

Her naturally calm disposition was piqued with curiosity. She was not a child to ask many questions, but today she was about to ask several.

"Why would we want to go there? We've been studying Alaska in school— isn't above the Arctic Circle some of the coldest places in Alaska?"

Julianne loved the cold, she had another plan.

"Yes, I think it is. Where they live is supposed to be beautiful. They live on a big lake that is frozen now. We'll take a long snow-machine trip to get to their house. That'll be fun!" I said, trying to sell her.

"Do they have any daughters?" Julianne had made several good friends here in the neighborhood and at school, Leah, Danielle, Nicole, and others. Julianne has the gift of friendship.

"They do have a daughter. I think she's twelve, maybe thirteen. I haven't met her, only one of their sons."

"Oh, where does she go to school?"

"She is homeschooled."

Julianne knew about that, we'd homeschooled her for second grade.

"How does she even get her schoolwork?" Julianne is a practical person, like Rita's side of the family, who are Midwestern farmers.

"In Alaska, if you live in the bush, they have teachers that teach you and send you your work in the mail, or the family comes to a town if they don't get mail and picks it up."

"Daddy, what's the bush?"

"It's places in Alaska where people live away from roads and towns or even villages. Some people in Alaska live off in the wilderness, just their family and that's it. Some people even live alone."

"Why? That must be lonely."

"I guess that's why we're going to visit Eric—to find out what living in the bush is like." I knew better than to try to close the deal then. I'd let her think about it, talk to her mother.

"You know some of my friends at school are going to Hawaii for spring break. Can we?"

I knew she had a plan. "Not this time, Juge. Maybe some other time. Okay?" Her mouth tightened; she was plotting her next move.

Charter companies fill up jet after jet after jet full of Alaskans headed to Hawaii for their end-of-the-winter sun and sea break. The Islands are not far, just head south. The humpback whales that spend the summer near Seward winter around the Hawaiian Islands.

"We've been studying the Native groups of Alaska. Do you know how to spell Inupiat?"

"I-N-U-P-I-A-T."

"Is Eric an Inupiat Eskimo?"

"No, they are white."

"How cold will it be there?"

"I'm not sure, honey. It could be twenty to thirty below zero."

She set her jaw. Where had I seen that expression before?

"Dad, you'd rather be in thirty below zero than Hawaii?"

"Well, no. Well, someday we'll go to Hawaii. But, all right, yes, this week I would rather be in twenty-five to thirty below zero," I answered, pathetically.

Rita arched her eyebrows and looked up from the salmon and pasta dish she was creating. Rita knew all too well Julianne's easygoing ability to lay the foundation for an argument.

"Dad . . ." There was a confident, even slightly condescending ring to the way Julianne said it. "You're kidding, right?"

"No, we should experience the bush. I'm pretty sure it will be good."

"Pretty sure, Dad?"

"Yes, Julianne, pretty sure. This Eric seems like a nice man. Your dad never really knows what will happen when he goes to the places he goes to. So we'll all find out together."

I remember thinking, "Send this kid to law school." It was like being led into a trap on the stand by Perry Mason.

It wasn't just Julianne who wondered about our destination. Friends, long-time Alaskans, all had their doubts, and almost all of them made comments to me. Keep in mind that Alaskans don't use words like *severe* or *dangerous* often.

- "You're going to the Brooks Range. Coldfoot. Beyond Coldfoot. I've never even been to Coldfoot. With Rita and Julianne! How well do you know these people? Be sure to let someone know when you're leaving the road and when you're coming back. If we don't hear, we'll call out the state troopers."
- "Do you know that's above the Arctic Circle?!"
- "From Fairbanks, you'll have to travel the Haul Road. Do you have any idea that in the winter the Haul Road has a few huge trucks, carrying equipment back and forth to Prudhoe Bay, and to the pipeline? Do they even allow private cars on that in the winter? The Haul Road is gravel, and rough, rough. Those trucks can throw up all kinds of rocks, smash your windshield. Don't get in anyone's way down one of those long hills. It is a rare thing not to have your windshield broken going up the Haul Road."
- "There is next to nothing once you leave Wasilla, which is not far north of Anchorage, all the way to Fairbanks. That stretch [it would be three-hundred-plus miles to Fairbanks] will seem like the drive through Seattle compared to the Haul Road. Be sure to carry all kinds of below-zero-rated sleeping bags, at least one for each, food, water, clothes—always, always have your gas tank full. If you can, carry extra gas in plastic containers strapped to the top of your car."

For the most part, real Alaskans, who have lived here and not been broken by its extremes, are not excitable. Alaska is a place where you need to keep your wits about you. Many things can happen to challenge your existence. So I was a bit surprised, and eventually my surprise grew to concern, as more people told me to be careful and attentive going above the Arctic Circle in winter. In Alaska, there are many different climates. You can go over two thousand miles in some directions and still be in the state. The almost nine hundred miles we'd be traveling would take us into a different world of cold and isolation. It could be as cold as anyplace on earth and as isolated as anyplace in the world. Heat and extraordinary isolation seemed to me to be survivable. And, I told myself, if there was abundant freshwater and food to harvest, being stranded or lost somewhere could almost be enjoyable. But, the thought of being lost or stuck or held prisoner in total isolation and outrageous cold, where everything's either frozen, hibernating, or on the verge of starving, was for me one of the most awful scenarios I had ever entertained.

One afternoon before we left, I was down at AVTEC, the local technical school, on the stair-stepper. Next to me was a student, a Yupik Eskimo from outside Bethel. We got to talking while we sweated off some winter hibernation fat. I told him where we were going, that I was taking my wife and daughter. He seemed to pick up his speed.

"You ever been in a really, really cold place?" he asked after what seemed like a long silence.

"Not really." I slowed down; sweat was dripping down my face and head. Another Eskimo guy who was shooting pool had put on a hypnotic techno-dance CD. Why did this young guy seem concerned?

"You must not let yourself, your center self"—he rubbed on his heart and chest—"get cold."

The young Eskimo got off the stair-stepper and came and stood next to me. He did not look at me when he said, "You stay on the road, whatever you do."

He walked away and shot three games of pool; he slaughtered his friend, almost running the table each time. This young, helpful Yupik was an exacting shot.

I stayed on the stair-stepper at least a half hour longer than usual, sweating, worrying, trying to wall out rambling thoughts of being lost in below-zero weather without communication devices, defensive weapons, or any real experience with the life-robbing cold.

Two weeks later, we left. We would meet Eric and some of his family in Fairbanks and follow them to Coldfoot. Then we'd take snow machines more than sixty miles to their place, down something Eric called the winter trail. First we drove from Seward to Anchorage. There was no way we would have stayed on the road without four-wheel drive. I'd bought our used Explorer from Hertz in Anchorage. If we'd only been in Alaska in the summer, almost any funky vehicle would have done, as long as it was big enough to protect us if we ran into a moose. Tragically just a few miles out of Seward, a long-married couple in a compact car had hit a moose and the woman had been killed. Driving in winter in

Alaska required a better vehicle. I would not risk the life of anyone in my family any more than we were just by being here. Several times on our way to Anchorage, the car went into a slide, and twice we would have spun out and worse if the on-demand four-wheel drive had not locked on when the back tires began spinning and sliding out of control. Some longtime Alaskan drivers passed me going at least seventy-five. These maniacs seem to know how to keep it on the road. The definition of *road* in the winter we were having this year is, you don't see any pavement; the driving surface is ice and snow with some occasional salt.

In at least six places in the mountains along the road from Seward to Anchorage, the destructive evidence of this winter's avalanches was sobering. Whole slashes of mountainside and valley were cleared and flattened by the snow's sliding destructiveness. Trees up to a foot and a half thick had been uprooted and snapped off in milliseconds. The snow had been cleared to the road's edge, though guardrails that had been crumpled or twisted had not yet been replaced.

A deserted car lay stripped of its tires, its windows broken, on the side of the road before we got to Turnagain Arm. Back in the summer, a local Anchorage lawyer had driven somewhere out here, mysteriously became disoriented, and gotten lost in the woods. Her family had come looking for her from Alabama. Most people thought she was dead, but eventually some gold miners found her naked, cold, and hungry under a blue tarp, which she'd gotten from one of their mine sites.

Another wild-child Alaskan driver sped by us at seventy-five. How did they keep it under control at that speed, even with studded tires? We passed a coyote eating something dead and frozen on the lake on our right. Three moose lay still in the willows on our left. The moose came down low into these valleys to eat the bark off the willows.

"Are we there yet?" Julianne asked.

"No, we've got a long trip ahead of us, honey, then we'll spend the night in Fairbanks. In the morning we'll meet the people we'll be staying with and follow them almost four hundred more miles. You'll get to meet their daughter."

"Okay, Dad."

Like her mother, Julianne had brought her JanSport backpack full of things: CDs, Game Boy, snacks. The child is prepared.

"Dad, do you want to listen to Britney Spears or Macy Gray?"

"How about Macy Gray."

"Okay, Dad." She put it on and started playing Donkey Kong.

YOU ARE NOT GUARANTEED

Lately I had been enjoying the sound of the roaring Turnagain Arm winds searching their way up and over the surrounding mountains. Past Girdwood, silver-gray clouds were lying straight above the lined-up mountains. The mountains looked like wolves' teeth. The sun, red and bright orange, was like a spotlight shooting straight across the earth as it appeared for another day. It lit the underneath of the gray clouds a softer, pastel red and orange but blasted bright light on the mountainsides. I had to pull over and marvel, something we often did here in Alaska.

We slushed our way through Anchorage, Eagle River, and Wasilla. Between Willow and Trapper Creek, Julianne had fallen asleep and Rita was reading a book written by an Alaskan wilderness B&B owner/chef. The land was flattening out and becoming darkly wooded. Several moose appeared at the edge of the road like giant shadow spirits. How could something as big as they are be hard to see?

"Dad, I'm thirsty," came a sleepy whisper.

We passed a road with about twenty-five mailboxes at the end of it all nailed to one horizontal board, and then we came to a Tesoro gas station in Sunshine, Alaska. Talkeetna was not far to the east. This station and restaurant next to it seemed to be Sunshine, Alaska. Public showers were available here for locals with no running water: local homesteaders, old hippies, young hippies, and the self-sufficient with no electricity or no well. Around here in the woods is a large group "living on the land." At least four customers inside needed showers; two had on frayed flannel shirts with holes in the elbows and no coat. All had matted hair and smelled like wood smoke. It was a warm four below. An old, yellowed stuffed polar bear was by the entrance to the bathrooms, along with lights that were too bright. Racks of Chee•tos, Doritos, and sodas lined the walls.

I grabbed a couple Power Aids and a water for Rita and went to pay. On the counter was a jar of red licorice, some lighters, Duracell batteries, some Altoids, and a pile of fliers, two or three sheets each, stapled together. I picked one up thinking it might be some local petition for people who wanted no limit on the number of sled dogs in their yard, or no limit on the speed they could travel on their snow machines, or no limit on what they could grow in their greenhouse. I've learned much about America by reading what's tacked up on bulletin boards inside neighborhood stores or printed on petitions and pass-outs for everyone on the counter.

It turns out the three stapled sheets of paper dealt with how to get free food, an odd offering in a quick stop where food is at its most expensive. At the top of the paper was the line "Instructions for Road-Killed Moose Application."

It was from the Alaska Department of Public Safety, Division of Fish and Wildlife Protection, Big Lake, Alaska. Underlined, in capital letters and in bold type, the next thing it said was **ONLY ONE APPLICATION PER HOUSE-HOLD PER YEAR MAY BE SUBMITTED**. Does this mean each household that applies can only get one road-killed moose per year? When the caller from Fish and Wildlife Protection calls, you better be ready to go, get, and butcher on the spot whatever moose, or part of the moose that is there, no matter where it is.

The application sheet spelled out in typical in-your-face Alaskan style the following: "You are not guaranteed to receive a full-grown, adult moose with only minor injuries. You may be called to pick up a small calf moose, or perhaps only half of a train-killed moose."

When a train hits a moose, it doesn't slice it precisely in half, like a meat saw does a beef carcass; it does severe and crushing damage. When the snow is deep, as it can be along the Alaska Railroad main line between Fairbanks and Anchorage, the moose will gather in or near the tracks for relief. Wolves have a big advantage over the moose when the snow is deep, especially if there is a crust on top that will support the wolves' weight. Sometimes so many moose are on the tracks the railroad sends a special advance car in front of the train to drive the moose off. Sometimes the moose don't move or, if they do, they get right back on the tracks.

The instructions continued, "What you receive is the 'luck of the draw,' so salvage what you can. Do not call and ask to be placed back on the list because you don't feel that you received enough meat—many people receive nothing." A full-grown, healthy moose in its prime can yield the lucky roadkill harvester four hundred to five hundred pounds of excellent, healthy, low-fat meat packed with protein, minerals, and vitamins. When cut off the bone, some meat would be ground up into "mooseburger," with some for stew meat, steaks, roasts, and more. Comparing it to the price of beef, averaging $4 a pound, that's $1,600 to $2,000 worth of meat. Naturally, that's why everyone wants the full-grown, just barely road-killed moose. Some locals joke the train-killed ones are just tenderized.

If someone signs up for roadkill in Alaska, he better live up to his end of the deal. "Note: If you agree to respond to a roadkill after being called, then FAIL to respond, you will be permanently removed from the roadkill list."

What if a fourteen-hundred-pound moose is hit and dies in your front yard, in the parking lot of your restaurant? Whoever's next on the list must adhere to the following rules: "You must remove the hide, head, legs, and meat from the kill site. The gut pile is to be moved well off the roadway and, if possible, out of sight. [The gut pile is one of the brown bear's favorite snacks.] It may not be left on private property. Failure to comply could result in a citation being issued and your name will be removed from future roadkill lists." Can you imagine little Timothy sharing with his fifth-grade class that his family was removed from the roadkill list because they failed to move every bit of the gut pile from the parking lot of that gas station?

The only other instruction was on page 3. It ordered the roadkill recipient, "Save the front teeth (lower front jaw) from your moose. [A picture showed where to cut the jaw off right behind the teeth.] Bring the front teeth along with this form to Alaska Department of Fish and Game, Palmer, Alaska." The state also wanted to know the sex of moose, exact location of kill site, and date of kill, and they wanted it all within ten days.

What if we hit a moose on the way to Coldfoot? Why wouldn't *we* get to keep the meat, especially after what it would do to the Explorer? If the state of Alaska let people who hit a moose have the meat, some guy with a shop behind his house and a welder would someday create a bumper that would kill a moose in the road and not hurt his truck. Then people would hear about it and start buying these add-on bumpers. After that, instead of having to take a full week off and go hunting far out in the wild, some cheating Alaskans could harvest meat while driving to work. It could become a full-time business for the welder. The design might look so techno, so hip, that people Outside would start putting them on their Land Rovers and Navigators and even Lexus SUVs, instead of African bush guards. They'd get a cool name, like Wilderness X Guards. There would be a flat-black model and a stainless one for California. But then, someone would use the Wilderness X to smash a police car in a high-speed chase and a good thing would have gone bad.

I'd read half the application driving north. There was basically no traffic, although reading and driving in Alaska can cause roadkill. I put away my reading and then allowed myself to become nearly overcome by what was outside the vehicle. Most of the time we were alone on Route 3. I wanted to be to Fairbanks before dark, when sliding off the road into a gully or hitting a moose could be catastrophic. If there was almost no traffic now, at midday, except for the occasional semi pulling double trailers and a rare personal vehicle, at night there would be almost none.

A WILD-EYED LOOK

As we drove north, Mount McKinley showed its dominating 20,320-foot-high self, as it can with rare clarity in winter. The land had opened up around us, and the mountains of the Alaska Range had become dominating to the east and west of us. Rita had her Andrea Bocelli CD on, and the power of his voice seemed to match the potency and clarity of the perfectly snow-white mountains. The air was electric blue and charged with purity. We were a tiny satellite flying through space.

Occasional ground winds flew atop the flat plains running up to the steep mountains, changing my visibility. Before the snow-filled winds swept across the flats, I had been able to see from Route 3 to the moon, but now visibility was only about ten feet ahead. Suddenly, driving inside one of these blows of wicked wind was a small, white car, a Honda Civic. Compared to the monster double trailers we'd been passing, it was like a rabbit in the road. Except it was a metal rabbit in a sideways skid, and its rear half was in our lane. Veer to the right, I thought. (No, there was no guardrail, just deep snow. It was sixteen below zero.) Slam on the brakes. No. I could see the Honda was full of people. Pull into the left lane, way over to the left. Go around it. No, just stay in the lane we're in, stay straight, and don't put on the brakes. The Honda fishtailed the other way, and we missed each other by about a foot. What if we'd hit them? There would have been major destruction to the cars and serious injury to the people. The awful part was, where would medical help have come from? How long would they have taken to get here? Could any helicopters have come to the rescue? What if Rita's cell phone didn't work?

What if one of us *had* been severely injured? Did they have sleeping bags in their Honda? My first-aid capabilities would have been tested in the extreme. What if no one had driven by for a half hour, an hour, or longer? There was no walking to find help. And this was on one of a few major roads in Alaska that went somewhere. In our vehicles we were warm and cozy and shielded from the extremes outside, so fooled. Yet, if there had been a different skid, we could have been out in the killing cold and the coming deafening darkness.

How far from help would we be out at Eric's? I did recall Eric saying they had a satellite phone, and he was a vet. That's almost like having your own doctor. Right?

I'd had this same thought on my first flight to Alaska. It had been incredibly clear below us as we crossed British Columbia and Alaska. There were thousands of mountaintops and valleys, no evidence of anything human. The temperature inside the plane was perfect, no survival clothing required. Need a coffee or orange juice or snack or magazine or toilet, your pampered human urge was satisfied. Yet, to crash-land and survive, what a shocking transition would be needed.

We passed the town of Cantwell; it was like a wind tunnel with a supercharger, this late in the afternoon. The surging wind was like the sharpest knife; it blew down the tight valley from the mountains that surrounded us. We passed the deserted entrance to Denali National Park, in summer as filled with travelers as it was now devoid of them. Rita reached over and put her left hand on my thigh. Her gentle touch startled me first, then thrilled me; then for no apparent reason I began to worry again about Eric and his family. I'd met Eric Jayne a few months before, with his eldest son, Mike, eighteen, at the Fairbanks public library. As a writer in residence with the University of Alaska, I often spoke at local schools, libraries, and campuses, promoting writing, reading, books, and communication. Earlier that day, I'd spoken at a state juvenile lockup, where some of the most serious underage offenders in the state were housed. I told the young men that if I had taken one more step a few times in my anger-laced youth, I could have been in a place just like this, and that they could recover from their mistakes. Later I spoke at Lathrop High School; Howard Lake Academy, an alternative school; some classes at the University of Alaska, Fairbanks, campus; and now the library. The crowd was large, including some professors, a few families that homeschooled their children, some college students, some retired people, and Eric and Mike. I didn't notice them until after I was done, when they stood at the end of a small line of people wanting to say hello. In front of them was an aggressive German woman, a writer, who lived alone in a log cabin; a history professor and his elegant wife; a bubbly young mother who had read some of my books in high school in Idaho; and two coeds from the cross-country ski team. Then at the end of the line were two brown-haired men, Eric and Mike.

There was something unsettling to me about them, or was it just that they were painfully shy? Mike looked at the ground when I glanced his way. He had the wide-eyed look of a tribesman who rarely saw strangers, who had no mirror to look in. Their flannel shirts had a few holes in them; their pants had some permanent stains. They clearly worked outside somewhere. Then the line of people was gone and it was only Eric and Mike left. Eric had a wild-eyed look, as if his spirit was too large for his body. I couldn't tell if his hair and beard had been combed. His voice was soft; he laughed nervously and was oddly precise when he spoke. Maybe he was just nervous, yet he seemed aggressive in an odd way.

Eric was about five foot ten; he shook my hand and was stronger than he looked. Mike was shorter and built like a battering-ram fullback. They didn't look alike, but they stood on the earth the same way. My paranoid side wondered if they were really father and son. My trusting side countered that they had similar builds. There were long pauses in Eric's speech; Mike said nothing. Eric explained that he'd always wanted to live in Alaska, that he'd grown up in Iowa; his father is a Methodist minister. Eric had established two veterinary practices in Iowa. He told me he'd read my book A *Walk Across America* and that it had inspired him to live out some of his dreams. He wondered out loud, after his longest pause, if I'd like to come visit him and his family in the bush. Mike had walked off. Was he bored, or had this separation from Eric and me been planned to give us privacy? Eric saw Mike could not hear us and mentioned that his children, of whom Mike was the oldest, were "bushy."

I must have looked perplexed by the word *bushy*, because Eric explained that living in the bush, being around only each other, not seeing strangers sometimes for months at a time, made them uncomfortable around people they didn't know. They felt unsettled in any town, even relatively small Fairbanks (pop. 33,000). They were so comfortable with each other, yet so uncomfortable with everyone else. They were unaccustomed to talking period, yet they were at home in the deep silence of the frozen world of the roadless Brooks Range.

I asked Eric to give me a way to reach him, automatically asking for his E-mail address. He didn't have one. He had a phone number here in Fairbanks; he did spay and neuter clinics here at bargain prices. He said I could probably reach him through that number. He had a satellite phone, but he wouldn't give me that number. I wondered why not, but didn't ask. He said mail was hard to get and sometimes they didn't get it for a few weeks or longer since they had to come to Coldfoot sixty miles on a snow machine to get it. I told him I'd get in touch if I was coming his way. Eric seemed almost too inviting, yet if he'd really read my books, any of them, he knew me. He never did say anything that would have proved he had read anything of mine.

I thought about going to their place, but I had reservations.

Then a few months later when I was at the end of the Iditarod in Nome, there he was, as if he'd materialized, as if he were following me. Of course, he wasn't. Come on, Peter. This is just what happens in Alaska, you meet someone and you run into him or her all over the state. He had that overflowing smile and his hair was matted down by an old sleeping bag. I really felt I had to experience the Alaskan life in the bush, it is so foundational to the unusual and original world of Alaska. This might be the perfect situation. But I wanted to check out Eric more. I offered to buy him lunch.

We went to a local Mexican place a few blocks from where the Iditarod ends at a burled-wood archway. Eric told me he'd taken his first trip to Alaska soon after his wife died tragically. He and his four children came up to Alaska and canoed down the Yukon River. They ran out of food, money, had to be assisted by Athabascan Indians who live in the villages along the way, took some major chances, but survived, stronger for it.

There was no pompous air around Eric. He reminded me of a mystic, a holy man from India who had taken a vow of poverty. Being around him was at times like being on nitrous oxide at the dentist—there were no big problems, no pain, smile, be happy. He might have had a personality that would make him an effective cult leader, though I couldn't tell. Eric was a mystery to me, and I don't meet many of those. Eric said if we could come and visit, he and his wife, Vicky, would meet us in Fairbanks and we could follow them to Coldfoot and then ride snow machines the sixty miles into their homestead.

Coldfoot was 255 miles up the Dalton Highway, once called the Haul Road, Eric told me. They're in the middle of the route. It's then 252 miles farther to Prudhoe Bay on the Arctic Ocean on Alaska's north coast.

Eric laughed and said that there would be plenty of food as long as we didn't get snowed in. The trail was covered with powder, as it had been earlier in the winter. They had become dangerously stranded until the local Alaska state trooper had come and saved them. I kept getting the feeling there was more Eric should or wanted to tell me. Why? Was he afraid to say too much, that he might scare me away? Was he setting some kind of trap? I didn't think so; I've watched too many Court TV crime stories. I decided after our meal that we'd visit them, and I told him so. He looked at me as if he had heard that before. He had said that no one had visited since they'd lived there.

As I walked down the frozen streets of Nome back toward the official finish line of the Iditarod, I wondered about trust and fate and people's intentions. I grew up trained to be suspicious of others, always questioning their intentions. Walking across America in the 1970s, into places as odd and unusual to me as a foreign country, I'd learned from hundreds of encounters that strangers could actually have good intentions. I'd learned to trust my first reactions about strangers and strange places. Often I didn't need a great deal of information or time with someone to decide to accept an invitation into his or her home. So why was I so worried about going to Eric's wilderness homestead? Was it something about him that I'd picked up on that made me anxious? Was it just because Julianne and Rita were coming along?

Back on the road, I was still thinking about emergencies. If something happened, what would we do? If Julianne or Rita was injured, how would we reach out for help? The only way was the satellite phone Eric had said they had. Even then, if there were a blizzard or windstorm or some other weather interference, no rescue plane would be able to land on the frozen lake. State troopers were far away. What if someone cut himself or herself with a chain saw, was bitten by one of the sled dogs, fell through the ice, broke a leg in a snow-machine accident? What if Eric and his family had evil plans for us? I was angry at myself for even thinking it, yet I couldn't stop the what-ifs running through my mind. There were no pay phones, no food except what they had, only their house for shelter, and guaranteed temperatures of ten, twenty, thirty to forty below zero. We would be as isolated as any of us had ever been, dependent—totally—on a family, the head of which I'd met only twice.

We dropped out of the hills and entered the cold-holding valley that is home to Fairbanks. Eric and his family had a small log cabin in town for when Eric comes in from the wild to do vet work in Fairbanks and in the surrounding towns, especially for mushers. The trip into town is at least a four-day trip for them, and they'd found they needed a place to stay other than a motel. So they had rebuilt the small log house to suit their needs.

We found a room for the night and I called Eric at the cabin. Some young female answered, his teenage daughter. I tried to joke a bit with her, but she responded with silence, answered my questions in one or two words. Eric was out shopping with Vicky, she said; she would tell him we had called. I wondered if she even knew we were coming to stay with them. I hung up, wondering about her tone of voice, if she was just shy. Her response definitely did not alleviate my concerns, concerns that I had not mentioned to Rita. Eric seemed too nice, yet too guarded; his daughter seemed anxious. I made myself sick that night thinking about all the bad things that could befall us. And I'd hung up without giving Eric's daughter, Elizabeth, our phone number at the motel. I called back and gave her the number; all she said was "Oh."

Eric called back a few hours later. He said that he and Vicky and this musher friend had been to Sam's Club buying dog food and supplies. He gave me directions to their place, said to meet them at about 8 A.M., then we'd drive the 250 miles to Coldfoot and spend the night there. He mentioned something about spaying someone's dogs that evening.

In the morning it was dry, windless, and the snow crunched under our feet. An ambulance went by us on the street; I'm not sure why, but it's difficult for me to reconcile extremely cold weather with blood, high emotion, and passion-motivated injuries. In cold weather all things seem frozen, stiff, slowed down, hibernating, even the terrible things people do to each other.

We drove to Eric and Vicky's little cabin, only a half mile from where we'd spent the night. Julianne, Rita, and I had each taken long, hot showers; we were quite sure there would be no running water, much less hot water, out at their homestead. I was having a problem imagining where any water would come from out there in the Brooks Range where it was normally twenty-five to thirty below zero, and quite a bit colder at times. I doubted they had a well—that took electricity. The ice on the lake would have to be a couple feet thick. How could you get through it, and if you did, would it instantly freeze over again?

As we pulled into their street, I saw a small log home with a truck parked out front. How did that thing even run? I thought. In the back were five or six sled dogs, young and thin. A dark-haired, slender guy was leaning into the back of the pickup, lifting one of the stiff-legged huskies out. A young woman held on to the collar of this dog and another, crouching on the below-zero ground. Both of them wore double flannel shirts and jeans; the guy's outer flannel shirt appeared to have been attacked by a chain saw that spewed oil. They either lived out in the bush and hadn't washed their hair in a few weeks or were going for the Jamaican wanna-be look.

Now I remembered that Eric had mentioned to me that a friend of his, a young musher who'd just run the Yukon Quest, was loaning them some of his dogs. Eric would doctor them, fatten them up, and his kids could use them to learn mushing. Eric had said last night they were going to send the dogs on a truck that hauled freight to Prudhoe Bay. The trucker would drop the dogs in Coldfoot.

I pulled in behind them and got out. The guy, whose eyes flashed, "I'm an Alaskan wild man and that's my gig," walked up and held out his hand. I'm not sensitive to dirt, I live on a cattle farm, but I wondered if I'd ever seen such a dirty hand. A germ fanatic would have driven back to Seward right then. His hand looked as if he used it to shovel ash from his woodstove; in fact, the best smell emanating from him was wood smoke. He had dog hair all over his clothes; maybe he had had a six-dog night last night. Who knows if he and the girl live out in the bush—they may have slept in the truck using the dogs as living blankets.

"My name's Hugh, you must be Peter."

"Yes, I am. This is my wife, Rita, and out daughter Julianne." I felt guilty that I was so repulsed.

Rita and Julianne are both very clean; you won't see dirt on them for long. Julianne even carries a plastic bottle of waterless antibacterial hand soap. Julianne went over, diplomatically avoiding his hand, and petted the dog he was holding. I could tell she was thinking, "What is Dad getting us into?" I avoided Rita's eyes.

"Did Eric tell you what happened?" Hugh asked. He was a slight, supercharged guy, full of energy.

"No," I answered, not being able to read him well enough to determine if "what happened" was a good thing or bad.

"Well, the freight truck won't haul the dogs, only the dog food. We will have to fit the dogs in the vehicles somehow. Plus, I'm going with you to mush the dogs the sixty miles from Coldfoot, where we'll leave the cars to head to their place."

Hugh walked over and opened the door to our four-wheel-drive Explorer and looked inside. We had brought enough equipment, survival gear, cameras, you name it, to fill the entire back.

"You think we could fit a couple of my dogs in with you?"

Right then the side door to the house opened and a young, blond teenage girl walked out. Even she wore just a light coat. She walked toward us, although she looked away, down the street, anywhere but at us. This must be Eric's daughter, Elizabeth, who was twelve.

Hugh spoke again. "I think Elizabeth is riding with you also."

I looked around to see what kind of vehicle Eric owned. Surely, being a vet and making this brutal round-trip from Coldfoot to Fairbanks all the time and traveling around this part of Alaska to do his clinics, he had an outfitted four-wheel drive or a Suburban or something large. Maybe they could fit all Hugh's dogs in with them if we didn't have any room. They would have to have something supertough, even if it was really used; all metal, big enough to sleep in if you ran off the road in winter when someone might not come by all night. But in the driveway sat a tiny red Dodge Neon. I wouldn't drive that thing around Anchorage. I'd be afraid taking it on a snow, ice, and rock-and-gravel road like the Haul Road, which would rattle and shake it to death. Almost every animal that you might hit would seem bigger than it. Surely this wasn't all they had. Eric was probably out doing some last-minute shopping. Being disorganized and living where they lived would be life-threatening. You can't run out from the wilderness and buy that flour you forgot or ran out of. It might take a week to get out and back.

The teenage girl walked to within thirty feet of all of us and stopped. When I looked at her, she looked down at the ground as if she'd never looked into a stranger's eyes before. Then the door opened again and out walked Eric and a slim, brown-haired woman. She looked put together, wearing warm snow pants and matching coat and wool hat. She walked slightly behind Eric as if he were a shield.

"Hi," he said, walking toward us. Eric seemed to be an up person, always optimistic, energetic, smart, and a bit scatterbrained.

I introduced him to Rita and Julianne. He introduced us to Vicky, his wife, and Elizabeth, his daughter, who still stood off in her own sphere.

"Do you guys have any extra room in your car for a dog or two?"

"Maybe," I said. "Hugh told us about having to transport them."

"I guess I should have checked the freight company a few days ago," Eric said.

I opened the back of the Explorer and some snowshoes, felt-lined boots, and other things fell out, like a gear avalanche.

"My dogs have never ridden in a closed-up car very far. They may get sick on the way," Hugh said.

"I'll give them a shot, tranquilize them, that'll be better," Eric offered.

I unpacked all our stuff, laid it on the ground, and, surprise, fit a dog cage in the back. Eric picked out two of the smallest dogs, tranquilized them, and put them in it. The other four would ride with them, in the Dodge Neon, with Hugh. Elizabeth would ride with us.

They had almost no luggage, just a few small bags. Although Hugh was from Chicago, he looked as if he'd lived all his life two hundred miles from anything or anyone, as if he could burrow down into a huskies' den and live underground with them. Yet Hugh was engaging, and he had a plan. He wanted to be a big-time musher, and knowing Eric, a vet, could be a large assist, because vet bills can mount fast. Hugh had angles and was always working on selling them. He was a bush-dwelling Alaskan player. He did have a newsletter and I think he said he even had a Web site. He pulled a newsletter out of his pocket and gave it to me to read. It emphasized the romance of the wilderness, dog mushing, and the people who sponsored him. He said he was always looking for sponsors.

Eric would drive the Dodge Neon; Vicky would sit in the front seat, with one dog on her lap. Hugh would sit in back with the three largest dogs draped all over him. What little luggage they had could be crammed in any available space. I still could not believe they'd be driving a Dodge Neon up the Haul Road, built in the 1970s when the Alaska Pipeline was constructed.

Eric read my perplexed, concerned looks well. Right before giving me last-minute instructions to follow him, that we'd stop at the last truck stop to fuel up and use the bathroom, he tried to calm the deep doubt freezing my face:

"You know, we had an almost new Suburban but we loaned it to these two German students, these attractive young women we ran into at the truck stop at Coldfoot. They told us they needed to get to Fairbanks fast. Turns out they lied, went north the few hundred miles to the North Slope and the Arctic Ocean. They about trashed the thing, then totaled it rushing back to Fairbanks to catch their plane.

"I guess we should have known better. They almost got killed, rolled the thing down a steep embankment. They just left it there and hitched in to the airport." Eric laughed his slightly-out-of-control, just-a-bit-hysterical laugh, like "Yeah, I can't believe we got into that one." Turns out the women split the country and the scene of the accident, and there were all kinds of problems with the insurance coverage, so the Dodge Neon would have to do.

We drove up into some hills on the way out of Fairbanks. Some of the finest homes in the area were in these hills, where it could be twenty degrees warmer in winter, since "heat" rises and the difference between minus twenty and zero degrees is great. After a few miles, on a hilltop, there was the truck stop. Once we left it behind, there would be basically nothing all the way to Coldfoot, so it was important to fill the gas tank until it overflowed. Eric had told me this twice.

After we gassed up, we all got something to eat; this was the last hot food and coffee for a long, long time. I still wondered if my instincts about the charismatic Eric and his family were correct. We could still turn around, make some excuse. My darkest doubts could build him into a Charles Manson–type leader, with Vicky and Hugh his followers. Elizabeth looked nothing like him; she must look like her mother. I tried to speak with her, joke around, to bring out whatever was behind her discomfort. Nothing came out to play. Vicky was quiet, yet assured. Hugh was the faithful attack-dog type; he would obey blindly and do whatever Eric wished. Peter, shut off that imagination.

"Eric," I asked over my second coffee refill, "who's taking care of your sons?" There were three of them out at the cabin by themselves now, their eighteen-year-old, fifteen-year-old, and nine-year-old.

"We have a young man who lives with us. He was kind of a street person in Fairbanks when I met him, but he's from a real good family back East. He's meeting us in Coldfoot, if we get there when we're supposed to. He's taking a break; it's tough staying out at the cabin and being in charge." Eric laughed.

The young man, Tyler, would snow-machine to Coldfoot and hitch a ride with truckers headed to Fairbanks from Prudhoe Bay and be gone while we were there.

"How do the boys get along by themselves like that in the wilderness? Don't you worry about them?" Rita wondered.

I was surprised Rita asked this pointed of a question. She doesn't ask people personal questions even when they're best friends. She is a listener, a feeler. Was this an indication of her level of concern? Normally she is fearless.

"Oh, they do great," Eric answered quickly.

"Remember that time you had to rush back because Pete accidentally cut Mike with his knife, really deep into his leg?" Vicky asked.

"Yes. I had to charter a plane in and sew Mike up," Eric said, remembering. "I had to sew up the muscle first, then the skin. It was a bad wound. It took several stitches. Pete's always sharpening this big knife of his. I guess Mike walked into it somehow."

Everyone climbed into the Neon after they rearranged the sedated dogs. Ours seemed more sedated than theirs. I couldn't even hear ours breathing. They pulled to the edge of the parking lot and their brake lights went on while they waited for us. If we followed them, we'd be heading into a frozen, lonesome, huge land where we would have no choice but to rely on them.

The coffee I'd just swallowed turned to acid. After hearing about the stab wound, or "accidental" knife cut, I wondered again why I was taking my youngest child and wife into the deepest, whitest wilderness homestead in America with these people whom I didn't know. Was Vicky trying to warn us? Come on, Peter, anyone can cut his brother accidentally with a really sharp knife. But if anyone could, why hadn't I ever cut one of my brothers or sisters? We certainly fought enough. I'd only met Eric at the library speaking event. For all I knew he wasn't even a vet, Vicky wasn't his wife, and Hugh was heaven knows who. . . .

MY TRUST IN STRANGERS

I'd been putting my faith in strangers rather blindly my whole traveling life. After all, everyone I know now was once a stranger. There is nothing devious about Eric's intentions, they just want us to visit, I kept telling myself. Eric feels that he knows me from reading my books. I had no problem taking substantial risks, trusting my intuitive instincts—when it was just me. It was Rita's and Julianne's trust in me that had me building up bad outcomes out of anything that didn't make sense.

I got out of the car and washed the windshield, again, to buy some time. Julianne had been and now was even more excited about this adventure, just the three of us. She wasn't saying anything, but she is so trusting. Finally finished with the windshield, I got in and followed them north. About five miles down the road the dog, or dogs, farted or, worse, had diarrhea. It was too cold to air the vehicle out for long. Juge had offered Elizabeth her Game Boy to play with, and Elizabeth took it, shyly, and played a game, maybe two, before telling Juge that she got really, really carsick, that she'd have to stop playing.

I asked Elizabeth what she did during the winter. She said she did school-work, that she helped Vicky quite a lot. I asked her if Vicky was her stepmother. She said she was. We passed the only possible turnoff, a road that went to Minto. Minto Flats, the gigantic wetlands and hot springs, was nearby. Wolverine Mountain was to our west. With all the ponds and creeks and marshes, it became obvious why Alaskans did their land travel in the winter when the ground was frozen and coated with snow and traveled on the water during the short season when water became liquid.

Maybe fifty miles out of town, Eric pulled over, steam flowing from under his hood. He popped the hood; something was wrong with the car. He said the car had been overheating lately. Hugh and the three dogs were wrapped up together in the backseat in a maze of sleep. It was probably the warmest sleep Hugh had had in months. Eric said he thought the mechanic was supposed to have fixed the car. He pulled out a gallon jug of water, poured it into the radiator. I fast-forward to our possible situation: the engine block cracks, the car's done. We have to go back to Fairbanks, adding Eric, Vicky, Hugh and the four huskies, that would be six huskies and seven people in the Explorer. How vulnerable we were on this winter road. But after ten minutes or so we began the trek again.

Julianne kept trying to talk to Elizabeth, but she said few words and her face was clearly strained by the strangers who surrounded her. I wondered when was the last time she had been in a tight place like our car with no way out, where there were only unknown humans. No matter how friendly we were, she did not seem able to relax.

"Elizabeth," I asked, "what's the ride like on the snow machines into your house?"

"It's long."

"Is it cold?"

"Usually."

"How cold?" Julianne asked.

"It can be forty-something below, but twenty-something below is more normal this time of year." That was better. She seemed intelligent. Even at home, being the only girl with three brothers, she probably didn't talk much.

"Is that cold?" Julianne wondered.

"Not really if you're dressed for it," Elizabeth said.

I wondered where these winter clothes were because Eric, Vicky, and Elizabeth were now dressed like friends of mine would dress on a "cool" December day in south Texas. What if we were stranded or broke down on this road? Since we'd left the truck stop, we'd only seen a few double semis. But I had to assume they knew what they were doing. Everyone, including lifelong Alaskans, told us not to even consider leaving Fairbanks in winter headed north without a full gas tank, extra gas if you could haul it; sleeping bags; some water; food; and if possible a satellite phone. Our friend Pat Ivey, who works at the University of Alaska, ordered me, and she is not the ordering kind, to call her when we got back to Coldfoot. She told me that if she didn't hear from us in a week, she would call out the state troopers. She'd been in Fairbanks for decades and had read too many stories about what can happen to stranded people around here.

The frozen world we were driving through in our rubber-tired, metal, plastic, and glass bubble appeared lifeless. I knew in my mind that somewhere out there, warm-blooded creatures struggled to survive. I looked for tracks in the perpetual snow and saw almost none crossing the thin line of gravel that gave us access. The road was surprisingly smooth at times, though sometimes the potholes, hidden by blowing snow, jolted us. The worst were the washboardlike ridges in the road that we hit, shaking our brains and making the car want to fishtail.

We were between Troublesome Creek and the Yukon River when steam started to pour out of the tiny red car again. We were so alone and the outside was so tough that I did feel as if we were on another planet. Their Dodge Neon and Eric's happy-go-lucky temperament made me think of a cartoon I hadn't thought of in years, *The Jetsons*—Eric was George Jetson, the Dodge his little spacecraft.

We stopped and Eric emptied the last of his water into the radiator; he held the plastic milk jug straight up to drain out the last drops. Where would we find more? Eric hadn't planned on the car overheating this much. I had some Power Aid; could you pour a sports drink into a radiator?

"Eric," I asked, "what if something goes wrong with the engine, who would you call to come get you?"

"We're so far from anything, if I couldn't fix it, I don't know, we'd have to flag down one of these trucks, leave the car, and get a ride back into town. I didn't plan to have to haul all these dogs, so I don't really have many tools." He scratched his head. "This satellite phone we've got—the company is Iridium—they've told us they're shutting down, they've gone bankrupt. It hasn't worked lately."

I didn't respond, just felt another porcupine quill stuck into my growing mass of worry. Now, overheated somewhere on the Haul Road, I find out there may not be any way to reach anyone once we get to their place.

We took off again quickly to cross the Yukon River; we could hear some large semis coming from far off. The Yukon is wide and is the second-longest river in the United States. In the summer it's a liquid passageway, but now it was a frozen highway. This bridge was one of only two across the Yukon. Eric and his children's first experience with Alaska was floating six weeks down the Yukon all the way to Mountain Village by the sea, shortly after his wife, their mother, had died. The river, the isolation, the constant danger, and the kindnesses of the Native peoples along the way had offered some relief from what must have been intense grief and sadness. They all learned that there was no escaping the gray pain, even in Alaska, though it was as far away as they could get and still be in their own country.

Just after we crossed the Arctic Circle, the Neon began overheating again. There was no way we could thaw some snow, we had no metal pot. Eric found a little road and turned off. Where was he going now? After driving through some woods we came into a man-made clearing with a metal garage and a trailer where someone lived. It was a pipeline maintenance place. Eric knocked on some doors, tried opening a few, nothing. It seemed no one was around and everything was locked up. Then he walked around the side of the metal building and came out with his jug filled with water, followed by a medium-built man in clean overalls. They both looked under the hood, then the man went in and brought out another plastic jug of water. I stayed in my car the whole time, and as we got ready to go, the man looked hard at us. I wasn't sure if he shook his head or not.

Slightly past where the winter road turns off to go to the native community of Stevens Village, the Neon overheated again. We only had about fifty more miles to Coldfoot. Eric added more water. By now I was glad to step out just to stretch into the freezer that covered this whole topside of the world. This cold, an invisible aggressor, penetrated and stiffened almost every bit of me, yet the fantastically fresh air made me more alert.

Julianne was now telling Elizabeth a story about how our cows back in Tennessee were able to fend off aggressive coyotes that wanted to eat their calves. She told her that we'd lost two dogs to coyote attacks, one her Kenai, a wire-haired fox terrier. Elizabeth mentioned this summer they'd seen two possibly rabid wolves on the rocky beach of the lake just below their house. I was re-lieved that she and Julianne seemed to be getting acquainted.

Coldfoot, Alaska (pop. 13), was named by early gold miners, some of Alaska's most aggressive and fearless pioneers. Most had to walk here from Fair-banks, and by the time they got to the Coldfoot area, they had gotten cold feet, literally, and were overwhelmed by the inhospitable climate and mountainous, desolate conditions that seemed endless. Today, Coldfoot is a lonesome truck stop built with prefabricated buildings and its own power generators. A state trooper and his wife live here, over by the airstrip. There is one motel, which looks like a long, long trailer; they used these structures to build the pipeline in the 1970s. People say that during the pipeline-building days, Coldfoot was like a combination of the Wild West and a space colony built inside a freezer. Eric mentioned as we walked into its only restaurant that he hoped the place didn't close. Coldfoot was where they could get fuel, catch rides, keep their car, get work done on broken-down snow machines, and stay over before making the trip to the homestead. It was basically impossible to drive in from Fairbanks and then take the big risk of running the last sixty miles on the winter trail to their homestead all in one day. Too much could happen on the trail, like getting stuck in the dark. There were winter bears, such as the one that had attacked Eric's friend Bernie and his dog team out of Wiseman last winter, and there was the dreaded overflow. I didn't know what a winter bear was, and I didn't know much about overflow, but right then I didn't want to.

We sat down and ordered a hamburger. Who knows what we'd be eating out at their place? There is something about eating a hamburger and homemade soup at what feels like the last outpost on a frozen planet that makes it the best food you've ever eaten. Though part of the enjoyment may have been related to the relief at arriving in Coldfoot. Like bears eating all they could hold, having no way of knowing how much energy they'll need to hibernate, Rita, Julianne, and I ate as if it were our last meal.

Eric said he needed to go up Wiseman (pop. 21), about ten miles farther up the Haul Road. He wondered if we wanted to go or if we'd traveled far enough for one day. He said he'd received a message from someone here that Bernie there needed one of his sled dogs sewn up; apparently it had been in a fight with one of his other dogs. Eric said Bernie and his wife, Uta, were originally from Germany, and that they had been living here, surviving off the land, for fifteen years. Eric mentioned that Bernie sewed fur hats made of marten, wolverine, and mink. Vicky said that although she loved Bernie and Uta she is adamantly opposed to trapping. Eric said that after that run-in Bernie'd had with the winter bear, an old, starving grizzly, he might make a few hats out of it. It had attacked his dog team, and he'd had to kill it.

"Oh, yeah, and then after that," Eric said, suddenly remembering, "I need to go to the state trooper's place and spay two of their dogs." Now there was some positive news. Going by the state trooper's house, that's got to be a good sign.

We all went to Bernie's. Eric rode with us after we took the two reviving sled dogs out of the back of our vehicle. We'd already had two rocks chip the windshield; the crack had already begun. It is considered almost a miracle to drive any distance on the Haul Road and not crack your windshield.

The sun was now behind the mountains to our west, out where the Gates of the Arctic National Park and Preserve, a designated wilderness of 7,523,888 acres, was located. As Eric had told us, there was almost no privately owned land for hundreds of square miles in all directions. To the southeast was Yukon Flats National Wildlife Refuge, that's 8,630,000 acres. To our northeast was the Arctic National Wildlife Refuge, which is 19,285,923 acres. There was also plenty of Native-owned land around.

Eric had bought his land, about fifteen acres, from the University of Alaska without ever having seen it. The first time he saw it, he hiked in during the spring, a dangerous time when hungry grizzlies are emerging from their dens. He had no idea how demanding a trip it would be; he did not carry a gun and said he'd never been so afraid in his life, it seemed a bear was behind every tree. Now he said he can actually sense where the bears are when he's roaming his land.

Everything that they would bring to their land had to be carried in, mostly on a trailer pulled by a snow machine. Eric or someone in the family had to haul in every nail, every board, every window, every quart of fuel, every pound of flooring, every everything to the shores of Lake Chandalar where they lived. Most people Outside have no idea how the nails and windows and doors and bricks got to their home, much less brought it all there themselves.

SURGERY

"Whatever I do," Eric said, after politely listening to Julianne tell him about the avalanches that had trapped us in Seward this winter, "we have to go by Trooper

Bedingfield's house. They have been wanting to get their dogs spayed for a few months."

"How do you spay someone's dogs? Surely not at their house?" I asked.

"Yes, I'm the rare vet that makes house calls out here in the wilderness. I'll spay the dogs right on the kitchen table, or anywhere they want. I owe him; he came close to saving our lives early this winter, he and his sons."

"What do you mean—what happened?" Rita asked.

"This winter began very early. I've seen it snow here in August, but in late October and November, we got dumped on. We got over four feet in two days, on top of over a foot we already had. We've got snow in places up to your waist. We don't usually get that much snow up here."

"I like deep snow," Julianne said.

"I do too, Julianne, but this snow made it almost impossible to go anywhere. We hadn't brought our fuel out [to the homestead] in fifty-five-gallon drums yet. That runs our generator so we can have lights and power. We hadn't brought out our food, either."

"I wouldn't think there could ever be too much snow for traveling on snow machines," I said, confused, not suspicious, not really.

"The snow here is usually powder, it's so cold. Unless it's mixed with water from rivers or creeks that overflow on top of the ice. That's called overflow, and it can be deadly, almost like concrete. But in the deep powder the snow machine will sink and stop, and then you have to stomp down a trail ahead on snowshoes or lift it back on the trail. Can you imagine how long it would take to go sixty miles?"

So far Eric had never sounded anxious, just calm. What would it take to get him to raise his voice or get upset, hit something, or give up? There was so much for him and his family to do. He had to be responsible in order to live in the wilderness, have all these children, and build a vet practice that covered more square miles than that of any other vet in the United States, maybe the world.

"The state trooper whose house we're going to tonight spent four days breaking a trail from Coldfoot with two of his sons. One would break trail until he was exhausted, then the other would. We were headed to them from our side. We finally met. If their family hadn't made that effort to reach us, I'm not sure, but it could have been bad, maybe really bad, especially if we'd been dumped on with another foot of snow. This winter has had one of the heaviest snowfalls in many years."

"Has there been much snow since you all left? What's the condition of the trail now?" I asked.

"I don't know; this young guy that helps us and stays with us will be bringing out a snow machine sometime later this afternoon—he should be here by now. He'll tell us. Sixty-one miles from here, through the mountains, a lot of different weather can happen. It could be sun here and blizzard forty miles down the winter trail. We'll just have to start and see what happens." Eric fell silent, and I sensed that he didn't want me to ask any more questions about the snow and the trail.

We drove on to Bernie's in a world of terrifying or soothing quiet, depending on your reaction to this piece of the planet. We'd seen few animal tracks in the over 250 miles from Fairbanks, except for moose tracks around the willows at the creek and river bottoms. Wiseman was an eclectic collection of tiny log cabins, most with at least a few outbuildings. None of the outbuildings was far from the deep snow. Wood smoke rose out of the few that had people living in them in the winter. Human trails were packed down into passageways to the dog yard, the woodshed, the generator shack, the storage shed. Bernie and Uta were happy to see all of us; visitors in winter are a splendid treat for them. After we ate, Eric would sew up the sled dog's head. He was not paid; someday there would be an act of kindness from them, a place to stay in a blizzard for a son or a big hot meal. Maybe he did it just because the few who braved this place needed each other, and they all knew it and protected their relationships.

Their tiny cabin, the part Bernie and Uta inhabited in winter when it could be so cold, was made of peeled logs by homesteaders decades before. There were a couple small windows, a hanging houseplant, a built-in bed, a table, and a tiny sleeping room off this main room for them and their three-year-old daughter. In Alaska many houses are tiny; who needs so much interior space when you have the world's most exhilarating, extraordinary, inspiring, dangerous, pristine, eye-popping exterior space outside. Besides, who can afford to heat it all. For the most part, Alaskans don't live their lives inside. They don't need big-screen TVs and surround-sound to watch the Discovery Channel or *National Geographic Explorer* to bring them the peace and balance of nature. They don't need to escape the creeping intrusion into their personal space. They've got all they could ever need waiting just outside their door, or in the case of Anchorage, a thirty-minute drive away. Bernie first came to Alaska from his home in Germany as a fifteen-year-old on a hunting expedition with his father. Surely he came from a wealthy family, certainly the professional class. He loved Alaska so much he came back to work as a packer, then assistant guide. Then like many before and since, Alaska had him in her grasp. Uta and her adorable blond, red-cheeked daughter served us moose-meat spaghetti, an Alaskan-size bowl of it with woodstove-baked garlic bread.

Afterward Bernie went outside where it was close to thirty below zero and got his injured sled dog. The skin on top of its head required twelve stitches. Bernie, his body a tough string of sinew and muscle, his face lined by surviving in this climate and prematurely aged, cleaned off a table in his workroom, attached to the living portion of the cabin. A Coleman lantern provided some light, and Eric put on a Petzl headlamp. He administered some local anesthesia, as Bernie held the calm dog. A large grizzly pelt hung from the wall, stiff, not tanned. It was the winter bear that had attacked his dog team. A winter bear is usually an old bear who is unable to get fat anymore, its teeth worn down to nothing. The dog was fine; we drank some tea and said our good-byes, then drove back to Coldfoot to Trooper Bedingfield's place.

Their house was owned by the state and built right next to the plane hangar next to the airstrip. The Endicott Mountains rose up to the west; Coldfoot was nestled in a narrow valley. A tall chain-link fence surrounded the house; so many lights were on inside that the snow-covered yard was brightly lit. Because of the reflection off the snow, the light was amazingly bright. The tall fence was left over from the state trooper family before them, who'd had small children and been concerned about bears snatching them from their play or the kids wandering off into the forever wilderness around them in every direction. Inside this little house lived five people, almost one-half the population of Cold-foot.

Eric knocked on the door, a rare occurrence surely. Immediately we could hear the quick yap of small dogs. A beautiful woman opened the door, a surprise out here in the rugged bush; she seemed quite friendly. Eric introduced us to Lynnette, Curt Bedingfield's wife and postmistress at the Coldfoot "post office," possibly the recipient of the least mail of any post office in the United States. Although Lynnette had been born in California, she had moved to Alaska when she was eight months old. The house was impeccably neat. Grow lights were shining on her year-round lettuce plants, and since it was March and time to think about spring, row after row of baby cabbage and carrots and flowers were also emerging from potting soil. Their home was attractively decorated and gave a whole new meaning to the idea of light therapy. Their living room and kitchen, which opened to each other, would make a perfect place for the surgery Eric would soon perform on their dogs.

Trooper Bedingfield came out from the back bedroom still in uniform. His head was basically shaved; he was trim, quick-stepping, and seemed genuinely pleased to see Eric and Vicky, and even Rita, Julianne, and me. In the winter around here, visitors must be a luscious gift, unless you're human-hating hermits, which they obviously were not. I thought that it was a positive sign that the trooper and his wife seemed to really like Eric and Vicky. Watching them interact made me feel more secure. At least the trooper would know we were here and what we were doing—I made sure to tell them. Their eighteen-year-old son, Jeremy, was sitting on the sofa. Their younger sons, Isaac, seventeen, and Simeon, fourteen, were on a school trip. Their school, which served Coldfoot and Wiseman, had about fifteen people in it from K to 12.

"Thanks for coming by, Eric," Lynnette said.

"After what Curt and your sons did for us, it's the least I could do," Eric responded, and Vicky nodded.

What Curt had done, and it turns out Curt goes way above and way beyond the call of duty for the people in his gigantic territory, was possibly save their lives. Trooper Bedingfield's territory is 73,000 square miles, roughly 350 miles wide by 210 miles deep. His territory is bigger than New York State, Connecticut, Rhode Island, and New Hampshire combined. Curt's responsible for an area almost twenty thousand square miles larger than Michigan, except Michigan has over 9 million people; his area of responsibility has about forty-five hundred. The majority are Natives living in some of the most isolated places on the continent: Arctic Village, Venetie, Bettles, Deadhorse, Anatubik, Kuletucvik. He patrols most of it in one of two planes, a PA218 Super Cub or a Cessna 185. Eric told me that Curt is an amazing pilot, and he must be.

There are so few ways out here for people in desperate need to reach out for help. Curt would not have heard about Eric's dire need if Tyler, their helper-caretaker, had not been trying to get back to the homestead from Coldfoot. It was early winter; they already had a foot and a half of snow. Then in two days fifty-three inches fell from the gray-white skies. It took a week and a half to open the runway by the trooper's house; during that week and a half there were no emergency flights or any flights at all, period, out of Coldfoot.

Someone from the truck stop had called Curt and told him that Tyler, twenty-four, the long-haired, wide-eyed caretaker, could only make it about six miles out of Coldfoot. Several times he had turned back, exhausted and increasingly concerned for Eric and the family, and for himself. Tyler had been trying to break trail by himself for over two weeks. Moving through over five feet of snow, up to your neck, on a snow machine is almost impossible. You run into it, it's powdery, free-flying, but you bog down, then disappear and tip over. Then you have to move your several-hundred-pound machine; you climb off and sink into the snow yourself. If sand could be as light as this snow, then imagine going sixty miles through five feet of sand. After a trail is beaten down, it's still really tough. There are always portions blown over by wicked winds coming out of the mountains.

If Tyler had been at the house with the rest of them when all the snow fell, no one would have known that Eric and all his children were running out of food and fuel and dog food and everything. Run out of fuel, eventually you can't cut wood. They don't cut that much wood in advance, and you burn through so much so quickly to keep yourself alive in the Chandalar Valley. Weather authorities at NOAA (National Oceanic and Atmospheric Administration) believe it has been one hundred below zero here. Curt said during this past winter in Coldfoot, a "warmer" place, it had been to sixty-seven below zero. Running out of food, when there is nothing around in winter to hunt, would have been desperate. You wouldn't want to think about what you might bring yourself to eat.

Curt got the family survival gear together, their two snow machines, and marshaled his two youngest sons, Isaac, who was dreaming of being a Navy SEAL, and Simeon. Both were born and raised Alaskans, about the best rescue squad anyone could have. Tyler worked with them too. For his sons, Curt told me, going out for a few days or a week or however long the trail-breaking rescue might take was about the best treat they could get. These were not young men who want to lie around.

It took them four long, brutal, fun, hilarious, exhausting, dangerous days to break the trail to the point Eric had reached on the other end. Once Curt, an expert on a snow machine, ran into what he thought was a stretch of virgin snow and disappeared into a riverbank. Only a foot of the snow machine's rear end was left sticking out. His sons thought this was funny, and he was fine. It took the four of them two days to get to the south fork of the Koyukuk River. One of them had to walk forward on snowshoes, sometimes sinking to over chest deep. Curt is six feet tall and was forty-one then. He is built like a middleweight weight lifter. Snowshoeing in deep snow will wear down the average person quickly. Just lifting the snowshoes covered with snow, the snow not wanting to let go, tires you terribly. But there was nothing average about the effort the Bedingfields and Tyler made. First one would snowshoe ahead, then another would run the snow machine like a maniac full blast following the tracks, into a trail you can't find. In the winter there are only vague ideas where it might be because of the opening in the trees. Across open fields of swamp or tundra, the only way to guess your way through the five to six feet of powder was to try to remember where the trail went, how close to the spruce woods, how far from the cliff, where it crossed the creek, how it took off down a steep bank, when it made sharp turns. Through *sixty-plus* miles of unmarked trail, how could anyone, even Curt, who is used to flying over "featureless," unmarked places, remember much of anything?

The boys loved it, gunning the snow machine down a short "takeoff" ramp of new trail laid down by snowshoeing until the snow inhaled them like a cumulus cloud, and they'd finally fall over on their side. At Boulder Creek they lost the buried trail for over an hour. Someone like Rita and me lost in these conditions—which come on without warning, since Eric had no TV, no radio, no way to get advance weather warnings—would almost surely perish.

On the fourth day, Curt and his sons met Eric just twelve miles from his cabin. Eric was snowshoeing; his snow machine was buried somewhere for the hundredth or five-hundredth time. The best Eric and one son could do was two miles a day. He had to leave either Pete or Mike back at the cabin to keep the home fires and generator going. At that rate, realistically there would have been no getting out, and in the next few weeks more snow would come.

Curt said the journey they'd made to open the winter trail was "extremely hard" and that if you didn't pace yourself, you wouldn't make it far. That's the equivalent of Muhammad Ali saying George Foreman could punch. Hard-core Alaskans rank their experiences in hard-core Alaska the way any extraordinary person ranks what they do, in a wide range of normal. I hoped we would not be called on to do any deep-snow, way-below-zero rescues.

I thought about calling off our trip right now. I had a conflicting list in my head: Why should we go? Why shouldn't we? Why: because Eric seemed kindhearted and giving. Why not: because if he was so kind, why would he subject his family to the risks of this kind of life? Why: Eric would now have a sled dog team, if Hugh could make it out. Why not: the dogs can't make it through the deep snow pulling a sled any easier than a snow machine. Why: experiencing life in the bush was something we all wanted to do, we just wanted to make sure it was with someone who had their world in order. Why not: Eric drove a Dodge Neon in these crazy conditions. Why: Curt and Lynnette and Bernie and Uta, two proven wilderness couples, seemed to really like Eric and Vicky and their family. No matter how long I thought about it, there was no avoiding the fears, the doubts, and the concerns.

A tiny dog, looking like a cross between a Pomeranian and a red fox, came trotting in as if she owned the house and the moment. Curt had been stationed in Kotzebue, the largest Inupiat community in Alaska. One of the villages in that territory was Kiana, on the Kobuk River, just up from Kotzebue. Kiana is many Alaskans' favorite bush village. Because Alaskan villages in the bush are so remote, small dogs are easier and much cheaper to bring in; you could put a Pomeranian puppy in your pocket. Over the years, these dogs, especially the small breeds, have developed their own gene pool. They are too small to be crossed to the local sled dogs and too quick to be eaten by them. Curt and Lynnette had gotten their dogs in Kiana.

"This is quite a bear dog," Curt said, and smiled as he watched little Foxy check out each of us. The mother weighed about twelve pounds; the daughter, Kiana, a puppy, weighed maybe eight pounds.

"When we got Foxy, she had never been inside a house before; she lived outdoors year-round, tough, tough little dog," Curt said. "When a bear comes near our house, she will chase it as far as her little legs will carry her. You should see her catch rabbits, probably had to hunt to survive in the village she came from."

Eric picked up little Foxy. She had long red hair. Eric rubbed his two fingers on top of her head. Her eyes calmed, her breathing relaxed. Lynnette was moving a bit faster, her motions more animated; these were her little girls in the world of her four human males. Curt had gone to the back of the house and came out in a tight T-shirt with short sleeves that showed off his excellent condition and large muscles. He looked as if he could do fifty pull-ups.

Lynnette cleared off the already clean countertop. Eric got out a needle and pulled in the appropriate amount of anesthesia. Lynnette and Curt were not leaving or going into the other room. They were both petting Foxy, exhibiting the great love and affection they had for her. I suppose some family members stay with their loved ones until the drug has had its desired effect, then they leave before the shaving, the cutting, and the exposure of internal organs.

Foxy went completely limp, her little tongue dangling seemingly lifeless out of her mouth atop her sharp, white teeth. Eric, being such a sensitive and thoughtful person, always watching for a response, always aiming to please, looked to see what they were going to do. When they were clearly staying, he began. Vicky shaved the area on the belly where Eric would make the incision; Eric unrolled his kit of surgical tools, sterilized and shining. Lynnette stepped back a respectful distance, while Curt stood closer. I had seen my children Rebekah, Jed, and Luke born via C-section and Julianne come out naturally. As long as nothing went wrong, I thought, all would be fine.

Immediately after the incision was made, Eric and Vicky looked at each other. They said nothing, but Eric began thumping with his fingers on tiny Foxy's chest. Foxy had stopped breathing. Eric would later say that in his career he had spayed and neutered over fifteen thousand dogs, and two dogs had died, with one colossal difference: the owners were not standing there.

"She then began doing something called anginal breathing. This happens with the brain's realization that life is soon to end. Foxy began taking these last gasps," Eric said later. At this point, I still hadn't realized anything was wrong.

"I knew instantly I must reverse the anesthesia, and I gave her a shot directly in the heart. Then there are different places that will stimulate the breathing reflex, a thump on the chest with your thumb, pulling the tongue, tickling the throat. I did all three," Eric said. He sure did—that's when I knew things were really wrong. Eric and Vicky looked to be getting sick to their stomach with concern.

"When they start getting reversed, coming out of the anesthesia, they begin to blink. Foxy wasn't blinking. Curt and Lynnette have been so nice to us. The last thing I wanted was for anything to go wrong with one of their dogs. I'd rather my own die. It was awful watching their little girl Foxy die," Eric said.

I saw Eric's lips moving as he gave Foxy a shot directly into the heart. He later told me he was praying, fervently, and Eric doesn't pray about much. He is capable of handling so many situations. He said if Curt and Lynnette had not been there, he and Vicky would have been screaming, "Breathe, breathe, breathe."

Foxy revived; she'd been shot in the heart with yohimbine, made from the bark of a tree in Africa. It's a central-nervous-system stimulant, makes the subject hallucinate. Eric had even overdosed her. Now Foxy was wigging out; her big brown eyes almost seemed to be spinning around inside her head. She was barking at imagined intruders, she was panting fanatically, she was jerking her cute little head around in a completely out-of-control way. I practically expected her head to spin around. She reminded me of this man from Brooklyn who'd taken three hits of LSD at Woodstock; it took four of us to carry him to the medical tent. We found him writhing around on the ground—he thought he was a snake. Lynnette held Foxy tight and took her into her sons' room, which was smaller and less brightly lit. Julianne and Rita went in with them and they petted her until she came down from her wild trip. Then it was Kiana's turn.

Curt picked up Kiana; she was quite a bit smaller. We were all looking for some smooth sailing on this spay, considering Foxy was only the third time in Eric's fifteen thousand plus spays there had been any trouble. They laid her down on the kitchen counter. Eric unrolled another surgery setup and put her to sleep. I could see his lips moving before anything happened. Everything went smoothly for Kiana, although Eric said she had a double wall of stomach muscles, something he had never seen before. Kiana was opened up, closed up, and began waking up. Her eyes were blinking a bit and she was breathing well. Then *she* stopped breathing. Eric gave her some yohimbine in a muscle; it seemed to help and then she wasn't blinking her eyes.

"She was dying fast," Eric remembered, "so I gave her a shot in the heart too."

She started breathing and woke up. Now there were two little red dogs tripping their brains out and being helped through it by Lynnette and Curt. Mother and daughter dog were almost fully recovered when we left a few hours later. They were no longer hallucinating and no longer capable of being bred. Curt and Lynnette wished us a safe trip. After watching Vicky and Eric relating to Bernie and Uta and Curt and Lynnette, and watching them handle the life/death/life situations of both Foxy and Kiana, I decided for sure that we would go with them in the morning. I still didn't think Rita had any idea I'd been wavering and wondering about going.

15

The Winter Trail

That night in our tiny, hot motel room with cheap brown paneling and thread-bare towels that were too small, we laid out our winter gear for the long journey in. They kept the heat so high all winter that the survival clothing we'd brought seemed absurd. Why did we need the boots rated to keep your feet warm from thirty-five to one hundred below or the superinsulated Cabela's Iditarod suit I'd purchased to train with Jeff King? It didn't seem that Rita and Julianne would really need their extreme-exposure snow pants and parkas from REI or the mittens or the fleece layers or the polypropylene long underwear or the wool socks. I'm not sure I'd ever seen such a pile of clothes that would be worn all at one time by three people, one of whom was a child. Oh, how we would need those clothes.

The morning was radiant, the sky electric blue, the sun sunflower yellow, and the snow virgin white. It was thirty-something below zero when we crunched over in our car-driving shoes to get our last meal cooked by someone other than Vicky or Rita. Rita is such an excellent cook that no matter where we go, she always at least assists in the kitchen. Rita made our last phone call inside the truck stop restaurant; she called her folks on the family farm east of Lansing, Michigan. Her dad said that if the weather held, they would be planting corn and soybeans in a week or two. You could never plant corn or soybeans here.

When I got out of the breeze and held my face toward the sun, I could almost imagine some warmth was associated with it. Otherwise, this image of a fish market in Tokyo that I'm sure I'd seen on TV kept replaying in my head—I felt as if I were walking around in a huge freezer filled with gigantic, rock-hard bluefin-tuna bodies.

Tyler, their helper, had brought another snow machine into Coldfoot. Now all three of theirs were here. Tyler had been staying out at the lake with his twenty-something girlfriend, a cute Alaskan wilderness woman, and Eric's three sons, Mike, Pete, and Dan. Their other two machines had been here for over a week. Would they start after being left that long in this cold? How did they charge a battery out at their place on the frozen lake? The boys were left alone until we arrived, with no way out except for walking. Eric obviously, or hopefully—I guess I didn't know him well enough yet—had supreme confidence in his sons' ability to survive. We ate and went back and put on our polypropylene long underwear, layers of wool socks, fleece jackets and vests, snow pants and jackets. We walked as stiffly as astronauts did in their boots and space suits.

Eric had us bring our gear and pile it up on a snow-covered, plowed-off area by a workshop. Their pile was diverse and massive, most of it fuel, food, and supplies. There were two fifty-five-gallon metal drums filled with gas, flexible sacks of flour, cases of tomato sauce and vegetables. There were some boxes of spare parts for life-supporting equipment. Just about everything they had was life-supporting; there was little in their home, at this point, to be used for leisure, to pass the time, to escape the pressures of the crowded world. They'd already taken care of the escaping thing, although Eric did not consider their lifestyle an escape, but a fulfillment of a dream. And Eric didn't need to look the part of the rebel or act it or talk about it or get anyone's approval, he was *doing* it. There were generator parts, pieces of snow machines. If just one bolt breaks somewhere on the snow machine that is required for it to run, what do you do? The closest parts store is three hundred miles away and there's no phone booth on the winter trail. What if one of the snow machines broke on the way? They are notoriously difficult to keep running when used hard. There would be no way to add another person onto the one or two that ran. I guess we could drop our load and put the two people from the broken machine on the sled. Eric and Vicky had piles and piles of stuff. Eric had two white plastic sleds, flexible, strong, and thin. He lashed everything to them carefully, since packing balanced loads was crucial. Tyler and Eric packed while we stood around banging our cold feet on the snow, wondering what lay ahead. Hugh, the guy with the sled dogs, had just pulled the hook that held his team and mushed by us. He looked like someone you'd see at a poetry slam, someone who could do three of them in three separate cities, three nights in a row, without sleep. Hugh must have been hell on substitute teachers.

"See you all on the trail," he shouted over his barking, hyper team.

"Dad, this is going to be fun, isn't it?" Julianne said, watching Hugh disappear into the spruce woods. We could hear the barking long after he was out of sight.

"Yes, honey. I think so too. Can't wait to get going," I said. Julianne would ride behind Vicky.

Elizabeth would ride with her dad. They both had on beat-up brown Carhartt overalls. Rita and I would ride together. Vicky walked over and instructed Julianne in a gentle way how to ride behind her. Just hold on tight, especially uphill, she said, especially on sharp turns and down steep slopes crossing frozen rivers. She told Julianne the snow machine would sometimes get sideways on the edge of the trail and they might tip over. Vicky said tipping over in four feet of powder snow was fun. She appeared to be a sensitive soul, shy, discerning, and honest. When Vicky and Eric had met, she was working at Iowa State University. She had her own little "zoo" of animals and Eric was her vet.

Eric and Tyler had everything packed. Eric looked like Michael McDonald of the Doobie Brothers, before he went prematurely gray. Eric had some gray hairs in his beard now and around his temples, but mostly it was bushy and brown. He pulled the eight-foot-long, plastic sled in behind our snow machine and hooked it up. Then he started it. *Bing, bing, bing,* a sound that a cold snow machine makes, filled the silence of our frozen world. It started immediately, though, and it was the biggest, most powerful machine. (Rita and I combined weighed the most, all because of me, of course.) We were about to do some advanced snow-machining and I had almost no experience. I'd gone a few miles down a frozen road and a packed dog-mushing trail at Jeff's and that was it. Eric told me to follow him and just do what he did. Sounded simple enough. For Eric, no challenge was a big deal—obviously, otherwise how could he live out here as he did?

Two of the snow machines warmed up, but Eric seemed to be having a problem with the third one. He could not get his started. He pulled and pulled. He lifted up the hood, looked around, and came over to us.

"I've got to fix something that's broken," he said. He had that look on his face he had had the previous night when Foxy was dying and he was thumping her chest. He was just slightly frustrated. Eric had the same kind of almost-never-flustered, Midwestern-farmer temperament my brother-in-law Aaron has, and Rita. I've calmed down 100 percent, well, more like 300 percent, compared to the way I was when I grew up in the Connecticut suburbs of New York City.

Eric took some substantial-looking part out of the engine compartment and laid it on the twenty-five-below-zero ground. He went inside the garage of the truck stop and, twenty minutes later, after borrowing some of their tools, had the machine running. It seemed to me that it sputtered, but they all ran differently. He returned the tools and we were off. It was thrilling, the first mile or two; the trail was well used. Eric would later tell us that he was worried about at least two of the snow machines because "there were broken things on them."

We moved with ease along a creekside through evergreens, then over the creek, up a hill. We came into some open flats at the base of a range of four-to-five-thousand-foot-tall mountains. They were smooth, rounded-off, and white.

We traveled like this for hours, single file, gunning it up narrow mountain passes with steep drop-offs, across frozen open swamps, through passageways into the cold-stunted woods. It was so severely cold that what trees could grow here did so slowly. Eric would stop before especially steep slivers of winter trail and come back and tell me to be sure to accelerate as fast as the snow machine would go. If I got stuck with this heavily loaded sled, it would be a major hassle to get both the snow machine and the sled back down the hill. On the first one, we made it, then slowed down substantially. Even if Rita fell off, Eric told me, just keep going. She could always walk up these steep inclines.

Then we came to possibly the worst piece of the trail, across a creek with steep, almost vertical, banks on both sides. Eric had already said twice that this spot was dangerous and difficult. First it was tough getting down without crashing. If you went too fast down the bank and then hit the flat, ungiving ice, it could be a bad wreck. You could break a ski, break some bones flipping the snow machine and sled and metal, fifty-five-gallon drums loaded with gas on top of you, the two-foot-thick ice below.

Worse, this creek at this crossing point was susceptible to overflow. What creates overflow is that, early on, the creek or river freezes over. But springs and other water sources continue to feed the creek, so more water is flowing underneath the ice than there is room for it. So, the water breaks through somewhere and flows on top of the ice. Often the overflow is camouflaged by fresh snow. Say you stay out of it but your snow machine sinks into the overflow a foot or two. You can't move the snow machine. It gets colder and colder, the overflow freezes. It is already a granular slush and can soon harden like concrete. If you do make it through the overflow, then you must hit the bank on the other side and rocket out without flipping the snow machine over on yourself. We made it, we all made it. The overflow was just to our left; Vicky and Julianne hit a bit of it, but they were light and powered through it. I let out a small yelp when we were all on the other side and had stopped to get instructions from Eric on the next obstacle. Eric told us that a long, narrow section with a tight trail lay ahead. Whatever you do, he warned, stay right on the trail I make. We did that section with no apparent problems.

Right before we crossed the south fork of the Koyukuk River, we took the halfway-point break. It was not far north to the headwaters of the south fork and Horace Mountain (elev. 5,446 feet). Eric got off and flopped backward into the deep snow alongside the trail. In all directions all we could see was hundreds of miles of undefiled snow. Eric made a snow angel. I fell in on the other side of the trail and did the same, as did Julianne. Vicky and Rita walked down to get some cover from the riverbank. Elizabeth sat on the snow machine. How many snowflakes lay on top of each other in this country? Never had I been around snow like this. I could drop a quarter into it and it would drop through the snow to the bottom.

Eric was excited about having a dog team at their house. I couldn't believe they wanted one. Where would the food come from? There wasn't much game out here; it was too cold for much to survive, much less thrive. I lay still on my back in the perfect snow, the sun soaking into me with its faraway power. I opened my eyes to find Eric standing over me.

"In the late seventies when I was sixteen, my friend and I, we bicycled across the United States from the West Coast to the East Coast. We collected signatures on a petition from people who believed in putting this part of the country into wilderness," he said. "Now I live here."

He'd been inspired to do that by my book *A Walk Across America*, he told me. Rita and Vicky walked back from taking a pee, a big job with all these layers. I found myself feeling guilty for being so cautious. For the past couple of days, I'd been feeling like a wolf around a trap. Several things just hadn't looked right. But now I'd shaken that feeling, and I felt relieved. We rode on.

We'd dropped down into the frozen wetlands of the upper Koyukuk. Arctic Village was less than a hundred miles northeast. When we ran through about eight inches of fresh powder, it flew up and parted like the lightest waves in the world. We created clouds of snowflakes behind us. It was a beautiful series of sensations, combining movement, sight, the cold air on my face with the warm

Eric and Julianne taking a break on the winter trail in the Brooks Range. Photo by Rita Jenkins

heart and body of Rita holding on behind me. We rode as one. It felt so free, somewhere between riding smooth ocean swells and flying.

Another couple hours and we were to the edge of Chandalar Lake. Eric stopped us right before we drove atop its two or three feet of ice, which was then covered by two feet of snow that had been sculpted by the wind into wavy ridges. He said that on this end of the lake there could be dangerous overflow, even a hole in the ice from a spring bubbling up in the shallows. We sped onto it and crossed the danger zone without running into overflow, staying to the center. We were like a little caravan and we hoped our arrival would be victorious—another trip down the winter trail with no breakdowns, no emergencies.

Seeing the lights of our snow machines, as I'm sure their boys could by now, after a few weeks of seeing nothing new may have been exciting. How many people in our world could go a week or two, or a month or two, without seeing a headlight, even if it's just the headlight of a snow machine? Or Mike, Pete, and Dan might really enjoy being in the wilderness alone. When we were about a mile away, close enough to see their house and its blue roof, built up on a high bank, Eric stopped and waited for us.

"Julianne, congratulations. You're the youngest girl to make it this far on the winter trail." She was nine and a half.

"Oh," she said, and smiled, though all that showed through her wool face mask was her mouth and bright blue eyes. "Thanks, it was fun." Julianne, like her mother, is a woman of few words. Julianne had adapted quickly to riding with Vicky, moving as one. Vicky turned and patted her on the shoulder with a snow-covered mitten. We blasted the last mile and floored it up the steep bank of the lake to their home. Their home was no little log cabin; it was impressive, almost like a mirage in the desert. How could they have built that way out here?

The Jayne homestead on Chandalar Lake is twenty-five miles south of the Arctic National Wildlife Refuge, about thirty miles north of the Yukon Flats National Wildlife Refuge, and about thirty miles east of Gates of the Arctic National Park. Directly behind the piece of lakeshore rises a mountain over six thousand feet that is home to several snow-white Dall sheep. They like the windblown heights in winter.

The world around us for millions of acres, now our world, was different shades of white, in different shapes. The lake was supposedly flat, but the wind had created intricate waves and ridges atop it as its currents curved the snow precisely. They were symmetrical, as pretty as white on white can be; it almost felt bad to run over them on the snow machine. But the next wind would perfect its creation all over again. The wind was one of the rulers of our new world. The mountains all around were rounded as foothills and pure white. Their lines were smooth and beautiful like the curve from Rita's thin waist to the top of her hip and down to the beginning of her thigh. The mountains here were not sharp and steep, but seductive, inviting. Of course, they weren't actually welcoming. Go to them, alone, or even with someone experienced, this time of year, and risk dying. Even the horizon appeared silver-white, the lowering sun a cold yellow with white and silver rings around it. The sunlight here at this time of the afternoon was cold like fluorescent lights.

All three boys were standing outside waiting for us. Mike, the oldest, was the stocky one, like a young bull. Pete was maybe an inch taller at five feet nine inches, but wiry. Mike looked straight at you, while Pete snuck a look. They immediately began unlashing the cargo, which was coated with a crust of snow and ice crystals. Dan, nine, their adopted son, was small but obviously strong. He was standing off to the side until Pete told him, in a tough tone, to come help. It was nine below zero—I remember looking at their thermometer—and the three boys had on just long-sleeved, cotton shirts, no hats, no gloves. I guess everything, even below zero, is relative.

The house was not a log cabin, the easiest structure to build out here. Eric and his sons had built a frame house. The siding was made from cedar shakes from Oregon, and its reddish orange color drew me to it, everything else was so white-cold. And it was not a little bitty space but appeared to have quite a bit of room. Four dormers came out of the blue roof, indications that Eric was a talented carpenter. He had made his living as one before he was a vet.

Every nail, every window, each door, the Canadian wood furnace, every tube of caulking, each screw, every piece of roofing, every inch of electrical wire, they had transported to this spot. The same went for every tub of Sheetrock mud, the toilet, every piece of blue metal roofing, every four-by-eight-foot piece of easily broken Sheetrock. All of it they had hauled here personally, almost all of it on the winter trail on a snow machine trip like the one we'd just made. Some of it, not much, had been flown out in a Beaver with floats and boated over in their little outboard. Why would anyone want to do such an extreme amount of work just to live here? It's a huge undertaking to build your own home five miles from a Home Depot. Eric and his family, apparently, had a rich mix of skills and talents, daring and courage, and a deep need for the uninhabited deep-white silence of the Alaskan bush.

A NO. 9 LEVEL RISK

It's not enough just to have a need for Alaska; to make it you must have a rare blend of many abilities. Near here last fall two men had been dropped off in search of their vision of the wilderness life. They thought they had what was required to tame it, or at least survive in it. They'd chartered a bush pilot and his Beaver, the Alaskan workhorse. The pilot flew them and their supplies in and landed on the north fork of the Chandalar River. No one knows why, but they'd chosen a spot seven miles upriver from a long-deserted mining camp called Caro. For some insane reason they chose a basin of landscape that trapped the cold. Since they were squatting, they may have just seen a spot off the river that the pilot thought he could land on and said, "Down there." Surely they didn't know it was one of the most frigid places on earth, thought to have reached one hundred below zero. Certainly they didn't think the spot they chose was void of all edible life in winter, but it was. There was nothing to hunt that whole fall, winter, and spring. They must have been dangerously mistaken since they had so much ammunition and guns to hunt with.

You can be a hundred yards off a road in Alaska and break a leg and never be found. Where these men went, between Thazzik Mountain and the Hadweenzic River, there was no hope of being found. How did they ever expect to get out? They even brought in a woodstove that weighed over two hundred pounds. They would be dead by now if State Trooper Curt Bedingfield, the one who had rescued Eric by breaking trail, had not spotted their green canoe on a routine flyover while checking on wilderness moose hunters. They had no way to communicate with anyone. If Curt hadn't flown over that fall afternoon, there was basically no chance he would have flown over that spot again in his seventy-three-thousand-square-mile territory. If their canoe had not caught some sunlight, if Curt had been concentrating on something in front of him, he would never have known they were there. They had made the ultimate mistake: they had not contacted Curt before they'd headed into the best or the worst Alaska can offer.

If they hadn't been rescued, just maybe one day after they'd died some Native men from Venetie, downriver on the Yukon flats, would have discovered their tortured little cabin. And maybe there would have been the remnants of a starved body, or two starved bodies, depending on if one had reverted to cannibalism. That is if a wolverine or grizzly hadn't found the bodies with meat still on the bones. There would have been some of their equipment left depending on how many years it took for anyone to venture this deep into the wilderness. But if had been another winter or more, the sod roof of their cabin would have fallen in. That would have hidden the things they'd brought with them from Las Vegas and wherever else. If the young man Jon Krakauer wrote about in the book *Into the Wild* took a No. 5 level Alaskan risk, these fools took a No. 9 level risk. A No. 10 risk would be to jump out of a jet somewhere before Anchorage from thirty thousand feet with a pillowcase for a parachute.

They had done little research besides having read some books, and they didn't have any winter survival skills; they'd come from Las Vegas. Coming to Alaska to make your dream come true and expecting to plunge in as deep as these men had is the mark of a true fool. The leader, Thomas, fifty-two, had tried Alaska in the summer once before and couldn't make the wilderness thing happen by himself even then. This time he brought Ray, thirty-two, with him. Ray didn't have the anchor of family keeping him connected to any place. Thomas dreamed of finding gold, getting rich beyond his most deluded fantasies. Ray must have been an easy sell, or perhaps desperate to disappear. They were sixty feet from the bedrock, which is where gold is; they only had two gold pans and a hand sluice box and no other way to get to it. How are you going to mine gold when it's forty-five degrees below zero?

Getting dropped off where they did, when they did, with the supplies and skills they had, was an elaborate, slow-motion suicide plot. How could anyone be so arrogant about nature's power? They had no—zero—mining experience; there was a million percent better chance of striking gold in Vegas at the quarter slots. They weren't more than fifty miles from Eric and his family, but they might as well have been separated by an ocean. These men hadn't brought in a snow machine, nor a set of snowshoes or a pair of skis. They could not have come to a place of greater desolation and difficulty. There was not one way to get out once they were snowed in. They did bring with them six heavy cases of fruit in metal cans, to fight off scurvy, when all they needed was a pound of vitamin C pills.

The first time Curt met them, in September, he analyzed their setup. He didn't want their deaths on his soul. The first crazed mistake they'd made was to have covered the roof on their log cabin with moss and dirt. A medium wicked wind would have blown it all away, and if not that, the ice would have broken it in on them. Curt told them they needed to build a sod roof, about a foot thick, by laying sod on top of spruce poles as a foundation. They had even brought with them two tiny windows.

Thomas, the fifty-two-year-old, was the apparent leader. He lost sixty-two pounds in the approximately six months he and Ray survived in Alaska. They were living out there illegally, not unusual in the Alaskan bush, but couldn't afford to charter a plane out, even if Curt arranged it for them. Plus they didn't think they were in any danger. They had this wilderness-pioneer, gold-miner, trapper, live-off-the-land dream. Alaska makes people hallucinate, it takes hold of you, it makes some believe there is no gravity. They can enter the power and purity of it and be uninjured, jump from a mountaintop and not land on the rocks below. These two men didn't know until Curt told them that there was almost no game where they "homesteaded." They never saw a moose, even a rabbit, in over six months. They also hadn't bothered to find out they had settled into a place so cold that seventy below zero wasn't unusual, even one hundred below in that paralyzingly cold valley. When Curt flies, he checks the temperature at two thousand feet, where it is warmer than it is on the ground. One day at two thousand feet it was twenty below over Coldfoot and forty below over the basin where these men who dared frozen death lived.

Envision living in their fourteen-by-fourteen-foot spruce-log cabin, built near the river. The lower down in the basin the colder it was. Windows are covered with layers of plastic and so provide only a little escape, diversion, and if there's nothing moving outside, maybe even a bit of inspiration, even if it's the adrenaline-based fight-or-flight response. You're shut inside the log cabin, the cracks chinked with moss and mud, except you didn't know what you were doing and for who knows what reason, the chinking falls out. You could have read a book about cabins in arctic conditions, but you didn't. When the mud falls out of the cracks, it is frozen, unusable like a brick. The moss is covered with deep snow, and besides it's too cold some days to even go out. The cold attacks your hands and toes, wants to flash-freeze them. You stuff the cracks that let in the unrelenting invasion of killer cold with scraps of clothes. You don't have extra clothes, though. The unbelievable cold is tracking you down; it's invisible but finds you anyway and steals your tiny bit of comfort. You get these feelings—you know at first they are silly—that you want to kill the cold, or whatever causes it. You think about loading up your rifle and shooting at it. But you can't kill winter; no one can change the tilt of the earth. So you blame your dilemma on Thomas, the guy who sold you on this deranged dream, a frigid, fiendish nightmare.

Speaking of Thomas, the one who lost over sixty pounds, he wakes up because the woodstove can't heat the place. No matter how much wood they burn, it's around zero inside. He's lying there thinking about how little food is left. Plus, no one knows if that state trooper will ever be back. You haven't seen anyone but each other for so long you wonder if he was ever really here. Even if he said he would check on us, he might be a masochist and just let us starve to death. Or he could die in a plane crash; there are plenty of those in the Brooks Range. That trooper, he seemed too nice, really; no one's that nice anymore.

Thomas's thinking, "If I get up and eat some food, will Ray hear me? What if I just kill Ray? Think how much more food there will be, but then Ray cuts and hauls a lot of the firewood and is strong, hauls water." The cold has already made the skin on Thomas's hands crack open. He covers his head from the cold and thinks, "Let damn Ray get up and stoke that damn woodstove that can't keep us warm." Why did they make the cabin so big? By now they had cut it in half, by hanging wool blankets that they could have been using to keep warm, to seven feet by seven feet. As Thomas lies there, being slowly tortured, he turns and an air space opens from his sleeping bag and the awful cold comes in to try to rob his body of warmth, of life.

At times sleep is unwanted because the thought comes back about creosote building up in the stovepipe and catching fire. Creosote is an oil generated by burning wood, and it builds up in a crystalline layer on the insides of stovepipes. If the pipe gets too hot and catches fire, the cabin will almost surely follow. Then they would be without shelter, except for a small tent. What if the wood-stove was crushed by the burning cabin as it fell in on itself, the ammunition all went off in the fire, the guns were burned up, and you only got out with the clothes you slept in? Then you couldn't even kill yourself with a bullet.

A day for these men, knowing the cold was outside waiting to get them in the forever silence and white isolation, was an immense exercise in maintaining sanity. You could scream for a week yet no one would hear you. You could try to shoot at a jet flying over, but your bullet wouldn't reach. You cannot call anyone, there is no road, no trail; five feet of snow closes you in as if it were a thousand-foot-deep ocean. You begin hitting the spruce tree with an ax while you cut firewood, trying to kill it because it is looking at you.

It's too cold to go out but you must, otherwise there's no wood, no water, no life. Maybe that would be better. Isn't it true that before you freeze to death you get warm all over? You haven't bathed in months, you stink, and your clothes are now mostly ash gray.

Why do people put themselves in places like this? Why did Eric?

By the end of November when Curt went back to check on them, they had no food left, just $37. He knew they'd be low on food, so he brought them a hundred-pound sack of flour, some beans, sugar, and rice. He bought these goods with his own money in Fairbanks; he hauled them 250 miles to Coldfoot. Curt wondered before he went back to check on them in November if maybe one would have killed the other in a fit of cabin-fever rage. But they didn't try to kill each other until the end of the winter, which is when the most domestic violence happens in Alaska. Would-be explosions controlled by discipline are controllable no more.

Thomas and Ray get another visit from their guardian angel around Christmas. He brought them a turkey and some sweet things as he dropped out of the sky and landed on skis by their cabin. Curt made one more drop of food to them one clear day in February. Right before Curt got there, almost terminal cabin fever had set in. Ray had attacked Thomas with a butcher knife because he thought he was eating too much food. Maybe Thomas stole two of the molasses cookies that Ray, the good cook, had made; they were to be eaten only on Sundays. They had been burning kerosene but had run out. They got some dim light from burning one candle at a time, and then those were gone too. After that there was fuzzy, dim daylight, and then too soon every day came the awful, silent, freezing dark. Solitary confinement in the worst prison in the United States would have been like a pleasure compared to their miserable months.

Once they began depending on Curt, they had to worry about whether the bad weather could settle in and stop his flying. Their failure was crushing them. What promises had Thomas made to Ray? When did the younger man figure out this Alaskan dream lined with pocketfuls of gold nuggets was a ridiculous idea, maybe even a malicious lie? Many Alaskan dreams have had foundations of sand like Thomas and Ray's.

Curt was able to contact Thomas's family, and they sent him a plane ticket to come home, defeated but lucky to be alive. Curt could only find Ray's father, who was bedridden and, someone said, couldn't speak. Ray ended up at a homeless shelter in Fairbanks.

On March 12, Curt flew them out in the Super Cub one at a time. They had to leave almost everything behind, as so many shattered Alaskan dreamers have done before, whether they were almost totally unprepared and thought they could survive because they had a book about someone else doing it, or prepared, indomitable, but ran out of luck and angels.

LAKEFRONT PROPERTY

Standing there, looking at Eric's home, having spent the last few days with him, Vicky, and Elizabeth, having seen him operate and relate to people, I felt better about the firmness of the foundation of his Alaskan wilderness dream. Before we even opened the door to their house, I heard a strange sound coming from inside, a kind of rapid tapping, like hitting a screwdriver, or several of them, against a wood floor. Tap, tap, tap, tap.

Elizabeth opened the handsome, handmade door into an arctic entry. Beyond the entryway, the house opened into a large two-story room, with a freestanding wooden stairway to four small bedrooms, the children's. The floors

Mike takes the dog team for a little run near the Jayne house in the Brooks Range.
PHOTO BY PETER JENKINS

were plywood, usually considered a subfloor, although I couldn't imagine carpet with all the animals. Because that's what the tapping came from, their six dogs, several they brought with them from Iowa. One was a red husky. These dogs lived inside with the Jaynes' six cats. The first thing I thought, or the first two things, were that I couldn't believe they hauled food out here for all of them, and that Rita and I are allergic to cats. Eric, being a vet, probably never thought to ask.

There was a room about twelve by twelve feet framed in and covered with plastic, sort of a room within a room. Elizabeth, who was now talking more and smiling, explained that when she had first moved out here, a year ago, the whole family had lived in that room, with its own small woodstove that burned short pieces of wood. I hoped they were careful about burning dry wood with little creosote. Curt had told me about another wilderness family who lived between here and Arctic Village. They had an extra cabin built, fully stocked, well away from the one they lived in, just in case. There would be no putting out an established fire, and it would be forty-five below and dropping. And all your clothes would be burned and you'd have gotten out with just what you slept in. I'd never thought about a fire out here. There were so many circumstances I could not even imagine. If a fire burned down the Jayne house, there was a meat cache built up on a ladder a few of us could get into and a few summer cabins across the lake.

Hugh and his dog team were not here yet. Eric thought he might spend the night on the trail and wouldn't worry about him until tomorrow sometime. Hugh had run the Yukon Quest this year with a few of the dogs he was mushing now; he could handle the winter trail.

The downstairs room wrapped in insulating plastic was Eric and Vicky's, but they let us stay in there. They stayed on a mattress on the floor in a downstairs room the dogs and Tyler usually slept in. The dog hair in there was thick. The house was neat and organized, it just wasn't finished on the inside. No paint, no trim yet, no vacuum. There was a TV in one of the kids' rooms for watching videos, but there were no networks or cable channels or talking heads coming into their home from NBC or CBS or ESPN or HBO or C-SPAN. The invisible microwave signals from the satellites could not even reach them. No one could call at dinnertime, or any other time.

Eric was not worried about Y2K. He is not a religious fanatic, although he is possibly the most balanced human I've ever met, a combination of the spiritual and practical. Eric and Vicky are similar; they appreciate life in the wilderness with their animals. Eric is not living out here with his family because he expects the world to end, and he is not looking for gold. If he found a vein of it, gleaming out of the side of some mountain peak he and the family had hiked to one summer afternoon, he would probably never mention it to anyone, but instead die with the secret. He's not running from the feds or taxes or the law.

In his high school yearbook in Des Moines, it said he would someday end up in Alaska. As a child, he had maps of Alaska on the walls of his bedroom. He read classic books about the great white north and was smart and practical enough (that farm-belt Midwestern thing) to realize that Alaska is like nowhere else. It requires more than many have to give. You find a person who can survive in the bush of Alaska for several years, and thrive, not gradually go insane or physically deteriorate, and you have found someone extraordinary. These distinct people cannot, however, be judged by their looks, their clothes, their appearance, their degrees, and their pedigree.

The boys banged the encrusted snow off our bags and carried them inside and set them on the floor near the kitchen table. Any piece of furniture out here was like a jewel-encrusted throne in a museum. The effort needed to get a kitchen table here was enormous; imagine a four-poster bed, an antique oak wardrobe. All the dogs came up and sniffed our stuff; the part–basset hound seemed the most intelligent. His name is Fred. I hoped they weren't going to hook him up to any sled. The oldest cat was on a stair, out of the way of children's feet, but in the hot air. Sit down and it was in the forties; stand up and your head was in the low sixties. We kept our fleece and coats on inside almost all the time except when we were sleeping. Quickly Rita and Julianne learned from the behavior of the cats. Sit on the stairs, heat rises.

Not long ago, Eric had built a separate room on the north side of the house and assembled a Canadian-made wood furnace that he had hooked up to ductwork. Living out here, I would learn that much of the best cold-weather equipment and gear is understandably made in Canada. Before Alaska was connected to the rest of the United States by road during World War II, many Alaskans had more of a connection to Canada than the United States. Many Alaskans have always felt they were a separate country, like Texas, and some Alaskans, including major state leaders, would like to be.

Eric asked Pete to start the generator. Their bank of huge batteries was losing its charge; the lights were dimming and soon it would be dark. In the summer, the endless daylight and sometimes-bright sun provided them with almost all the power they needed. Eric had a small windmill that generated some electrical power as well. He could read an article and look over the diagrams in *Popular Mechanics* or *Mother Earth News* and build it. So could Pete. Mike told me one of his dad's hobbies was fixing up old houses. Mike and Pete had been able to do "the easy stuff" in building since they were eleven or twelve, such as framing up walls, and lately, hanging Sheetrock. This freed up Eric to do the more complex stuff. That's why Eric didn't mind leaving the boys out here to fend for themselves occasionally. Pete could fix about anything Eric could; Mike was the entertainer, the "gourmet" bush cook. All this had taught them independence.

Eric was so humble, so self-effacing, so hardworking, so generous, in a way sort of godlike, that it would be difficult to disobey him. Often when he asked his kids to do something, he would say, "Sorry, but would someone start the generator" or "Sorry, but whose turn is it to sweep the downstairs?" Eric's courage to tackle this world with his family, to be radically different from most people today, must have been somewhat inspired by his father, a Methodist minister. He is no normal minister, although there is really no such thing. Eric's dad is a lobbyist for the Methodist Church to the Iowa legislature. Eric joked that Iowa could be considered somewhat conservative, but that his father is called the "white Jesse Jackson." He lobbies for equal rights, abortion rights, gay rights, liberal ideals. Eric said his father does not back down but is not obnoxious about his stands, just committed to them with his heart. He gladly rocks the boat, respectfully, in a place not known for rocking the boat. Iowa has every nuance of the human condition; it is just not as evident as in, say, New York City, being camouflaged as it is by the veneer of "normalcy." In Iowa, you stand above, beyond, or below your fellow man mostly by your actions. Eric's father not only encouraged him to ride across America on his bike at sixteen, he told him he thought the trip would enlarge him.

Elizabeth, seeming much more relaxed, had combed out her thick, dirty-blond hair, which had been stuffed under a worn wool hat on the way. She and Julianne were headed outside to record the temperature. It was an Alaskan homeschool project Elizabeth was doing. The sheet she used said, "NOAA Record of River and Climatological Observations." Here at the Jayne home on January 1, the high was $-20°$, the low $-32°$ F. On January 2, the high was -28, the low was -42. On January 4, it heated up to -1 and cooled to -22. The second week of January must have been like living in a freezer with the lightbulb burned out. January 8 gave no indication of the killer cold to come: it was -2 high, -20 low. Then January 9, the high was -26, low -36. The low on the tenth was -39; the high on January 11 was -37 and the low was -44. On the twelfth, the high—there has got to be a better word—was -40 and the low was -45. On the thirteenth, the high was -41 and the low was -48. The last week of January, Pete and Mike probably went snow-machining in T-shirts: the highs were between 9 and 23 and the average low was about 5 degrees above.

The girls came back inside, and so did all of the dogs. The sounds of all their claws on the plywood, six sets of paws, echoing around the cold house, is one I'd not heard before and one I will never forget. The fluctuation of these temperatures and the Jaynes' lack of advance warning, such as the Weather Channel or government recordings, make planning activities always a risk. Even cutting wood, which they do ten miles away, cannot be planned until the day or hour in question.

Mike decided to go check on Hugh, to see if he'd made it to the lake yet. Pete sat down at the table with Rita and me. Vicky was making some large pepperoni pizzas and had already finished some homemade dough. Eric was doing something in the workshop, off the kitchen. Just a few minutes before he'd told Mike and Pete they'd have to go get water in the morning. They'd chopped a hole in the thick, thick lake ice and covered it with canvas and cheap tarps. They'd probably have to chop open the hole wide enough to fit the five-gallon buckets, I thought. Eric was concerned that they'd burned so much of their supply of wood; he said there would have to be a trip to cut more, hopefully tomorrow.

As Pete sat at the kitchen table, it took quite a few minutes for me to get him talking. Out here for four months without going to Fairbanks, he was bushy. His skin was white, his hair black, and his cheeks red. He looked like a choirboy, the kind with a sixth-degree black belt and three girlfriends.

"When did you first come out here?" I asked him.

His smile was subtle and made me feel confident. "About four years ago I first came here—this was when we were living in a small town in Washington."

I'd asked five or six questions before this one, and he'd just answered, "Yes." "Not really." "Kind of." "Okay." I had decided to wait until he got used to us.

"Dad and I, we came here right after Thanksgiving. It was so tough coming in here; we had to break trail and it was twenty-five below. It was so bad we left our sled with our supplies back on the trail. It kept getting stuck.

"Then when we got here, there was nothing here. I was eleven, really I just wanted to go home. Dad had built a food cache: a shed built off the ground, high up so animals can't break in and eat all your food. It might be eight feet by ten feet, maybe ten feet off the ground."

Pete exhibited superior self-confidence, especially when he was not around his two brothers.

"We had to live in that food cache. We brought a small woodstove to put in it. It had no windows, there was not much room. We hauled logs from across the lake to use as foundation supports for the house."

One of the four-legged cats leaped onto the table. Pete immediately but gently threw it off.

"It's really intense when I've been out here for a few months and go into Fairbanks. There are so many people I don't know. All these cars. So much moving all the time. Too much noise and confusion," Pete said, his bright eyes glowing with self-awareness.

Suddenly the dogs all started barking, with more barking outside. Hugh had mushed the sixty-plus miles and was here. He was so tough and energized, he bounded in as if he had just been out for a half-mile walk. He ate some of the fantastically tasty leftover pizza and we all went to bed.

16

Life at the Homestead

In the early morning, the kids' chores began. Eric wanted Mike and Pete to go across the lake about two miles. I went along to help; we were going to retrieve some doghouses to keep the team in. Over there was their only neighbor, a Vietnam vet, a caretaker of a few cabins owned by a man from Fairbanks. It was a weather station for NOAA. Mike and Pete told me that the depth finder on their boat, which they used to catch lake trout, showed that the lake was more than four hundred feet deep. Their depth finder only goes to four hundred feet. In the summer, they set a subsistence gill net offshore from their house and catch fish to eat.

We took two snow machines across the lake and one of the long, flat Siglan sleds. Big Dave, the caretaker, who never left because he had to make weather readings every few hours, seemed glad today to see someone, anyone. He was the Jaynes' only possible winter visitor and lived with his Siberian husky. The caretaker across the lake, and there had been several, was always the subject of much conversation at the Eric Jayne homestead. If the current one, Dave, was a bit grumpy one day, he'd try to tell Mike and Pete how to snow-machine the winter trail, except he'd never done it. When it was clear and the northern lights shook the sky and wiggled in purple and green, they were often right over the top of the caretaker's cabin. If the Jaynes happened to be watching the dance of the lights, they might see him circling round and round and round on his snow machine on the lake. They interpreted this to mean something was bugging him; maybe it was a way to think through his past. They could only guess. If he was in a mood to be around people, they'd hear a knock on their door, something so unexpected as to be unimaginable. If you want to live where no one will ever come to your door to sell you something or try to save you, move to the Alaskan bush. If Dave was in a good mood, the outside light of his cabin was on; if not, just a dim glow came from inside. Where there is little human interaction, one notices little things like this.

In Alaska, most people don't delight when others are broken by life in the last frontier, but they do have a refined vocabulary to describe it. Some seem almost to enjoy observing the downward spiral. Another caretaker across the lake, two before Big Dave, was so anxious to leave, so determined not to spend an extra minute here, that he chartered two planes at once, dueling charters, all the way from Fairbanks. Apparently he made them think there was an emergency. You never know if a charter will have the weather conditions to come, or the incentive, so when you're about to lose your mind, you make sure someone's coming.

"It's interesting about some of these caretakers," Eric said. "A lot of people like to blame others for their problems, but out here there's no one to blame. People run out of blame, then they realize it has to do with them, and it really gets to some people when they realize that. It's hard to deal with. People think, maybe, they come out here and they will escape all that's wrong with their lives, and they get here and seem to find out it's the same problems here as wherever they come from."

Eric told us about Stuart, who'd arrived just to fill in for the "full-time" caretakers who were taking a vacation, but they'd bolted and never returned. There was no wood, no snow machine. He was about forty-five, reclusive.

"Stuart never became unhappy," Eric said, his voice becoming intense for him, which wasn't very intense. "It's just the longer he stayed, the more messy the place became. I guess it shows that some people stay clean and keep clean because of peer pressure or job requirements, because this guy spiraled on the cleanliness and order scale. It was gross. There was old food rotting all around the cabin. Clothes rotting, inside and out, lying in piles. He was pretty ripe. He wasn't even doing the weather. Sometimes we'd go over there at one o'clock in the afternoon, in the *summer*," Eric emphasized, "and he'd still be in bed."

Eric described him as heavyset, short, and said he probably didn't take a bath for eight months. After he left, the owner, Walt, had to take almost everything out of the cabin and burn it. Stuart was here from December through the summer. How does Walt find caretakers for a place like this, and what does he tell them about it?

"The most bizarre caretaker was the man who claimed to be a World War Two veteran yet he was only forty. He left notes in the cabin that said he was going to go to Germany and save them from the Jews. The man was on medication, except he forgot to bring it with him," Eric said, raising his eyebrows.

The caretaker parade across the lake was like the Jaynes' own off-off-Broadway one- or two-man plays. The plays normally had similar last acts: the character or characters losing self-control, self-esteem, and sometimes themselves to temporary insanity. Dave was only in act 2. The only thing Eric worries about is that one of these caretakers will snap and take it out on Eric's family, especially if he happens to be gone, especially if Elizabeth and Vicky are there. I knew exactly how he felt.

Mike, Pete, and I dug out about eight old doghouses from three feet of snow; they were built out of logs. Behind his snow machine, Eric had hauled out a wooden sled so they could all learn mushing. A couple of Hugh's dogs had come from Athabascan musher Jerry Riley, who'd won the Iditarod in 1976. He came in eighth in the Iditarod in 2001, amazing for his age. Jerry, tough as double moose hide, was trying to help Hugh get started.

Mike, Pete, and I pulled two doghouses across the lake at a time as Dave, the present caretaker, critiqued our methods from the window. We made four trips; each time the doghouses fell off on one snow lump or another. The whole surface of this side of the lake, more exposed to the wind, was a series of carved lumps, like moguls. Julianne and Elizabeth were zooming around spying on us. Elizabeth was teaching Julianne how to run the snow machine.

Elizabeth's main job was to care for the animals. Based on how unusually difficult it was to get yourself here, much less pet food, I was constantly amazed at how many dogs and cats were a part of this family. Just a couple days before we'd gotten to the Jayne homestead, their beloved yellow Lab, who had been Vicky's back in Iowa, died at almost sixteen. He'd become so infirm Mike or Pete or Eric had to carry him outside to make the snow yellow. He'd go and then immediately fall over, he was so weak. Vicky had said that she thanked God he died in his sleep. One night I stepped out on the front porch to look for the northern lights and stepped on his frozen body, covered with a blanket. They would have to wait until spring to bury him. Eric joked that spring lasted a week, summer three weeks. They'd lost two dogs this year, since Tutt, the Pomeranian, had been killed by wolves.

Elizabeth fed and watered and paid attention to other animals, such as Handsome, a three-legged cat that someone had brought to Eric's vet clinic after it had gotten caught in a trap. He was ten and could hop up the carved-wood, circular stairway Eric had built to where the heat was.

And there were Skippy, Sweet Bones, and Stumpy, three cats that they'd adopted from another of Eric's vet clinics in Washington State. Eric and his family had made an intermediate transition to the Northwest before making the final leap here. There was Red, the retired sled dog that had come inside the house one day following funny Fred, the part–basset hound. Sled dogs aren't supposed to like it inside, but not Red. He immediately loved the easy life and refused to live like a sled dog anymore. Just watching Fred come into a room and, ba-dunk, steal everyone's attention was worth the trip out here. Fred came from the Fairbanks animal shelter. There was Truman, the Mackenzie River husky; shy Lisa, the total mutt; Buddy, the fourteen-year-old part-sheltie from Iowa; and Shelley. Elizabeth not only readily handled all the responsibility as a twelve-year-old, but she is also an excellent student. She will probably graduate from the state homeschool system by the time she's fifteen.

Late that afternoon, an hour before sunset, Eric said the conditions were right for him and me to take a couple snow machines up to the head of the lake and beyond. It was the last week of March and would be light until after 8 p.m. We were gaining about seven minutes of daylight per day now, forty-nine minutes a week. Gaining daylight is something counted and counted upon all over Alaska. The sun was painting the snow pink and a pale peachy color; there was no wind. The air was so perfectly pure that the mountains appeared a thousand miles away or right next to us.

We took the lightweight machines since we were not hauling anything but ourselves. Riding through the fresh six inches on top of the four or five feet of snow underneath was a luxurious feeling. It had enough mass to hold us yet it felt like flying through clouds atop the ground. The snow gave in to our weight ever so lightly so that our movement was smooth, silky, and effortless.

We rode atop the tableland right before it dropped off into the lake. Eric mentioned when we stopped at a sudden clifflike decline that all kinds of bushes and tundra and rocks and even boulders were underneath us, and this deep snow is what made traveling on this magic carpet of snowflakes so awesome. Of all the freeing and inspiring movement I've done in my life, moving atop this deep powder was as thrilling and inspiring as any I'd ever done. Moving across water, no matter how slight the resistance, couldn't compare. Flying through the air, diving off a high cliff was too fast and too short with too much bang at the end. Walking and running were far too plodding.

We rode off little cliffs, our way padded and buffered by the four to six feet of powder. We flew across sections of blueberry bushes that would be a maddening, impossible tangle in summer. We saw a dark gray, almost black fox. It was hunting slowly, then started running when it saw us along the hard edge of the lake. Its fur was so luxuriant, deep, and shining against the white-on-white of everything else. The fox would run fifty feet and stop, look at us, run a bit more, and watch us.

When we came to the beginning of the frozen lake, we could see that no humans had been here for months, because there was not a track, no evidence at all. Then we headed into the north fork of the Chandalar River. There were bare places where potent winds had blown off the snow and exposed the ice. The icy spots were turquoise-colored, and solitary beautiful, like a Navajo-carved piece of turquoise lying on the fur of a sleeping polar bear. We knew there was water underneath, somewhere. Farther up, as the valley narrowed and the walls of the surrounding mountains became steeper, we began to see a few tracks. It looked as if a moose had been feeding on the reddish willow branches. A couple of wolves had come through, sticking to the willows and rabbit tracks. A half mile up we came to the tracks of a relentless wolverine.

On our way home, we decided to go across the lake for a ways, then zoom up onto the land where the snow was more fun. We found deep places we would start sinking into, yet we always powered our way out. No wonder winter, when the rivers and lakes and ponds and swamps that cover Alaska are frozen, is many people's favorite time of the year. Snow like this brings freedom, the chance to wander and explore, race sled dogs, follow the caribou herd. It gives people the ability and the time to visit neighboring villages.

We got home, red-cheeked and refreshed, and Rita and Vicky had made some homemade cinnamon rolls, the best I've had anywhere in Alaska, and the Alaskans love their sweets. I ate my second cinnamon roll while all the dogs and one cat waited for a crumb. This place reminded me of a painting that hung in my Sunday school classroom when I was six or seven at First Presbyterian Church. It showed all the humans and all the animals lying down together in

The Jayne family: Mike, Dan, Pete, Elizabeth, Vicky, and Eric. Photo by Peter Jenkins

peace. I always liked that picture. The entire time we were here, I never heard one growl or hiss out of the dogs and cats.

The four adults drank tea after dinner while Eric told us vet stories. One was about a senior citizen, a sweet, widowed Iowa farm lady, who was in the sometimes-deep confusion of early Alzheimer's. She was convinced her dachshund had fleas, so she would bring it to Eric once a week. One time she covered the brown dachshund with shaving cream, even in its ears, to kill those pesky fleas. And there were the calls late on Christmas Eve, usually from some widow. Eric knew what they really needed was company. He would always go to their home and bring a few children. They would visit and eat the Christmas cookies the lonely old woman had made, the sugar cookies that had been her husband's favorites. Eric would ask about her sick pet and she would say that it was better. It was hard to imagine Eric saying no to anyone who asked him for help. In a way, living out here being such a sensitive soul might have been a relief in this world so quick to use you up.

About an hour into Eric's stories, Mike came down the stairway. It moved a bit under his weight. He waited until his father stopped speaking; he kept glancing at me. Since we'd moved those doghouses and stoked the wood furnace together, we had bonded a bit. Apparently he had something to say and he wanted us to witness it. Something was up.

"I am going to graduate from this home school this year, right?" Mike said, his muscled neck set sternly. I remembered how uncomfortable it could be for someone his age to talk to adults.

"Yes, that's right, Mike, if you get all your work done and turned in," Eric said.

Now Mike spoke directly to me. "If I do, then I want to get an old sailboat, fix it up with some of the money I got when Mom died, and sail around the world. Dad tells me you did a boat trip. You know that movie *Legends of the Fall*, when Brad Pitt's character took off on that boat, that's what I want to do. What do you think about that?" Mike asked. He said it all in one breath, as if he didn't want to stop for fear of losing the courage it took to speak his dream out loud.

"Sounds like a major change from life out here," I said. I wasn't sure what I should say. Eric might want him to stay and help here.

"Yeah, it does," Eric said. "I think it would be a great thing for Mike to do."

Now that I knew how Eric felt, I could speak freely. "I've got a friend, Scott Bannerot, that's been sailing around the world for the last few years. When I get back to Seward, I will try to contact him, see what he says. I think he's in New Zealand. That sound okay?"

"Sure, that would be good. Thanks."

Relieved, excited, Mike went back upstairs; he and Pete were watching one of the new movies we'd brought with us from Fairbanks.

I had to get up a couple times that night and go to the bathroom, which was some kind of Swedish self-composting model, except the composting part had frozen. While I was up, I always had to step out on the front porch and hear the silence and look for the northern lights. Everyone was asleep; no dogs were moving across the plywood floors. As a person who loves quiet, melody, and peace, never in all my traveling had I ever been in a place so still, so void of noise. The light crunch of my feet—I had on wool socks—could probably be heard by a wolf a mile away, or so it seemed. I wanted so much to hear a wolf howl in this vacuum. I thought I could hear snowflakes landing. The cold didn't get to me as I stood waiting to see the lights, Vicky's frozen Lab lying in peace next to me. Then the lights were there, green and pink and blue, they wobbled and darted and flamed and disappeared.

In the morning, Eric's loud voice woke me. Rita and Julianne already had their eyes open and were listening, you couldn't help it. I got up and went into the kitchen where Eric was speaking as firmly as I'd ever heard him. Pete and

Mike were going into Coldfoot; Mike would get off at the truck stop and hitch a ride to Fairbanks. There he'd hook up with a musher and work as a handler with him. Pete would have to come back by himself, a journey filled with possibilities. To make matters worse, it was already snowing and blowing and conditions were gray light. *Gray light* meant that in the snow there was no shadow, no way to see the trail clearly. It is easy, especially across open places, to get lost. Then if you panic and strike out farther without being sure of your way, you can become terribly lost, so far off the trail that anyone looking for you will not find you. This trip would require substantial mental toughness, and of course, physical stamina.

Eric spoke an order to Pete: "You get lost, just stay put. Don't get brave and then get even more lost."

Eric was obviously concerned but also excited for his sons. If he hadn't been, he would never have let them go. Running the winter trail alone was a boyhood-to-manhood rite of passage out here.

"Do you have a gun, in case you run into a winter bear?" Eric asked.

"Yes," Pete and Mike answered in unison respectfully, not with a whine.

"Watch for overflow. Remember, if you get stuck and you're not back by near dark, I'll be coming to look for you," Eric said.

Pete smiled as Eric ran down the list of instructions and warnings. Pete's blue eyes shone as confidently as those of any fifteen-year-old I'd ever met. He would be traveling over 120 miles on a snow machine, today, if nothing went wrong. So much could go wrong, but also so many things were right about him undertaking this responsibility. If he did it, he'd be the youngest person ever to do the winter trail solo. But it wasn't about being the youngest, it was all about having confidence in what he could do himself. Pete knew he could fix the snow machine, he knew how to make out the trail in gray light, he knew he wouldn't panic if he got lost. Right before they left, Eric asked Pete if he had any matches. He felt around in his pocket. It was the one crucial lifesaving thing he had forgotten. He got a box of wooden matches so if he did get stuck, a fire could be started and he would keep warm.

After they left and we ate breakfast, Eric and I went and cut wood about eight or nine miles away. It took us a couple hours to load up the Siglan sled with dead spruce logs. We brought back about a week's worth of fuel. Then it was afternoon, and the light began to wane. Everyone kept opening the front door and looking for the headlight of a moving snow machine. I saw one; it was

Big Dave going around in circles on the lake. All of us got quiet, not wanting to ask about Pete. I noticed Eric went outside every fifteen minutes and looked and listened. Eric could wait no longer; he suited up to go find Pete. As he did not return, we began to worry.

After about an hour, I saw another moving snow-machine light. At first I thought it was Dave, back to his circling, but then I saw that there were two. It had to be Eric and Pete. Pete was almost home when Eric had found him. A huge cheeseburger, a mountain of fries, and the census taker had delayed Pete. The census taker was unprepared, or unwilling, to come down the winter trail and actually eyeball the seven people at Chandalar Lake, so Big Brother asked Pete a lot of questions, took up his valuable time knowing he was expected back, and didn't even pay for his burger.

To think a census taker was snooping around in the wilderness made me feel sick, even violated, oddly. Out here in this white temple, a person can ride the snow and soar in the vapors of snow crystals kicked up. You can turn off your machine and what you hear are millions of notes created by nothing. It struck me as grotesque that some census worker was wanting all kinds of personal details, far beyond how many souls were living out here. Was there no place to get away from the incessant data gatherers, the governmental snoops? This encounter notwithstanding, it was easy to see how proud Pete was at having done the return trip on the winter trail alone.

That night the northern lights pranced in our blue world lit by moonlight. What did people think of this night light before they understood what it was? Was it contented spirits dancing in heaven? Did anyone think they were spirits trying to come back into the world for their loved ones? Could it be your mother who had passed away two winters ago when the caribou never came, leaping, the one in the sky that was yellow and red?

I understand why Alaskans get so sick of people being hung up on Alaska's winter darkness. The light from the moon as it bounces off the whitest snow is another form of illumination, of revelation, that more than makes up for the missing sunlight. Everything is bathed in shades of blue. The summer sun for several hours in midday around my farm is oppressive, its glare closes my eyes, makes me shield myself with sunglasses, hats, and shade. The blue light showed me plenty: strings of caribou, clouds moving, definition of mountainsides, frozen lakes, maybe even a wolf slinking into the darkest blue of the forest. Then when Alaska's winter sun comes out, its low angle makes for an almost three-hour sunset. Sometimes the mountaintops all turn pink and gold. They are rich shades of these colors that I'd seen in pictures thinking they had been manipulated by filters.

Julianne and Elizabeth had been waiting all day for Pete. Mike and Pete had run the new dog team yesterday before they left. Pete had no experience, Mike only a bit, but they ran the dogs up and down the lake. The girls and Dan wanted to get in on it, but Pete and Mike weren't ready to be hassled by them. Pete promised if it wasn't too cold, he'd hook the dogs up and teach them how to mush in the morning.

Vicky made the best pancakes in the world that morning. I'm not sure if it's the cold and the lack of humidity, the lung-filling perfect air and hard work, but food in Alaska tastes better and you seem to need more of it. I wonder, does it have anything to do with the coming of winter, the body picking up signals about a need to hibernate?

Pete and the girls untied all the dogs, put on their harnesses, and then hooked them to the sled. Red, the retired sled dog, wanted to run; he was jumping and barking. Pete tried Fred; he didn't have a clue. He pulled to the side, in the way of saying, get me out of here. He lay down while all the huskies lunged and barked excitedly. Pete finally took Fred out of harness, and he became a retired sled dog without ever pulling the sled one foot.

Pete ran the team off the hill and down onto the frozen lake, quite a rush since the dogs seemed to like to run down it. There was about six to eight inches of fresh powder. The big brother was impressively patient as a teacher. When the girls finally took off, it was hard to say who was leading whom. They got off the snow machine trail and bogged down. Pete would run through the snow to help them, sometimes having to get ahold of the leader and lead him through a drift. Elizabeth and Julianne had bonded quickly; they might as well have been the only girls in the world. They mushed around their end of the lake, each taking the lead while the other sat in the sled as passenger. Then Rita took off with Julianne as passenger.

Rita and Vicky, both gifted at creating food from the barest basics, had been baking bread and making tender sourdough rolls. When we came in, the counter was full of whole-wheat creations, and the delicious scent from all of it filled the room. All the nonmushing dogs were loitering, waiting for any possible snack. Eric walked in from the food cache with a hindquarter of a caribou that Tyler, the "vacationing in Fairbanks" caretaker, had shot earlier in the win-

ter. He carved off caribou steak after caribou steak, throwing each delighted dog
equal bites of the bright red meat.

GETTING BUSHY WITH IT

As we talked for hours after dinner, someone turned on the radio; the only station they got was from Japan. If you were alone and superlonely, maybe you'd
listen. But we were listening to Eric, telling us about his plan to take another canoe trip down the Yukon this summer. He would take Dan and Elizabeth and
stop in each Native village on its banks and offer his veterinary services to the
people in Rampart, Tanana, Ruby, Nulato, and so on as far as they traveled.
There was no regular vet service in these villages. Sometimes Eric would be
paid and sometimes not. He would also stop at the many family fish camps,
where every year salmon were caught, cut up, dried, and smoked.

We didn't want to go. We had become connected to this family and fond of
winter in the Brooks Range. The next morning, we were packing our clothes
when Eric came in, still as shy and polite and unassuming as always, and asked
if anyone would like a shower. You would have thought he'd asked if any of us
wanted to fly or live forever. We had not felt water, except on our one washcloth. Eric said he had gotten up early and heated a large pot of water. Pete had
hauled some extra water from the lake, a rugged job, even for him. Water
weighs eight pounds per gallon, and getting it at fifteen below zero, scooping it
out in five-gallon buckets, then hauling it upon the snow machine makes for
real appreciation of each cup.

Eric had a camp shower, like a rubber hot-water bottle. You fill it with warm
water, then hang it in the shower stall and get naked. It was chilly in their bathroom, but who cared, warm water would soon be dripping on me. Rita and Julianne went first. Rita had not taken off her wool cap since we'd been here. She
is a stylish woman; this was probably as long as she'd ever gone in her life since
she was thirteen without seeing herself in a mirror. Just hearing the precious water, heated by the miraculous generator, powered by precious gas, every ounce of
it hauled out here on the winter trail, was a major episode in our lives. Every
other shower I've ever taken would be considered better by objective analysis,
but they weren't. This was the best.

To shower, to be warmed by water—what pleasure the warm little streams running down my needy body were. I heard water dripping off my body onto the tub as I'd never heard it before, what a ravishing sound. I used as little as possible wanting to be warm and wet but also needing to get clean. It was more than a treat, rare to many in the world. Why was I so unappreciative so often?

In a way, taking that shower at Eric's summed up what was so meaningful about our experience. The silky, precious, caressing water Eric warmed for us we loved for how difficult it was to get to us. We loved it just as we loved his home, each bit of warm air, slice of bread, lightbulb lighting, and motor or generator starting. When the sun shined, it not only shined on us but on solar panels for us. I had a new appreciation for plastic buckets to haul water, metal forks—so many things. The list is long.

We all cleaned up, dried our hair completely, which took me a minute and Julianne an hour. Julianne gave her Game Boy to Elizabeth; we hugged Vicky and said our good-byes. It is always sad to leave when you connect the way we had. This would be a family adventure we would remember all our lives. We got our cold-weather gear on and loaded up the sled for the voyage back to Coldfoot and took off feeling as if we were different people from the ones who had arrived several days before. It was gray-light conditions; I could not see much, if any, definition in the trail. This meant even though I was right behind Eric, I could not see the trail. I just followed his red taillight. If he went off a cliff, I would land on top of him when we came to the bottom of our fall.

Julianne asked if she could drive one of the snow machines back. Eric said that he had noticed how well she had learned to run one since she had been here and maybe he'd need her help on the way back. He mentioned that he weighed more than she did, though, and you needed the heaviest person in front. We crossed creeks; Eric and Juge got stuck trying to get up a steep hill. Juge walked up; Eric made it the second time. We lost the trail a few times in the featureless world. Rita and I missed the trail in a really tight spot with a cliff on one side and a steep, tree-studded hill on the other. We slid on the frozen waterfall that ran through it, and we and the snow machine slid down the hill. The snow cushioned us, as if we'd jumped into ten feet of feathers. It was all Eric and I could do to lift the snow machine back onto the trail in waist-deep snow. If Eric had not been with us, we would have been stuck twenty-five miles from their home, thirty-five miles from Coldfoot. The four of us moved as a swift unit down the trail. There was no fear of flying, only freedom in our confidence. We handled all our obstacles with humor and focus and high energy, and we made it in excellent time.

No building rises into view in Coldfoot. The mountains in Alaska dwarf all man-made objects. We pulled our snow machines up to the front door of the truck-stop restaurant and walked in, still coated with some trail snow. Julianne walked into the little truck stop with an increased boldness in her step and body language based on her accomplishments here above the Arctic Circle. All the people inside were staring at us, or were they? A few of the truckers were smoking; a man wearing a flannel shirt sat in the corner, a pile of papers in front of him. He was staring rudely at us. As I walked by him on my way to the bathroom, I noticed the papers were census forms. I'm not sure why, but I thought of flushing him down the toilet.

When I came back, he was grilling Eric. Was my response to these unknown "crowds" and this personal-information collector part of being "bushy"?

When I sat down across from Eric, the census taker asked, "Do you live out at the lake too?"

"No," I said. Rita got up to get a coffee refill she didn't need.

The census taker was in his late forties; he seemed to be trying to be subtle. Either someone had told him that rural Alaskans could be slightly to totally rebellious, or he knew it from experience.

"Where do you live then?" he asked me.

"Ah, I'm a secret agent. I can't tell you, I'm on assignment. You know, you should head down the winter trail and go interview Dave. He's a Vietnam War vet," I said. "He might enjoy answering your questions. He might take you for a ride on his snow machine."

"No, thanks." The census taker giggled. "That young man Pete answered all my questions."

Rita was watching us from the counter. I'm not normally this aggressive with representatives of the government even if I want to be. Being bushy was the only excuse I could come up with for my awful, rude, prying behavior.

When we'd warmed up and had our hamburgers, I went to our vehicle and dug around for my address book. I had promised Mike I would give Eric instructions on how to contact my friend sailing around the world. I did put them in touch, and Mike ended up sailing with him from Tonga, north of New Zealand, to Fiji. He's going back again the summer of 2001 to sail from Fiji to somewhere else in the South Pacific. Mike had a great teacher in his dad when it came to realizing that you *can* live your dreams.

We loaded our gear into the Explorer and took off down the Haul Road. It was like cruising down an eight-lane interstate compared to where we'd been. Before we left Coldfoot, I called our friend Pat at the University of Alaska. She sounded a bit breathless, she was so glad to hear we'd made it. I almost laughed at her concern, but then I remembered how paranoid and uptight I'd been. She said if she hadn't heard from us today, she was going to call the troopers. Curt would have been able to assure her we were fine, if he had not been out patrolling somewhere in his seventy-three-thousand-square-mile territory.

We passed a couple of heavily loaded semis that couldn't make it up a couple of the hills on the first run and had to back down to make another attempt. I thought of Eric and his family most of the 250-plus miles to Fairbanks. Eric is not a talker; his life is spoken through his actions. Talk is cheap and easy; making dreams real takes hard, humble work. Dreams in the Midwest are acceptable, just keep them to yourself. Maybe tell your family, but don't just talk—do something about it.

Eric had been telling himself, then his family, then his friends, since he was eleven that someday he would live in Alaska. He could not have known then why Alaska drew him. No picture can truly re-create its vastness, its severity, and its profound beauty. But he stared at the maps on his wall. He rode cross-country on his bike at sixteen, gathering signatures on a petition to put more of Alaska into wilderness. He had no idea how much of Alaska was already untouched or that the term *wilderness* has significantly different meanings in Iowa and Alaska. There are basically no wild places left in Iowa, but that's about all Alaska is. He knows this now.

Eric's fantasy of living far from crowds is no longer his childhood dream. He bought his land without seeing it, though he knew it was on Chandalar Lake, which would provide clean water, the essential necessity. He walked to his land the first time and was terrified by all the signs of bear, the wolves howling at night. He learned how difficult it would be living over sixty miles off a road. Most people wouldn't even have attempted that first hike alone in winter, and if they had, many would have given up the idea right then. Not Eric. He realized what he needed to do to get supplies to their few acres on the west side of the lake. Like all pioneers, he faced tiny hassles, moderate challenges, and seemingly monstrous problems. They did not deter him; he altered his plans, adapted to the world above the Arctic Circle. Some parts of his decades-long dream were something like he'd imagined, but many were far different. The challenges only helped reveal who he and his family truly are.

His dream was not his children's; they became big or small parts of it. They followed him because children follow their parents. Eric could not have made their home without his children, without Mike, Pete, Elizabeth, and Dan, nor without his love, Vicky. Each of them has realized he or she too can do the impossible. They've built their own house, hauled their own water, learned how to gather power from the sun and the wind. They have learned they do not need Madison Avenue's product placement to have a fantastic life. Fashion, what's fashion? They've learned you can get more from the northern lights or a successful traverse of the winter trail. There are no mirrors to gaze into to worry about whether you're too thin, you have a couple zits, your hair isn't the right color. Your mirror is the expression on your family's faces; your family includes your dogs and cats. How they look at you is what matters.

What kind of car or SUV you drive means nothing, except how it gets you up the Haul Road. For the Jayne family, the Suburban made a lot more sense than the Dodge Neon, but the Neon got them where they were going. You make do with what you've got. The Swedish composting toilet may work, someday. Eric and Pete and Mike, they'll study the problem and invent a solution. Someday the Sheetrock will be up all over the house. You learn not to throw spoiled-brat fits over unfinished walls, where the pink insulation covered by the vapor-barrier plastic shows. You know what a "miracle" just one piece of four-by-eight-foot Sheetrock is out here in the Brooks Range because you've hauled out so many on your sled behind the snow machine. After following their dad and husband and helping to build his dream, I'm sure when his family members' dreams want to come to life, Eric will be there to encourage them and assist in any way he can.

We spent the night in Fairbanks, and by the next night we were back in Seward. One thing you learn in Alaska, if you're going through Anchorage, which we had to do, you stock up with stuff. We did, even eating our favorite lunch at New Sagaya.

17

On the Edge of the Land-Fast Ice

A Native friend who knew me well enough to know that I could come to a place like Barrow not wrapped in preconceptions, but to look and listen, had arranged for me to visit this northernmost community in Alaska. I was to call whaling captain Oliver Leavitt's home, and there was a good chance I would get to join him and his crew for several days on the edge of the ice. I wasn't sure what might keep me from going, but I was willing to come to Barrow anyway.

Everything in this Eskimo city of over forty-two hundred people was the northernmost something in the United States; the northernmost Mexican restaurant, the northernmost video store, the northernmost motel, the northernmost fax machine, the northernmost commercial airport. (From Seward to Barrow was over eight hundred air miles.) Here was the northernmost public school, church, sewage treatment plant, library, the northernmost search-and-rescue squad. There are lots of searches and rescues in this frozen white world.

Before these people knew of things like libraries and pizzas, before these things became parts of their lives, Barrow was a life-giving place. The people on this Arctic Ocean coast didn't care how far north it was, for them survival was all about what came by here on an annual migration. The town has always been almost a type of shrine to the bowhead whale. A magnificent, deeply respected, long-lived living thing, this whale gives its life just off the land-fast ice so that many people may live. And it has done so for well over a thousand years.

Barrow (pop. 4,276) is the community in Alaska with the coldest sustained temperatures; it has 322 days per year, average, with a low temperature of thirty-two degrees or less. In Barrow, when the sun comes back from being gone, it creeps above the horizon and steadily climbs and then sinks again, never setting from approximately May 10 to August 1. That is no sunset for eighty-four days. What do the young romantics in need of a sunset do? They do the same as all the Inupiat people who have lived in this white world of intensity; they don't live like the rest of us. They have their own beautiful language, their own customs, they don't want to do it like anyone else, and they know who they are and that's who they want to be. They accept the pizzas and the Mexican food and the videos, but they fight to keep their world the way it has been.

When the sun finally does start to set, it lights the world less and less until it stays away permanently from approximately November 18 to January 23, sixty-seven days. So Barrow has the beach in the United States with the most daylight, a beach with big, curling waves, sometimes. It is eight hundred air miles from Barrow to the North Pole. Things on top of North America have different meanings than they do where I live. Thick, thick ice is good. The sea ice breaking and forming leads—openings—is even better. Snow is beautiful. It makes for better traveling. Raw meat is good. Walrus stink flipper is gourmet eating. Seal oil to dip the aged raw caribou in is good. Every lake and river is frozen—that's good. Five below zero is warm. Fur is good; caribou hair worn inside, against the skin, is better. To sit still for days is enjoyment. To be silent, to listen, is desired. To harpoon a whale is about as good as it gets. What was desired and good here was different from anyplace else in the world I'd ever been. It was truly an original place. Would I be allowed to enter?

Barrow is the "capital city" of the North Slope Borough, by far the richest in Alaska. When they lost their lands, the Natives of the North Slope organized a government, got some big-time lawyers, fought the oil companies and the state, and set up a taxing mechanism to get a tiny piece of the oil produced off what had been their land. Their area covers one hundred thousand square miles; it is a forever-spreading expanse of tundra, all above the Arctic Circle. It is an essentially flat, treeless place but not featureless. During the summer thousands of lakes and streams offer habitat for millions of birds and water for caribou. Snow is on the ground from September to May.

The ancient annual event I hoped I would soon observe was staged on a breaking slab of ice that in winter stretched all the way to the North Pole. It was spring; the ice would be breaking, separating, and forming leads for the whales to come through. This event/adventure/mishap/celebration has been going on for at least a thousand years before the United States of America was even a thought. Though these Inupiat people have been perched here for several thousand years, today they must obey the laws of Washington, Juneau, and the International Whaling Commission.

It's April and the ocean has appeared again. Once again, the bowhead whale is coming. It is time to move to the edge of the shore-fast ice as their people have done and done forever. It is time to take the whale so the people may live. And please don't try to tell these people to be vegetarian or eat potato chips or pasta or cook like Emeril or Betty Crocker or follow some U.S. government chart. They don't want to be like you; they want to be like their great-great-great-grandfathers and -grandmothers. They don't want to be melted into the melting pot.

I called Oliver's house and got his wife, Annie Leavitt, a woman whose overflowing life force comes through loud and clear even on the phone. The way her motor runs, it is obvious she could survive if everything was shut off and closed and life went back to the way it was five hundred years ago. She told me a couple of young men, her nephews or some relatives, would pick me up soon and haul me out to the whaling camp. The crew was already there, she mentioned—and told me to bring my warmest clothes. I would get to go.

Snow machines were zipping around town on the snow and ice that was all over. There were also quite a few cars and trucks. Most visitors would have no idea what was going on out on the ice. A couple young Eskimo guys with white parkas with wolverine ruffs came toward me in a snow machine at full speed, pulling a wooden sled. They stopped; one asked me if I was Peter Jenkins. He looked about fourteen. I said I was; they told me to climb in and put my duffel and daypack into the sled. And, they said, try to get comfortable in the sled somehow.

Before I could though, the driver let snow and ice fly and wailed out to the edge of town toward the frozen ocean. We dropped off the high bank and down onto the land-fast ice. I was banged around so much my brain hurt. The ice gave not at all; the flat freight sled flexed only a tiny bit. I tried to support my weight with my arms, using them as shock absorbers. I tried to lean against my bags. I worried the banging would jar something loose in my camera or my video camera. Could the fillings in my teeth be rattling out?

Naturally these teenage Eskimo guys drove at one speed, full throttle. Why not? Being whipped across the ice was fun to them and their elastic bodies; why would it not be to me, the white man with the pale eyes and the red goatee?

Oliver Leavitt, the whaling captain, wanted me out at his camp, and whaling captains are important people in their culture. These young men were going to impress him with their on-time delivery. I was one of the few non-Eskimo visitors allowed at the ice's edge, at the sacred site of the most important, annual event in all of coastal Inupiat Eskimo life. Oliver scheduled his vacation to do this. He is a leader of these people and their many businesses.

When Oliver, fifty-five, had been a boy, he had heard his elders tell of trying to get a whale to give itself to you so your village could eat, which meant survival. Not getting one could mean starvation. Oliver remembers, too, asking his elders often if they wanted coffee or tea because the only time their tent or home was warm was when someone was cooking. Today, there is no fear of literal starvation, but there is concern for the starvation of the Eskimo spirit. They don't want their culture to be lost. Being around them made me realize how little of my own culture I had any idea of, much less practiced.

It was April 26, 2000, but I wasn't out at their camp long before day and night and date and year no longer mattered. Time doesn't matter on the edge of the Arctic Ocean. What matters is the condition of the ice. The ice that had stretched all the way to the North Pole was now breaking apart, making openings for the bowhead whales to come through on their annual migration north and east to the Beaufort Sea. The whale, and to a lesser degree the many sea mammals that thrive here, are the main reason these Inupiat people have thrived. When most of Europe was still a bunch of heathen tribes, a bold whaler pointed out to me, the Inupiat people waited on the edge of the land-fast ice for the whale to come to them.

Bowhead whales are the only large whales living only in the Arctic. They have massive heads with a thick bone structure that they can use to break through a foot of ice. That is the reason they can survive in this land of ice. As creatures that must breathe oxygen to live, it enables them to survive in a world where sea ice is dominant. Their heads are about 40 percent of their total body length; they have up to twenty-eight inches of blubber to keep them alive in this chilly climate. A forty-foot-long bowhead weighs one ton per foot—that is eighty thousand pounds of whale. Today, as it always has been, when a whaling crew kills a whale, the people will use almost all of these eighty thousand pounds. Today these people live in wood-frame houses; they used to use the bones to support their sod homes. Oliver chains one of his dogs to a whale rib mounted in the ground by his house. A relatively few years ago, what the humans didn't use was eaten by their dogs, who were an important part of their cultural identity. Snow machines have taken over for the dog teams of old.

Unlike the humpback's, this whale's skin is smooth like a black skipping stone. The black skin of the whale has always been many people's favorite part. Called muktuk, it is rich in vitamin C. The men of the crew who were hosting me at their whaling camp told me it tasted like coconut. I would try muktuk, I was told, if they got a whale while I was here. The blubber was used for fuel and food. The whale's internal organs were prized. The heart was eaten; it could be the size of a big man and weigh two hundred pounds. Portions of the intestines were used as well, the kidneys and liver too. The membranes from the whale's liver were used to cover the Eskimo drum frame to give them a pulsing, relentless beat for their dancing.

The killing of a forty-foot bowhead that weighs eighty thousand pounds would be a cause to thank the highest spirit. If there were five hundred people in the village, which would be a large number, and forty thousand pounds of the whale was usable, that would be eighty pounds of food per person. One thing the people did have a few thousand years before everyone in southern climes was a way to freeze their catch year-round. They just dug a room out in the permafrost twelve feet down and had their year-round walk-in freezer.

If I had not been accepted and trusted by Alaska's Native leadership at the beginning of my trip, I would never have gotten this opportunity. To come out here to the ice meant I would be living for a time with this crew, sleeping on the floor of the tent they all shared, eating their food at the end of the land-fast ice. Land-fast ice is still connected to land; sometimes it too breaks away from the mainland and floats away. The crews travel by snow machine, hauling the sealskin whaling boats that they use to glide silently in the water toward the dark streaks in the sky. Every piece of ice and the ground is silver and white and is reflected as white in the clouds in the sky. But the leads that the whales travel through are dark, almost black, like the cold, deep sea, and the darkness is reflected in the sky. It shows up in the sky for many miles, and the whalers follow the dark streaks in the clouds to choose the best spots to locate their campsites.

The edge of the ice is not stationary. The currents flowing in the ocean can be intense, and the wind can blow the massive, two-to-three-feet-thick sea-ice chunks and building-size icebergs wherever it wants. Sometimes the whalers must vacate their campsites as rapidly as humanly possible, take down their tent and observation posts. Free-floating icebergs or, worse, village-size pieces of ice weighing millions of tons can slam into the shore-fast ice. The collision of these potent powers creates wreckage and death if humans are in the way. It can also cause the shore-fast ice to break off, and suddenly you're floating toward Russia. Many Inupiat people over the years, while seal hunting or, in lesser numbers, whaling, have been standing on the ice when it broke away; no one ever sees them again. Today the North Slope Borough has one of the most elite rescue squads in North America. The flatness and the white and the storms and the stubborn independence of the people make for lots of rescue situations.

The bowhead whales that the whaling crews seek seem plentiful, though no one knows how many there are because there are no exact ways to count them. If the lead is too wide, they are almost impossible to harpoon by hand out in the ocean. The narrow leads force them to come up to breathe in a smaller space, sometimes no wider than a creek. Whitlom Adams, a member of a crew who's in his early eighties and who has the most peculiar, contagious laugh, told me about a whale his crew got in 1955, when he was a young man. When they butchered it, they found a carved ivory and jade harpoon point embedded in the blubber. The Eskimo whalers had originally used ivory, jade, and slate as harpoon points. The coastal Eskimos had traded with the interior Eskimos for caribou hides and jade from a nearby mountain of jade. But the Eskimo people had stopped using jade and slate in the 1850s, after the Yankee whalers from the eastern United States had arrived in 1848 and introduced them to metal points.

So that meant the jade harpoon point had been broken off in Whitlom's bowhead whale over one hundred years ago. No one knows exactly how long a bowhead whale lives, but they live much longer since the Yankee whalers left Alaska in about 1915. The Yankee whalers had nearly eradicated them, killing more than nineteen thousand between 1848 and 1915. It has been estimated that about twenty thousand whales lived in the area when the whalers arrived.

In addition to the metal harpoon points, they left behind descendants as well. Some of the whaling captains from Massachusetts and other ports on the East Coast started families in Alaska. Oliver Leavitt, the whaling captain who had invited me, was a product of one of these families, begun by a famous Jewish-American whaling captain from Massachusetts named George Leavitt.

This white world is not truly white. The ice has edges of pale blue and clear green and icy silver. It's not flat but has been bent and broken from the impact of drifting ice from the sea. As difficult as it is to make sense of this, I am on a snow machine heading toward the seawater that holds the most numerous concentration of sea life on earth. In the Arctic, green plants are the foundation of life. At first there looks to be no green anywhere—how could there be in the frozen-over ocean? But in the sea, tiny plants, phytoplankton, are food for krill, tiny shrimplike creatures eaten by whales, squid, and fish. The squid and fish and other crustaceans are in turn eaten by the sea mammals, seals, walrus, belugas. These oceans on top of Alaska, spreading out from Barrow, provide the nutrients to sustain all this life, so it is possible for the Eskimos to have existed here for so long.

I seriously considered asking my "drivers" to slow down. They were sitting on a cushioned seat, and my cushion, although larger than theirs, didn't have enough padding. My internal organs felt as if they were being shaken into a much smaller cavity. It might only have been a couple miles down the trail through ice and pressure ridges, over the deep cracks, around where violent movements had pushed ice mounds into blockades of rubble. A few fresh inches of snow had accumulated on the snow machine trail. Finally the guys slowed down; ahead was a dark gray line up in the clouds. It was the open water reflecting up in the sky. I could see a large canvas tent; some snow machines were parked near it, a few attached to freight sleds. Some square blocks of ice had been cut out by a crew member and placed at the dark water's edge.

My drivers took my bags out of the sled, I climbed out, and they took off. This world was not a place for young people; they were excited just to go near the camps, hoping someday they would be chosen to be members of a crew, hoping someday they would be strong enough to throw the harpoon. In earlier days the elders had drawn the silhouette of a whale in the snow to teach the young men where to aim the harpoon. At least forty crews were up and down the edge of this unstable land-fast ice for several miles north and south of Barrow. Everyone was totally focused, reverent, hoping that this spring a bowhead whale would give itself to their crew.

TO WAIT

The dominant color where I live is green, green in every shade. Other colors, such as the brown of the tree trunk, are minor players. Here there is no green, no color at all but the pale colors of the ice, and the whalers wear white covers over their parkas to camouflage themselves from the whales' eyes.

The crew had set up a wooden seat on the ice like a long bench with a back.

Oliver Leavitt awaits the bowhead whales near Barrow. PHOTO BY PETER JENKINS

Canvas tarp had been laid over it to block the wind that could rob even these Eskimo men of body heat and—fur side up—caribou skins for the crew to sit on. From here the whalers watched for approaching whales. They were migrating through here from the southwest, so the bench faced south. Someone sat on this bench at all times, watching and listening and being still, quiet, even silent.

A couple of silver thermos bottles were lying on the hides. When thermos bottles first came to the Arctic, they were cherished; the people built fur-lined bags to protect them. But the most important man-made item on the ice was their boat, a twenty-two-foot boat, all wood and painted white on the outside, light blue inside. Almost every crew had a similar boat, but with just a wooden frame and a sealskin covering. The boats are pointed and narrow and perched on the edge of the ice; they must be ready for launch by the crew at any second. For the crews to get a whale, seconds and fractions of a second matter.

Oliver greeted me coolly. He was sitting on the caribou skins, his wide, tan face and black hair standing out from the white of his parka and everything else. Friends had told me, and by now I understood, not to expect much talking at first with Native Alaskans. There would be more silence than words. For my first day on the ice, I sat by Oliver on the caribou skins and mostly just observed and listened.

I was startled by the beauty of their world, the beauty of the perfectly clear ice, ocean, and sky. It was different from anyplace else in Alaska I'd been so far. There were no mountains, no trees. There was no green or vegetation at all now. Practically all of the Arctic is a frigid desert. The reason so much water soaks the top of this land after snow and ice melts is because of the permafrost. This forever-frozen ground is sixteen hundred feet deep in places. All rain and snowmelt stay close to the surface. So flying over the land around Barrow, you see what appears to be an endless collection of lakes, ponds, creeks, and rivers.

My first day with the Leavitt crew we saw thirty to forty whales, at least. And those were just the ones that happened to breathe as they came by. The lead at first was maybe a half mile wide. On the other side of it were floating slabs of two-and-a-half-foot-thick sea ice that were once connected to the land-fast ice we camped on. In the midst of the lead was a shimmering, frozen margarita blend of newly forming ice and some aqua blue icebergs. They seemed to move faster than the slab ice; they probably caught the wind with their bodies. It was almost supernatural, watching the aqua blue icebergs, tall and jagged, bright and brilliant, moving against the backdrop of the dark gray sky and the ice topped with a fresh coat of powdery snow. All the icebergs and slabs of ice were moving southwest, the opposite direction of the bowhead whales. Winter was over, and if the whaling crews could fill their small quota of whales allotted them by the International Whaling Commission, they could provide many tons of the healthiest of food to their people.

I overheard Oliver talking to his brother-in-law, Hubert Hopson, who, although he was in his late forties, still looked strong enough to take on a polar bear with a spear. He was known as a great hunter, still a designation of honor, not long ago the highest honor that could be paid to an Inupiat. He was complaining that the TV in his house always seemed to be on, it was like a too loud "member of the family." Oliver said he could sit here and look out at the moving ice and ever-changing lead, looking and listening for the whale, and be perfectly satisfied. His regular job took him to Portland, Houston, Anchorage, and Washington, D.C. He said he would rather be here at the edge of the land-fast ice than anywhere else in the world. Oliver's brother-in-law, who reminded me of a soft-spoken Mike Ditka, nodded. At least they were speaking English. If I had not been here, they would have been speaking their language, which they did at times even with me sitting there. When I half-jokingly said I had no idea what they were talking about, Oliver said, "Too bad," half-jokingly.

My rear end was incredibly warm, as if some kind of heater were in the

The lead is closing and it's time to retreat near Barrow. Photo by Peter Jenkins

caribou skins. Oliver saw me putting my bare hand on the caribou fur and lifting it off, cooling it, and putting it back on it. He told me caribou fur, which had insulating air in each hair follicle, keeps your body heat from leaving, keeps the people alive. Not long ago, their coldest-weather clothes had winter caribou hide, fur in, as the lining. He said these hides here were old and nowhere near as insulative as they used to be.

I noticed him looking intently toward the dark strip of open ocean before us. Just then there was an exhale, and the black silhouette of about a third of a bowhead whale came out of the new white ice forming beyond the open water. It was over a half mile from us. Oliver said that before they'd launch the boat, the whale had to be almost right next to us. Oliver had stopped looking at the whale; his experienced hunter's eye knew instantly that it was too far away. He could see the lead shrinking, which meant the wind and/or the current was bringing the free-moving ice closer to us. Now the migrating whales would have to come up right next to us.

Getting ready, Oliver spoke to his fellow crew members even softer than he did before. Several stood near the boat. About half the crew appeared to be in their late twenties or early thirties. Oliver's son, Billy-Jens, a tall and powerful young man, was the harpooner. There are so many Billys in Barrow, Oliver told me, that they call him by his full name. Billy stood ready.

The harpoon was in the bow of the tiny whaling boat, which looked like a rowboat. They would propel it with oars. Another harpoon, attached to 250 to 300 feet of manila rope and a bright pink rubber float, rested up against a block of ice nearby. Sometimes a whale would come so close to the edge of the ice, they could harpoon it without getting into the boat. More often than not though, the whalers spooked the whale: it saw them or heard them and dove. In fact, the sealskin from the bearded seal used as the skin of most boats but Oliver's was intended as camouflage.

Oliver had a forceful presence, was a stable leader with a rooted power. He also seemed to have some sort of psychic quality, an ability that certainly the best leaders must possess to read people and their intentions. I know I don't look anything like John Denver, who was a vocal opponent of commercial whaling in the 1980s, but I was white. I was not here to try to change what they do, just to observe. But people from the Outside have continuously and aggressively attempted to aggressively alter the Eskimo world, which had adapted in so many ways over many generations. It was not the Inupiat people who had senselessly destroyed the bowhead whale just to get the baleen (a substance found in the jaws of whales and used for corsets and hairpieces) and the blubber to make oil, it was the Yankee whalers. At one time, Oliver said, baleen, which the Eskimos didn't even use, was one of the most valuable things in the world per pound.

They had been whaling forever, and the whales always returned. They considered the whale their brother; they used the whale efficiently and had therefore been able to survive with relative security. Then after the bowheads had nearly been wiped out in other cold places, such as around Greenland and Norway, the Yankee whalers came to the Arctic. Then Russians came and forcibly claimed the land; though they never got to Barrow, they sold the whole place—which they didn't own—to the United States. Then more recently, other Outsiders who claimed to love the whale and its song, who had probably never even seen a bowhead, wrote songs about whales, established organizations, and through the manipulation of world politics, got their hunt stopped in 1977. For decades, Oliver and his people have fought for the right to do something that is so foundational to their existence as to be a matter of life and death. They are keenly intelligent and practical people; they were some of the first Alaskan Natives to realize the need for a powerful posse of today's allowed warriors—lawyers. The longer I was with the crew, the more I could understand why they could be suspicious of me every time they saw me sitting there.

Now the lead in front of us was about twenty-five feet wide at its most narrow. The current must have strengthened because the ice was moving south faster. Whales were coming up to breathe in the silvery haze of new ice, broken-off slabs of flat sea ice, and icebergs. Just the black, irregular ridges of their backs rose out of the water. When they exhaled, a silver plume rose up. Oliver clapped his hands, which is supposed to attract seals, and it worked—a small seal poked its head out of the water, its eyes large.

These Inupiats' lives have always required massive amounts of patience. They wait for hours and hours for the seals to come to their breathing holes. They cannot have much warning, there is no sound until the seals are there. There is almost no warning when the time comes to try for your whale. But you cannot lose your focus, become moody, or need to be entertained. You must look and be ready because at any moment it emerges from the water and there is your chance. One hundred years ago, if you were ready, you and your family might live. If not, you might starve to death. The ability to concentrate and be still was absolutely necessary no matter how cold, how hard the storms blew.

Oliver and his crew, all whalers, do not do what they do in order to brag, to take pictures or video, or to have their catch mounted. (Think of the house that it would take to display a whale—maybe Bill Gates's place would have a wall big enough.) We sat on the caribou skins for hours, hours that would turn into days. Oliver and Hubert found it slightly peculiar that ESPN makes such a big deal about programs that show people catching one-and-a-half-pound large-mouth bass, or even five-pound bass. That they could at any moment catch and bring to their people a hundred-thousand-pound whale has nothing to do with any kind of trophy.

Oliver told me many stories as we sat on the edge of the ice and waited for a whale to come. One time, he and fellow whaling captain Jake Adams were down south. South to them isn't south to me. They can travel almost fifteen hundred air miles south and east and still be in Alaska. They were fishing somewhere around Bristol Bay at the base of the Aleutians for king salmon. Also staying at their remote lodge were a father and a son from Minnesota. The father, in his seventies, had never before been to Alaska; the biggest fish he'd ever caught was a four-pound walleye in one of the freshwater lakes of northern Minnesota. After three days the gentleman finally caught a king salmon that weighed close to forty pounds. That night at the lodge this white-haired man, shining with pride, had a few drinks, Tanqueray on the rocks. Then he had a few more. He began to brag about his king salmon, a mighty wild fish indeed. He was getting borderline obnoxious, Oliver said; his son tried to get his dad to quiet down, kick back. But he wouldn't. Then he started to focus his arrogance on Oliver and Jake.

Jake's a restrained, sensitive, yet powerful man. The old man wanted to show somebody up, and he got in Jake's face.

"What's the biggest fish you ever caught?" he said to Jake, almost growling.

Jake didn't really want any part of a contest, but the man persisted. The Native people hold their elders in the highest reverence.

"I said, what's the biggest thing you ever had on the line, anyway?" the man from Minnesota said, punching with his words.

Jake could tell the man would not let up. So he told him: "Oh, about fifty tons."

"Fifty what?" the white-haired man said, thinking Jake might have said fifty pounds, bigger than his king salmon.

"Dad," the son interjected, trying to diffuse the situation, "this man is an Eskimo whaler. He said fifty tons, that's one hundred thousand pounds."

The man got quiet and left the dining room shortly thereafter. Jake didn't rub it in, he was proud for the old man. A king salmon could feed several members of that man's family. But a bowhead whale can feed many more.

TO KNOW ICE

When a crew like Oliver's or Jake's does get a whale, there is a tradition about how the whale is divided up. First they pull the whale to the edge of the ice. Then the word goes out and many people, a hundred or more, start making their way to the place on the shore-fast ice. They will help to pull the whale out onto the ice using large ropes, a block and tackle, and much muscle. Then the butchering begins. The back third of the whale is reserved for the captain and crew. However, this meat is used for three separate celebrations—their summer festival, which includes the jubilant blanket toss; a celebration at Thanksgiving; and one at Christmas. This clearly shows how the whale reigns at the center of this thriving culture.

Two fourteen-inch "belts" are cut from the whale. One goes for a village-wide party the captain and the crew put on. The captain flies the crew's flag from his house; often, a block-long line of people are waiting to come into Oliver and

Annie's small home for their taste of the whale. The meat and muktuk and blubber from the other fourteen-inch belt goes in equal shares to all of the crew for their personal use. Then the close to two-thirds of the bowhead left is divided equally among the other crews.

You don't get to be a member of a whaling crew because you want to; you can't pay to join. Basically, you have to be family and you have to be very capable. Everyone has a job; the whaling captain is absolute boss. In fact he must supply and pay for all equipment and food, cover any costs. On Oliver's crew is Hubert, who is considered one of the best hunters on the North Slope. There is Oliver's son, Billy-Jens, twenty-seven, the harpooner. There is Ambrose Oliver, twenty-seven, Oliver's nephew. He is what Oliver calls a generalist; he does whatever is needed. Johnson Booth, forty-nine, is married to Oliver's cousin. Lester Suvlu, in his early thirties, a good all-around hand, is some kind of cousin. And Leo Kaleak, in his early thirties, is also part of the crew.

Oliver's crew had other full-time jobs, of course. Hubert and Johnson worked for the North Slope Borough government as administrators of capital improvements, overseeing building projects. Billy-Jens was a carpenter's helper, a general laborer. Leo works in the oil fields. Ambrose is a trained mechanic but does mostly odd jobs. Lester works for the Barrow police department, and Oliver Leavitt handles governmental relations and is chairman of the Arctic Slope Regional Corporation. If they had to choose between their jobs and whaling—well, they just wouldn't. They have built lives that mingle the ancient with the new and do well at both. They do not seek anyone else's approval about their way of life.

There were long moments of silence on the ice, or not quite silence, but moments without human noise. The winds blew from far-off places; the new ice made a light crackling sound when it collided with the land-fast ice. The icebergs spoke softly as they went by, but all knew of their power. Eider ducks flew by, their wings hissing in the wind; the whales exhaled from many different distances around us, and their breathing was one of the world's greatest sounds to Oliver and his people. The ones that breathed too far out might give themselves to another crew or live on to return next spring.

Every part of me that touched the caribou hide felt like a sun-warmed rock on a cold fall day. Even though I wore my Trans-Alaska boots, my feet resting without moving on the three-foot-thick ice got cold sometimes. I had expected this part of Alaska to be the least attractive, most boring, least inspiring. Instead I was inspired, awed, humbled. Last night as I had slept in the tent with those who didn't have to stay up all night, a fresh snow had fallen, three or four inches. It had coated all the irregular chunks of ice that had been broken apart and pushed into piles by the immense strength of the moving ice. The whalers used these little "mountains" of ice as lookout posts. I could see far down the coast; on every pile stood an Eskimo in his white parka with its wolverine ruff standing watching for the whales. We did not have a lookout "mountain" near us and so just watched from our bench.

Today, the second day, the ocean-blue water showed in thin bands between the ice with a light chop on the surface. Between these open leads were moving icebergs surrounded by new ice. Since it's moving, it gives the impression that the whole surface is shimmering. And amid the shimmering silver are the huge icebergs and the black backs of the surfacing whales.

At different times the men of the whaling crew ate and slept. The tent was warm, with a propane heater and the heat of a floor full of snoring or silent sleeping whalers and me.

Hubert offered me some raw, aged caribou, a slice of hindquarter, when he saw me watching what he ate. He told me to dip it in seal oil. Instead of using heat, many meats are prepared with extreme cold, aged to a person's liking. It's like cheese; some like bland cheeses, some like ripe blue cheese. Hubert had noticed me stomping my cold feet on the ice. He said if I ate this aged, raw caribou, dipped in seal oil, first I would feel a bit cooler, then my body would heat up like a furnace. It's an old trick the Eskimos learned long ago. My body did precisely that. One old whaler had told me that his favorite food was "stink flipper." You won't see Martha Stewart prepare this dish. They take the flipper from a walrus, put it in a box so no bugs can get to it, then leave it to "age." Some might use the word *rot*. Once aged just so, it is consumed as one of the highest joys in life. I wondered if anyone had some out here, would offer it to me now that I'd surprised Oliver by eating aged, raw caribou hindquarter dipped in seal oil.

It was hypnotic sitting and watching the slow-paced icebergs and whales and new ice flowing by us in the current. We experienced all types of weather while I stayed with Oliver's crew. The people never moved too fast. It was mostly about sitting and watching and being ready. That's why when I saw Hubert and Oliver stand up and stare out at the ice, then tell everyone to hurry, I knew something serious was up. I hadn't noticed, but the moving slab ice and icebergs had moved closer to us on the land-fast ice.

Oliver was barking out orders. He'd been calculating the current and ice movement and had determined that the icebergs and pack ice that had been flowing southwest, parallel to the shore and our resting place there, had shifted direction and were coming straight at us. I glanced over at the crews on either side of us; they were moving in all directions too.

Oliver told his son and two of the younger guys to pack up all the food, then take down the tent and pack it up. He told a couple others to load up the boat, then pull over the snow machines and sleds. We were striking camp, an elaborate job. Oliver's soft commands and the speed at which the crew carried them out had a definite sense of urgency. It was a gray, shadowless day, but it was obvious even to me that the big ice was coming to confront us.

Oliver didn't want to talk to me now, but he did. He told me to look at the house-size pressure ridges all around us. He explained this had once been all flat ice, but that moving ice now coming at us had caused these intense masses of ice wreckage. When stable ice is hit by moving ice, the force of the collision has to go somewhere, and ice breaks, shatters, goes up in the air in a jumble of ice blocks, some half the size of a two-story house. Oliver said no Eskimo would ever challenge this kind of ice: "Too much power," he said as he folded up the caribou skins. This world has much to do with understanding ice. There are more than one hundred words to describe snow and its many types and moods; there are almost as many words for ice.

Earlier, we'd sat together, the crew relaxed, and I'd looked out at the icebergs moving with the currents and the winds and thought about what would have to change to worry these men. Even as icebergs passed within fifteen feet of the edge of our ice, they knew immediately where their whaling boat sat, that the current carrying it was no concern. As long as the ice moved by us parallel, that was good.

The snow machines were started. It took the most work to heft the boat onto the bare frame of a sled and tie it down so it wouldn't fall off as we went over pressure ridges and ice blocks from previous ice tantrums. Billy was packing up the CB; Hubert had the delicate job of dismantling the harpoons. Oliver supervised. He had joked that he'd been demoted to steering the boat; his son had the fever to strike the whale. Oliver said it was time to use his brain and his son's brawn. Steering the boat is considered the height of skill because it requires you to predict the whale's behavior. In the Eskimo culture it seems important always to be self-effacing.

"This ice coming fast. Wind's getting stronger," Oliver said. "Not long ago,

The Leavitt crew boat near Barrow. Photo by Peter Jenkins

near my house, archaeologists found the bones of some of my ancestors, they were four hundred years old. They'd been crushed by the moving ice. Their chest cavities were all compressed, they had been asleep when it happened."

Oliver said some of the young guys in the crew might like to get back to Barrow anyway, get a chance to see their girlfriends, eat pizza at the northernmost pizzeria. Oliver remembered the time five years or so ago when a pizza place in Barrow used to offer to deliver anywhere. They had ordered several pizzas delivered to their tents on the ice several miles down the coast at that year's spring whaling camp.

The ice had exerted its dominance once again, and the people respected its power. We ran away from the possible destruction back to town. All of the gear was loaded; we crawled onto any available spot to ride back. I asked Oliver if I could walk. He said a polar bear had been around since the first whale had been landed. He said I could walk if I wanted, but polar bears stalk humans. I rode.

Whaling crews of today do a few things just the same as the crews of the past, but many things are different. During past whaling times, the whalers stayed at the edge of the land-fast ice from the first of April until the first week of June and did not go home. No tent was allowed; if there was rugged weather or a storm, the whalers had to create shelter by using skins or by getting under their boat. Raw food was not allowed, clothes could not be dried out, what meat was eaten was boiled. The rest of the family stayed on land and waited until a whale was struck and secured.

Oliver told me about a furious storm in 1957, a time when a person was measured by his dog team. The team hauled driftwood for heat and ice to melt for fresh drinking and cooking water. The whalers that spring had had to run for their lives as we were now. One whaler did not even have time to get his parka on; he dragged it and ran. The ice opened and closed, grabbing it from him. Ice was breaking up all around them. The crew had to leave so fast they had to leave their dog teams on the ice to perish. The sounds of the ice breaking, cracking, killing, crushing—it was far more violent than it had been this time, at least where our camp had been.

It is all about understanding the ice. As spring and whales arrive, the ice cannot be predicted and is at its most dangerous. At least two seal hunters disappeared while we were in Alaska. They go out on ice, maybe they are stalking a bearded seal, and the ice they are standing on at the moment is all part of one piece stretching to the land, and security. But it breaks off and they are suddenly on an island of ice that is moving away, lost in the forever of their surroundings. Like the bullfighter and the bull, the Eskimo must have intimate knowledge of the ice, this all-powerful force. The Eskimo hunter must get close to this changing, cracking, crushing, destructive force, as close as he can. To not take this risk meant starvation—to stay at home is not a choice. There was a real comfort in being on the ice with Oliver and his crew because they are confident in their knowledge of its behavior.

But sometimes for all the experience in the world, they are caught. There are many reasons; maybe the ice had not taken anyone in several years and people are getting too relaxed. Who knows why, but something happened to 143 people and all their equipment on the ice in 1997. If it had not been for the North Slope Borough's outstanding Search and Rescue Unit, which was founded in 1972, this moment when the ice did the unexpected could have caused one of the worst catastrophes in Alaska's history. For days Search and Rescue had been patrolling the ice. A long, continuous crack three to four inches wide went for at least thirty miles. All the crews had crossed it and were at their camps whaling. One crew had struck a whale, and that added to the population on the ice. The communal butchering had begun.

At midnight that crack popped and split; an island had broken off from the shore-fast ice and was adrift in the Arctic Ocean. On this forty-mile-long, floating "ice boat" were 143 people, 166 snow machines, 43 whaling boats, and all the gear that went with them. If something like this had happened before the Search and Rescue Unit had been established, this would have been an atrocity. E. Ray Poss Jr., Rescue's chief helicopter pilot and one of the most experienced rescue pilots in the United States, was asleep when the call came in. He launched immediately. First thing he did was contact his boss, Price Brower, an Inupiat who was at his whaling camp on the floating mass of ice. He located Price, but hovering at seventy feet the ice fog was so impenetrable he couldn't see him. On the ground Price could hear him, but without visibility rescue was out of the question.

Flying over at low altitude, eventually the helicopter rotors blew the fog away and then Ray could see Price. Then like an old-fashioned aluminum ice tray cracking open, right as Ray hovered over Price, the ice shattered into many more pieces, people on some, equipment on others. Ray radioed base, got their other rescue helicopter in the air, and their small helicopter too. All three helicopters flew for three hours. At times it was "0/0" visibility; other times they were able to see no more than one hundred feet. Finally everyone was rescued. They came back and went to bed.

Eight hours later, Price and Ray were awakened by people anxious to get their equipment, their sealskin whaling boats, their harpoons, their snow machines, their parkas, their tents, everything, off the ice. It took Price and Ray seven days, twelve to thirteen hours a day. Price's camp was the last one deconstructed and hauled out. In seven days the piece of ice that carried it had moved fifty-five miles into the cold and lonesome Arctic Ocean. It felt as if the whole population of Barrow gathered at a base camp twenty-five miles from town where all the equipment was flown for redistribution.

Ray and Price told me this story at their high-tech, immaculate hangars. Ray had moved to Alaska from Las Vegas, where he was one of the main helicopter pilots who had rescued so many off the top of the MGM Grand Hotel during that terrible fire in 1980.

"You know as a white man, and being relatively new to North Slope Borough, I'd be at the grocery store or getting gas, and the elders of the community would see me," Ray said, remembering. "The elders would come up and say, 'Ray, I want to thank you. You saved our lives.' I'd say thanks, no problem, thinking no big deal. But these men were in tears. But no wonder they felt this way—because several years before, when there was no rescue squad, people died when the same thing happened. These men knew the danger."

Ray paused, then added, "I had no idea the trouble they were really in. Then I didn't understand the power of this ice."

Price remembered that it was a shining moment for their Search and Rescue Unit. "There were forty-two crews on the ice. From ten miles north of Barrow to fifteen to twenty miles to the southwest, that's how far the crews were scattered. And then there were polar bears roaming around on this ice with us, looking for some fresh meat."

Everything was saved but one boat. Every whaling camp on that ice was intact, while if they had located their camps on other parts of the ice, the camps would have been destroyed. When Ray asked Price why, Price said in classic Eskimo understatement, "We know the ice."

Travel on the North Slope is so filled with risk that the North Slope Borough had purchased several personal operating beacons, or POBs, which are emergency location devices that they encourage people to carry with them when they go fishing or hunting. Even though no one on earth can find his way like an Inupiat Eskimo can over seemingly indistinguishable ice and snow, over the years many people have been lost. The helicopters are equipped with sophisticated heat-seeking viewing systems. They can see a white fox on white snow in a whiteout. These systems, called Flair, can differentiate the temperature of a snowmobile track two hours old from the snow next to it.

A young man who worked at Search and Rescue in general maintenance had gone caribou hunting. When the POB distress call came in specifying his location, just nine miles from the Search and Rescue base, they assumed because he was so close that he was severely injured. Otherwise he'd have ridden on in. It cost $6,000 an hour to search in one of their biggest helicopters. They launched, and nine miles out the pilot immediately saw a snow machine and two polar bears, but no person. They searched; still they saw no one. Their first thought was that the young guy had been eaten by the polar bears, a real possibility. The pilot, not wanting to waste time, switched on the heat-evaluation device. But then he saw something on a concrete monument nearby marking the spot where Will Rogers had died in a plane crash. As he circled, the concrete pillar came alive—an extra arm sprouted from the top of it and waved at them. The young man had climbed to the top to get away from the aggressive polar bears.

The whaling crew spent the night in Barrow. I ate some Mexican food at the farthest-north Mexican restaurant in North America. Another guy there, eating alone, turned out to be John Baker, an outstanding Native musher from Kotzebue. He was in town speaking to the schoolchildren; he is a hero to many in Alaska. We chatted during dinner, and when it came time to pay the bill, I reached in my pockets—oops. No money. John picked up the check.

Early the next morning, I was picked up by the same teenagers as before to head back to reestablish camp. My driver went faster across the ice this time. After this trip I might have to marry a chiropractor. When we got to where our camp had been yesterday, pieces of ice the size of small trucks were where the boat had been. The whaling crew next to us, who had set up in a small, covelike area yesterday, now found the cove filled with man-killer-size pieces of ice. They spent hours moving them out of the way with poles.

Everyone had a job, and camp was set up once again. We sat for a couple more days. One day we saw almost no whales, the next day we saw close to a hundred. The lead had become wider now, filled with new ice and icebergs and the surfacing black, rounded backs of the bowhead whale. Only once in all the time I was there sitting on the caribou skins did Hubert whisper to the crew that they should get ready. The harpooner climbed into the boat's bow and sat down. The crew moved to either side of the boat, ready to launch as silently as possible right as the whale exhaled. The whale might have heard something; for some reason it did not surface close enough for them to launch.

The Oliver Leavitt crew did not get a whale that springtime of 2000. They went to the edge of the ice together as much to preserve their way of life as to get a whale to eat. The whales gave themselves to other crews, and they shared the muktuk and the meat with the people, and there was bowhead whale to eat at special times during the year. Oliver and all whaling captains hope that if the world is still around in the year 3000, members of their families will go to live at the edge of the land-fast ice, seeking the bowhead whale.

18

Anything but Cyber Trash

Even in Alaska the cyber invaders find you and send you their crap. "Do you want to make $10,000 a week?" "Do you want to enlarge it?" I've got a Web site, so naturally people can reach me from almost anywhere in the world. They find you. Every place you ever shopped, they're after you. And there are those ten "contest notifications" that I had won a cruise to somewhere sent to me all in the space of two minutes. Depending on my mood, sometimes I just hold down the Delete key.

When will some marketer get politicians to outlaw the Delete key? Somehow they have figured out how to subvert it. I have to press Delete about ten times to just get rid of one of these crap mails. Anyway, more than once I have been pounding the Delete key when suddenly a familiar name comes up in the From area, or some interesting line in the Subject box. Usually it is already deleted by the time I react, and I have to retrieve it from the Trash. That's what happened this time. I returned from being away ten days to find my E-mail loaded with cyber pollution. I was deleting the hell out of it when I saw a familiar name go by. I retrieved it; there were two from my youngest sister, the ever creative and resilient Abby, who is a designer in and around New York City.

I started deleting again, and as they flew by—"Subject: The Fat and Cellulite Reducing System!"—I saw this: "Wow. Welcome to Alaska." I retrieved it from the Trash, and it was from a Dean Cummings, a teacher in a small Eskimo village named Deering. I'd not heard of Deering, but I found it in my *Alaska Atlas & Gazetteer*, page 132. It is much closer to Russia than to Seward, about 170 miles from Russian waters in the Bering Strait and Russia's first landfall, Big Diomede Island. It's a bit over thirty miles south of the Arctic Circle, about 125 miles northeast of Nome, and 536 air miles from Anchorage. Of course there is no way to drive a car there.

I read this Dean Cummings's E-mail, alaskadean@hotmail.com.

Peter Jenkins! I haven't heard that name for several years. I live in a small, remote Eskimo village in Alaska for going on three years now. I teach grades 4, 5, and 6 in a coastal village of 150 people.

But before all that, let me tell you where I know you from. I went to school in Florida, at University of Central Florida. Just before I graduated, my buddy Damon and I drove across the U.S. in my Chevy. We spent three months with vague plans of going to the Grand Canyon. But at each stop along the way, we met people who would recommend a new place to us, and almost without fail, we'd take their advice.

Incidentally, one of the hottest tips we received was from a guy in Nashville. We were visiting my uncle Harry in Franklin, TN, and we met this guy in a music store in Nashville. He showed us his scars from the sun dance ceremony at Rosebud Indian Reservation, then told us to go see Rex Toulusee at the Havasupai Reservation on the south rim of the Grand Canyon. But that's a whole 'nother story in itself . . .

Anyway, when we returned home three months and 17,000 miles later, my roommate Jay gave me your book to read. He said, "Hey, man, this dude reminds me of you." So I read your book *A Walk Across America*. I enjoyed it immensely. I also learned from it.

Six months later, I finished college and stayed around for three more months to take a photography class and save money. Then, it was off to Alaska, going for broke all the way to the Arctic Circle.

So tonight, when I heard your interview on APRN [the Alaska Public Radio Network], I knew I had to write to you. I'm at the school where I work. This place is amazing. Like yourself, I enjoy a place more for the people I meet and the relationships I discover than for the awe-inspiring natural beauty it holds. We have more than our share of both!

Good traveling while you are in Alaska. If there is any way I can help you while you're here, let me know, and I look forward to hearing of your travels. Dean Cummings.

Dean sounded legitimate. I'd been hoping to meet some teachers in Alaska. I'd heard all kinds of stories about teachers and their adventures and misadventures. Often Alaskan dreamers from the outside, from Florida or Ohio or Texas or wherever, get a job teaching in some radically isolated Native village in the Aleutians or in the bush. Some bring the "I'm going to save them" attitude, a sun-lit vision of "noble savages" in a village that they can save from their primitive state. More than one teacher with a contract has landed in a village and never gotten off the plane. Many last only a year. I wondered what this Dean's story was, how naive a dreamer he was. He could not have come from an environment more the extreme opposite of Alaska—hot, paved Orlando, Florida, the home of the fantasy park. Alaska's a fantasy for many, and much of it is a park. I'll take Alaska, and so would Dean.

Later that night after I unpacked and hung out awhile with Rita, whose peaceful spirit I'd been craving on the road, I E-mailed Dean back. I just asked him to tell me about his Alaskan world. What I received, in a long E-mail, was an unexpected and illuminating journey through Deering's, and Dean's, year.

Subject: It's cold up here.

Hey, Peter, thanks for writing back. Deering has 150 people in it, 45 of them are school age. The school here has four full-time teachers. Pat Richardson teaches pre-K thru third grade with about fifteen kids. She's been here for sixteen years or so. She spends summers in Oregon. Her husband also lives here in the winter. I teach fourth thru sixth grades with fifteen kids. I also coach the cross-country running team, the wrestling team, and the Native Youth Olympics team. Also, I'm in charge of various other activities and fund-raisers. My favorite one is the wrestling club, which is basically my whole class. We sell pop at basketball games and wrestle every once in a while. . . . Eric Smith teaches language arts, social studies, and shop to the seventh- to twelfth-graders. Michael O'Neal teaches math and science to the same group. That whole group is about fifteen kids, so they split them up into junior and senior high.

Deering is built up on a "spit," right on the coast of the Kotzebue Sound, which is not far from the Bering Strait. It's tundra all around us, right out of the textbook. The people here subsist on seals and caribou and salmon. The fishing and hunting up here is incredible. Before I got here I'd done almost no hunting or fishing. The other day, Eric and I rode our snow machines up the river valley—Deering lies at the mouth of the Inmachuk River—and saw close to twenty-five moose. We have a resident herd of musk oxen. They were reintroduced to the Seward Peninsula, I think about twenty-five years ago. They have thrived. One herd lives just outside of town, less than ten miles usually. Two falls ago, one even ventured into town. We had to call Fish and Game. They sent a guy out with a tranquilizer. He shot the animal, then we (myself and four others) loaded him onto a front-end loader and carried him a mile out of town. He's alive and well still.

Last fall, the herd wandered onto the bluff just west of town and milled around the cemetery for about a month. They are definitely here to stay. My friend Diane spins qiviut, their insulative underhair, into yarn. People go out and collect it on the willow trees after they have rubbed it off there. I have a scarf made out of her yarn, and it is warm! (Just a little scratchy.)

Jim, the hunter, got two wolves last week. He hunts for a living. Spring, when the rivers open up, he takes his four-wheeler up and down the rivers, or he travels by boat. Last summer, he found a complete mastodon skull. In the past, he's found teeth, skulls of extinct bears and Ice Age bison, and even the skull of a saber-toothed tiger! He's always got some new discovery to show off.

The village is Native. With the exception of the teachers and their families, and one other guy, Charlie Brown, the maintenance man, everyone here was born in the area, grew up here, and mostly, they don't plan on ever leaving. So, yes, I have seen some incredible things, and I feel very fortunate to have spent the last three years of my life here. I don't have any immediate plans to go anywhere, either. Still so much more to see.

Before I even finished the E-mail I got on the phone and called the airlines. There were flights from Anchorage to Kotzebue, and then I could get a six-seater into Deering. I read on.

Just yesterday, I went exploring and discovered some amazing geologic features. I traveled about forty miles south of town on my snow machine in twenty-below weather. The source of the river is twenty miles out of the village, and I'd never been beyond that before. What I saw back there floored me. Treacherously deep ravines, and magnificent lookouts. My plan for this winter is to make it as far back as Imuruk Lake. It's a large lake, over five miles across in both directions. I want to camp back there. First, though, I want to become familiar with the country between here and there. Getting lost is a very real concern here, with distances being as great as they are and normally no one around.

I made it to a landmark known as Asses Ears. It was named by the turn-of-the-century gold miners. You see, after the golden beaches of Nome tapered off, the gold miners kept trekking north. They came to Deering, then known as Ipniatchak by the Natives. The gold miners established a port here and did quite a job of exploring. The relics they left are reason enough to visit Deering. Three bucket-line dredges still stand at various places on the river. A whole ghost town of cabins still remains, and its history is recent enough that some Deering old-timers can still recall working there.

You never know what will come over the computer via E-mail, and who's sending it, but I was impressed that this Dean Cummings, a teacher originally from Florida, seemed to have intimate knowledge of life in a small Native village as it revolved around the school, and even more around subsistence.

This time of year is caribou and wolf and wolverine hunting time. The limit of caribou is six per day, and many is the sled you'll see returning from the backcountry piled high with meat. The lifestyle here is still very traditional, so the men hunting and returning with a sled full of caribou are probably supplying meat for several families at a time. Later in the winter, as the days get longer, people will be ice fishing for shee fish. These are twenty-to-forty-pound whitefish that even kids can catch. Last year, we took about a dozen kids camping in subzero weather to catch shee fish, and every single kid caught at least one!

With spring come the breakup and the return of the birds. We all enjoy catching ducks and geese. The ocean doesn't break up until after June. It's still safe for snow machine travel even after the snow has melted and grass is greening and spring flowers are visible.

When the ocean does break up, the boats start coming out. Seems like the favorite season here is oogruk hunting time. *Oogruk* is the native name for bearded seals. These behemoths can weigh close to a thousand pounds. I went out with a couple of friends last year looking for oogruks. We took this flimsy, eighteen-foot aluminum skiff far offshore into the ocean and thick ice flows. We'd motor up to a solid-looking piece of ice and cast an anchor up. Then we'd all climb onto the floating island of ice and find a high spot to look around from. That was a truly memorable day in my life.

By this point, I had decided I was definitely heading to Deering. I took a break from reading and E-mailed Dean, thanked him for his fantastic communication, and asked when would be a good time to visit. I read on.

One summer I didn't leave. I stayed in Deering. Even though it's June, we're still riding snow machines. I went camping with a guy named Subluk Barr, his wife, Dodo, and his brother, Connie. We rode snow machines out onto the ocean and down the coast about thirty-five miles. Once we left Deering, there were no other people. We camped out at the mouth of Cripple Creek. Then we inflated a Zodiac with a nine-horse engine to get to the mouth of the Goodhope River. That's where the fun really happens, because this time of year, all the migratory birds are returning and building nests. For generations, the birds have fed the people up here. We tramped around on the island carrying shotguns and plastic grocery bags. Eggs. That's what we were after. The four of us walked until our legs were sore, wading through deep muskeg and swamp, and collected eggs from the nests of seagulls, geese, and eider ducks. The goose eggs especially were a find. You could recognize the nests by the down, and when you put your fingers down inside, the warmth held in there was just amazing. It really felt like there had recently been a blaze in that spot; the earth the nest was on was still warm. That down is such an amazing insulator. We stayed out there three nights and just returned to Deering on Monday, June—what was it?—the seventh, I guess. . . . Foxes came close to our camp. Moose could be seen just across the creek, and the sun never set. It won't until July 10. The ride on the ice was pretty hairy. It's getting late in the season. Subluk and Connie kept telling me that their dad was known for traveling in these kinds of conditions, and they had learned from the master. I did feel safe, even crossing big cracks, with black water down

below. Just give it some gas and close your eyes! Subluk is fifty-one, Connie is in his forties, and they really have been doing this all their lives. It
was Subluk and Dodo's twenty-eighth wedding anniversary too. We ate
lots of eggs while we were there, and Dodo plucked two brants and made
soup too. Last night, I roasted a Canadian goose. Tasty!

If someone had told Dean at the fraternity parties at the University of Central Florida that he'd write an E-mail like this about his Alaskan experience, he
would never have believed it. Alaska is bigger than most any dream; like mine,
when his dream came true, reality was much better than the dream. What a rar-
ity, but that's Alaska. I read on.

Late summer is fishing time. The salmon are coming up the rivers. We
mostly see seine nets here. My first year here, I went out with five women.
(Fishing is women's work.) We pulled in about three hundred salmon in
one netful. My friend Omie and her sister Eckie showed me how to use an
ulu to filet the fish and hang them to dry. After three nights of backach-
ing labor, I finally cut all of my share of the fish, and I ate good for months.
Also, even though I could never quite meet their standards of ulu proficiency, I did learn enough to turn heads on the riverbanks in more urban
areas.

Fall time is moose hunting. Eric and I got one last September. I sent a
hundred pounds or so to a sausage place in Anchorage. That's been one of
my staples this year. Not to mention the steaks and roasts and soup I've
been eating!

Also during fall, people pick berries by the bucketful. First, blackberries
and salmonberries. They call salmonberries upiks. Then, blueberries, and
finally, cranberries. Also during this time, various other plants are harvested. I have a friend here named Millie. She goes "trading." Apparently,
it's an ancient tradition. The mice on the tundra gather the roots of the
mussu plant. They store these in their holes. Well, Millie cuts up vegetables such as carrots and celery and goes looking for the mouse caches. She
knows just how to spot them and distinguish them from the other nonde-
script little rises on the tundra. She cuts open the mouse cache and takes
the mussu, leaving her vegetables in trade, always careful to cover the
hole just how she found it.

After reading about Millie, I called Rita over to read it. I knew she'd be fascinated by Dean's tales. She was watching her favorite show, *Emeril Live*, the only TV show she sits still to watch, but she agreed to read it before she went to bed.

Later in the fall and in early winter, people go ice fishing. Early winter, like Thanksgiving weekend or for the month prior, they catch tomcods. These little fish you can catch dozens of in an hour or two. We just pile them up on the ice, careful to keep them apart. That way, when they've frozen, they are frozen separately, so as not to have a big chunk of frozen fish, but rather, individuals. Who wants to thaw out fifty fish just to boil up five?

I know I haven't covered every single activity throughout the year . . . what about spearfishing for trout, or gathering up the flightless molting ducks, or gathering their eggs. Hunting spotted seals with a .22 and a harpoon, a hybrid of ancient and new hunting tactics. So much goes on, you have to come see it all!

My family is always a good audience for my stories. I spent Christmas in Fort Worth, TX. Every time I was introduced, my family member would say one of two things: either, "This is Dean. He lives with Eskimos in Alaska," or, "This is Dean. He's the one I've been telling you about!"

Amazing. Man, where else do you find this kind of stuff? I mean, I'm sure that plenty of other people in the world are doing these types of things, but to actually take part, to be there—that's why I came up here.

Tell you what, I've got to go. It's Sunday night, my lesson plans are done, but I've got chores at home to do and I have to get some sleep. Looking forward, Peter, to hearing from you again.

GO TO DEERING

Deering. I would get there and meet Dean and Eric. The longer I traveled in Alaska, the deeper I was drawn into the maze of it all. It appeared that Dean and Eric had become a real part of village life. Over the next few months Eric and Dean sent me more E-mails. Eric's address gave me some hint into who he was: idahohippy@excite.com.

Months passed. Pieces of their E-mails often floated into my mind.

From Dean: "It's really amazing to stop the snow machine and turn off the engine and look around and all you see is frozen ocean. Like nothing else in the world!"

From Eric:

The snow is so deep along the riverbanks that you are actually riding your snow machine on a crust that looks like it has small willow branches sticking through it. In reality these are the tips of willow trees deep under the snow. It's common to step off your snow machine and sink up to your armpits. It can be really time-consuming digging out your stuck snow machine. Let's see, at the beginning of the month Dean and I rode our machines to Kotzebue, and if you pull out a map, just draw a straight line between the two and you will see pretty much the route we took. With the ocean all frozen it takes several miles off the trip, but you are always wondering about that one bad spot that could be anywhere around you. Some places you are simply picking a route through large chunks of ice that have been pushed upward kind of like the movements of the earth with plate tectonics. This time of year is nice, you never run out of ice cubes. Everyone has big chunks of ice they have carried from the river. Typically this is piled up outside the door to your house. A few Saturdays ago we had one of our five Saturday school days for the year.

They told me later when they knew me better that sometimes they would do anything to get out of the village, fighting feelings that were a combination of cabin fever and village fever. Two good-looking young guys, twenty-seven and twenty-nine, naturally they got the urge. Sometimes they got so feverish they'd head out in a blizzard across the frozen ocean to Kotzebue, the largest town in any direction. There, certain weekends there were dances at the Lions Club. Basically it was them, a few married guys with their wives, and a large number of Eskimo women who wanted to dance until night became day. They never had to ask anyone to dance, it was all they could do to dance with one woman at a time, especially a few hours into the dance, after some alcohol had been consumed. Sometimes six women would be lined up, all wanting to dance at once. A few times, after the dance had ended and they'd turned down all kinds of offers, they had to run their fast snow machines full throttle through the snow-covered streets of "Kotz" to escape a carful of good-looking women wanting the dancing to move to another level.

Eric and Dean said they'd never imagined such a thing, but teachers hold a special place of respect in Alaska. In Alaska, as I've said, you don't do something outside your village without your entire hometown knowing about it. Plus their bosses live in Kotzebue. Dean and Eric both said the people of Deering knew before they got home whom they'd danced with that night.

On Valentine's Day, both our older daughters called us. Brooke, who's in her early twenties, called us with news. We had noticed that she seemed happier in the last several months than in a long time, and we didn't think it was because we were gone. Brooke wanted both Rita and me on the phone to tell us she was in love, and that someone had given her a very special present this day, a big rock. A guy we'd not yet met, Trey Buttrey from Thompson Station, the little town north of us, had asked her to marry him. She had said yes. It was wonderful news, and we told her how happy we were for her.

Later on Rebekah also called. She'd spent some time with us in Alaska, but now was back in the States at school. She asked how we were doing. She told me that she had decided she'd like to come up for spring break, sometime in March. I said great, told her I would love to go off somewhere with her. There was a pause, and then she said that she would rather go somewhere by herself, perhaps to some village way out.

This moment when your child no longer needs you should be cause for celebration, even in the *last* frontier. I should have been thrilled that she wanted to go somewhere constructive and have an adventure, rather than do some MTV spring break thing. But I felt a prick of sadness, a slight blue mist coming over me when she said it.

Come to think of it, I had noticed distinct changes in her since last summer when she'd spent a month in the southeastern Oregon wilderness on a National Outdoor Leadership School trip. The effect on her seemed similar to the changes I'd seen in young men after boot camp. On our kayak trip in Aialik Bay and in Cordova, she had seemed more assured, more secure, more confident in her ability to take care of herself, to be by herself. It may have also had to do with her finding success in college; she had not had a positive high school experience.

Dean, Eric, and Cody on Main Street in Deering.
PHOTO BY PETER JENKINS

I tried not to let my first reaction show over the phone, but Rebekah misses almost nothing. Eventually I got over it on the phone, got more excited; I told her sure, I would think about it and call her back. I asked her if she had any preferences; she said no, just someplace radical.

I thought about what my parents must have thought but did not say when I, the eldest of their six children, told them I was going to walk across America, and then I sat down to think of a plan for her. I thought of possible places, places I'd been. The Brooks Range and Eric's place. Hydaburg and Tina and her sister, Jody, and her boyfriend, Tony. Or what about Neva and Per? No, she wanted to go somewhere she hadn't been. I called some friends I'd made in Fairbanks who were from an Athabascan village on the Yukon, but they said they wouldn't recommend sending Rebekah there in the winter.

What about Deering? But I didn't think it was a good idea. I hadn't even really met Dean and Eric yet. I knew that in small-village life in Alaska, there was often no resident police, only sometimes a VPO, a village police officer. I talked to a few friends; they said they would be cautious about sending their twenty-year-old daughter to a village near the end of winter, when any acting out would be at its worst, the frustrations of light deprivation and being closed in having built up all season long.

I began to wonder if there was anyplace I'd feel comfortable sending Rebekah. A week later she called to see if I had made any progress. I told her I hadn't. She said that time was passing. "Come on, Dad, you can do it," she said in a slightly mocking but motivating tone.

I kept leaning toward the idea of Deering. Surely Eric and Dean were tough guys to have done all they'd done with their Eskimo hosts. Many teachers in Alaska do not get so involved in the hunting and the gathering, in village life. Eric and Dean would know how to watch out for Rebekah. No single available women were in Deering, though, and it had been a long winter. Rebekah would be the only single white woman in town. Where would she stay? I knew Eric and Dean both had their own homes. Maybe a woman or a family could take her in, give her some cover. I worried so much about this, debated all the possibilities. I didn't want to be overprotective, yet I wanted to be as careful as possible. She planned to be here in only a bit more than two weeks. I E-mailed Eric and Dean to see what they thought.

Dean and Eric,

I would suspect that my experience in Alaska has been similar to yours; the longer I am here the more profound and intriguing and personal and surprising the experience becomes.

As I think I mentioned to you guys, my daughter Rebekah, twenty, is traveling with me sometimes on her vacations from college.

I think it would be great for her to spend some time by herself in a village, and I am wondering if you think she could come stay in Deering. She is getting here on the weekend of March 10 and staying through that next weekend. I realize sending an attractive twenty-year-old into a small village has its potential pitfalls. I also realize my wanting to send my daughter so that you guys could show her around would require trust on my part, but I think that can be handled.

Rebekah could fly in on Saturday or Sunday to Kotzebue, March 10 or 11. I trust you guys enough to send my daughter there and realize also that you know how to watch out for her and who is who in Deering; you know what I mean. Let me know. Peter.

They E-mailed me back in a few hours and said sure, they'd love to meet her and would arrange everything. They certainly seemed excited; they'd responded awfully fast. I couldn't help but remember myself at twenty-seven or twenty-nine and tried to imagine living in a totally isolated Eskimo village of 150 with no easy way out or in. What if some guy wanted to send his twenty-year-old daughter for me to "take care of." It would be like a dream come true. Plus I knew, and they didn't, how attractive, cute, and quick to make friends Rebekah is. They told me about a wonderful Eskimo woman named Stella who worked at the school. She was in her fifties and lived alone; they even mentioned that she taught Sunday school. Were they trying too hard to assure me? I did feel that they would be on their best behavior, knowing I would be coming there after Rebekah did. Not that I'd ever really find out what had gone on, but still, I'd be there, meet them. After I got to know Eric and Dean, they told me that the word *trust* had sure stood out in my E-mail. I decided to send Rebekah there.

FROM REBEKAH

Deering

I still can't believe my father sent me, alone, his just-over-a-hundred-pound, twenty-year-old daughter to the Arctic Circle, to two men in their twenties who hadn't seen a single white woman in a long time. Two men whom he had never met. My father had never even seen their faces. Everything we knew about them was from E-mails and phone conversations that my dad had had with them from Seward. We knew they were both teachers in the village, that both were originally from the lower forty-eight, and that they made up two of the six white men in Deering. One of them was a fan of Dad's, had heard that he was traveling in Alaska, working on a new book, and had E-mailed him encouraging him to visit Deering. Scared? I was.

First of all, it was spring break when I went up to Deering. Several of my friends were headed to Florida and Cancún to get wasted and sunburnt, maybe even tattooed. I was headed to a place where the water was frozen but where the sun still burnt, where the scarring came from blisters caused by the below-zero wind. I don't believe I would ever have gone to Deering had it not been for NOLS.

Before Dad and I embarked upon the wilds of Alaska together, he had heard about the National Outdoor Leadership School (NOLS) from his friend Skip Yowell, the guy who co-founded JanSport and who knows everything about the almost underground world of adventure sports and schools. It didn't take much convincing before Dad realized that NOLS would be a wonderful thing for me to do to prepare for the extremes of Alaska.

NOLS helped me find the confidence within myself to do such a thing as go to Deering alone, without my father to protect me, without my mother to guide me, and without my friends to keep me company. NOLS helped me find the voice within myself that encourages me to persevere, to stay strong, to never give up. And what is most invaluable about what I found on my NOLS trip, out there in the high desert of Idaho and in Oregon paddling the Owyhee, making my own way through the treacherous, hot backcountry, is that voice within that screams, "You can do anything. Anything!" Before NOLS I would not have gone to Deering as willingly or as self-assuredly as I did. I would not have been so free of fear as I was out in the middle of nowhere with a bunch of hard-faced Eskimos. I did not know anyone or anything, and I loved every single precious minute.

My mother, as well as a bunch of her lady friends, loves and trusts Jesus. My mother and twelve of these friends put their hands on me and prayed for me before I left. Yeah, I was a little apprehensive. I didn't know these two guys. My dad didn't know these two guys. I had imagined them, though. In my head they were handsome and rough and manly, the kind of men written about in those supermarket romance novels, in the books without covers in some ninety-nine-cent pile at any Goodwill store. They were also intellectuals far off the "I'm escaping" beaten path. My mother, as she listened to my anxiety, told me I was romanticizing the situation. At the same time, of course, she agreed that it really was romantic. So there I was, a young, adventurous, long-haired girl going up to a village in the Arctic Circle of 150 Eskimos, alone, to stay with Stella, the fifty-five-year-old, indigenous-to-Deering Eskimo woman: the woman who would protect me from the men (Dad and I never verbalized that, but it was what we both had concluded). Sometimes you have to expect the unexpected.

When I got to Deering, Stella wasn't even there. I was informed that she had gone down to Oklahoma to visit her children and grandchildren. This meant that I would be staying with Dean and Eric, the two handsome he-men I had created in my nonstop imagination. But that was okay. Just fine. Because when I stepped off that Bering Air bush plane, away from that young, ever-so-cute, flirtatious pilot who had let me sit in the copilot seat, I saw Dean Cummings, the lean, twenty-seven-year-old playboy who had a perfect smile and an artist's hands, and Eric Smith, the quieter, long-dark-haired twenty-nine-year-old whose expressions were those of a tormented rebel and a tender, careless hippie all rolled into one. They were not on horses. They were on Polaris snowmobiles. And I couldn't believe they actually were both cute and tough-looking. They certainly knew what they were doing on those snow machines.

They were waiting for me with an extralarge, army-green, down-filled coat. I had stepped off the plane in a lightweight North Face jacket. How they knew I would need that big green coat I do not know. But they did. I was a little nervous. What would I say? I got over that as I soon discovered that I was with two true long-lost-brother types. They weren't going to hurt me, rape me, take me miles away from the village and chop me into wolf food. I was going to be all right.

One morning, I slowly stood up from Dean's old, worn-out couch, my bed for last night, and whispered a silent thank-you to the cloudless sky that I have felt safe here, and not at all far from home. The plan for the day was to travel by snow machine to Buckland, the closest village, about fifty miles east of Deering, and then down to Koyuk. Dean and Eric wanted to take me to Koyuk to see the famous hot springs. The plan was to stay there for the weekend at an old cabin and enjoy the hot springs and maybe even catch a glimpse of the Iditarod mushers who would supposedly be passing through.

Eight miles out of Deering, Eric and I stopped on a small rise in the frozen ground, turned off the snow machine, and waited for the others—Dean, Toni, and Matt—to catch up with us. Toni and Matt are a couple from Kotzebue whom Eric and Dean have befriended. Once the others reached us, word spread. I was cold. I couldn't feel my fingers or my toes.

I'd felt this numb before, within ten minutes of putting my feet on the ground in Deering. Eric had stashed me on the back of his snowmobile to head back to the village from the lone building that was the airport. When we'd reached Eric's place, a little red house half-buried in snow, I'd asked him, "Will I get my fingers back?"

He smiled and said, "Yeah," as if it were no big deal. I admit, it made me a little mad.

Today we were only eight miles out of the village and I was having these scary am-I-about-to-lose-my-fingers-and-toes thoughts. We still had a couple of hundred miles to go to the hot springs. Once Dean caught up and heard the news, he took off my boots and socks and put my feet up his jacket, under his shirt, and in his armpit. Whatever works, I thought. No problem. It was a different sort of romantic, my feet in some guy's armpit. Toni and Matt were trying to warm my hands with their hands, and Eric was standing there smoking a cigarette. We stayed like that for a while with my toes inside Dean's shirt until Eric convinced Dean that I shouldn't take the trip to Koyuk because I didn't have the right gear. Eric said I would be miserable if I tried to go, and I agreed—besides, I wasn't about to put myself in jeopardy. I understood that I knew nothing about this land other than how cold and dangerous it was. I was disappointed. Dean was disappointed. But I got over the disappointment rather quickly because not going meant Eric and I would have a long weekend together. No Stella. No Dean. We said our good-byes, told them to have fun, and off we went.

My favorite moments were riding on the back of Eric's Polaris, bumping over the hard, cold tundra, when my fingers and toes were warm, my body presented to the big blue sky and the still sea. Behind Eric, who, by the way, likes to drive his Polaris really fast—you could almost say irresponsibly—I smiled underneath my red and beige fleece scarf and gleamed happily because no one could see me: not the Eskimo kids who were playing in the snow, not the occasional passing snow machine, no one. No one knew my happiness, my feelings of pure joy. In just this one day, I knew the emotions of a lifetime. Everything about this village is beautiful: the frozen sea, the rolling tundra, the lack of trees and endless white horizon, the darker-skinned people. I am in awe. It is simple—I thought I had found heaven.

I felt overwhelmingly at home flying into Deering, experiencing the exhilaration that the Arctic Circle brings, that the frozen sea brings. I believe my calico curls have found themselves a home here among the isolation, the below-freezing blow, and among the men who have fled so far from their own homes to find solace and themselves here.

Should I be surprised that after only forty-eight hours I concluded that I could marry one of these men (it doesn't matter which) and build a life here surrounded by these silent, feisty Eskimos? I could be a wife, have nowhere to walk or drive to, other than this one, one-mile road. I could be happy inside, through the dark, depressing, aurora-graced winter, reading all those books planted on the school's classroom shelves. But after I'd been there a while longer, I realized that what Deering actually showed me was my own strength, my own desire to go, to see, to travel and experience other places like this, again and again.

NO MORE HONEY BUCKETS

Rebekah loved her spring break in Deering, and *love* is not too strong a word. Now it was my turn to fly over the still-frozen Kotzebue Sound, part of the

The Deering cemetery sits on a hill overlooking the town and the frozen ocean.
PHOTO BY REBEKAH JENKINS

Chukchi Sea, in possibly the same little plane. From this height it was hard to differentiate between the frozen ice and the frozen tundra, although it appeared that's all there was for hundreds of miles. When I finally saw Deering's maybe forty or fifty houses and a couple public buildings, it looked to me like a colony on a frozen planet. In a couple minutes we'd land in this town, built on a sand spit formed by the draining of the Inmachuk River. As we lost altitude for landing, I could see where the wind had sculpted the snow into frozen white waves. Someone at the Kotzebue airport had told me that thousands of caribou were right at the edge of Deering. They'd heard they were part of the gigantic Western Arctic Herd which numbered over four hundred thousand animals. Maybe I'd seen them from the air.

Dean, in the spirit of *A Walk Across America*, which he'd been reading to his fifth- and sixth-graders, walked with them to the "airport," which was just a strip, a bit more than a half mile out of town. Two of the girls, Mary and Diane, both on Dean's wrestling team, asked me a hundred questions and said they were my bodyguards. One of them called me Stone Cold. Dean told me Stone Cold was their favorite WWF wrestler. Dean was tall, well built, energetic, and handsome. Rebekah had never mentioned what either of them looked like, come to think of it.

Dean told me I was going to stay at his house. He lived next door to the best ivory carver in Deering and across the street from Eric. The ivory carver also collected mastodon ivory in the summer, which could sometimes be found lying on the bottom of local rivers and creeks. He also searched for dead walrus skulls, which sometimes washed up on the beaches, to carve on. Pieces of these beaches might not have had a human footprint on them for fifty years, or ever. As we got to town, I saw that some of the tiny homes, most of which had been built by the government, were practically covered by snowbanks. People liked to keep them there as an insulative windbreak.

As I walked down the narrow gravel road that held everything that was Deering, a couple homes had freshly killed caribou lying on their snowbank. They may have been killed and skinned by a nephew for his auntie who cannot hunt, or by a son for his widowed mother and she hadn't cut it up yet. Eric had a large Alaskan malamute chained to the house he rented; he had painted the house barn-red. His was one of the only freshly painted houses in this section of Deering, which the guys called Downtown. Eric's dog, named Cody, was the size of a small bear and was every kid's favorite in the village.

The school was the center of this community. In a few days school would end for the summer, and the one member of the Deering senior class of 2000 would graduate. There are four full-time teachers in Deering; one of them, Pat Richardson, has been there for sixteen years. Her husband is a member of the National Space Society. Every year the NSS has the International Space Development Conference. Most members of this organization are not space cadets but serious people interested in the colonization of the moon and Mars, in space tourism, in outer-space B&Bs. You could immediately see that Deering was similar to a space colony, totally self-contained, thriving in a hostile environment.

Dean took me down to his house and showed me my bed, an old sofa. He let slip that Rebekah had used it. I had thought she was staying with Stella, the fifty-something Sunday-school teacher. My first reaction was this tiny home was empty and the sofa was in such tough shape that the Goodwill truck wouldn't take it. Then I thought about how one gets a sofa to outer space, I mean Deering. Obviously, you can't fly it in as extra luggage. It wouldn't even fit in the plane that comes to Deering. Was it hauled from Kotzebue across the frozen ocean on a sled? The freight bill alone to get it here must have been large. I had a new appreciation for the sofa. I began to look at everything in Deering larger than a suitcase the same way you'd look at stuff in space. How'd they ever get that four-wheeler here, that big-screen TV, that freezer, that generator? The difference between Deering and the moon, though, is that when the ice is gone, maybe some essentials, such as diesel fuel, sofas, big-screen TVs, and the one little pickup I saw, can float in on a barge. This is also one reason why when big things in a Native village like Deering break and can't be fixed, they tend to stay wherever they broke down. There's an old water truck right at Eric's house that has been there for several years.

It's not only a substantial challenge to bring stuff to outer-space colonies and villages like Deering, it's tough to get rid of what is not needed. Take human waste. (At least in Deering the stuff is not weightless, a whole separate challenge.) Getting rid of human sewage in Deering required some sophisticated engineering solutions and was a real challenge for whatever firm accepted it. It may have been an engineer trained at the University of Alaska at Fairbanks, as they have one of the finest engineering schools in the country dealing in the specific problems of arctic conditions.

Until recently, waste was deposited in a "honey bucket," not something that required an engineer. When full, the honey bucket, normally a five-gallon plastic pail, had to be hand-carried out onto the sea ice and emptied. They say that sometimes the stuff was frozen even before it hit the ice. Imagine, it's forty-two below zero and the honey bucket has to be emptied. You've waited long enough; there's no more room.

When Pat Richardson's husband goes to the International Space Development Conference in 2001 in Albuquerque, surely they will have a lecture by a space sewage expert. After all they have speakers on "space pharmacy," "space tourism," "economically self-sufficient space settlement on the moon," and "taking advantage of Martian chemistry." How well attended could the panel on "space sewage and its challenges" be? Probably pretty well, considering the seriousness of the problem. Some of the cosponsors this year were Boeing, Embry-Riddle Aeronautical University, the Air Force Research Laboratory, and the U.S. Department of Energy. Deering would be an excellent location for the U.S. government to put a training center for people going to live in space. It would also help in case there is alien life somewhere, because for some the adaptation to Deering's culture and way of life is difficult and challenging. Dean and Eric would receive outstanding grades for their adaptation; other teachers have not done well at all. Sometimes a teacher from the Outside wants to do it just the way he did in Las Vegas. What alien do you know who would want to do it the way they do it in Las Vegas?

Elections in Alaska generate almost as many unusual political debates and promises as they would in a space colony. Politicians make many promises. In Alaska someone running for office might say, "If elected, I promise to try to get some of the government-owned land for the people." Only 1 percent of Alaska's land is privately owned. "I promise to do something about the wolves." Some Alaskans are concerned because an overpopulation of wolves has brought these mighty, brilliant predators into villages looking for easy meals, like dogs. Some worry will children be next? "I promise to fight for subsistence." Subsistence, the hunting and gathering of food to survive, is one of the most hotly debated, controversial issues in Alaska.

In the eighties, while Wally Hickel was running for governor of Alaska as an independent, some politicians were for keeping marijuana legal, some were for making it illegal. Although marijuana lost and Wally Hickel won, many Alaskans put this bumper sticker on their vehicles advertising the election results: "Pot got more votes than Hickel." It's true.

Honey bucket is one of Alaska's sweet words for not so sweet. It was and still is the receptacle for no. 1 and no. 2 in hundreds of Alaskan villages. It could be a five-gallon plastic bucket with a custom-cut wood seat. If the person is too heavy for plastic, then the honey bucket could be metal.

When I arrived in Deering to hang out with these two teachers, Dean and Eric, I didn't even know what a honey bucket was. In Barrow they'd put in a sewer, burying their sewer lines deep and even heating them. I found out what these lines had replaced in the first couple hours I was in Deering, sitting in Dean's little house along the road that was Main Street, the only one people lived along. The houses were all little wood boxes. Dean's house was tiny, one small bedroom, a small living room–kitchen, one room that was shut off. Dean, Eric, and I sat around talking, hearing the villagers pass by on their four-wheelers on the way to the only store. Only one person seemed to have a car, a small pickup. The rest traveled on four-wheelers or snow machines.

Deering is blessed to be a recipient from a major campaign plank of the present two-term governor, Tony Knowles. When he first ran for governor, he courted Alaska's Native community. Often in Alaska, politicians get elected by tiny margins. Somebody in Knowles's campaign came up with this political promise, which was repeated over and over anywhere in the bush where the honey bucket was filled and emptied: if elected, Knowles promised to do his best to put the honey bucket in the museum.

What museum would display honey buckets? Would they be honey buckets that famous people had sat on, or the most unusually designed honey buckets curators could find, say one painted with peace signs from the sixties or one that had been clawed by a brown bear and survived to be used again?

That promise may not sound like much to you. But if you'd been emptying a honey bucket all your life, in the winter at thirty below and in the summer when the mosquitoes are swarming, getting rid of it might just be enough to get your vote. Tony Knowles *was* first elected by a small margin, with a big assist from Native Alaskans. Now that political promise has actually been kept in Deering and many other villages. In Deering there are no more honey buckets—instead there is the human-waste blaster. This technology hasn't been around long enough to have a name; it should be called the honey rocket. With every invention there are bugs, if that's the right word, to be worked out, or pushed or flushed out. In this case they are blasted out. Putting in a sewage disposal system in a place that has permafrost and sometimes gets to fifty below zero is no easy task. This new high-tech honey rocket was the first thing I noticed when I walked into Dean's house. It was all over the walls, so to speak. In fact, when the new high-tech honey bucket was first installed in uptown Deering, in a couple houses instead of sucking it all *out* of the house, it shot it all up *into* the house like a mini-geyser. A couple people told Dean and Eric the suction was so great they worried about their small children playing near it. What if one adventurous little girl had her hand down in the toilet when the blaster went off, when it was flushed?

Running up the walls and across the ceiling in Dean's house were water and sewer pipes. A powerful pump was attached to the front wall. These pipes were in full view, not in the walls or hidden in any way. The new technology was displayed for everyone to see. It did cut into your ability to hang pictures, but that's all right. If the pipes were black, it could look techno. What if a pipe burst? It's bad enough if that happens underneath the house, much less over the kitchen table.

It's a type of vacuum. The biggest problem adjusting to this marvelous new honey blaster was the blast itself. When someone flushed, it sounded like a small jet taking off. The loud vacuum pump kicks on, then the even louder water pump kicks on; there is a loud sucking noise. Do not try to talk while the honey rocket is going off. Then if you're like Dean and you don't like hauling water to keep your tank filled, which is also open and right in your living room, it runs dry and there is an incessant sucking sound as the pump searches the empty tank for water. Visualize having friends over for a card game or a candlelight dinner of fresh caribou and seal oil and salmonberries, and someone flushes. There it is, it goes off, everyone stops talking and waits until the honey rocket has done its very appreciated task. But it's a small price to pay. Waiting to talk or being awakened or missing a score made by Alaskan Scott Gomez in the NHL play-offs on ESPN is worth it compared to the relative silence of the old honey bucket.

Some light sleepers in Deering have passed new rules since the honey rocket came to town: "No flushing at night while I'm asleep or else!" One of Dean and Eric's best friends in Deering is pre-school teacher Millie, a Native woman born and raised in Deering. She had an idea, one of those bright and shining moments when civilization is advanced if only someone will listen. She has one of the gentlest voices I've ever heard. She said one day as we were laughing about the honey rocket, "If they can make a silencer for a gun, why can't they make one for this?" What political potential this idea has, and if the solution is worked out by the right engineer, it could be cheap.

MOUSE TRADING

Teachers that come to the Alaskan bush from hometowns in Florida or Idaho, like Dean and Eric, or other places Outside should have certain personality traits to maximize their experience. They should possess the wayward, flexible spirit of the explorer, the ability to be thrilled by the unknown, and the "I don't care what people think" attitude of the rebel.

In Dean and Eric's case, these attributes were evident early and often. Dean grew up the son of Texans who'd moved to the small Florida beach town of Indian Harbour Beach, just south of Cocoa Beach. His dad was an engineer who worked for Harris, a company that did work for nearby NASA. The engineers of Dean's dad's era wore the short-sleeve white shirts, blue slacks, and certain type and color necktie that we all know.

Dean was born in 1973. He remembers wanting to be a surfer. His parents gave him the impression that nice kids don't surf, nice kids have short haircuts.

Dean grew his hair long but was in the gifted programs and got good grades. He didn't have to try hard to get good grades; he probably heard something once and remembered it. He got 1370 on his SATs but hung with the punk crowd, the out crowd.

Dean recalled that his Alaska dream began when he was in second grade. Their *Scholastic Reader* had a story about land selling in Alaska for $2.50 an acre. He and his friend decided right then they would move to Alaska. In fourth grade, this same friend called Dean and asked if he was ready to go, they could ride their bikes to Alaska. Dean wasn't prepared then, but one night in fifth grade he did decide to go. He packed his daypack, had $4 in change, and took off at 4 A.M. before his parents were up. The only problem was, he didn't know which way to go or quite how far it was. He went south on Route A1A and in two hours realized he needed to turn around and head back for school, which started at 8 A.M.

Around this time Dean decided he wanted to build a rope swing. For whatever reason, he didn't ask his parents, or if he did, they wouldn't get him what he wanted, the necessary ten-foot piece of nylon rope. He included this desire in his Christmas letter to his grandmothers in Texas; they both sent him a piece of rope. He made a swing, and he remembers that it took him high into the sky.

After graduating from high school, he followed his first major girlfriend, one he had loved from the moment he saw her in tenth grade but didn't date her until his senior year, to college at the University of Central Florida. That didn't last long, the girlfriend, but he lost his dreams for Alaska in the world of fraternity life, partying, and drinking, probably a bit too much. He'd gone to major in engineering, but dropped out for a semester and came back wanting to be a teacher.

One of his grandmothers bought him a college graduation present, but died before she could give it to him. It was another piece of nylon rope. He knew what she meant by it—she meant it as inspiration, to remind Dean to follow his dreams. Getting that short piece of rope sparked some of his dreams all over again, especially the one about going to Alaska. That rope's the reason he got this job teaching in Deering, and that rope has proved to him that sometimes your dreams can be even better when you actually live them in the daylight.

Eric grew up in Salmon, Idaho. Growing up in a place named Salmon gives you a step up in Alaska on some guy like Dean, who grew up rarely wearing more than shorts, a T-shirt, and sandals. Eric's family is an influential and conservative family around Salmon; he grew up on a part of the family ranch. Salmon's near Montana, about ninety miles north of Sun Valley, and has about three thousand people. Eric told me his family was strong and involved and included lawyers, judges, city council members. He said he decided that his role in the family was to take the place of his black-sheep uncle. His ideas for living involved perpetual fun and stretching mischief as far as he could. In a family that had short hair, he too grew his long. Eric's got that sparkle in his face, that little-boy charm, that makes people like him right off. Both Eric and Dean could be classified as chick magnets, although obviously that ability was not one they wanted to develop or they would never have moved to Deering, where all the women are taken. Even if they weren't, as a teacher you're off-limits. Dean said he didn't begin appealing to females until his sister, always the classy dresser, told him he needed to start tucking in his shirt.

When Eric was locked in his room and grounded, he climbed out the window. When his car keys were taken, he took his dirt bike and a flashlight. He and his friends, the Salmon class of 1988, showed a creative side. When they wanted a day off, they marched through town protesting to get Martin Luther King Day off at school. Eric said there wasn't an African-American for one hundred miles, but they succeeded. On a hill overlooking Salmon is a huge S, visible from town, with a number signifying the year. In 1985, a few of them snuck up there one night and changed S85 to SEX. There was a government teacher that Eric and a few buddies liked to torment; they spray-painted his pigs Day-Glo orange, green, and purple.

Eric shocked a lot of people when he entered the army. He served in Desert Storm, and then right out of the army, he went to Boise State. He majored in Party 101 through 110; first semester his GPA was 0.0; second semester it was 0.25. He liked his psychology course, probably learned about himself. He ended up graduating from the University of Idaho, the family's choice in higher education. Eric says that his rebellious days now help him to work with so many who are turned off by school, education. In college he met a guy whose dad and brother fished in seine boats in Prince William Sound out of Valdez. Eric became the skiff man. He'd sit out there, write songs, and think about what he was going to do with his life. Sitting there one day, Eric decided he would teach in Alaska. And that's how Eric's and Dean's paths crossed and they came to live across the street from each other in Deering.

There was a knock on the door—it was Reggie. Reggie follows Dean and Eric everywhere they go, which is simple to do in a place like Deering. It is impossible to hide, unless you take off on your snow machine looking for four or five thousand caribou, which we did, or go to the plateau above town and look for the musk ox herd, which we also did. Riding along with a caribou herd that numbered in the thousands across the snow-covered tundra was one of my most profound moments in Alaska. No matter how far we followed them there was never a fence, not for the hundreds of miles they roamed during their yearly migrations. To see the herd of musk ox with this year's crop of baby musk ox protected in the center of the herd when anyone comes around was more inspiring than I had thought possible. Their long, flowing hair and their stocky, powerful bodies moved so forcefully atop the tundra. They like being up on the ridges and hilltops where the winds, not only friend to the Eskimo but to them as well, blew the snow away to make it easier for them to feed on the tundra.

Reggie, a large and powerful young Eskimo, is in junior high school, but he has the build of a man. He remembers not only Eric's and Dean's birthdays but their parents' as well. He remembers when Eric's mother came to visit. Reggie wants to play the guitar and sing just like Johnny Cash. He comes over to their homes, often a couple times a day, to pick and grin. He never thinks twice about wanting to hang out with his teachers, any time of the day or night. Both Dean and Eric have big and caring hearts and never turn Reggie away; they give so much of themselves. When he saw my microphone and found out I was from Tennessee, he wanted me to record him singing Johnny Cash. I did. One night, Reggie's mom and grandmother invited Dean, Eric, and me over for dinner. Reggie's mom is the cook at school. Since the people of Deering, especially the kids, so seldom see a stranger, every time I walked down the one and only street that the houses are on, I had a parade of kids following me or calling out, "Hello, Peter Jenkins."

Of all the stories I heard and the people I met in Deering, the stories told to me by Millie, an Eskimo and preschool teacher, best illustrated the intimate relationship these people have with their world. The abundant life and the seasons that affect them are what rule Deering. I had to be around Deering awhile before Dean could get the people to tell me stories. They saw me at graduation, at the end-of-school picnic, their kids told them I'd spoken in their classroom. Everybody in town, especially the children, loved Rebekah; she had come before me and laid the groundwork. I couldn't be too bad if I had a daughter like Rebekah. Right before I was to leave Deering, Millie told Dean it would be all right to bring me by her mother's house so we could talk.

Gladys Iyatunguk is Millie's mother. Both have some gray hair, but I'm not sure how old either woman is. Both are totally alive and involved in living their lives as Eskimo people of the tundra and ocean and rivers and ice. Millie's voice is like a whisper but has incredible strength. I think this Eskimo way of speaking, soft, slow, focused, and songlike, comes from being listened to and from living surrounded by so much beautiful silence and life.

They told me about mouse trading. Gladys said the first part of September, they go into the tundra looking for where the mice have been gathering a root called mussu from a grass that grows in bunches. They look for slight disturbances in the ground where the mice have been building their caches, mouse-size, underground storage places where they store food for the long winter months. Mussu is a root from a grass with purple flowers, pretty flowers, Gladys said. In the fall the flowers and leaves drop and all you see is the stem. Gladys said when they find the grass growing in gravel, the roots are tough.

The mussu has been gathered for hundreds of years for food. Gladys had learned from her mother and aunties when they went out in the tundra to pick mussu. Gladys said we needed to try some; she had some mussu in seal oil frozen in a plastic bag in the freezer. Millie pulled it out of the freezer, where it sat next to the Neapolitan ice cream. The roots were as thick as a pencil and white. Gladys said they are sweet; I thought they tasted like a raw or boiled peanut. Gladys liked them best soaked in seal oil.

Gathering this mussu is called mouse trading. To me it illustrates the people's fantastic appreciation of their environment. Most people would never see what they find. This illustrates how they observe the subtlest of details in nature and understand what it can do for the people. It's called mouse trading because first they must find the mouse's home. They gently open the cache, which shows itself as a bit of freshly dug dirt, to reveal what is inside. Gladys told us that some mice pick the mussu very clean and stack it neatly, while some are sloppy and don't pick the roots perfectly clean of the little "hairs" that grow on them. All mice are not the same, she said, and smiled—just like people. Gladys's eyes are bright and lively. As always in any Native conversation, the elder, Gladys, did most of the talking.

"Sometimes you use your fingers to feel around in their burrow feeling for the cache and, *eey*, you feel a mouse."

As they are kneeling on the ground, gently entering the mouse's house with their fingers and taking its mussu, they do not just take. They trade. Before they leave on their four-wheelers, Millie leaves cut-up potatoes and carrots and celery in the mouse cache so the mice will have something in return. To trade like this with such a tiny creature that has no way of demanding any equality or any fairness shows such concern that survival is tough around Deering, for mice as well as people.

Normally Millie and Gladys gather about six quart-size bags to last for a year. It is not cooked, but eaten with seal oil or plain. Millie said she liked it best eaten with dried fish or boiled meat. After our mussu, Millie and Gladys served us some of the best food ever to come out of Alaska, a bowl full of salmonberries. Dean and I thanked them for their story and their time. I would try to integrate the concept of mouse trading into the way I lived, I thought as we walked across the street to Eric's for tea.

In a couple of days Dean, Eric, and I would be leaving Deering. Eric has an old Volkswagen bus; and he and Cody and Eric's daughter were going to spend the summer on one long road trip. Dean was going to take the year off; he wasn't sure what he was going to do. He would try to strike up a relationship with an old girlfriend in Tampa; if that didn't work out, maybe he would go to a wooden-boat-building school near Seattle. I thanked them both for what they'd done for Rebekah and me and for introducing us to their world. I left the day after Eric and Cody did. Cody is such a large Alaskan malamute it might cost more to fly him to Anchorage than me.

19

Hobo Night

It was Hobo night at the Yukon Bar in Seward. I had heard a couple college students who worked at Icicle Seafoods call it "the church of Hobo" since he played every Sunday night. The Yukon is about three blocks from Resurrection Bay. Hobo Jim, Alaska's rebel folksinger, has made his living for a couple of decades playing the saloons, festivals, and fairs in every fishing village, town, and city in Alaska. He came to Alaska as a hitchhiker, looking like Che Guevara. In the seventies his shoulder-length hair and full beard were as black as a Greek fisherman's. His last name is Varsos; his father is of Greek descent, his mother Scottish. His beard may be mostly gray, but he can still outperform just about everyone, playing before five thousand or seventy-five. He is such a gifted entertainer that listening to his CDs isn't enough. He enchants people; the audience has more fun than they can remember, even when he's yodeling. I've seen him sing and play guitar for three hours straight, threatening to take a break but never doing it. Before the night's over, he'll probably be singing from on top of a table.

Some people followed Hobo around in Alaska the way people Outside followed the Grateful Dead. Wherever he was playing, Homer, Soldotna, Palmer, Seward, or some biker bar near Girdwood, they showed up. Some people have been going to his shows since they were eighteen-year-old cannery workers just planning to summer in Alaska. Now they're in their late thirties, they never went back to wherever they came from, and they've been fans of Hobo's all this time.

We had Julianne and Luke, Rebekah and Aaron with us. Almost everyone from our family was back in Alaska now, except Jed and Brooke. Jed was in Governors School in Tennessee studying theater and Brooke was planning her wedding. The Yukon Bar's ceiling is covered with dollar bills that people have autographed with the town or city they're from; I'd put one up right over the front little round table where we always sat. We got there early so the kids could hear him do some songs; they'd make requests before they had to leave. As usual, Julianne would request "The Iditarod Song." Hobo was running a bit behind tonight; he'd got caught in some construction traffic. We sat and watched him unpack his amp and speaker. He slung his trusty guitar over his shoulder. That motion made me remember the time Hobo and his friend Mike Sipes took me, Rusty Jones, and Rusty's friend Gerry Fatzer on a walk in the wilderness.

It was in 1996, and we'd made a "guy trip" to hang out with Hobo. That brief walk challenged me, and my tame world. Not far down the trail, it terrified me. We were staying at an isolated log lodge on Lake Tustamena owned by two of Hobo's friends, Mike and Linda Sipes from Soldotna. Hobo had written some of his most famous songs on napkins at their former restaurant. Linda is a gourmet cook; she and Mike are both wine connoisseurs. Mike, an intense guy, is originally from California and reminds me of a Special Forces colonel I once knew. You would never ask Mike about his life, but you would trust him with yours. I would be doing that shortly. I would never have thought as we took off from their lodge near the banks of Bear Creek that some of us might come back wounded, or worse.

There were five of us. Shafts of sunlight broke through the swaying spruce and sent spikes of angelic light to the forest floor. It was possible that no human had ever set foot in parts of that forest before. The bouncing beams of sunlight highlighted isolated spots of the wilderness. The trail brought us to the middle of a meadow filled with tall grass and wildflowers. On either side of it were deep, dark evergreen woods. About fifty yards off to our left was a small stand of slightly bent white birch trees, and amid the trees stood a mother moose. She moved nervously, looking down at the ground below her, then behind her into the dark forest. Suddenly, a newborn stood up, unsteady on its long, spindly legs. She nudged her calf into the light and out into the natural meadow, surprisingly, toward us.

The grass on either side of the trail was neck high. The temperature was perfect, low sixties, and wildflower and spruce scents sweetened the air. Mike slowed down and pointed to a fresh trail that intersected ours—at a ninety-degree angle—coming through the middle of the high grass.

"The brown bears are in here right now. They cross this trail going to the creek, which is just about fifty yards off to our left, to feed on the salmon. When they get enough, they go back into the woods to sleep in the shade."

"Really," Rusty said.

Right then I could feel my nerves jumping a bit. We walked about fifty feet more and reached a big circle of bare ground, like a small bomb crater, about ten feet in diameter. What had once been deep, thick grasses were gone. An indentation in the surviving grass on the edge of the crater marked where something had lain down, and a hole about two feet wide and three feet deep had been dug in the crater's middle.

"What happened there?" I asked.

"Oh, nothing much," Hobo answered. "Some brownie dug that up looking for the yellow jacket nest in the ground. They like to eat the larvae." That was when Hobo swung his "elephant gun" off his shoulder into his hands the same way he'd just swung his guitar.

"How can they stand getting stung by those wicked yellow jackets?" I asked.

"They have outrageous pain tolerance," Mike answered. "You can't imagine what they can take." I did not want to imagine. Mike mentioned that first the black bears come to this creek seeking the salmon. Then the supreme creatures, the brownies, come and chase the blackies away. Or eat them, whichever the blackies prefer.

We passed several more of the brown bears' trails intersecting ours. What if we met one face-to-face? Although the largest brown bears can be ten feet tall and weigh over a thousand pounds, if one was walking in the tall grass alongside us, we wouldn't see it until it was right on top of us.

My short-lived state of nature-induced nirvana was gone. We passed several more bear-made craters. Inside two of them the dirt was still damp—they had just been dug.

"Mike, what is the worst thing that can happen to us out here as far as these bears are concerned?" Rusty asked, worst-case-scenario lawyer that he is. We were only about three-quarters of a mile from the cabin, and Mike had said we'd hike about five miles up and back.

Mike stopped and gathered us around. He had some Italian-made shotgun over his shoulder. Hobo and Mike were definitely not the lie-down-and-play-dead types or the bear-bells types; most Alaskans know better.

"The worst thing is coming up on a big, old male brownie lying on a kill. They will kill a moose and let it lie there until its gets rank. They are so strong they have been seen carrying a dead eight-hundred-pound moose off the ground slung over their back."

I got hung up on the thought of how powerful and fast a brown bear must be to be able to kill *and* carry a moose.

"They get real protective over their kills. They probably think humans are there to take it away from them." Suddenly two huge black ravens cawed at each other; I nearly jumped up into the tree next to me.

"Probably the next worst thing that could happen is to come across a mother bear with twin two-year-old cubs. The two-year-olds are big enough to kill a man or two and act like curious teenagers. They might run up to you, take a swat at you, maybe just testing you or wanting to play, but one swipe with those powerful claws and they can rip your head off."

"I hope we get to see some bears," Rusty actually said after that. He's been a successful lawyer too long, I thought; you cannot outnegotiate a brown bear.

"It's doubtful we will see any bears," Mike said, "but if we do, you three stand behind Hobo and me. They usually smell us and take off before we see them. They have an excellent sense of smell and not very good eyesight."

We came to a part of the trail that went up on a narrow ridge, into a dark hemlock woods.

About halfway through it we flushed some grouse. The sound of their flapping wings as they rocketed out of the dense hemlock was a new sound to me, and I didn't think of benign little birds when I first heard it.

Mike pointed to our right. In the deep shade of a grove of hemlocks the ground was torn up, but not like a crater. Everything was disturbed, the dirt, the mat of rotting hemlock needles, the rotting trees that had died and fallen, even small saplings. Mike knelt down.

"Look here," Mike said. "Look at this black fur. Look, here is the mama's skull, and her teeth. Look over here, a piece of foot bone with the claws still connected to it. Over here is a cub's skull; no, two of them. This must have been awful when it happened."

"What happened?" Gerry asked with his Swiss accent. Gerry hadn't said much.

"Only thing I can figure, this fur and skull and whatever else is left was once a mother black bear and her cubs, and something killed them violently, and then ate them. It had to have been a brown bear."

I picked up one of the long claws from the mother and put it in my pocket.

"Brown bear claws are about four times that big. Believe it or not, there are more people mauled by black bears in Alaska than brownies," Hobo said with a teasing grin. Some Alaskans, I now realize, seem to enjoy seeing people from the Outside respond to the dangers that they live with so casually.

A line of willows was ahead.

Mike threw up his hand and stopped us. "Be real quiet now, we're almost to the creek."

We came to the creekbank; the water was about five feet below. Still shielding us from a clear view of the creek were the willows. Mike threw up his hand again and motioned us toward him.

He whispered, "Look up there."

To our right, standing in the narrow and shallow creek, was the largest bear I had ever seen. It looked about twice the size of a large black bear. Its fur was golden brown and glistened in the sun. It was spawning season; we could hear salmon splashing, driving themselves up the clear creek. Because there were so many, it sounded like something much larger, something charging. We could also see many of the salmon's bright red backs poking out of the shallow water as they swam.

At first the bear was ambling along the creek. Then, with no warning, it came running almost right to us. Chasing a salmon, it stopped and grabbed it.

Then another bear, more than twice the size of the first, stepped slowly off the bank into the creek. It seemed to stretch from one side of the creek to the other. Oh, God. She or he—probably she—was no more than seventy-five feet away. The "smaller" one was just twenty-five feet from us. I could hear the bones of the salmon being crunched as the smaller one ate.

Mike now had his gun off his shoulder and ready. He turned just enough to look in our eyes and whispered, "Do not say anything. Do not move."

A third brownie, about the size of the first, came into the creek right behind the enormous one. Must be a mother and her twin two-year-old cubs. The mother crossed the creek to the other side and disappeared. Had she smelled us and was now stalking us? What I felt to be my last seconds on earth slowed to freeze-frame after freeze-frame. I remembered some advice I'd gotten once, supposedly as a joke. If you go for a walk where there are brown bears, always go with at least one person you can beat running. I began to try to figure whom out of this group I could beat down the trail. These bears can run as fast as a quarter horse. If all three chased us, I'd have to outrun three of these guys!

The second cub ran down the creek toward us. The bears moved with terrorizing speed and power; I now understood how they could be lying down on a kill one second and on top of you the next.

Then the big mother reappeared. All I could see was her incredibly wide, golden brown head. She was standing on our trail, but just across the creek. She could be on us in two ground-swallowing leaps.

I remembered what Mike had said about why it was especially bad to run into a mother and her twin two-year-old cubs. A cub could see or smell us and run up to investigate. If they attacked one of us—swiped and knocked us down or bit onto our heads—and we had to shoot it, then, as Mike said, the worst hell would break loose. The mother would charge us, perhaps the other twin too. Mike said he didn't ever want to have to find out how he would respond in that situation.

The mother bear headed into the creek. We were all frozen in our spots. Mike, no more than twenty feet from her, had his shotgun ready. I heard a bone-crunching sound, then she stood up, and all I could see was the back of Mike's head, her head, and a salmon in her jaws.

She dropped back down out of sight. Then we could hear a terrible splashing sound coming from our left. The two cubs were chasing each other back up the creek, or was something chasing them? Hobo had said that the brownies get in awful fights on the creek and that males could easily kill and eat these cubs.

Then, the mother stood up again. She seemed to be looking right at us through the cover of the willows. Just as quickly, she dropped back down. Had she seen us? Had she caught our scent and was circling around to attack us from behind? I heard more splashing sounds, louder than before. All three of them were running up the creek, back where they had come from.

Hobo touched my back and I almost jumped over the willows and the creek and the moon.

"I've been living in Alaska since 1972, and that's as close as I've ever come to death by bears."

"Did anyone take a picture?" Rusty asked.

"I did," Gerry said.

"Mike, we are turning around, right?" I asked.

"Nah. I want to take you to the top of the hill by the spring, so we can look back at the lake."

We crossed the creek on top of a fallen log. On the other side I asked Mike why the bears didn't see or sense us. He licked his finger and held it in the air.

"What little breeze there is was blowing into us and away from them. They never smelled us, which was a good thing, believe me."

We got back to Mike and Linda's lodge around 10 P.M. I lay in bed and thought about our little "after-dinner walk" to the creek. I remembered portions of it as vividly as any experience I'd had. I felt more alive in certain seconds than in whole months of my life, a life that has been used by my readers as a model of adventure and self-determination. I could not fall asleep. It was not being afraid that kept me awake; it was because I felt so alive. I felt the early groanings I have come to recognize as internal messages drawing me to a place. Lying in bed that night, thanks to Hobo and Mike and that walk, I was getting the feeling that Alaska was a place I would need to explore.

That hike was more than three years ago. Tonight was a time to celebrate life and Alaska and that most of our family was together again. Hobo was master of this ceremony. He was tuning his guitar, about to begin. He plays so hard that people lay bets on how many strings he will break in one night.

Hobo's done about all there is to do in Alaska. He built his own log cabin on the Kenai Peninsula. He's been a commercial fisherman, he ran for mayor of Homer. He has composed some of the best songs ever written about Alaska. He's been a cowboy on one of the few ranches in Alaska. He and his wife, Cyndi, have lived off the land. Hobo's been around enough to benefit from countless rings of the bell in the bar. When the bartender rings the bell, someone who has just come in with a large load of king crab or halibut or returned from a month in the oil fields of the North Slope is buying a round. He's an antique-book collector; he is a student of comparative religion.

As soon as Hobo tuned his guitar, the audience would begin making requests. Hobo always looked for Julianne or Luke right away, knowing they would have to leave. Julianne requested "The Iditarod Song." The whole bar would stop what they were doing and sing along to Hobo's Alaskan classics. In the best sense of the word, being at a Hobo performance was like being at a far-out adult summer camp. Most people in Alaska don't seem to worry about being hip; if it's genuinely good, that's enough.

I watched Julianne as she sang every word along with Hobo:

> *Well, way up in Alaska, the state that stands alone*
> *There's a dog race run from Anchorage into Nome*
> *And it's a grueling race*
> *With a lightning pace*
> *Where the chilly winds do wail*
> *Beneath the northern lights*
> *Across the snow and the ice*
> *And it's called the Iditarod Trail.*

College students, couples, people covered with eagle tattoos, boat captains, white-haired folks—we were all singing, waiting especially for the chorus. Mike and Linda Sipes were here tonight too. They remembered when Hobo wrote this famous song.

"Dad," Luke said, hitting my arm, "here comes the chorus."

The noise of the bar's many conversations died down and the people switched to singing the chorus:

> *I did, I did*
> *I did the Iditarod Trail.*

After the kids had their sodas and a few Hobo songs, I ran them back to our apartment. When I returned, Hobo was doing Dylan's "Forever Young." Then he performed some German drinking songs that were sing-alongs. Hobo played a song he wrote for his wife, Cyndi, called "Backwoods Girl." He yodeled. If people had told me pre-Hobo that I would like yodeling, I would have told them they were nuts. Hobo's so original, he's just right for Alaska, and that's why we love him.

I would make my request before he got the place in high gear. His job is to get the place rowdy, good rowdy, and keep it that way. My request was too reflective for later in the night when everyone would be howling and dancing and spinning their partner. I always asked for his song "Wild and Free." Since I want my funeral to be a party, I have asked Hobo to play this song at my funeral:

There's a part of me
Wild and free
In my heart there's a wild wolf howling through the tall pine tree
It's a long cold trail that I've been on
Just doesn't seem to be an end to this way I've been going
I can see that road spreading over the land
I see a young boy standing with a suitcase in his hand
It was long ago the boy was me
I was running like a wolf in the mountains
Wild and free
I've got in my mind that it must have been the times
That made me to wander away
From a family that I love
And a warm roof above
But everyone else around does say
It's just me
Being wild and free.

Hobo is an outstanding guitar picker, in any style. People would yell out Hendrix, and he'd switch instantly into "Purple Haze." He always plays an acoustic guitar. Many of his songs were bluegrass style, but he could do chording like Dylan. He'd play his guitar Mississippi blues slide-style using an empty beer bottle. And he doesn't need sheet music or lyrics.

After a couple hours he'd start playing songs that would infuriate the politically correct among us, and most everyone would sing along. Fortunately there aren't generally many PC folks in Hobo's audiences. One, by an Irish songwriter friend of his, is called "Deform Farm." It's based on "Old McDonald Had a Farm," except animals on this farm have been experimented on by the CIA. The characters in this song are a snake with a lisp, a narcoleptic pig (Hobo snores), a dyslexic sheep that says "ab, ab," and a Tourette's syndrome chicken that says things a chicken shouldn't say. Hobo introduces this song and suggests that any hypersensitive folk or members of one of the two PETA organizations in Alaska may want to leave. Alaska has two PETAs, one Hobo belongs to and one he doesn't. There are People for the Ethical Treatment of Animals and People Who Eat Tasty Animals.

A dentist from Soldotna and his wife, Dan and Reean Pitts, came in and surprised Hobo. They sat with us. Over the years they've heard him hundreds of times. It's not that Alaska is short on entertainers, it's that Hobo is that entertaining. From night to night, performance to performance, you never know what he will say. Sometimes this is related to the number of drinks admirers send up to Hobo. Normally he just sips on a white wine. But his fans know if they send him shots of tequila or Matoxa, he might be more likely to leap onto their table, play standing on one foot, or invite people to come and sing with him, one of his songs or one of their own. One time after too many shots of Cuervo Gold, he even let his good friend Ben Ellis, the guy who had introduced me to Seward, get up onstage and do his Dylan interpretation. People who were coming into the Yukon Bar that night when Ben was "singing" said they saw flocks of seagulls and ravens leaving downtown Seward.

Usually bunches of young cannery workers come to wherever Hobo's playing on the coast. They are sunburned white kids with dreadlocks, almost preppy-looking college students, or people who could have come to Alaska because they're running from the law or something else. When Hobo launches into a particular song, they throw their fists in the air and howl in understanding. Every time I was at the Yukon after this song, some guy brought Hobo a fresh pack of salmon roe, one of Hobo's favorite foods.

> *My name doesn't matter*
> *There are many like me*
> *Who come up here to work in the old cannery*
> *Packing fish in the summer*
> *Then we leave in the fall*
> *Then we're done with the cannery call*
> *And we're done with the cannery call.*

Hobo's a wise enough performer not to close with one of his most passionately delivered songs, one of Woody Guthrie's. Until I heard Hobo's version, with commentary before and during the verses, I'd never thought of this song as revolutionary.

But when Hobo would start singing that "this land is your land, this land is my land," mentioning for non-Alaskans in the audience that only 1 percent of Alaska is privately owned, the place would erupt. There is some serious concern and even developing anger over the way Alaskans see the federal government clamping down on their land and our land. Hobo's song points that out. He is the rare entertainer who is willing to challenge his audience, even make them uncomfortable.

Hobo does a couple songs after "This Land Is Your Land" for pure entertainment. Maybe "Gloria" or a cowboy song with the sing-along chorus "Yippee yi a, yippee yi o, ghost riders in the sky." If the audience didn't sing loud enough, he'd wonder aloud if this was a convention of accountants. He'd chide the people and tell them they were just a bunch of yuppies. Usually by now there are three Seward guys in the bar wearing realistic-looking rotted teeth, tie-dyed, fake Afro wigs on their heads, skintight cowboy jeans, and cowboy boots. Hobo instantly shifts into Willie Nelson's "Mama Don't Let Your Babies Grow Up to Be Cowboys" when they appear. These three guys head onto the dance floor and do some kind of cowboy-style buck dancing. When one begins to sing along, Hobo segues perfectly to the *Beverly Hillbillies* theme about a poor boy named Jed. The bar bursts into applause. As the Afro-wigged guys dance, Hobo, playing the *Beverly Hillbillies* theme instrumentally, then says, "You know, you look like a cross between Jed Clampett and Jimi Hendrix." Then some Tennesseans scream they want "Rocky Top"; tonight Aaron requested it. After "Rocky Top," Hobo segues into a meticulous version of the *Deliverance* theme song.

After these hysterics Hobo gets all of us to sing Bob Dylan's "Knocking on Heaven's Door" and masterfully slows the place down. People slow-dance, including Rita and me. The bell goes off—it was actually rung by the owner. The whole place gets a free drink. To end the night, Hobo does "Hava Nagila." Tonight Hobo had given an Israeli hitchhiker a ride into town and brought him along, and he jumped up and danced alone.

In many ways, this night with Hobo illustrates Alaska. Songs about mushers were sung by children in a bar, songs about cannery workers were sung by cannery workers with dreadlocks, songs about a Native shaman were sung by a native shaman; songs were sung by some of the most handsome guys in town wearing fake rotten teeth and tie-dyed Afros making fun of themselves. There was Bach and Bob Dylan and Woody Guthrie, "Mustang Sally" and songs about gold miners and the Alaska railroad. The federal government was trashed, the whole place yodeled. Hobo did some Hank Sr., some Johnny Cash, a song about a Spanish stallion, and my favorite, "Wild and Free." I never knew there was so much of both left in the world until I got to Alaska. Thanks, Hobo.

20

XtraTuf

After spending her spring break in Deering, Rebekah was ready to take off on her own, create her own spot in a universe where people are the planets. She wanted to spend the summer in Alaska. A couple months ago, I'd gone to Kodiak Island, stayed with my friends Captain Jimmy and Joy Ng at the Coast Guard base there. I'd lectured a couple times at Kodiak College for Professor Leslie Fields. Leslie had mentioned something to me about trying to find someone to help her with her children and the house this summer out on their island. She and her husband, Duncan, a lawyer specializing in fishing issues, and his extended family are set-net salmon fishermen. I told her that Rebekah had worked with children, as a nanny and at a day-care center. I mentioned she had been to Deering for spring break; that kind of thing impresses Alaskans. I gave Leslie Rebekah's number in Tennessee. She called Rebekah, and they hit if off over the phone.

Now, today, I was driving her to Anchorage so she could catch her flight to Kodiak Island to spend the summer working for them. I hugged her, she hugged me, I told her I loved her, she told me she loved me, and we both knew that to be so. I remember thinking as I walked back to the car that being a parent is tough in so many ways; you never really want to leave your child but you must. Sometimes you must even encourage the leaving.

FROM REBEKAH

July 18: One thing has been accomplished thanks to my travels in Alaska: I have over-come my fatalistic fear of flying. I'm even at the point now where the smaller the plane, the better. The more creaks and grunts it makes, the better. Flying has now turned into an adventure. It certainly was adventurous when, sitting next to a cigar-smelling fat man, a sports fisherman up from Florida gator country, I flew over Kodiak Island in a small, old nine-passenger plane. The destination was Larsen Bay, a scarcely populated, much talked about cannery town in bush Alaska. From there, my southern-flying buddy was headed out to a remote lodge where he would spend his days catching some of the finest salmon in the world. I was headed to Harvester Island and the Fields family.

Riding in the plane, on this mellow northern July day, I could barely breathe. The things I saw, the majesty! Everything I could see was a brilliant green, and the water-falls, there were so many. The rivers—oh, how they curved as if they were made for me. As we were forcing our way through the tumultuous, rocky air, I thought, this is it. This is the most beautiful place I've ever been. Yes, there's rain, as you might have heard, but it only adds to what this place is. There are mountains with snow, mountains without. Some are a fresh and water-fed green, a luscious, luscious green. Some are bare and a grayish brown, only with slanted rock. Some are hidden, some are small. And of course, there's the water, everywhere I look, surrounding me.

As I climbed out of the toy plane in Larsen Bay, I looked around trying to discern who Leslie or Duncan Fields might be. My dad had told me that Leslie was a petite woman with short dark hair and that she had an intense, dramatic look to her. Looking under one of the plane's wings, I found her, not far off my father's description. She was walking toward me in a long, red raincoat and she was wearing makeup, a surprise to me. I hadn't expected an Alaskan bush woman and mother of four to be wearing blush and lipstick, to look so pretty.

"Leslie?" I asked.

"Yes. Rebekah? I thought you would have darker hair."

"Yeah, it's got some color on it."

I liked her immediately. I turned to my bags, and together we carried them over to what looked like a broken-down, abandoned pickup truck. Except it couldn't be because there were kids in its bed and more climbing up. All of their eyes were on me, checking me out trying to see if their new nanny was cool, if I was the kind of nanny who would sneak chocolate to them when Mom and Dad weren't around. Duncan, Leslie's husband and the father of all these bush-eyed children, was looking through a large, blue dry-bag sorting out letters and packages, their mail.

"Rebekah, it's good to have you here." That was all he said, but it was enough to make me feel welcome. In a sweet, gentle voice I introduced myself to the children.

Duncan and Leslie Fields on U'yak Bay. Photo by Rebekah Jenkins

"Hi. I'm Rebekah." *I looked toward the oldest-looking boy, who had blond hair and big, pleasing eyes. "What's your name?"*

"Noah."

Another, younger boy standing beside him said he was Elisha. He was little and cute and brown-haired.

I asked another child, "And your name?"

"I'm Naphtali."

She was the oldest and the only girl, the queen with a capital Q. She had beautiful amber-green eyes and olive skin with long limbs and sandy blond hair.

I thought to myself, how am I ever going to be able to pronounce that name? I must think of something else to call her, or only talk to her so I didn't have to call her by name.

I looked into the remaining child's eyes. He'd stood there all the while behind the others and stared, sizing me up.

"And what's your name?"

He stared at me bashfully and in a quiet, almost voiceless sound said, "Isaac."

So there we were, all together, in the back of this worn, golden-colored pickup headed for who knows where. We stopped only minutes down the gravel road and parked next to the strangest-looking vehicle I have ever seen, a yellow-and-black-tiger-striped, two-door whatever. I wondered what kind of place I was in. Out of the ol' pickup truck we all climbed. I was only following everyone else. I had no idea what was going on. Leslie appeared from the cab of the truck and spoke to me while un-loading all-different-size bags and duct-taped boxes.

"We're not going straight to Harvester Island. There's this picnic every summer for all of us who fish out of Larsen Bay. So that's where we're headed, as soon as we get the skiff loaded up. We should be there several hours. It's a rain-or-shine kind of thing. Oh, do you have any other shoes?"

I was in flip-flops, which are definitely not the right kind of footwear for bush Alaska.

"I've got these!"

I fished around in my bag for my standard brown XtraTuf rain boots that Dad had bought me in Seward. Leslie watched me curiously, not knowing what I was looking for.

"Those will be perfect! They'll be great for fishing," she said.

It sounded good to me. I was ready with my knee-high plastic boots, waiting to be shown what this fishing family's life was about. We loaded the aluminum skiff that was anchored down past the wooden sidewalk between the one store that the people of Larsen Bay have to shop in and the red-roofed buildings of the cannery.

I hadn't really noticed much due to all of the excitement in the fifteen minutes since my arrival. As we were walking over the rocks to the water and the anchored skiff and up onto the wooden boardwalk of Larsen Bay, I did begin to notice some things. A lot of young people my age were walking around in bright orange rain/fishing gear. Some were talking on the few pay phones. Some were sitting on the benches in front of the old buildings and windows of the Larsen Bay boardwalk. I assumed they were mostly college kids up for the summer to work. I assumed that they were somewhat like me— that, thanks to good fortune, they had ventured to the wilds of Alaska to find something.

And then there I was at the annual Larsen Bay picnic in the midst of real live fish-ermen and fisherwomen. Everywhere I turned were young men with beards. Otis Redding was playing on a small CD player. All the young men were congregated around it. It was still raining, but no one cared or even seemed to notice. Instead, everyone was standing in the food line clothed in bright orange and yellow or lime green, talking to fellow rough and tough fishing friends. Leslie and Duncan were who knows where. At first I immediately latched on to the kids, Naphtali especially. I asked her who these people were and what usually happened at this sort of gathering. She didn't have too many answers. She was more interested in playing with her friends and her cousin Rachel, who lived right across Uyak Bay on the mainland of Kodiak, about seven hundred or so yards from Harvester Island.

Eventually, I made myself talk to the men and women who were holding the babies, because babies are one thing I know. All the bearded, attractive, weathered, and wet *young men were a different story. I've got no brave heart there. Nope, I stuck with the babies. I googled and goggled with them and more than occasionally snuck a glance in Otis's direction. Overall I liked being there, although I felt both at home and lost at sea in this crowded, colorful land of XtraTuf Alaskans.*

Before I knew it, we were headed out the bay to their island where I would live. I put on some borrowed bright orange overalls and was thrown and bumped around by the waves and slapped by the wind, all the while feeling the hard raindrops freckle my traveling face. Harvester Island is a 380-acre island that rises up from the fin-whale-populated waters of Uyak Bay. It is covered with raspberries and simple meadow flowers (later I would come to pick them so that we could look at something pretty at mealtime). There are horses, one named Rocket, the other named Winddancer. They have been brought out for the summer so the Fields children can learn how to ride. Duncan had to ship the horses out to the island by boat. There are trees with eagles nesting, a white-planked house that sits a hundred upward yards from my new abode, the dock house that Leslie and Duncan built over twenty years ago when they first made Harvester their summer and fishing home. They are the only houses on the island.

One of the first books I read on Harvester Island was a small book of Leslie's poems. She is a writer like I want to be. I often sat on the dock and read her words.

MONDAYS ON THIS ISLAND
by Leslie Leyland Fields

Mondays on this island are like any other day or hour.
Choose the century.
It could all be the same scatter of gravel on the beach,
The same shatter of the sea into foam,
The hiss as it gathers for the next.
The summer sun is no clock
And the birds only hint at the seasons,
Their flights mostly circular,
Following the currents that move in giant spirals
Arcing from this shore into the gulf and back again, again,
Neither hot nor cold, only temperate, moderate,
The climate of any island, at any time.
I am told the grass here is brown in winter,
That the darkness settles like a bear against the sun,

The mountains sink white into sleep.
Summers they say are brilliant.
The mountains burn and always the sun, the sun.
I have not seen this.

Right across Uyak Bay, I can see boys, lots of bearded boys who look like they are straight off the cover of GQ. They are young and stout and from all across North America. They are the crew members. They work for the Fieldses and reside all summer on Bear Island, the ten-acre candy store of an island just two miles beyond my boatless reach.

And, oh, the family, the Fieldses, these people I have come to know so quickly. Right away they became family to me. I have come to serve them, to be their nanny/cook/maid/friend/daughter. I have come to learn this island kind of life.

I love this poem of Leslie's about my girlfriend Naphtali, their daughter:

BEFORE LEARNING TO COUNT
(For Naphtali, Age 3)

You were out till midnight last week
fishing with your father and me.
It is the herring you remember most—
tiny thing, caught among the salmon,
dead, but in your small hands
as you held them to the sun
shining back his emerald and opal prisms
to the sun,
he was almost
swimming again.
When you were done,
you set him down among the salmon
in the bin, petted him good sleep.
Later, at the tender, you did not see us sort
and toss the worthless over.

Soon you will have a job—
bailing and cleaning kelp from the boat.
After that, you will get the white cotton gloves,

children's small, to hold and hook the net
while others pick fish and count. Then you
will pick and count fish and
count 6 days till closure,
7 nets left to mend,
823 pinks from net #5
60 seconds before noon on opening day
3 hours of sleep lost last night
4 nets still to pick in the dark. . . .

Ten years from now, if I hand you a herring,
you will instantly know its weight,
what the canneries are paying per ton
that year, and you will remember, as you toss it over—
this one doesn't count.

This place, all of it, with its indifference and perfect photography light, shall be good for me, the timid loner in me. I plan to write for two hours a day. Not so much to ask from a girl like me, who fears the sitting, the silence, and what writing brings. But I will play that deep hide-and-seek game of the mind to come up with the words that I need to help me detail and describe what I see.

July 25: I've been on Harvester a week, or has it been a year? A lot of jumping on the trampoline today. The kids and I made up Olympic routines. I think we're making up for the fact that we can't actually watch the Olympics, since there is no TV on the island. We went on a picnic for lunch. Leslie and I talked about the things women talk about in the kitchen while we prepared dinner. We had a family prayer. The sun shone, the wind blew. I talked too much. I washed dishes; I gathered rainwater from the trash cans that are set out to collect it down on the porch, then put it on the gas stove to heat it. I go through that whole process every day just to wash the dishes. I listened to Andrea Bocelli. I took a picture of the sun as it faded away around 10:45 P.M. I thought about the GQ boys and my new friend Tammy, Leslie's niece, who are all on Bear Island, and what they might be doing. And now I'm back in my blue and yellow Kelty tent that I put up on the third day I was here. I decided that I didn't like the dock house. Too creepy. I'd rather be in a tent anyway.

It's late now, around midnight, and Naphtali is here in the tent with me devouring one of her books by flashlight. *She reads a book a day. I have never met anyone like her. I remember the first full day I spent around her and I was stunned at her vocabulary. She was using words that even people my age don't use. She is twelve but sometimes I swear she is much older than I am.*

Across the bay I can hear the crew's voices, their laughter. They're having a cookout at Uncle Wallace's, Duncan's brother. Wallace has a shower, a real toilet, and a washer and dryer, the only washer and dryer working around here because of a drought. The crew is there doing laundry. I don't feel that I am missing out. I am just enjoying living this island life and acting like a kid again. There is so much kid in me. I am enjoying chasing the kids and not having to pretend that I am something I am not. Naphtali and I did take a banya last night. A banya is a sauna fired by wood. Ooh, was it ever wonderful. There has been a water shortage so bathing has been very limited. We're taking a banya only once every seven days. I got to wash my hair and pour hot water all over my body. I didn't even care that the water was bug-infested. I was only interested in being any kind of cleaner than what I was when I first went into the banya. I enjoyed every second.

I am tired from the day and tired from rehashing it and want to dream. All this dishwashing and landscape and energy overwhelm me at the end of the day. One more note: the kids don't call me Rebekah. They've decided to call me Leaf. I have always wanted another name. I like Leaf. I think I'll keep it when I fly back down south.

July 30: Dad's coming in two days for a weeklong visit. Duncan took all the children down to Bear Island today for the afternoon because fishing is closed. So Leslie and I were left to our tiredness and sisterhood. We talked and talked of many plunging things; of dependence and why women bond and how dangerous friendship can be between women because a woman can stop relying on her spouse to meet her emotional needs and come to depend solely on her female friend. I've seen this in my relationship with my mother. We fight the same wars, we women, and I think as time moves on the island, Leslie and I will armor up together as well and become sisters too. It is nice to be with Leslie, for she knows me even when I do not have the words to show who I am or what I mean. We are a lot alike. We both write poetry. We both are sensitive, even to the smallest of life's things. And we both are warriors.

I will never forget it. Duncan and I were almost to Harvester Island, and there was my daughter, standing there with everyone else, waving hello. I felt like crying but I didn't. I was coming to her world. The moment I got off the boat,

The Fields's children stage their own Olympics on Harvester Island. Photo by Rebekah Jenkins

Rebekah and all the kids came down wanting to show me everything on the island that they loved: the eagle's nest in a tiny, wind-smashed tree; their two horses; the place where her tent was—one horse had apparently knocked it down, thinking the tent was in its territory. I saw the dock house where Duncan and Leslie had lived before they built a house themselves. Their house reminded me of that house in the Andrew Wyeth painting *Christina's World,* with the young woman sitting in the field looking up at it. I saw the area out in the bay where they'd been seeing all the fin whales spouting, and I noticed the clarity of the ocean. I was shown the banya, the house, the kitchen where Rebekah did the dishes, the trampoline, and the books the kids were reading. I could easily see that Rebekah had become part of this family; what a beautiful thing to watch her as she so elegantly moved in this universe. I felt thankful that she was allowing me to see a bit of it.

Right before I left, Rebekah and I and the kids walked to the top of the island; it reminded me of a small green volcano in shape. It was a tough walk, but it seemed that from the top we could see the whole world, together and separately.

21

Unalakleet

You better have a fantastic sense of humor if you live *out* in Alaska. The farther *out* you are, the more laughter you need. That three-day storm just met the new three-day storm, your flight's canceled for a few days. The bears pulled your net out of the river and ate everything in it. You can't find your way back to the village from Bethel. The snowbank now covers your house. The king salmon barely showed up in the river. Smile, life is good. The farther out in Alaska I got, the more smiling, joking people I seemed to run into. This was especially true in Unalakleet, Alaska, on Norton Sound on Alaska's western coast.

Probably the whining, super-uptight types died off long ago, when life was so much tougher. Not long after Christ died, a Roman orator said, "Many who seem to be struggling with adversity are happy; many, amid great affluence, are utterly miserable."

A friend of mine from Nome introduced me to Boyuk Ryan, who lives in Unalakleet and is mostly Eskimo, $^{13}/_{16}$, to be exact. He has the dancing eyes of the Eskimo, and he is always ready to deliver a story. One morning he was sitting in the backseat of an eight-seater plane, the kind that takes people and freight from village to village all over Alaska. The plane was full; a few people were on their way back from Anchorage and were loaded down. There was a delay, could have been a hundred reasons. Most of the passengers were relaxed and waiting for the pilot in silence, but a few, well, maybe they'd had a bit too much fun in Anchorage, they began to complain. "Where is the pilot?" they said. Ten minutes later they regressed to "Where is the pilot, why are they always late?"

Then one said, "If I knew how to fly this stupid plane, I'd do it." Boyuk, who is as relaxed as he is intensely energetic, got an idea. He got up from his seat in the rear, squeezed his way into the pilot's seat, and said, "I've flown on this plane enough times, I've watched these pilots—I think I can fly this thing."

He reached above his head and flicked some switches. He turned on motor No. 1, then motor No. 2. He wore old jeans and jogging shoes. At this point, the complainers spoke up. "What are you doing, man?"

"I'm going to fly us to the village. I think I can do it," Boyuk said, sure of himself.

"No, please, we'll wait, okay?" said a few of the now worried passengers.

"That's okay, I believe if I just push down one more switch and pull on something, we can go. We'll fix 'em!" Boyuk fumbled around on the panel.

At this point one woman and one man, not Native, got quite excited. They pleaded with him not to do it. Boyuk moved the plane forward just a bit, then informed them that he truly was their pilot and the freight they'd been waiting for was now ready to load. When I first began flying in Alaska, the experience that would become so casual was an adventure in itself, having to tell how much I weigh, flying through and over outrageous countryside. Now being in Unalakleet was nothing out of the ordinary, and Alaska itself was more like home to me.

During the Iditarod while I was following Jeff King, I'd stayed a few days in Unalakleet (pop. 798). It is close to Nome and the finish line, but still distant enough that the race is far from over. It is the first village the racers hit on the frozen Bering Sea, a place that can be brutalized by roaring storms coming from Russia or even farther west. Jeff said it was one of his favorite places in all of Alaska, that the people were open, friendly, caring. As usual Jeff was right.

When I first visited Unalakleet, it was March; normally I think of March as spring. In Tennessee the earth begins to seduce you again with its warmth. Little hints of green replace the brown and gold of the dead pasture. In Unalakleet, March is still raging winter. I recall sitting in a log cabin lodge at the edge of town drinking a coffee at Browns, the only place to get breakfast. I've never heard the winds howl and moan and whistle and roar as they did in this village. Man-made objects creak and shutter and rattle and flap. Across several snowbanks, I could see the top of a tiny wooden building, painted an odd green, that housed the post office. Walking by, you might not be able to see it because the wild winds filled with snow and ice crystals hid the building, but you'd know it was nearby because the American flag in front flapped so loudly. In front of the post office was a snowdrift so high it was almost up to the peak of the roof.

When you're in an Eskimo village like Unalakleet in the winter, you could curse the founding families for choosing this wind-whipped location. But now that Rebekah and I were here in the summer, we blessed their names, whoever they were, and understood how wise they were in settling Unalakleet, Deering, Kotzebue, Barrow, and Shishmaref, and hundreds of other villages. Just try leaving the strong breezes of the coastline in these communities in the summer, however short summers are, and you will know why even the caribou climb high into the mountains trying to stand on the remaining snowfields, why they go out on the remaining ocean ice, why they practically go insane.

I'd been warned about the mosquitoes around here. It's only the females that suck your blood, but there were so many inland around Unalakleet that I think I could go crazy staying too long with them in the bush with no way out. Several hard-core Alaskans, not Native, told me the mosquitoes were put here by God to keep people out of these parts of Alaska. The short summer season of the bloodsuckers and the flesh-biting gnats is another reason we were here now, in June. One of the two incredible women I'd met in Unalakleet this winter would be around the village now, both to avoid the bugs and because the king salmon were coming into the river soon and it would be time to make smoked salmon strips.

As I contemplated the women I'd met in Alaska, I thought of two I wanted Rebekah to meet, women I would hold up to anyone looking for a role model. When you're a parent, you give a lot of thought to whom your children hang out with, whom you'd like your children to meet. Both of these women lived in Unalakleet; one I met at the post office while mailing a postcard to Jed and Luke, one I'd met after I attended a basketball game between Unalakleet and Point Hope. One was Eleanor Sarren, postmaster of Unalakleet, and the other was Eva Ryan, Boyuk Ryan's mother. Both were descendants of old blue-blooded North American families, respected families, families full of highly intelligent, accomplished people. One family has been in North America for hundreds and hundreds, maybe thousands, of years. One has only been around a few hundred, but in North America if you're smart and well educated, you can go places quickly.

Both families are filled with high achievers. There are professional airline pilots, archaeologists, world-class authorities on whaling and maritime artifacts. They have won numerous awards and been on the cover of national magazines. The mother of Eleanor, the postmaster, graduated from Vassar and was on the cover of *Glamour* in 1941. Inside, it read, "Dorothy Shapard, New Orleans debutante, has brown-gold hair, complexion fair as the moon—her beauty secret is a quick cleaning with Woodbury Soap before a date . . . her date book proves it." One of Eva's sons went to medical school and is a leading orthopedic surgeon in Anchorage. Her daughter graduated from Wheaton College and is a health aide in Unalakleet. Her sons and son-in-law are some of the top commercial pilots in Alaska. Eva herself won one of the top awards given to a person in Alaska, the Hunter and Fisher Award, given each year by the Alaska Federation of Natives. Eleanor's father was educated at Andover, Harvard, and UC Berkeley, and he founded Plimoth Plantation. He was a pioneer in the field of historical archaeology. He dreamed of celebrating "the legacy the Pilgrims gave to America, including their relationship with the native peoples who helped them survive the hardships of the rugged New England Coast." Today at Plymouth Rock in Plymouth, Massachusetts, there are not many Native Americans left, if any. In Unalakleet, there are about eight hundred and just a few whites. Most of the whites work for the Eskimo people as teachers or, like Eleanor, as a civil servant.

If you had to ask the Native people of Alaska—say Albert and Walter Kookesh of Angoon in southeast Alaska; or Jerry Riley, Athabascan of Nenana; or Bill Thomas, a Tlingit from Haines; or Eva Ryan, an Inupiat from Unalakleet; or Max Malvansky, an Aleut from St. George in the Pribilofs; or Tina, her sister Jody, and her boyfriend Tony from Hydaburg on Prince of Wales Island; or Oliver and Annie Leavitt from Barrow—what is the most essential thing that must be protected to save their way of life, they would probably say subsistence. That is, their ability to be able to subsist on what they draw from nature, the ocean, the lake, the river, the tundra, the mountains, the valleys, the ice, the edge of the land-fast ice.

They know what Eleanor's father knew. The Native people lost their way of life back in Massachusetts. Now artifacts in museums and actors portray what was once their world. They appreciate all Eleanor does to serve them, to sort and send their mail, to bring in what they want from the outside world. Eleanor has even married one of them. And that's why Eva Ryan is so proud of her Hunter and Fisher Award, even though she's too shy and humble to have gone and gotten it in Anchorage when the award was given at the annual Alaska Federation of Natives (AFN) convention. They mailed it to Unalakleet. It does hang on her wall, though, surrounded by the pictures of her many grandchildren, young people who spend much time with her, who look at her as their hero.

Rebekah and I called Eva when we arrived; she was busy collecting driftwood with her four-wheeler, the SUV of Unalakleet. She goes to the beach when tides are right and collects driftwood to cut up with her chain saw into manageable pieces to stack for winter. Winter is never not on your mind in Unalakleet. All the hunting and gathering that goes on in the summer is to prepare for winter.

We called back that afternoon. Eva invited us to come by. She lives behind her son Boyuk and his wife, Vicky, who is originally from Ohio. Inside and out, Eva's house was neat and spare. I noticed some brightly colored knitted afghans on the two sofas. She asked us to sit down and complimented Rebekah's hair. Her voice is strong, filled with a radiant warmth. Her laugh made me feel that I could do anything. She told us about this award that she had been so surprised to get.

"My friend called me up one day," she said, "and asked me if I read the AFN newsletter. I said no." The way she said *no*, it was as if the word had sunshine on it.

"She said, you're nominated for Hunter and Fisher of the Year. Oh, no, I said, now everyone's going to find out I hunt and fish all the time." I wasn't sure how Rebekah would respond to this talk of hunting and fishing, not really her kind of thing.

Eva won the award in 1998, the first year it was given. The award was statewide; there were several nominees, mostly men. Eva forgot about the nomination after a while, but then when they told her she had won, several tried to get her to go to Anchorage to accept it in person. With as many planes as her son and sons-in-law own, I'm sure they could have flown her there. But she said there was no way she was going to stand in front of all those people. This is why Eva spends so much time in nature—she loves it much more than cities or towns.

"When the weather's nice, my daughter calls me up and asks me, 'What kind of mischief are you getting into today, Mom?'" After almost every sentence Eva laughed her all-over, feel-good laugh. It should be recorded and played for sad or sick people all day long. Already Rebekah was smiling.

"The reason she calls is because I never stay home. All the guys in this village that hunt have been real nice to me. A lot of times I'm the only lady that goes with them," Eva said, and laughed.

"Are you a pretty good shot?" I asked.

"Yeah, I think I am. I keep up with the guys." She laughed again loudly. She explained she uses a .257 or a .270. For moose she uses a .270, but these days, now that her grandsons are old enough, she lets them hunt for the family. One of her grandsons, Donald, whom I recognized from the basketball game I'd been to this winter, came over. He said he was hungry and Eva told him to raid the fridge. She mentioned that Donald always seemed to be around when someone needed help. At his young age, in fact, he'd already saved a few lives and even found someone dead.

Eva explained that she'd started hunting after she got married. Now her two sons-in-law call her and invite her to go with them. They each take their own snow machine way out north past Shaktoolik to around Koyuk, ninety miles or more each way.

"One day my son-in-law said he was going out to hunt caribou. Then it got stormy, started blowing. We split up. He went over this hill and I went another way. I thought I took all my bullets with me. Then I got to a herd of caribou and shot one. I ran up to my snow machine to get my shell bag, there was nothing. Now it was beginning to blow and snow hard. I had to hurry and butcher this caribou I'd shot." The warmth of Eva's voice made the room feel small and cozy. Rebekah was now completely focused on Eva's story; I was somewhat surprised she was so tuned in.

"I was in a hurry to get the caribou meat and get back before the storm got too bad. Then this big bull caribou came and stood in front of my snow machine and was shaking its head at it like it was gong to attack it. I had no bullets, no ax. I was afraid it would attack my snow machine. So I snuck over and started it, hoping that would scare it away. Nothing." Eva smiled; she is a powerful and confident woman. She was many miles from Unalakleet and a bad blizzard was blowing up a head of courage.

"My son-in-law, I had no idea where he was. I was afraid that thing could attack my snow machine and break it. I'd be stuck out there. So—"

"Eva," Rebekah asked, "how far were you from shelter?"

"I don't know, far, but it was losing visibility, too." Eva is maybe five foot five; her hands and face are wide. She is magnetic, the kind of person people wanted to be around, no matter what your age. Even her "with it" grandchildren wanted to be with her as much as they could.

"It started blizzarding. I had this homemade ice chisel. The chisel, it is a big piece of iron. You use it to make a fish hole in the ice. So I revved up my snow machine and it just shook its antlers at the lights. The whole time it was just a few feet from me. I was scared it might come at me.

"I was getting to be a nervous wreck. I knew if I started to move, it would probably charge me, so I went behind it and I had the chisel. I snuck up, it was just watching my snow machine. I clubbed it as hard as I could on the head. Then it dropped and I hit it some more. That was the only way I could get rid of it.

"I never get nervous when I'm out hunting but . . . I had to then butcher both of them. I don't know what was the matter with that caribou. From then on, I never leave without bullets in my pocket. When I got back to camp, I told my son-in-law what happened. He had never heard of a caribou doing that before." Eva was fifteen miles from camp when she got the caribous butchered and packed.

"You know, I am very stubborn and I really don't like to talk much; now I can't stop talking."

Rebekah nodded in agreement. I wasn't quite sure what Rebekah was thinking now. Even though she's my daughter, she is often a mystery to me. There was a knock on the door—it was Boyuk.

"You still talking to Mom?" he asked. "Wow."

"Okay," she said, "that's enough talking."

The three of us walked out together. Eva said she needed to get her racks, where she hung the king salmon strips, cleaned and ready. A front-end loader towed a huge aluminum boat on a trailer past us, filling up the road. It had been used for the herring season that was just ending. We said good-bye to Boyuk and began walking in the dusty dirt road into town. A few four-wheelers passed us as we walked. Rebekah was quiet for a few blocks, then spoke up just as we'd reached the store.

"Dad?"

"Yeah."

"You know that commercial, 'I want to be like Mike'?"

"Yes, I do. Michael Jordan, right?"

"Well, I want to be like Eva."

"Really? Well, me, too."

Eva Ryan at home in Unalakleet. PHOTO BY PETER JENKINS

We walked a couple more minutes to the post office. Eleanor had said she'd be done with work about now. A beautiful Native woman in her midtwenties who cut people's hair stood at the counter, holding a round-faced baby who was about seven months old. Eleanor was cuddling him, asking her how was he getting so big, was he eating strips yet? In the interior they call this smoked and dried salmon "squaw candy." Eleanor weighed the little boy on the electronic scale. The three others in line also wanted to hold him, give him a kiss. Everyone was talking about when the king salmon would arrive in the river. Normally it's here by now. Based on U.S. government regulations, the post office should have been closed, but Eleanor had long ago converted much of her life to Eskimo time. It is one of many reasons why she has been so accepted in Unalakleet.

Eleanor Hornblower came here just for a visit in 1979. She grew up around Boston. She was educated in private schools to prepare her to become a leader in established society. She remembers being a brown-haired, bright-eyed girl; in maybe third or fourth grade, someone at school had her stand in front of a back-lit screen. She thinks a photo was made, but the idea was to analyze her posture. It was essential to hold yourself erect, chest up, chin up, nose tilted. She remembered being taught that what showed on the outside of you, your family, and your house were what mattered.

Her mother, as bright and beautiful as a woman could be, grew up in New Orleans. In 1937, at Sophie Newcomb College, which is now part of Tulane, she was spotted by someone scouting for David O. Selznick, who was doing a movie called *Gone With the Wind*. They wanted her to be one of Scarlett's sisters. She chose to go to Vassar instead, to lose her Southern accent. Eleanor's parents split up; her mother became involved with a well-known Italian French-horn player in the Boston Symphony.

Her mother had been on the cover of national magazines, but Eleanor was interested in being a photographer, not in being photographed. When it came time for Eleanor's debutante ball, as she made her formal entrance into society, she could not take her boyfriend. His family was not in the black book, or the blue book, or whatever color it was—the book that listed which families were acceptable and which were not for a date of Eleanor Hornblower's. Eleanor thought it was absurd; one of her boyfriends' parents taught at MIT. She does remember dancing with her dad, who had encouraged her through his letters to move anywhere her heart and soul took her.

He wrote this letter to his daughter when she was nineteen, about Rebekah's age when we first arrived in Alaska. Eleanor has saved it all these years.

Dear Eleanor,

I find it very difficult to write a definition of an acceptable philosophy of life and equally difficult to be critical of anyone's. It seems to me that philosophy changes with the age of the individual, the objective of the person, the exposure to others and the degree of affluence (or poverty) of the ones involved. The happy people I have known and respected have usually been so engrossed with their work that they have had little time for casual associations. They rarely think in terms of money and because they are able, money flows to them. . . . If there is no objective, no drive to excel, that individual will probably be the unhappy one—he or she has no philosophy of life in which he or she feels strongly about and so will drift until the magic moment comes that motivations sets in. . . . There still remains the problem of getting your birthday present to you since you have not left a forwarding address. Lots of love from me to you,

Dad
24 Apr. 70

She graduated prep school in 1969, the year of Woodstock. It sounds like a long time ago until you mention Woodstock. It was the year I graduated from high school. I could relate to Eleanor in many ways; I had a girlfriend then and I wasn't allowed to be her date for her debutante ball either. A friend of mine, Craig McAllister, and I went to a thrift store, bought a couple sets of tails and some new high-top, black Converse sneakers, and went anyway. Everyone at that chandelier-encrusted ballroom in Manhattan was too polite to throw us out. We got the place jumping.

Eleanor went to college in Wisconsin, where she could major in photography and weaving. After graduation Eleanor became a commercial photographer for a large, multinational corporation located in Waltham, Massachusetts, and stayed in this familiar world for a few years.

Every so often her dad, a stockbroker whose passion was Plimoth Plantation, would write or speak of adventure and inspiration to his daughter, who craved it and wasn't finding it where she was. She looked up to her father. The Reverend Peter Gomes, Plummer Professor of Christian Morals at Harvard University and Minister of Memorial Church, said of her father in the *Proceedings of the Massachusetts Historical Society*, "It was Harry's lavish investment of himself in all its wonderful and generous complexity that was his ultimate gift. In the extraordinary vitality of that institution in Plymouth, known the world over, we can see the life recollected of Henry Hornblower, II." Eleanor read these things about her father, heard him speaking to her, and became determined that she would someday do something with her own life.

Her radical change started when a friend from college sent her a picture from Unalakleet, Alaska. It was of a snowbank that almost covered entire houses. On top of this snowbank you could see a roof, some doghouses, and the face of a lone husky. Eleanor pinned up the picture in her office in Massachusetts, and eventually the picture and her friend's invitation to visit pulled her to Unalakleet. Her friend worked for Head Start and lived in a cabin that was smaller than the pantries in the houses of the people with whom Eleanor had grown up.

When Eleanor got off the plane in Unalakleet—just the trip must have been startling for a young former debutante—no one was around except a tall, "really good-looking" young man. He walked up and said he was her ride. His name was Johnny; her friend was up the frozen Unalakleet River and Johnny was to run her up there on his snow machine. Eleanor was prepared for Massachusetts cold, but it was way below zero here. Soon, on the river, she was frozen. What happened next may be one of the best ways I've ever heard to make an immediate connection with a person. Eleanor's feet felt like blocks of ice, so Johnny, who had brought her to this place he loved, did all he could to warm them: he opened his parka and shirt and put her feet on his strong, angular body. They became a couple not long after that.

Johnny is Johnny Sarren. He has a heart of gold, and his smile is half from the devil and half from God. Housing has always been tight in Unalakleet; just getting materials to build is incredibly expensive and difficult. Johnny and Eleanor first lived in a tent out on the river, then they moved the tent to the spit on the other side of the river's mouth. A wind blew the tent away, including everything inside, such as Eleanor's full set of Nikon cameras and their Coleman stove. Johnny did much of the cooking; he's their son's choice for cook, even now. They finally got a place to live above the Youth Center, which they ran. Eleanor never believed in too much furniture, mainly because it's so hard to come by. She used an open drawer for both her sons' baby beds. She had her family—it was a struggle, but there was much about it she loved.

Eleanor loaded Rebekah and me into a friend's truck for a ride out the road. Up on a hill, looking back, the ocean seemed so large, like space must be to a satellite. The land spread out before us too, the Nulato Hills to the northeast. Eleanor was enraptured when she spoke of the crunch the tundra makes when you walk on it. She collected Hudson Bay tea out here and remembered giving her sons insect nets to collect butterflies and other creatures. They built a cabin out on the river where they could go to escape the village, catch silver salmon. They lived out there for a while, but it became too difficult for Eleanor to snow machine their boys into school every day and back, nine miles each way.

We turned back toward the outskirts of town. This side of town had the new homes, brighter colors, small, double-pane windows. I could see a woman with long black hair walking barefoot down the gravel road, away from us. As we got near her, I thought I heard crying, then a kind of desperate wailing. As we approached her, we had to slow down because she was oblivious to us. There were so few cars on the roads; year-round, most got around Unalakleet on four-wheelers or by walking.

Eleanor knew who she was. Everyone who lived here knew everyone, but Eleanor, as postmaster, *really* knew everyone.

"Oh, she's been drinking," she said.

When the barefoot woman heard us and moved to the side, she clawed at her long black hair, wailed, and cried.

After a minute Eleanor said, "You know, much of what goes on here is seen. Where I grew up, that same things went on, it's just that you didn't see the person walking down the street."

We pulled into a gravel road—all the roads were gravel—near Eva's house where we were planning to meet up with Eva again. I detected the marvelous smell of wood smoke coming from someone's fish house. Eva and her daughter Linda were standing out by their drying racks and smokehouse. By their feet were twenty-one king salmon. They were holding their ulus, curved knives, and there was much work to be done, cutting these kings into strips, hanging them to dry, then smoking some of them. One of Eva's nephews came by, wanting some salmon stomachs, an early-season delicacy. We all watched Eva's masterful cuts with the ulu, perfection with every cut. No wonder one of her sons is an orthopedic surgeon.

Eleanor needed to get home, see about her youngest son, who'd been tubing on the river with his friends in their wet suits. Her older son had already left for California where he was going to college.

"You know, one of the reasons I've stayed here this long, and who knows how long I'll be here, is because life here is so out in the open. I like it better that way." Eleanor hugged both of us and went home. We hung around Eva and Linda for a couple hours until they finished cutting up all the king salmon.

As Rebekah and I walked the hundred feet to the little fishing lodge where we'd rented a room, Rebekah spoke up. She had been quiet but attentive all afternoon, which is her way.

"Dad?"

"Yes, honey."

"I changed my mind. I want to be like Eva *and* Eleanor."

22

Landing on a Roof

I had second thoughts when I saw the mountains in front of us. It was the Alaska Range and we were flying toward it in a plane that seemed about the size of a lawn chair. I'm not much for keeping track of dates and times, but I know exactly what day it was—September 7, 2000, and we'd taken off at 1:08 P.M. It was now somewhere around 1:30 P.M. I'm sure of this because I was in the plane with my father-in-law, Jerry Jorgensen. Jerry keeps exacting lists and records; he's a farmer and must know exactly what day it is. He needs to know how much rain fell in this rain gauge from year to year in the fields by the Kubiaks or the Chamberlains and everywhere else. He must know how many bushels of corn came from each acre, and which variety of corn, was that Pioneer or DeKalb? I didn't know there were so many types in the world. He needs to know precisely how much fertilizer to apply on this field and that one. Since corn sells for about the same money as it did twenty years ago, but nothing else in farming does, it's imperative to be a detail person, to crush every penny, to work every moment, in order to succeed.

The first few miles of this flight was nice, the first few minutes, that is. To begin, Jerry just doesn't like flying. And if he knew where we were going right now—if I did—we might be turning around. In life, sometimes it's better not to know. Then we were over Cook Inlet, though as we looked down, it looked more like an ocean. Flying over, I'd seen white, angelic-looking beluga whales here before. As much as I'd flown in Alaska, I don't know why I was so nervous. So far the sky was clear, the wind moderate. We were headed toward a gigantic mountain range. Maybe it was that this was my last trip before leaving Alaska and I didn't want to test my standing with God or fate or another aircraft engine, even this Cessna 185.

Or my apprehension could have had something to do with being responsible for Jerry. When you picture Jerry and me together, think of the *Odd Couple*. He recently turned seventy, and he's the most precious cargo in the world to my mother-in-law, Dorothy (which is Julianne's middle name), and to my wife and the rest of his six children and his twenty-seven grandchildren and two great-grandchildren. Jerry was sitting in the copilot seat. Twenty minutes later, I didn't think that was the wisest choice.

Once we crossed Cook Inlet, we were flying low over small lake- and pond-dotted wetlands. I was looking for brown bears and saw one running at the edge of a lake. I saw a pair of trumpeter swans, flying elegantly below us. I looked forward and noticed Jerry was looking straight ahead at the mountains capped by snow and ice rising sharply to over seven thousand feet. Either he could not move his head from fear, or he had a stiff neck, or he was enraptured by the view! From sea level to over seven thousand feet happened in less than fifty miles—quite dramatic, as a proper English person might put it. Some of my more irreverent friends would have burst out the unprintable.

Our pilot was John Clark. He was tall and serious, to comfort us, until he started "entertaining" us with stories of his adventures. Beluga Lake was to our north. Did the beluga whales come up from Cook Inlet into that lake?

I began looking forward too. John had said we'd go through the mountains in one pass or another, or turn back. There was no way to go over these, some of the giants of Alaska. The passes have localized weather coming off the glaciers and valleys and mountaintops, and everything can change, requiring quick turnarounds, or worse. I didn't want to hear about worse; I'd already heard from Hobo and other friends who were pilots. I hadn't said a word to Jerry about it. John didn't let us down, so to speak; he told us a story through our headphones about landing on someone's roof.

It seems John was coming into Anchorage for a landing one day. It is the busiest private-plane airport in the world. Floatplanes are landing in the lake all over the place, Cessna 180s and Piper Super Cubs and Twin Otters coming and going constantly, especially in the summer and fall. John's single engine died on the way in. At this point, I thought about reaching up and pulling the plug on Jerry's headphones, or turning the volume knob on it near the side of his head. From so many years on tractors and combines, especially before they had cabs, Jerry's hearing isn't the best. Maybe he wouldn't ask John to repeat himself.

Before I could decide what to do, John readjusted his mouthpiece, so we could hear him even better. John said that he was losing altitude fast, and below him all around were planes, white birch trees, some spruce, some houses. Like all fine Alaska bush pilots, he looked for the best place to land. To you and me some of the places they land seem insane. He realized, he told us, he wasn't going to make the runway. He looked for anything level, away from the trees. One idea he had was to fly between two trees and take the wings off first, which he did because the fuel tanks are in the wings. What he did then was find the flat roof of a two-story house. He brought the plane down "gently," didn't even break through into the bedrooms. The house belonged to a family of Korean Americans; the only one home was the grandpa, and he didn't speak much English. Whoops, I thought, taking father-in-law into Alaskan bush, not starting out too well. Bad story choice, John.

Then we flew over Chakechamna Lake, which is more than ten miles long. On our left there were long and narrow glaciers, unnamed, growing between the mountaintops of the Neacola Mountains. With steep mountains less than a mile away on either side of us, the winds were focused, banging us around. At least it was clear here. John seemed much more focused. We were headed for Merrill Pass, one of the most treacherous in Alaska. Something like thirteen planes have crashed in here. I didn't mention that to Jerry. It was so narrow—how could a plane ever turn around in some of these spots if weather ahead blocked them? All this was flying by sight; there's no instrument-flying here.

I'm not sure where we were and Jerry wasn't taking notes. His powerful right hand had a hold of a handgrip. It's fortunate Cessnas are made with the toughest materials. I think we were near the headwaters of Another River. I wondered who named it that. Somewhere before or after Goldpan Peak, 7,450 feet in elevation, John began talking again. The mountainsides were so close together I hoped for stable air. It was like flying into Shangri-la. John told us that this was the most dangerous place in one of the most dangerous passes in the world because it was so narrow. About halfway through it made a turn to the left. If the clouds socked in this area, turning around was a bad idea, and going forward even worse. John said to look down; I expected to see some wildlife, but instead saw two planes that had crashed and never been recovered. Wonderful, I thought. Jerry had relied on me to take him to a place where he could live out one of his lifelong dreams. I don't think peering down on two completely wrecked planes on the floor of some wicked mountain valley was part of it.

Then we made the sharp turn, and everything below us and above us and beside us was snow, ice, glaciers, wild waterfalls, gray steep stone, sheer rock walls. Horrible places to crash. John seemed delighted. This guy is nuts, I thought. No, it was just such a relief to be able to see. When you're flying through this pass, you don't know what the conditions are until you get there. Can you imagine flying in here without being able to see 50 percent of what's waiting and unforgiving?

He pointed to our left. After a tall, sharp peak, there was a flattened mountaintop. Lying atop it far above the valley below was another wrecked plane.

"Now there, look." His voice came in too clear, the rough air was smoother. "That guy almost made it."

There atop a snowfield, atop a mountain, was a crashed plane, looking innocent.

"That pilot realized too late and at too low an altitude he wasn't going to make it any further west into Merrill Pass, so he tried to make it over that, but obviously didn't. You must be thinking in here all the time," John said.

That was the problem right now, thinking.

John crammed us through the pass and we were over the headwaters of the Merrill River. The tiny, steep valley widened, then widened some more, into the Lake Clark Wilderness. Then we popped into the Stony River valley, lush, swampy, green—prime moose habitat. The next mountains with names on the other side of this valley even deeper into the wilderness were the Revelation Mountains. On either side were mountains called Babel Tower, the Angel, Golgotha, Mount Hesperus, and the Apocalypse. Somewhere back in that pass Jerry may have thought we were in the Apocalypse. Almost no one, even Natives, lived out here full-time. The only village anywhere nearby was Lime Village (pop. 47).

No matter how closely I searched the land below, I could see no evidence of anything man-made. There were natural meadows, stretches of blackened tree trunks where forest fires had been called burns, mountains that shot up like rockets, a river dividing itself at times around gravel bars, deep, dark forest. John said as many wolves and other predators lived down there as anywhere in Alaska. Then finally I saw a couple cabins, one with smoke trailing out of it. We flew lower and lower directly over the river, lower still, slower, slower, lower, and then landed gently on a sandbar on the side of the river. We had arrived at Jim Harrower's Stony River Lodge, and like everyone who comes through that pass for the first time, we were delighted to be here. Jerry, being a man of the ground, seemed especially happy to set his feet on the solid stuff.

A couple people stood near the runway. Don, a former guide, was now basically manager of this place. Patrick had just pulled up with a four-wheeler and a cart to haul gear. We could see a small tractor and some elevated fuel tanks. How did they ever get any of that out here? They had taken the tractor completely apart and flown it out piece by piece in the small planes that are the lifeblood of this wide-open world. These guys who flew around the Stony River drainage, in sight of the Revelation Mountains and the Apocalypse, over Tundra Lake, landing on bodies of water that would shrink your underwear to one-third its size, were some of the best bush pilots in the world. Since Jerry wasn't even a big fan of flying big commercial airlines, it was good that it would be a few days before we took off again. We were planning to go into one of the most isolated places in Alaska I'd ever been.

A trail led into the woods and away from the landing strip, and at the end was a collection of wood cabins with rough-cut siding. The oldest-looking one was a log cabin. Some of the buildings were built in the style of a Western saloon. How did they build places this nice out here? Jim Harrower and his people had hauled in a portable sawmill and everything else they needed, each large thing taken apart, flown in, and reassembled. Jim's an exacting and precise man; he's a dentist, a renowned bush pilot, a Dall sheep hunter, a world-class outfitter who also offers eco-tourism. I'm not sure which of these things requires more precision, but Jim's life involves doing extremely daring things precisely.

We were here because I had called an Alaskan friend of mine, Kevin Delaney, and told him that my seventy-year-old father-in-law—"the old farmer," as he called himself—had a wish, and Rita and I wanted that wish to come true. Jerry farms many acres near Lansing, Michigan. He began farming for himself right out of high school and married my mother-in-law in the early 1950s. Their first child was Rita—we're both the eldest of six children—three boys and three girls. Under the definition of *work ethic*, you might find Jerry Jorgensen. He would be embarrassed by that; a Midwesterner and on top of that a farmer, he doesn't like to draw attention to himself. I'm proud of him, so I guess I can. I wouldn't want him to get aggravated with me and throw up his dukes, but I think I can outrun him, possibly, as long as he's on foot. I've been hunting with him in Wyoming, and when he's on a four-wheeler, you need God on your side to follow him. Deer hunting is one of the few things Jerry does for the sheer joy of it. I take that back—he gets great joy out of plowing the earth, harvesting a high-yielding field of soybeans, or seeing a healthy newborn Holstein female calf born at their dairy, Ri-Val-Ree Farm. *Ri* is Rita, first daughter, *Val* is after Valerie, second daughter; and *Ree* is after LeAnne Rennee, third daughter.

Jerry doesn't like to be far from the farm. He raised his family in the farm-house he was raised in, then he and Mom moved up the gravel road, still on their original 240 acres, to the corner of Moyer and Morrice Road, into the house Jerry's dad and mom moved to when Jerry and his new wife had moved in. You look out any window of their house in spring, summer, fall, and you see either alfalfa growing, corn growing, or Holstein cows gazing. In winter the land rests. But Jerry is never idle.

And that would make it tough on him as we waited around the lodge for our guide, Larry Fiedler, to come in from the wilds where he was with another client, Bruce from Wisconsin. They'd been gone over nine days to a spike camp on some lonesome lake on the edge of the Lake Clark Wilderness Area.

My friend Kevin had been a hunting guide for Jim Harrower when Kevin was new to Alaska. I'd asked Kevin to suggest an outfitter who could take my father-in-law and me into the bush. Jerry has always wanted to hunt in Alaska, and since he's a deer hunter, he would like a chance at the largest member of the deer family, the moose. Jerry's a purist; he wanted to be as far out in the bush as we could get. He'd heard people did float trips, but he wasn't interested. I told him that going into the bush could be extremely demanding, that there was no way we could do it without a guide; he said fine, get one. After I'd met Jim Har-rower and one of his young guides, Arno, from Germany, I called Jerry. I ex-plained that if we were going to go out as far as he wanted, we'd have to do some serious walking through bogs, swamps, tundra, up and down mountains through seemingly impregnable forest. There would be no bridges on the wild side of the Alaska Range, the west side, but plenty of rivers. These kinds of trips, searching for bull moose in Alaska, taxed the youngest and toughest Alaskans. The say-ing was too that the work didn't begin until you got your moose because then you had to pack out all the meat on your back, hundreds and hundreds of pounds of it. The hindquarter, for example, could not be deboned; carrying just one out could be over 150 pounds. Jerry didn't feel that he could carry one of those anymore, and I told him that I seriously doubted I could either, but that

I'd be his secondary packer. Larry, whoever he was, would have to take the biggest loads.

This, my last experience in Alaska, was meant to be a tribute to my father and my father-in-law. Jerry was the only one still alive. My dad had died on December 5, 1999, about six and a half months after we'd come to Alaska. Speaking at his memorial service was one of the most impossible challenges I've ever faced. I still pick up the phone and start dialing his number, but there's no phone service where he is. Often, I felt like a parentless child, even though I wasn't. I was so blessed to have all the family I did; I was just missing some anchors that I'd thought would never be gone. Since the death of my father, I was determined to give more, love more, be more available, sacrifice more. I didn't expect perfection, I just wanted to do more for those I love.

Jerry'd trained for this adventure for months, walking in his hunting boots, carrying his rifle, there on the farm in Michigan. He'd call us in Alaska, ask me how much exercise I was getting. He'd researched every type of clothing, worked up special loads for the bullets he would use at his own shooting range, using some machine that calculated velocity and all kinds of other things that were beyond me. So as we waited, I could tell Jerry was becoming frustrated. He began making comments that he'd never been so idle in his whole life. And that was true. He was ready to be out there doing what he'd planned for almost a year.

Being a planner and list maker, for the first time in his life Jerry began keeping a diary. It helped click off the minutes and hours and days that we waited for Larry.

On Sunday morning, September 10, Jerry wrote, "Eberhard Brunner and his German client arrived back in the lodge early last night. They hunted for moose at Grizzly Flats with no luck for 8–9 days. It is supposed to be a nice camp with good view and rolling terrain. Jim Harrower told Peter that will be our spot when Larry, our guide, is available. If weather changes, it should be good for moose."

After these long days of waiting, to hear that these two men spent eight or nine days and saw only one black bear way up on the mountain was not good. After all this planning and hoping, I surely didn't want Jerry not to see the moose he'd come so far to get.

Jerry's back was beginning to bother him. I fired up the sauna for him a few times and we took some walks on a trail beside the Stony River. Every so often

Jerry would stop and sit on a stump. He is a man of such pride, and of course he vividly remembers when he was in his prime. What a prime it was; he was tough and stoic and tireless. I walked at his pace, which was fine, but tried not to seem as if I were slowing down. Jerry often commented on what a walker I was, and that his feet were his weak link. Most farmwork requires upper-body strength, your hands, your arms, what's between your ears. Don't ever think today's farmers are dumb; they are some of the most intelligent, capable, productive, efficient people on earth. Since being Jerry's son-in-law, I will never wish for perpetual sunshine again either.

To come on this trip he had begun his hill walking on the annual July 4 trip to their cabin in the upper peninsula of Michigan, known as the UP to some of us. He and Dorothy, who have one of the best marriages I've ever known, began walking about two miles a day. I think Dad decided that when he turned seventy, he would spend that year preparing for and having one of the biggest adventures of his life. A few years prior he'd begun pumping down the herbs, which Rita had got him interested in. By herbs, I'm talking antioxidants and the like. Then he devised a walk two miles up and down hills in the UP, and then on the family farm. He carried a twenty-pound pack and then increased it to thirty. He carried his rifle, wore his new boots. The other days he did aerobic treadmill and stretching. He changed his diet and lost thirty pounds. He knew Alaska was a supreme challenge at any age, and he was right, as he usually is, in a humble way. He did his own Jerry Jorgensen Boot Camp, Drill Sergeant Jerry Jorgensen, Private Jerry Jorgensen.

And here we were with Jim Harrower, world-renowned Dall sheep hunter and Alaskan bush outfitter, and we'd been here seven days, looking at some of the world's most dramatic stone mountain peaks dusted with snow, my second termination dust. Below them were foothills burning with the deep reds of blueberry bushes. Looking through a spotting scope, we could see several black bears feeding. Below them were the yellows and oranges of Alaska's quickly passing fall. In five days, I'd seen changes. And always the silver-green Stony River rolled by, all this was good for sitting, meditating; taking pictures is not Jerry's thing. Action is, following through on a plan of action. I was here to see that it all came to pass. I could not be frustrated by anything Jerry said. This was all about him.

On Thursday morning, September 14, Jerry wrote, "Chris, the camp pilot, who usually flies for FedEx to Russia, has already made two trips by 9:45 bringing Harry, who is the hunter we've been waiting for to get his moose. Chris has gone to get Larry (our guide) now. Hopefully we will fly out in the P.M. if Larry gets ready to take two more hunters, 'us.' Peter has sauna fire started for therapy for my back. Harry, from northern California, got his moose. I took my 2-mile walk along the river while Harry was in the sauna. After a walk and my sauna, my back feels much better. The word seems official that 'author guy' and 'the old farmer' are heading out today. If so, I'll have a gun in hand tomorrow."

GRIZZLY FLATS

That evening Jerry's diary recorded the good news, "Don just loaded our gear in trailer behind ATV and headed for landing strip. It's 3:25 P.M. and put us on 1-hour notice to fly." There's always good with the bad. Chris flew Jerry, Larry, and a bunch of our gear over to Grizzly Flats, a flat spot halfway up a mountain with a valley below, the bare mountain above. They would have to land on a field of blueberry bushes and brush. Jerry was ready to land on anything, after all that waiting, as long as it wasn't a crash landing. Chris made a second trip to fly me in.

"We landed on tundra in blueberries and low bush cranberries. Peter came on 2nd trip with rest of gear with Chris in Super Cub about 6:00 P.M. Larry got water out of a fast stream about 50 yards down from our tiny cabin. After being there about an hour, Larry spotted a 55–57" bull moose wandering along ridge 250 yards from camp. We couldn't shoot him because you can't shoot the day you fly in. We had a Spam-and-cheese pizza for supper. We organized our gear and made plans for tomorrow's hunt, which means trying to find the bull. Time to turn in, it's 10 P.M."

Our new guy-home was dug into the side of a hillside, just under the top. At one time this little hut, about eighteen feet wide by twenty-eight feet long, was on top of the hill, but some storms blowing in from the former Soviet Union or the Bering Sea exerted their dominance over this man-made trifling combination of two-by-fours, plywood, windows, and insulation. It would have blown away but it was held down by cables. Now the backside of it was dug into the hillside. The front had five eighteen-by-thirty-eight-inch windows. Our tiny, narrow shelter faced almost straight south into a colossal valley that seemed to spread out into forever. This could not have been a more perfect home away from home for Jerry. We had shelter, it could snow, it could rain almost continuously as it had on Eberhard and his German client. The wind could try to blow us away. We had clothing to handle all this, but living in a small tent for a week was not what Jerry deserved for his biggest adventure away from Jorgensen Farms.

Our first day was sunshine and even at forty-five degrees the windows let in enough solar energy to warm up the place. There were four bunks. Larry and Jerry took the bottom ones. Larry decided after seeing me attempt to squeeze into the one over him that he should switch with me. He said something about thinking I was considerably younger than I am, so he'd given me the top bunk. Larry was a charming person you liked immediately. He was thirty-three, powerfully built, about five feet ten inches tall, 185 pounds. When he was in junior high, he won awards in the national Junior Olympics for weight lifting. Part of the concept of spending a few days at Stony River Lodge, other than waiting for your guide, was for Jim Harrower to check out the hunters he didn't know. He could quickly analyze a person's physical capacities, mental toughness, and shooting ability, everyone sighting in his rifle under Don's watchful gaze. Jim had put us in the perfect spot. We could sit on this knoll and literally gaze over several hundred square miles of country. Above us was open tundra-laced mountainside, rising to over five thousand feet. We were at about two thousand feet. Larry hoped we'd see moose below us. The land dropped off steadily over a thousand feet in elevation to the Stony River, which we could clearly see winding along. A couple times we saw distant smoke on some sandbar where wilderness hunters or adventurers were floating the river maybe five miles away. In certain directions we could probably see fifty miles or more.

Larry was our boss, Jerry was the reason we were here, I was the "do-whatever." Larry told us we'd be sitting on the knoll above the hut, a 360-degree vista. We would spend several hours every day with our binoculars to our eyes, glassing the little marshy openings and open tundra. Larry said sometimes if the sun was out, a bull moose's extremely wide antlers would reflect the sun and show up in the eternal green below like someone holding up a white T-shirt. It could show up as a tiny speck three miles away, larger if it was closer. It was doubtful one would come close as on the night we'd arrived. Bull moose use their concave antlers and large ears to hear the slightest noise, the way a radar dish focuses radio waves. Jerry wore two hearing aids; he'd already lost one on one of our walks. We'd have to whisper a lot, Larry said; that would be quite a challenge. I've always had excellent eyesight and am good at noticing the slightest movement. The first day we spent several hours sitting on the ground, kneeling, just watching. I spotted a golden eagle soaring up a slight valley behind us. A couple caribou were a couple miles up in the tundra. A small owl flittered over, hunting. Two female moose were in a lake three miles or so below us. Larry, who'd grown up in Kansas, told me that although Jerry was in outstanding shape for a seventy-year-old, we'd have to locate a moose within a mile, no more than two miles; if Larry thought it was right, we'd stalk it. From around 7 A.M. until midmorning we glassed the wilderness.

I'm not sure what the correct definition of wilderness is. That's one thing about sitting on a rock and staring into the wild: you can think about these things. The wild is a place where the balance of nature is about attempting to survive. Predators prey on weaker, slower, smaller predators. The wilderness is not the Garden of Eden, it's about taking and creating life. We humans are no different; some of us are so far removed from the killing part that we've lost perspective.

Some past hunter or guide had left a National Park Service publication out here under my foam mattress with some other reading materials. After a while you read anything, even the back of Spam cans. The publication said:

> To most of us, the vast stretches of forest, tundra, and mountain lands in Alaska constitute a wilderness in the most absolute sense of the word. In our minds, this land is wilderness because it is undisturbed, pristine, lacking in obvious signs of human activity. To us undisturbed land is unoccupied or unused land. But in fact, most of Alaska is not wilderness, nor has it been for thousands of years.
>
> Much of Alaska's apparently untrodden forests and tundra land is thoroughly known by people whose entire lives and cultural ancestry is intimately associated with it. Indeed, to the Native inhabitants, these lands are no more an unknown wilderness than are the streets of a city to its residents.
>
> The fact that we identify Alaska's remote country as wilderness derives from our inability to conceive of occupying and utilizing land without altering or completely eliminating its natural state. But the Indians and the Eskimos have been living this way for thousands of years. Certainly then, theirs has been a successful participation as members of an ecosystem.

We pick up Jerry's diary: "After lunch we walked north on the ridge on centuries-old game trails. Some wolf and moose tracks along the way, plus scrubbed-up trees. It's obvious with all the wolf and grizzly sign, their dropping loaded with caribou and moose hair, that the moose and caribou are under pressure. Larry said he's only seen 5 moose calves the last two years, a bad sign. We crossed three creeks and stopped at the Hell Hole about a mile and a half from camp."

I'm sure Larry wanted to take Jerry and me, with small packs and rifles, walking through this country on this ridgeline to see what Jerry could do. If it came time and we saw a bull moose below us, Larry wanted to know how fast Jerry could move. This trail was a wild-animal highway. They used it for ease of travel. Predators such as wolves could do the same thing we were doing: see a moose in the open, go and try to get it. The winter caretaker at Jim's lodge, Arno, said that the worst time for these moose is when they calve. The bears and wolves follow the cows and grab calves almost as soon as they hit the ground. He has found several fresh scat piles with baby moose hooves in them.

As we walked the trail silently, some past predator's spirit came upon me. In terms of history, it hasn't been long since my ancestors, covered in fur clothes, walked trails like this in what is now Europe searching for something to kill to feed their families.

Jerry: "I hope we will see the bull we saw last night, again. This country separates the men from the old men. Peter and Larry are both good walkers. They haven't had to carry me in yet. It is truly a great experience just being out here. It is down to 36° already at 9:30 p.m. Time to go to bed. For the third morning in a row it is 26°. However we have a sprinkle of snow and a very cold wind. I guess the windchill index is near zero. There was no need for towels, washcloth, and soap on the list, baby wipes are the standard option. Larry and Peter are freezing on the hill, where they are looking for moose, one or the other is coming down every half hour to warm a little. We started kerosene heaters for the first time." Larry had told us he does not like to start heaters; he keeps things spartan so hunters will not get too comfortable and not want to go out.

"About 11:30 (freezing still), Peter spotted a bull moose about ½ mile below us and moving left to right through the trees. We all get to see him but he was moving too fast to intercept. We are spending fourteen-plus hours a day glassing."

It had now been about four days of looking and searching the wetlands below, hoping to catch a bull moose move in the dense evergreens, hoping that there would be one coming along the trail. We'd passed several bushes and small, cold-and-wind-stunted trees that a bull moose had trashed with his antlers. They do this to clean off the velvet when they first appear, and to mark their territory. Right now the rut was either in or close, and bull moose were gathering up as many cows as possible. Larry told us stories about the loudest sounds one could imagine when two equally matched bulls had fought to gain control over potentially breedable females. Larry said the same thing goes on at some bar in Anchorage called the Bush Club. Jerry didn't hear that one.

Jerry: "We didn't see anything on the evening watch. There can't be many animals here."

Fortunately both Jerry and I greatly enjoy living like this. That night there was another dinner with Spam chopped up in freeze-dried noodles. It was time for a bit of humor; Jerry was getting a bit discouraged, which for a farmer is a hard place to get to. I told him how I sometimes called Rita "Jerita" and Julianne "Jerrianne," because they reminded me of him. That fell with a thud. It had worked before. Larry was writing a letter to his wife and new baby daughter back in Girdwood where they lived. I told him about a skit I'd seen on *Saturday Night Live* about Bill and Hillary watching TV. That one bombed. Dad watched sports, news, and probably more than anything the Weather Channel. I picked up a can of Spam. Jerry had said, without any levity tonight, that his wife would never serve him Spam. On the back of the can, there was actually Spam marketing. It said that it cost $15 to join the official Spam Fan Club for one year. For the fifteen bucks you get a "members only" Spam Fan Club T-shirt, membership certificate, membership card. (Can you imagine pulling that out when a state trooper pulled you over for aggressive driving?) They actually had recipes, a quarterly newsletter, and a number to call, 1-800-LOVE-SPAM. Larry was listening, he laughed. And so did Jerry.

Jerry: "Another clear and cold night, 21° this morning. Larry started to glass at 7:15 A.M. Larry started raking and calling about 8:50 A.M." Raking is beating an old moose antler or this hard plastic tube on the brush. It copies the bull moose when he is raking his antlers. He also called by sort of moaning into the tube. It supposedly sounded good to a moose.

Jerry: "Peter spotted a bull moose down in the flats. We quickly got together our gear and lunch and started down the mountain. After a rough and rugged ¼ mile we set up on a small ridgetop in the cover of some spruce. We saw him, he was a big bull (Larry estimates the antlers at more than five feet wide). He had 3 cows at least with him and was 500–600 yards away. Larry called him across one meadow and into a strip of trees. If he came out on our side of the trees, I was in a position for a 300-yard shot."

Huddled there, all three of us intensely focused, trying to be as silent as a moth flying, watching that glorious bull, so huge and yet so able to disappear. I could see it so clearly in my binoculars, its ears moving better than the most sophisticated radar dish, wondering where was that rival bull raking the brush. That rival was the expert Larry. The bull, I could tell, wanted to come and fight, beat back any rival, but didn't want to leave his hard-gained cows. We whispered to each other—it was hard to whisper to Jerry. We crouched there for what seemed like an hour, though it may have been only twenty minutes.

Jerry: "Unfortunately he turned around in the trees and went back to his cows. Why be greedy for another cow and a fight or risk getting shot? We then circled to a hill to the north of them about 300–400 yards from the area they were in. We stayed there from 11:00 to 4:45, calling every 30 minutes, but nothing showed."

We hiked back up the mountain, a rough, demanding hike. Larry and I glassed some more and spotted a cow and possibly a bull.

Jerry: "Tomorrow we hope to locate my bull again. It's all I can handle to make the trip down to the flats and back. Anyone thinking moose are easy or dumb should try hunting Grizzly Flats."

It was now Tuesday, September 19, a balmy twenty-seven degrees, Jerry recorded.

Jerry: "At 8:15 A.M., Larry is raking above camp trying to locate a bull for us to stalk. The regular coffee ran out so we are down to instant, quite a hardship on me. Larry and Peter located the 64" model and his three cows but they are deeper in the trees, 1½ to 2 miles away, and not an option for today. Also saw a 57" bull with one cow. We have until the 25th when the season ends for one of them to make a mistake. As tired as I've been, I haven't had sore legs the next morning. My back is normal also. I'm making this diary as complete as possible for my family, friends, and fellow hunters as my memory (plus many other things) isn't as good as it should be." That represents one of the many inspiring characteristics of my father-in-law. He didn't say "isn't as good as it used to be." He still demands excellence from himself and all body parts.

Another day passed. The longer we stayed, surprisingly, the less interested I was in the world out there. I could not have cared less about world issues, the news. I was concerned about my family but felt spiritually connected to them, enough to know if anything was wrong. I worried less about time passing and grew more patient. We were like a pack of wolves or pride of lions just waiting on the ridge for our chance. Jerry seemed to be in the same state of mind. For such an entrepreneur, it is not easy to let anyone else take over.

Jerry: "Weather has changed overnight. Temp now at 44° and looks like rain. Larry has seen the big bull again and we are planning our stalk, lighter clothes but including rain gear. While waiting for word to head out, I will catch up on notes I made using a 180-grain bullet as a 'lead pencil.' It's 8:45 A.M. and Larry has decided it's time to try a stalk on the big moose and his harem. Larry estimates they are about a mile and a half down in the flats. Another factor to consider is the bull is distracted by being challenged by the smaller bull who has only one cow. As we work our way down the mountain, Peter and Larry glass at every bench. When Larry would rake the brush and call, it got him really excited. I guess he now thought he had two challengers."

As we descended, walking as fast and silently as we could, I was surprised how fast Jerry moved. Larry was in front, the alpha male, then Jerry, then me. We tried not to get our feet too wet in the swampy spots, but there was no way around them.

Jerry: "Larry has insisted that he carry my JanSport pack over the frame of his big pack. Being that the guide is the absolute boss on a hunt, I accepted. His reason was valid, he wanted the old man to be as fresh as possible for the shot. Peter was instructed to carry my rifle. We moved along slowly, trying to be as quiet as possible through shoulder-high alders, hip-high willows, and low cranberry bushes, besides that we were walking on tundra and crossing swamp."

We were flying down the hill. Jerry was moving like a thirty-year-old.

Jerry: "After we got down to the flats about one mile down, there were only low elevation points to glass from. At one of the passes Larry realized Peter didn't have my gun. I was stunned, Peter was embarrassed. Peter *ran* back and luckily found it lying on a game trail we were following through some thick alders, which had apparently brushed it off his shoulder."

I almost got sick to my stomach when I felt on my shoulder for Jerry's favorite rifle and it was gone.

Jerry: "I regrouped with my .308 Norma Mag. We moved on a couple hundred yards to a nice little knoll."

Excitement alternated with worry. Things seemed to be all wrong. We hadn't seen the moose in twenty minutes; we had to go down from the top of one knoll, cross a creek, and go up game trails any way we could to the next knoll. Any second the bull could crash through into some opening, or maybe it had already disappeared. I was glad Jerry has a strong heart. We snuck to the top of the next hill.

Jerry: "Larry spotted the bull and a couple cows on a ridge to our right. I got in position by a small spruce and whispered I could make the shot if he stepped into the clear."

I heard "the whisper" from quite a distance away.

Jerry: "He did and I aimed for high on the front shoulder, which was a good thing because I estimated the range at 250–300 yards and it turned out to be 350 yards, plus. . . . Larry instructed Peter to stay put and he guided us to the area where the moose had disappeared. After a few minutes I spotted a palm and he was dead at 10:58 A.M. on our sixth day of hunting at Grizzly Flats. Larry was the real hero, his instincts and moose experience are what got the job done, plus his ability to communicate with an old man that can't hear in these type of whispering situations or see real well. The moose measured 65¼" across his antlers. He was 81" from top to back to bottom of his hoof. He was 9'3" long from tip of nose to backside of rump. He had very good palms with four frontal or brow tines on both sides. After skinning him and cutting up meat and storing it away from bones and gut pile on wood limbs and hanging antlers in tree, we got back to camp at 6:10 P.M."

There was a fantastic moment when we all met at the fallen moose. "The old Michigan farmer" was almost glowing with his moose. As is always the case with me, I felt a moment of reverence, almost a sadness, for the life taken. The whaling captains always thank God when they get a whale. I silently thanked him for what he'd given Jerry. I took pictures. Then the hardest of our work began. Jerry actually carried huge pieces of the moose meat over to our cache area fifty yards away. A moose gut pile as the guides call it is one of the most dangerous spots in Alaska. In time a grizzly would come and then it would be his or hers.

Jerry and his moose below Grizzly Flats. Photo by Peter Jenkins

Larry, with a small amount of help from me, made seven round-trips to the moose over the next couple days, packing out anywhere between 100 and 140 pounds of moose meat per load. Nothing is wasted. Larry estimated the bull weighed 1,500 pounds.

Jerry: "Was I nervous? No. Was I excited? I tried to be, but I think the only way that will happen is if I can see one of my many grandsons or granddaughters kill a nice whitetail at our UP cabin. I think satisfaction (or accomplishment like the end of planting season) is the best way to describe the moose kill."

A few days later, after all Larry's loads carrying the moose up the mountain, Jerry was beginning to think about home. It was Friday, September 22.

Jerry: "It's time to get out of here. I hear a plane now, hopefully one of Jim's. Larry's about out of whiskey, Peter's socks stink bad [I had hung them to dry right by Jerry's bunk], and my Hershey's bars are gone."

We were flown out of Grizzly Flats one at a time by John. Chris, the camp pilot, was now back flying for FedEx, his vacation over. I remembered as we took off from the bushes what Chris had said about trying to fly like a competitive gymnast. Each landing, each takeoff, striving for a perfect ten, almost never achieving it, but you never stop trying. The only difference is a gymnast always has the same apparatus.

We walked back into the lodge and hugged Denise and Jen, the fabulous cooks who didn't belong to the Spam Fan Club, and told Jim of our success. He was proud for Jerry and yet concerned for all the rest of his guides and clients from all over the world who were still out in the bush. But then the weather turned against our leaving.

We waited another day, and although pilot John said there was a good chance we would have to turn around either in the pass or at Cook Inlet or even Anchorage, we would give it the old Alaska try. We would fly in the Cessna, and Tony O. would fly the floatplane with three guides in it, Chad, Macen, and Larry. It was no problem taking off; the fog was farther east. We got deep into Merrill Pass and had to turn around. John and Tony, who was flying below us, were talking to each other; it looked as if they were too low. John had said you need to maintain altitude in case you need to slow way down to turn. Slowing down, I assumed, made you lose altitude. They decided to go back and try the pass to the north. We got through, and this time Jerry was looking around as if we were on a ride around a soybean field.

We came out of the Alaska Range and Cook Inlet was before us. John was listening intently to someone on the radio in a Beaver on floats. The pilot had just come from Anchorage and was heading west, where we'd just come from. He couldn't get back into Anchorage, he said; he was going to land on one of the many lakes below and just wait it out. We did not have that option. I could see a rolling, blockading bank of fog and clouds lying on the water in front of us. John wondered out loud whether he should go back. Tony said he was going to head in the opposite direction we should be going and go south down the coast. Maybe, he said, there would be an opening, a way to see our way across the inlet to the other side, then head north up that coast to Anchorage. Over there was the Kenai Peninsula and more places to land. There was nothing that I could see on this side to land on without it being a crash landing. John brought the Cessna down to below three hundred feet. I could tell he was concerned, but at least Jerry didn't seem to be.

We made it to Anchorage, just another minor moment in the life of Alaska. Everyone was just fine. We landed and taxied to the place John tied down his plane. Waiting there was Larry's wife and his new daughter, and Rita, Julianne, and Dorothy. We tried to tell them about our adventure as they told us about theirs. They had taken off on the Alaska ferry and just gone wherever they felt like. They loved it, ended up in Cordova.

Jerry: "After a good night's rest, we boarded a crowded 757 at 9 A.M. for the trip home. We are due to arrive in Lansing at 9:15 P.M. Alaska was a very rewarding experience in many ways. I have never talked with anyone who was disappointed with it."

As Mom and Dad walked out of sight down the entryway to their Northwest jet, I saw tears in Julianne's and Rita's eyes. Whenever Julianne felt the urge to cry, she would always look at me to see if I was too. I was. There went two of the finest people in the world, whom we loved dearly and whose lives would never be the same since they'd come to Alaska.

23

Leaving Alaska

We drove back to Seward as if we'd been living here all our lives. I got aggravated with some tourists driving too slowly, just as I had driven when I'd first arrived. Then I saw that they were looking up this valley to a glacier at the end of it. The clouds had parted and the sun was shining just on the glacier; it was raining on either side. This cathedral was slowing them down.

Rita, Mom, and Julianne had packed up most of our stuff while Jerry and I had been hunting. We had arrived here with one giant duffel each, and now we would need a U-Haul and every bit of room in the Explorer to get it all home to Tennessee. Aaron would drive; it would take him six days. Into that U-Haul, Aaron and I squeezed two massive sets of caribou antlers with the skull still attached. Rebekah and I had found one in Unalakleet on the tundra; Eleanor's husband, Johnny, had given us the other. There was a Haida drum made for me by Tony, Tina's sister's boyfriend. Painted on the deerskin drumhead in black and red was the eagle spirit. It looked as if the eagle had swallowed a man whose head was where the main body of the eagle should be. A friend from the world of ice had given me another Eskimo drum whose skin was made of walrus intestine.

I hadn't wanted to buy it, but we loaded up the cheapest TV we could buy at Fred Meyers. The kids had to watch their stuff, I needed to watch *Saturday Night Live* now that it was good again, and Rita needed her cooking shows. There were some "finds" from Seward's garage sales; we'd given away all we could here in Seward, including a couple bikes. Right before we left, I returned Joe Tougas's blue Schwinn mountain bike to him. It had done a lot to release my freedom-loving soul, which had become too sedentary. There were tubes with prints and posters. One was Rita's, entitled "Salmon in Seward," celebrating what a chef can do with a silver salmon. Another was from Juneau announcing the 1999 Alaska Folk Festival. We had a small box of Hobo's CDs and a couple fishing poles Jed, Luke, and Aaron had used. There were three boxes of super-cold-weather gear I'd worn mushing with Jeff King. I now had someone I could always pull for in the Iditarod and the Kuskokwim 300, and if I ever got a job repairing walk-in freezers, I'd have the right clothes and boots.

Rita had labeled several boxes Fragile. Inside were wedding presents from back in July when our daughter Brooke and her husband, Trey, had been married on Fox Island here in Resurrection Bay. At first they'd said they were going to get married, just themselves, in Jamaica, but then Brooke talked Trey into having the ceremony in Alaska. We rented a boat called the *Alaska Sunrise;* Trey's mother, sister, and niece came from Tennessee, and our whole family except Jed was there. He was in school. It was Luke's job to film the ceremony with our video camera; I was taking pictures. The captain of our boat, Tim Fleming, would also perform the ceremony. In Alaska, because as we now know everything can be so far away, anyone can marry anyone. Tim wasn't just anyone—he was one of our favorite people in Seward.

The surroundings on Fox Island were profound, perfect for a wedding. On the way out to the island we passed a humpback whale and her baby. The baby was leaping out of the water, breaching over and over. We took it as a blessing for Brooke and Trey. That was the closest to Seward I'd ever seen a whale. We had the wedding on an outside deck; mountains were everywhere, better than any wall, and the sounds of the sea on the pebbled beach were our organ music. We left, and Brooke and Trey stayed the night on Fox Island. They found a heart-shaped rock on the beach, and they brought it home as a remembrance of the place where their new life together began.

There were several boxes of slides that Rebekah and I had taken while exploring together and apart. Rebekah was already back in school at Belmont University. She had E-mailed right before we left, trying to explain how Alaska had affected her and thanking me for the opportunity. She wrote to me, "Dad, I suppose I should listen to you more often. Sometimes I think you know me better than I know myself. I guess it's the cut-from-the-same-cloth thing. Love, Rebekah." About Alaska, she wrote:

"Remembering Alaska. Now I sit here and know what Alaska did for me.

Luke after a fantastic trip fishing for silver salmon.
PHOTO BY PETER JENKINS

She made me brave. She made me soar. She made me drink myself into her innermost caverns and unbeatable mountain caves. She held me at first and I won her at my best and now we together have a truce and memories for a lifetime, things I will hold on to until I grow old and cannot remember my name or my children or how I once traveled the worlds of 'The Last Frontier.'"

In those boxes there were pictures and video and voice interviews on minidisk about everything that had captured us in Alaska. Tina and the totems in Hydaburg; my first king salmon; Eric and Dean of Deering; Jeff King's retired lead dog Kitty; Cordovan's Per, Andy, and Neva; Harvester Island; Julianne and Rita standing beside the snow machines on the way into Eric Jayne's in the Brooks Range. There was Oliver Leavitt and crew on the edge of the land-fast ice, the blue-blooded woman from Unalakleet; Jerry and his moose; Luke holding up one of the huge silver salmon he'd caught; Jed sitting on top of Mount Marathan; and so much more. There were boxes of books, like *Our Boots: An*

Rebekah and me. Photo by Eleanor Sarren

Inuit Woman's Art, The Wolves of Mt. McKinley, Bibles, and on and on, mostly bought at my favorite used-book store, Title Wave, in Anchorage. Once Aaron and I got everything crammed in, he put his collection of bald eagle posters on top of it all.

Rita and Julianne got out their charm bracelets to wear on the plane ride home. Added to them since we'd been here in the last year and a half was a bear with a salmon in its mouth, a sea otter, a puffin, a swimming salmon, and the supreme orca.

Down in the walk-in freezers at Captain Jack's, where Aaron and Luke had worked their first summer here, we had four huge boxes filled with vacuum-packed silver salmon, king salmon, red salmon, halibut, and lingcod. Everyone had caught some of it on our outrageously good family ocean-fishing trips on *The Servant* right outside of Seward. We would have to buy a new freezer when we got back to our farm, a place I loved and yet had not missed as much as I would have thought.

We were back in Tennessee in just a few hours, really. It was as if we'd only been gone the weekend. Or had we been gone a lifetime? It had seemed so difficult to leave, and yet it was so easy to come back home. Part of that was because when you've lived in Alaska, living in other places seems easier, less challenging, less threatening. The first thing I remember thinking was that I did

Captain Tim Fleming, me, Rita, Julianne, Brooke, Jody, Trey, Cayla, Aaron, Rebekah, Luke and Trey's sister Dora and mother Janice on Fox Island on Brooke and Trey's wedding day.

not have to look up so often, at mountains and glaciers, or stare out at the endless ocean and tundra. Alaska had enlarged each of us. Whenever I get in long lines or jammed traffic, I think of Alaska. When I feel that I cannot overcome, I think of her people. No one is ever the same after coming back from Alaska.

Epilogue
Jump Out of That Plane

Milling around in the hallway of the Franklin Road Academy gymnasium were just over seventy high school students in caps and gowns. Some had been going to school together here since kindergarten. Soon, Jed and his classmates from the class of 2001 would march, one by one, through double metal doors to take their seats for graduation.

After their senior prom just a few weeks ago, about half of these humans had spent the night at our farm. Jed, Luke, and Jed's friends Kyle, who is going to NYU, and Rob, who is going to the University of Tennessee, had come out that morning and gathered enough dead trees, cut up with my chain saw, to make a pile of wood as big as an Alaskan single-room log cabin. When Jed, Kyle, and Rob lit the woodpile that night, the flames from the sun-dried trees seemed to reach the moon.

The mercury lights glared from above and reminded me of the brilliance of a glacier's reflected light. Alaska was never far away from me. Since I'd been back, I'd noticed that there was a calmer center in me; I could be in tight, milling crowds like this one or under intense pressure and not feel like I needed to escape.

Tiger Williams, head of the upper school, gave out several awards, the same kinds of prizes that were going to students in every high school in the country. Frankly, our family has not been known as award winners. Most of us are too ornery or dance to the beat of some drummer that others don't hear. But Jed was awarded Outstanding Senior Boy. At the beginning, Tiger had asked the audience not to scream and whistle for their family members, but several families totally disregarded her. One person even used a foghorn—a bit rowdy for so many well-behaved people.

Then Courtney Beavers, valedictorian, got up to make her speech. Her curly brown hair seemed more windblown and wild than usual. She and Jed were both going to the University of Southern California. I remember her, year after year, skinny and shy, winning all kinds of academic awards. She began quietly, talking about how being done with high school meant she and the class of 2001 could begin living *their* dreams in the daylight. She then informed her parents, that she, her older brother, and three classmates, including Jed, had jumped out of a plane yesterday at fourteen thousand feet. I couldn't see Courtney's parents' faces when she informed them of her leap into the clouds. Our family already knew about it—it was Jed's idea, his graduation present.

As far as Jed and our family are concerned, as I suppose it is obvious now, the adventures, no matter what they are and where they take us, will continue to be just one step, just one jump, just one encouraging word, just one heartbeat away.